ANN RULE

In the Name of Love
and Other True Cases

Ann Rule's Crime Files: Vol. 4

WARNER BOOKS

A *Warner* Book

First published in the United States in 1998
by Pocket Books, a division of Simon & Schuster, Inc.
First published in Great Britain in 1998
by Warner Books

Reprinted 1999 (twice), 2001

Copyright © 1998 by Ann Rule

The moral right of the author has been asserted.

The names of some individuals in this book have been changed.
Such names are indicated by an asterisk (*) the first time each
appears in the narrative.

Lyric from "Unchained Melody" (Zaret/North) © 1955 Frank Music Corp.
Lyric from "What Now My Love" (Sigman/Delanoe/Becaud) © Editions
Rideau Rouge, BMG Music Publishing & Major Songs. All rights reserved.
Used by permission.

A CIP catalogue record for this book
is available from the British Library.

ISBN: 0 7515 2109 4

Printed and bound in Great Britain
by Clays Ltd, St Ives plc

Warner Books
A Division of
Little, Brown and Company (UK)
Brettenham House
Lancaster Place
London WC2E 7EN

www.littlebrown.co.uk

To Jerry Lee Harris
and

Oregon State Police Sergeant Ralph Springer,
who met only once in the unexplainable synchronicity
that defines our lives, but who shared a spirit of adventure
and a true concern for those who passed their way.

One is a friend I knew, and one is a friend
I never met.
Godspeed.

Acknowledgments

I thank Susan Harris for having the courage to look back into painful, closed spaces of her memory and for sharing that recall with me. I know that Susan would never allow me to acknowledge her without mentioning the investigator who became her friend for life: Gerald "Duke" Diedrich, FBI special agent (retired). Thanks, Duke, for your input and your fact checking—but most of all, I salute you for helping me demonstrate once more that cops have big hearts.

I am grateful to Assistant District Attorney Jon Goodfellow, Lieutenant John Whitson and Inspector Bob Connor, of the Alameda County District Attorney's Office, and to Captain Gary Tollefson of the Pleasanton Police Department. Even though they had more than adequate reasons to want to move on, they were gracious enough to walk with me through a case that had consumed them for almost a decade.

The investigators who solved the shorter cases in this fourth volume of my crime files have been friends for more than twenty years: Don Nelson and Doug Engelbretson of the Snohomish County Sheriff's Department;

Acknowledgments

Mike Crist, Bruce Edmonds, Benny DePalmo, Duane Homan, Craig Vandeputte, Danny Engle, and Al "Beans" Lima of the Seattle Police Department; and Ken Trainor, Ted Forrester, Robert Andrews, George Helland, T. T. Nault, and Norm Matzke of the King County Sheriff's Office. Over the years, I sat in one trial or another and watched Jim Warme, Roy Howson and Lee Yates of the King County Prosecutor's Office successfully prosecute felonies. The cases herein represent some of their toughest fights.

Much of *In the Name of Love* was written in "the winter of my discontent"—or, more realistically, "the winter of my three mudslides." With an increasingly portable office, I somehow made it through with the help of my rebuilding crew: Martin and Lisa Woodcock, Larry Ellington, Don White, Tom "Digger" Donovan, Tarlus Taylor, Merv and Cathy Leitch, and Mark Hansen. My neighbors are the kind that everyone longs for: Vicki Winston and Mark Iden and Margie and Bob McLaughlin were there in an emergency— and after.

As always, I thank my *first* reader, Gerry Brittingham, my assistants Donna Anders and Mike Rule, my photographer/ author/daughter Leslie Rule, my editor Julie Rubenstein, and my agents Joan and Joe Foley and Anna Cottle and Mary Alice Kier.

And my remaining offspring: Laura Harris, Andy Rule, and Bruce Sherles. My brother and sister of the heart, "Ugo" and Nancy Fiorante and my "main publicist" Lucas Saverio Fiorante, and my far-flung Michigan cousins (in the fond hope of a family reunion): Chris and Linda McKenney, Sara and Larry Plushnik, Christa Hansen, Terry Hansen, Karen and Jim Hudson, Jim and Mary Sampson, Bruce and Diane Basom, and Jan and Ebby Schubert.

I have been happily overwhelmed with readers' letters asking to be included in my newsletter mailings! If you are not on the mailing list and would like to receive my "sort-of-quarterly" free newsletter, just write to me at P.O. Box 98846, Seattle, Washington 98198, and I will see that you receive the next issue.

Contents

Author's Note

Each book in my True Crime Files series has a central theme, although the human beings involved act out their own variations on each theme in ways that continue to amaze me. This volume deals with love and what people will do for what they define as love.

Many acts are committed in the name of love, and love can mean many things: caring, passion, sexual obsession, friendship, jealousy, companionship, ownership, loyalty, tenderness, and—for some people—cruelty and revenge. Since time immemorial, convicted men and women have cried, "I did it for love!" and, in their own perception, they may well believe what they say.

In the Name of Love, the book-length title case in this volume, concerns the love between a man and a woman: Jerry Lee Harris and Theresa Susan Hannah. Every source I contacted in my research has validated my impression that theirs was a true and unselfish love, and if life were fair, they would have been together always. But life is seldom fair.

This book ultimately becomes Susan's story, the evolution of a woman who began her marriage as a rather dependent unambitious housewife—a description, incidentally, that she was proud of. But something happened to turn Susan's life inside out. Where many women would have buckled under the crushing weight of loss, grief, and terror, Susan Harris proved to be worthy of the title "heroine." She surprised almost everyone who knew her—most of all herself.

What Susan did in the name of love is the framework on which this book is built; she was a willow tree, slender and fragile-appearing, bending but never breaking in the gale-force winds that battered her, and then whipping back stronger than ever.

As you will see, Susan's ordeal was not an instantaneous tragedy; it was one that continued for years. I think that most women would like to believe we would fight as hard as Susan did to see justice done, and that we would have as much courage. I am not sure that I could have weathered such storms or that I might not have given up somewhere along the way when the assaults from a truly evil enemy went on and on . . . and on.

But Susan Harris never quit, even when she lost almost everything that had ever mattered to her. *In the Name of Love* follows her tenuous journey from despair to quiet triumph.

Susan's story didn't make the headlines outside of the Bay Area, but I heard about it, and it kept tugging at my mind in fragments of a song on the radio, in short AP wire stories out of San Francisco that found their way into Seattle papers, and finally in a phone call from one of the principal players. As one who believes in synchronicity, I had no choice but to drive four hundred miles to meet Susan Harris. Once I had talked with her, I was amazed at the connections that bound me to her—and to Jerry.

In this volume, in addition to *In the Name of Love,* you will find four shorter cases from my files, cases that I can remember as well as if I had covered them only yesterday. They all deal with some bizarre mutation of the dictionary definition of "love." They are "Murder and the Proper Housewife," "The Most Dangerous Game," "How It Feels to Die," and "The Killer Who Never Forgot . . . Or Forgave."

In the Name of Love

PART ONE

October 1987

Foreword

Theresa Susan Hannah Harris had never expected to be so utterly, completely alone. She had never been this alone in her life, so frightened and full of dread and yet desperately wanting to know the answers to questions that kept bubbling to the surface of her mind. Good or bad, she had to know *why;* she had to have some closure to the agony of not knowing where the man she loved had gone. The explanations that Susan—her family called her Susie—formulated about the mystery she endured were terrifying and grotesque. When she fell asleep, her dreams were worse.

Susan Harris was living in a mansion grander than anything she had ever dreamed of, a sprawling pink two-story estate with 6,200 square feet of luxury detail: six bedroom suites, six and a half baths, a game room, a fitness gym, a sauna, and a hot tub. When she and her new husband first saw the house at 3158 Blackhawk Meadow Drive, in Danville, California, both of them viewed it as the home they would live in for all the years ahead. Although Susan demurred at the price tag of almost a million and a half, Jerry Harris just grinned. He had always given her anything she wanted, usually before she even mentioned a wish aloud. The irony was that all she really wanted was Jerry himself. Meeting him, falling in love, and finally marrying him had been a modern-day fairy tale. Too good to be true.

Too good to last? Susan Harris wondered.

Alone at night in the mansion on Blackhawk Meadow Drive, she was afraid. There were no drapes or blinds over

5

the dozens of windows. Some had a view of the treetops below, and others focused up at the sunburned hill that rose beyond their backyard. They had moved in only three weeks before; she had thought they had plenty of time to decorate and buy window coverings. Now she felt as if there were eyes out in the night watching her. The high ceilings and the massive rooms made her feel lost, and her footsteps on the marble and granite floors of the hallways echoed eerily.

The kind of love that Susan and Jerry Lee Harris felt for each other transcended the ordinary. They fell in love quickly and they loved each other more as the years passed. Theirs was the kind of relationship that ballads were written about.

It would be no exaggeration to say they would have died for each other.

Susan and Jerry Lee Harris had so much in common, and, at the same time, so little. They had both grown up in working-class families, each had four siblings, and they were both born in Medford, Oregon. Indeed, they were born in the same hospital—Sacred Heart. His birthday was June 1 and hers was June 2. But Jerry was eighteen years older than Susan. He was a shining star, brash and confident and exciting, while she was a quiet, almost shy, planner who spoke softly and went about her life and education in a traditional way.

Susan was beautiful and slender, with a sweet face and long blond hair. Jerry was handsome, despite his three-times-broken nose, although Susan couldn't really see *what* he looked like when she met him. She laughed when she recalled her first sight of him. "He had a bushy beard, and there was no way of telling what he looked like underneath it."

There is no question that from the moment Jerry Harris first saw Susan Hannah, he never thought of another woman. He was a man inordinately gifted with intuition about most people, and he saw something in Susan that both startled and thrilled him. She embodied, perhaps, the one thing he had never been able to find in his world: romantic

love that would last for a lifetime. He had married three
times and seen each marriage fall apart, but he recognized
something in Susan, something that made him know they
Owould be together until the day he died.

Theresa Susan Hannah—no one ever used her full given
name—grew up as the middle child of five in a happy
family. Her father, Pete, was the supervisor of the Boise
Cascade sawmill in Medford, Oregon. Her mother, Mary
Jo, was a housewife. Their children were Kathy, Bill, Susan,
Joe, and Julie. While Susan attended college at Southern
Oregon State College in Ashland, fourteen miles south of
Medford, she worked weekends for her dad at the sawmill,
mostly doing janitorial work. She had one more year to go
for her B.A. degree in marketing.

One of Susan's friends at the Boise Cascade sawmill was
Sandra Harris, Jerry Harris's sister. Susan and Sandra were
close friends, and when Sandra got married at a small home
ceremony in May 1981, Susan was invited. She would turn
twenty-one in a week, and the man she had yet to meet—
Sandra's brother—would be thirty-nine a day earlier. Susan
knew only that Sandra had four brothers: Jerry, Jim, Don,
and Sandra's twin, Sandy.

Although Jerry Harris would travel to his sister's wedding
from his home in the San Francisco area, he and his family
had once lived in southern Oregon and still considered it
home territory. Jerry had spent the first twelve years of his
life in a hamlet in the foothills of the Cascade Mountains—
Tokatee Falls, Oregon. Tokatee Falls is as far removed from
Othe ambience of the Bay Area as any spot could be. Jerry's
dad, Jim, supported his family as a fur trapper. It was a
hardscrabble existence, trying to support a family of seven
by selling animal pelts. The Harrises finally left Oregon and
moved to Mountain View, California—near Palo Alto—
where Jim worked for a steel company.

Given the eighteen years between them and the fact that
Jerry had moved away from Oregon six years before Susan
Hannah was born, the odds were that they would never
meet at all. Had it not been for his sister's wedding, they
would not have.

Susan wasn't much impressed with Jerry. "All I saw was

7

that beard," she said years later. "His sister didn't like it, and she told him to go shave it off. He did—and when he came out of the bathroom, that's when I saw how handsome he really was."

Susan wasn't dating anyone at the time, and she was drawn to Jerry's electric blue eyes. "And he was so full of life; he was funny—and spontaneous."

There was something special about Jerry Harris. Susan admitted that to herself. She wondered what she would say if he asked her for a date, but that was a moot point: he went back to California without one word about seeing her again. Susan was both relieved and disappointed. She needn't have been. She hadn't heard the last of Jerry by any means.

"Later he called his sister and asked *her* to ask *me* if the fact that he was so much older than I was bothered me," Susan said. "I hadn't really thought about the age difference. He didn't look his age and he certainly didn't act it, so I told her, 'Yeah, I'll go out with him.'"

Jerry's notion of a first date was unlike anything Susan could have imagined. "He told me I could pick anywhere in Oregon to go—or he would take me to Las Vegas," she recalled hesitantly. "I'd been everywhere in Oregon, but I'd never been to Las Vegas."

After she said yes to a first date in Las Vegas, Susan was both excited and appalled at her uncharacteristic bravado. She barely knew Jerry Harris, and she was going to a strange city with him for three days. "I was scared to death," she said.

She soon found that there was no reason for her to be frightened. Jerry treated her like a princess.

"Jerry drove up from San Francisco and picked me up," she recalled, "and we went back there together. We took a ride in a horse-drawn carriage, and then we had dinner at a wonderful restaurant. Then we flew to Las Vegas."

Susan was relieved to find that Jerry was sensitive to her apprehension. "He was very much a gentleman," she said, smiling. "He had arranged for us to have separate spaces at the hotel. He knew how nervous I was. . . . He was so respectful—even in Las Vegas where everything is kind of bizarre and everyone is rushing around. He always opened the door for me, always walked on the outside of the sidewalk—old-fashioned manners."

They stayed at Caesar's Palace for three days, and Jerry enjoyed seeing the glitter and flash of Las Vegas through the eyes of a bedazzled Susan.

"We saw shows, I played the slot machines, and we walked all over. We listened to a number of local bands. I could see that Jerry was a natural entertainer himself, and he enjoyed listening to the groups that weren't famous yet. And of course we ate at some great places."

If she had had any doubts about Jerry's being almost two decades older than she was, Susan soon forgot them. He was the youngest, most alive person she had ever known. "He was naturally positive. You know how those motivational speakers are at conferences? Jerry was dynamic like that. His energy level was high all the time—he didn't need to sleep much. He was always on the go and doing something. In all the years I was with him, he never wasted time. If he was sitting down, it was because he was watching a movie, but even then," Susan said, smiling, "he would have to jump up and fiddle with the TV."

After their wonderful three-day first date, Jerry drove Susan all the way home to Medford. She hated to see him head back to California, but she didn't worry that he might not call her again. Already they both knew that they had begun an important journey of the heart together.

From that point on, Jerry Harris spent all his spare time in Oregon. He flew up from his home in Fremont, California, and he and Susan went fishing. He loved to fish, probably the most sedentary thing he ever did. Their lives would never be ordinary, and their dates weren't, either; they ran the gamut from big-city lights to the pristine serenity of the fields and forests of Oregon.

"At first when Jerry came up so often, I just thought it was because he liked to fish. We went trout—stream fishing—but he was coming up every weekend. It sounds so corny," Susan recalled, "the whole Prince Charming thing, but he really, *honestly*, was . . . I mean, I *knew*. . . .

"There was something about Jerry. It was instinct at first,

9

I think, but I came to appreciate him more later. It wasn't just how sexy he was and how attractive he was. . . . I really *was* lucky to have found a soul mate."

Jerry usually stayed at the Ashland Hills Hotel when he came up on weekends, and then he and Susan took a picnic lunch and headed out for the upper Rogue River. "He took me to Tokatee Falls," Susan said, "so I could see where he'd grown up, and he told me about being a little boy there."

Susan knew that what she felt for Jerry was absolutely real. It was obvious to anyone around them that Susan Hannah and Jerry Harris were completely in love. To Jerry, Susan was not "Susie"—she was "Sue," a special woman whom he had chosen above all others.

"She actually glowed," an old friend said, "and Jerry—he loved her. How can I describe it? It was kind of like—like an *explosion.*"

Susan felt the explosion too, although she kept going to college, determined to finish. She didn't know very much about Jerry's businesses at that point. She knew he had a nursery where he sold and rented exotic plants, and he also owned a small recording studio in the Bay Area. It didn't really matter to her how much money Jerry made. It was the man himself she loved.

She kept seeing Jerry on his weekend trips up to Oregon, but he complained that he couldn't call her during the week. "I lived in this basement apartment, and I couldn't even afford a phone," she said. "If we were going to talk, I'd have to call him from a phone booth. He got tired of that pretty soon."

Finally Jerry said that they had to take a chance. "Sue," he said, "either this is going to work out or it's not. Why don't you come down and live with me? If it's not going to work, you'll find out real fast."

Susan hesitated. She needed another year of college to get her business degree—but Jerry had a good argument about that. "Oh Sue," he said, "if you're really interested in business, you'll learn more about it being with me than you'll ever learn in college. And if you want to go to school, that's fine. You can go to college in California."

Susan felt he was pressuring her, but it was a good kind of

pressure. "He was so unusual, so charismatic, so *good* to me. He really took care of me, and I felt so safe and happy with him," she said as she remembered agreeing to go to California.

Susan's parents, Pete and Mary Jo Hannah, liked Jerry, but they were anything but overjoyed at the idea of their twenty-one-year-old daughter dropping out of college and moving in with an older man—without benefit of marriage. She had been raised in a traditional Catholic home. She had always stayed close to her family, but Jerry Harris lived hundreds of miles away.

Jerry was respectful to Susan's parents. He went with her when she told her dad that she would have to quit her job at Boise Cascade because she was going with Jerry. Pete and Mary Jo weren't the first parents—or the last—to hold their tongues and their breath over decisions their children made.

Jerry Harris and Susan Hannah had met at the end of May 1981. By the end of July, she had made up her mind to be with him. That last week in July 1981 seemed to be filled with romance. Prince Charles and Lady Diana were married in a display of pageantry that rivaled anything the world had yet seen. While enraptured viewers watched the royal wedding on television, Susan Hannah packed five suitcases and boarded a plane for San Francisco to live with Jerry Harris.

"I had planned to drive down to California," Susan said. "I had an old car. But Jerry said, 'You're not parking that old clunker in *my* driveway; you can drive one of my cars.' He gave me the brown Porsche."

Susan moved into Jerry's house on Chaparral Drive in Fremont. Jerry's spot in the south San Francisco Bay area in Alameda County was very different from southern Oregon. Even the trees and flowers were different. Susan loved it. But then, she loved Jerry, and anywhere he lived would have been fine with her.

Actually, she was a little shocked to see that Jerry's home was an almost empty bachelor pad. He had a big-screen television set and a bed with a mattress so bad the springs were poking out. That was it for furniture. But he had some lovely Tiffany lamps and hundreds of plants. The place was full of luxuriant green living plants—and not much else. Susan set about changing that. Together they began to furnish Jerry's house so that it was a *home*, too.

"By the end of our first summer, he had the house all furnished. He wanted me to stay with him so badly, and he tried to make everything perfect for me." Susan smiled. "He didn't have to do all that. I never thought of leaving him."

Even so, to the outside world, Charles and Diana seemed far more likely to stay together than Susan and Jerry.

Another young woman might have made the decision to run away to be with her lover easily, but it was completely inconsistent with Susan's usual pattern. Susan was too close to her family, too bound to Oregon and to her vow to finish college. And yet she had had to go; she knew she was meant to be with Jerry. Later, considering all that had happened, she was shocked that she had been strong enough to take such a vehement stand—to walk away from the first twenty-one years of her life without letting herself look back.

And there had to have been times when she asked herself if the ending might have been different if she had only said no to Jerry.

1

Everybody remembers one kid from high school who was a teenage entrepreneur, the one who was always looking for an angle, a way to make money, a ladder to climb that would take him above the pack. Jerry Lee Harris had been that kid in a hurry. Maybe it was the memory of living in Tokatee Falls and knowing that eating depended on how many pelts his father could gather. Maybe it was because he was the oldest child in his family, and he shouldered adult burdens early. Perhaps Jerry had a premonition early on that he needed to live his life in double time.

If he did, that was understandable. He wasn't very old when he was forced to realize that the time line between life and death could be measured in seconds; he had experienced it firsthand. Jerry Harris almost didn't survive to graduate from high school. He came so close to dying violently when he was in his mid-teens.

Jerry had his first brush with death after the Harris family had moved to California. Jerry went to high school in Mountain View. Eddy's Sport Shop was on the corner of Fairmont and Castro Streets, a familiar store for fifty years, kitty-corner to the high school. In the mid-fifties, some kids broke into Eddy's through a back window one night and stole a sleeping bag and two guns—a starter's pistol and a .22 caliber handgun. One of the young burglars brought the .22 to school. He bragged about how he was going to rob a drugstore. Jerry tried to talk him out of it and threatened to turn him in. Suddenly the kid swung the weapon around. Whether he intended it to happen or not, the gun went off

13

and Jerry was shot in the abdomen. The kid ran, but somebody came along soon after, found Jerry critically injured on the ground, and called for help. When Jerry was rushed to the emergency room, doctors shook their heads in amazement.

The bullet had entered near three vital spots. A fraction of an inch in any direction and the slug would have pierced a vital organ or severed his spinal cord, leaving him either dead or paralyzed from the waist down. But Jerry had incredibly good luck. Although surgeons found it too dangerous to remove the slug from his back, he survived emergency surgery and left the hospital with only a long vertical scar running from just below his right rib cage to his groin area to remind him of the shooting incident. In time, the scar faded so that he barely noticed it, and Jerry always seemed surprised when he went bare-chested and someone asked about it.

Jerry was too badly injured even to speak for days, so no one knew how he had been shot. The papers went to press with the wrong story: "Youth Critically Wounded by Sniper's Bullet." "I was gurgling blood," he remembered years later, incredulous, "and I heard them calling for X-rays! I figured they could just look at me and tell I'd been shot."

Eventually he was able to explain what had happened. Local residents who had been living in fear of a deranged gunman relaxed. The shooter went to juvenile detention. When he was released months later, Jerry and the boy who had shot him were called into the principal's office. Jerry was amazed that they *both* got a verbal warning. It was as if Jerry too had done something wrong.

Years later Jerry held a Mountain View High School reunion at a nightclub he owned. There, he ran into Jerry David who had taken over Eddy's Sport Shop from his dad. Jerry Harris grinned when he saw Jerry David. "I remember you," he said. "I've still got a bullet in my back from your store. Probably always will have."

After he was shot, Jerry seemed almost to defy fortune, taking chances other kids didn't. Since he had already had a miracle, perhaps he felt invincible.

More likely, Jerry was just a natural born risk-taker. He embodied the concept of a son who sets out to find a more exciting life than his father had. He loved his folks, though, and he wanted to make their lives better too. Jim Harris was a chunky guy with an Irish grin and a balding head; Jerry's mother, Lila Faye—always called Faye—was a tall, slender blonde, as pale as her husband was ruddy. She doted on Jerry, amazed at the crazy ideas he came up with and more amazed that he actually made them work, but she was secretly proud of him. Jim Harris recalled that "Jerry was never satisfied."

And he wasn't, but that was what made Jerry Harris run.

The blue-eyed kid with the cowlick in his sandy hair had a lightning-quick mind; he had always seen possibilities that didn't occur to other people. When he was nine years old, he threw "parties," but he charged his friends for the pop they drank. He and his younger brothers sold magazine subscriptions door-to-door. Later, in California, Jerry learned how to operate a motion-picture camera so he could film junior college football games in Los Altos. And he found a way to market game films to fans. Jerry was still in his teens when he became a stage director for weddings and funerals for Parker's Flowers in Mountain View. He lugged lavish floral displays into the churches and halls and funeral parlors. With a change of ribbon color, he could design arrangements suitable for either a happy occasion or to soothe mourners.

Jerry followed his dad into the iron and steel business, where he slaved as an iron worker, but only long enough to learn the business. He soon saw that the view was much better from the lofty offices of management than it was down where the air smelled of white-hot ingots and rebars.

Jerry Harris graduated from high school in 1960—the year Susan Hannah was born. When Jerry was eighteen, Elvis Presley was soaring like a rocket to the top of the entertainment world, a phenomenon the likes of which America had never seen. Elvis was then, and always would be, Jerry Lee Harris's idol. Jerry identified with the singer—on many levels. Like Elvis, Jerry grew up poor, and like Elvis, he was always devoted to his parents and con-

15

cerned about them. Although Jerry was six or seven years younger than Elvis, and although he never hoped to meet him, he felt a bond with Presley. Some of their resemblance to each other was natural; some may have come about simply because Jerry chose Elvis as a model. They were both brown-haired, blue-eyed, and handsome, but Jerry's nose had been broken several times and never set, so his profile was more rugged than Presley's classic look.

Jerry Harris had always loved to sing, and he had a wonderful, albeit untrained, voice. He sounded so much like Elvis Presley that it took a skilled ear to tell them apart. Jerry was far better than the mass of Elvis impersonators. He could have been a professional singer, but he sensed that he might be a little fish in a big pond in that arena. He admired Presley, he collected his records, and often he leaped to the stage of some club in the San Francisco area and belted out a few Elvis songs while amazed crowds gathered around. Still, there was only one Elvis; Jerry's personality was such that he could never be an imitator— he was one of a kind.

Jerry made a halfhearted stab at going to college and spent a year at Foothill College in Los Altos Hills, but academia just wasn't for him. He had too many ideas and too much ambition to spend another three years in college. He was in his early twenties when he started his first company, Northwestern Steel, in Santa Clara. He finagled a contract to work on the expansion of Candlestick Park in South San Francisco. Some of his work is still in place, and it withstood the force of the 1989 earthquake that terrified World Series fans and players alike.

Even though he had made his way into management in the steel business, that wasn't Jerry's ultimate goal. He was continually building on what he knew and looking for more handholds to pull himself up and out of middle-class life.

Before Jerry Harris was twenty-five, he had his own company. By the time he was forty, he planned to have it made. He was one of the small percentage of young men fighting their way out of a blue-collar background who had the brains and imagination to rise above the ordinary.

Again and again Jerry saw his luck turn around until it seemed that everything he touched glowed platinum.

If Jerry had flaws—and he did—his biggest one was that he liked and trusted almost everyone he met. He was ambitious—mightily ambitious—but he was also honest and generous. He was a rascal but he was a good-hearted rascal who seemed to feel some essential obligation to make other people happy. He could not bear to see anyone poor or hungry or unhappy. At the same time, he had no guilt feelings at all about living as lush a life as he could afford.

Jerry had a first very young marriage which produced a son, Mike. His second wife, Carmen, gave birth to their daughter, Tiffany. Later he married a woman who shared his mother's name: Faye. Although his marriages didn't work out, Jerry was devoted to both of his children, and his ex-wives never had a bitter word to say about him. He always took care of his kids, and he had the best of intentions about making time in his life for Mike and Tiffany. But he was a workaholic who often found himself working eighteen hours or more a day; if he had regrets about his life, it was that he had not spent enough time with his children. He tried to make up for that in other ways. He named almost all of his future enterprises after his daughter, Tiffany.

Jerry Harris moved into the business world instinctively. Many of his most successful ideas came about spontaneously. One day while he was working in his yard he realized that he couldn't keep up with the landscaping and his business interests too. He loved gardening, but he had so little time. It occurred to him that it would be much easier if he could just rent plants. And if he had such a need, he figured other busy executives did, too. That was how Tiffany's Limited Plant Rentals began. It was only one of his ideas that were innovative at the time but that are commonplace today.

Molly Clemente, who would later become Jerry's fiercely loyal personal secretary, started working for him part-time in 1977. She began as a typist in the sales department of his plant rental company on Mission Boulevard in Fremont.

Jerry and one salesman put bids out to commercial offices to supply plants and take care of them. They later moved their office to 101 Curtner Road in Fremont.

"Jerry or Chris would deliver the plants and set them up," Molly recalled, "and then they had a girl who would go out and water them and care for them."

Renting plants was, at the time, a brand-new concept. Today there are many companies that provide plants to businesses and remove the burden of responsibility from potential brown thumbs.

Not all of Jerry's ideas worked, however. He tried opening a little retail shop close to the nursery where he sold wicker baskets and statues to complement the plants he rented. He called the new shop Tiffany Interiors, but it never really got off the ground. After a year, he closed Tiffany Interiors and lugged his leftover retail merchandise to his plant rental location.

"Jerry got a bug about singing," Molly Clemente said. "He sang well, and he really enjoyed doing it. He wasn't real aggressive about it, but he enjoyed being in that atmosphere."

Spending time at small clubs around the Bay Area, Jerry heard the same complaint over and over: the singers had to share their nightly take with the musicians who backed them up, and they couldn't make a living that way, nor could they sing without music behind them.

"Jerry came up with the bright idea of recording for these entertainers," Molly said, explaining that he would give them a recorded background tape more dependable than any band—and cheaper. "He spent a lot of money, set up a little studio, and that was Tiffany Productions."

Jerry found an empty General Motors plant and converted it into a studio with perfect acoustics. Because he bought top-of-the-line taping and dubbing equipment, he was able to produce backup tapes that sounded as if a singer had a whole band behind him. (In essence, Jerry had come up with the concept of karaoke—canned music for nightclub patrons who yearn to be singers—a fad that boomed in 1990, although he did not get credit for it.)

"He really got into it," Molly remembered. "By this time, people had heard about it and he had a half dozen singers who wanted to sing to his music. . . . He even got into booking people in local restaurants and nightclubs. He would charge the club, oh, maybe $150 a night, and the entertainer would get so much and Jerry would make the difference—for the use of his music."

Jerry recorded his own voice, using his taped backup tracks, and he sounded great. It made a good sales demonstration. Not only could Jerry sound like Elvis Presley, but he could also imitate Ricky Nelson and Buddy Holly. He got a lot of offers to work clubs himself, but he sang only for free—at clubs, weddings, and an occasional funeral. Singing was his avocation, his hobby, not his business.

The music studio was so successful, however, that it was taking more of Jerry's time than he wanted to devote to it. The entertainers wanted newer arrangements constantly, and Molly said he grew disenchanted with the project. "They were bugging him," she recalled. "He just eventually got to the point where it was more than he wanted to deal with. He was still with the plant business, and something else had come up."

Jerry Harris probably had more friends than any one hundred ordinary men, and he was always glad to make new ones. He was doing well financially, his life was on track, and he just plain liked people. Late in 1979 a man named Al Jennings* dropped by the nursery. He shook hands with Jerry and said he had bought a home on the hill just above Tiffany's Plant Rentals. He had come to personally pick out plants for the new house. Jennings said that an old friend of Jerry's, Gabe Knott,* had sent him down to see Jerry about buying a number of large decorative plants.

The two men hit it off. Jennings seemed very interested in the agricultural aspects of Jerry's plant-growing business. During the late seventies, plant growing was considered an agricultural enterprise by the IRS, and there were legitimate ways to write off the inventory.

It didn't happen right away, but Jennings suggested that they go into business together, serving investors in need of legal tax shelters. They would sell seedling palm trees to investors. Their customers would then become growers who would benefit from the tax write-offs. Tiffany Plant Rentals would be paid to locate the seedlings and then to take care of the plants. Jerry had the greenhouse *and* the green thumb, and he was in a perfect position to be the hands-on nurseryman.

Al Jennings's management company, Agro-Serve,* would be the sales division. Jerry would be responsible only for growing the plants, which would be sold to the investor-growers when they were at the four-year maturation point. If Jerry needed them later on for his rental business, he could buy them back.

Jennings's plan worked so well that, before long, he and Jerry needed a separate company to broker the plants to the investors and to arrange for any loans the investors might need.

Jerry Harris could see no pitfalls in Agro-Serve—at least not in the beginning. His only responsibility was to grow and maintain the palm trees. He enjoyed running the nursery, and with Agro-Serve, he would have a much larger operation, with a guaranteed group of plant investors who would pay him for his services.

Molly Clemente remembered meeting another of Jerry's associates, Steve Bonilla, in 1979 when he walked into the Tiffany Plant Rentals office looking for Jerry. She called Jerry from the greenhouse, and she saw that he and the small, dark man knew each other. The two men visited for a while, recalling mutual friends. When Bonilla left, Molly turned to her boss and said, "Who *was* that guy?"

Steve Bonilla had looked for all the world to her like a mobster—a mafioso. Of course, she wasn't used to seeing men in three-piece suits with crisp white collars and expensive ties in the nursery. Jerry and his workmen usually wore jeans and work shirts. Actually, Bonilla would have been pleased by Molly Clemente's reaction; he had once hired a limousine and a driver to give the impression that he was closely connected to organized crime. As far as anyone knew, the only thing he had in common with Mafia members was his Italian surname.

Bonilla was Jerry Harris's opposite in every way possible.

Where Jerry had a typical Irishman's sandy hair and blue eyes, Steve's roots were Italian and he had dark eyes, and jet-black hair that was disappearing rapidly. As if to balance his receding hairline, Bonilla had grown his sideburns longer. While Jerry was close to six feet tall, Bonilla was about five feet six. He seemed a rather bland, awkward man—not handsome, not ugly. He had a deep cleft in his chin and a surplus of body hair. Where Jerry was confidence personified, Steve was almost obsequious.

Still, he gave Molly Clemente the creeps. Jerry just grinned at her and teased, "Well, I don't know if Steve is Mafia, but he may not be far from it with a name like Bonilla."

But when Molly looked alarmed, Jerry patted her on the shoulder, "Naw, he's just an old friend looking around to get into some kind a deal."

Jerry told her he had known Steve Bonilla since his high school days: Bonilla had gone to school with Sandy, Jerry's younger brother. "I guess he went to all the [Harris] family gatherings and stuff when they were kids," she recalled.

Bonilla's visit to Tiffany Plant Rentals was propitious for him. Jerry and Al Jennings needed someone to oversee plant sales, and Steve said he was already incorporated in a business called Independent Caterers in San Jose. Independent Caterers had lost its fleet of trucks in a warehouse fire. Bonilla said he would be glad to help with the palm trees. He renamed his corporation Sun State Tropicals.

Jerry Harris was adamant about one thing: Agro-Serve's investors had to be able to *legitimately* write off their agricultural venture. "None of them wanted to get in any problems with the IRS," Molly recalled. "Or with the Securities [and] Exchange [Commission] or anything like that. They had certain guidelines, and they ironed them all out . . . and their first sales were in 1980."

During the first year there were twenty-eight investors—doctors, attorneys, executives. Most of them took it on faith that they owned baby palm trees—which indeed they did: 8,500 plants in each "unit" purchased. They were tiny plants, yes, but they would grow into impressive trees that would be in demand by interior decorators and retail stores.

21

A few of the investors actually came out to Jerry's nursery to look at their plants. Jerry met them and took them out into his sprawling greenhouse to show them the fledgling trees that would mature in four years.

In the meantime, investors could legally write off the interest they paid on the loans that had enabled them to buy the plants, the maintenance costs they paid to Tiffany Plant Rentals, and their losses for any plants that failed to thrive. December was the only month in which they would sell the mature palm trees. That would allow the investors to write off their agricultural costs for the year about to end.

Jerry's expertise as a nurseryman let him pick the strongest plants—Sophrytzia palms. He bought the tiny seedlings from a grower he knew and trusted in Texas. By 1984, however, the palm tree business was *too* successful. Agro-Serve had taken on a life of its own. It had millions of palm seedlings and 345 wealthy investors seeking tax shelters. And it was Jerry who was responsible for potting the palm trees, "staging" them (moving them to larger pots as they grew), and most stressful of all, finding a place to put them. By the third year, he had more palm trees than he had places to put them.

He was making money from the Agro-Serve program, but he was just too good at what he did. All around him palm trees were thriving and crowding each other out. He had nightmares about being smothered by mountains of palm trees.

Jerry enjoyed growing things, but this operation had become a factory. And his real interest was with his music studio. He took pleasure in visiting nightclubs around San Jose, Fremont, and the East Bay Area where he could listen to other singers and sometimes jump onstage to sing himself.

Even more than he loved music and plants, Jerry Harris loved Susan Hannah. They had been together for three and a half years now. He wanted time to be with her. He had never meant for the palm tree business to take over his every waking hour.

Susan never complained about any of Jerry's business interests; she went along with him whenever she could.

They drove around the Bay Area and flew to other states, always holding hands, sneaking kisses, and laughing. Whatever Jerry wanted to do, wherever he wanted to be—that was where Susan wanted to be too.

2

This was Jerry's California world—the world that Susan Hannah had entered when she packed her five bags and flew to join him. She saw how other women flirted with him—some subtly and some not so subtly—and realized that Jerry could have had a hundred women just by crooking his little finger. But the only one he wanted was Susan. After a while, she believed that. Susan had seen him in Oregon where he was laid back and where he fit perfectly into the ambience of a small town. Aside from the dazzling trip to Las Vegas, their dates had been rustic—fishing trips and picnics. She had known Jerry as a country boy, and now she saw him as a businessman and as a popular habitué of nightclubs.

Both men were the real Jerry, but Susan knew him in his heart. No one else really understood that. Anyone laying odds on the longevity of Jerry and Susan's relationship would have been betting a long shot. They fell in love too quickly; their worlds were too different. Susan gave up everything for Jerry. She worried for a long time that he might grow tired of her now that she was part of his daily life and not some almost unattainable young woman who lived far away.

Susan realized early on that Jerry was a workaholic; he never tackled any project that he didn't put all his energies into. If it wasn't the nursery, it was the recording studio. He always tried to pack one more errand in, only to have that lead to two or three more. Jerry wasn't the kind of man who could be counted on to be home for dinner, or even home within a half hour of his estimated time of arrival. At first, Susan was relieved that he ate dinner out so much. One secret she had not shared with Jerry was her complete lack of experience as a cook. "He said he couldn't cook either, and I thought, *Oh, no . . .* and so we learned how to cook together." Susan smiled, remembering.

She soon figured out that her best chance to keep Jerry home a little longer was in the morning. "Sometimes I would cook a big breakfast and entice him to stay home—he liked my cooking. I screened his calls and decided if the message was important enough to interrupt our morning. His secretary knew I did that. I changed our number many times. Our phone was always ringing; everyone needed Jerry for something."

Susan had no pretensions about having a career herself. She was a woman who would, perhaps, have fit more comfortably into the idealized female role of three decades earlier. Her choice was to be the woman behind the man; she was perfectly happy with that kind of a relationship. Had she been married to another kind of man, she might have seemed too compliant. But Jerry appreciated what she did for him.

After years of living in his unfurnished bachelor digs, Jerry loved having an immaculate house, and Susan ironed all of his shirts herself and kept his closet organized by color. She lined his shoes up perfectly. She spent about three hours each morning doing housework because she enjoyed it.

"Jerry was romantic. He brought me flowers at least once a week—especially if he was late in coming home. They were never roses, though; they were the type of bouquets you get at the gas station or the 7-Eleven, but I thought it was sweet," Susan said. "He brought me chocolates, too."

Susan learned early that the way to a man's heart really *was* through his stomach. "If I wanted Jerry home for dinner, I would call him at the office and let him know what

I was cooking. He loved any kind of pasta. Sometimes—not often—he would come home for lunch. He was so appreciative of all my meals and my attempts at new dishes. He always said thank you, and if something didn't turn out, it was okay, and we'd just order a pizza or something. I cut his toast into heart shapes. I trimmed his meat loaf with parsley in the shape of a heart, and I put a love note on his napkin."

But even though Susan Hannah knew that Jerry loved her above everything else, she was sometimes a little envious of the world outside. Jerry drew people to him like a magnet, and he loved getting into long, involved conversations— often with complete strangers. He had an insatiable curiosity about other people's lives and their problems.

Susan remembered the time she and Jerry were having a drink in a bar, and Jerry struck up a conversation with an obviously downhearted young man. The boy wanted desperately to get to Reno so he could propose to his girlfriend, but he said he had no money and no transportation. "Jerry loaned him his Mercedes and gave him money to go to Reno and propose," Susan said. "The guy got married, and he brought the car back, and he was as happy as could be."

Jerry Harris never met a stranger, and he sometimes drove Susan crazy with his surprise visitors. She soon learned to cook whole meals and keep them in the freezer, just in case. "He not only invited friends and colleagues home for dinner without letting me know until the last minute, but on occasion he would meet some guy from out of town—a traveling salesman, maybe—and bring *him* home. Everyone was welcome in Jerry's home."

Susan learned to be accommodating. *More* than accommodating. Her finest moment may have been when Jerry explained that his ex-wife Faye had promised a friend some years earlier that if she ever came to the San Francisco area, she would have a place to stay. The woman, who lived in Chicago, had kept Jerry's business number. "One day," Susan said, "Jerry came home and told me that this young woman wanted to come out to California and make her way. By this time, Jerry's ex-wife was newly married and not interested in the prospect of having a houseguest."

Annoyed, Susan tried to explain to Jerry that he didn't

have to be bound by some invitation his ex-wife had issued years before. "Well, he talked me into it," she said, "because he convinced me I would be a good influence on this woman. So she flew out and I picked up a total stranger and she *lived* with us for a couple of months!

". . . But then my cousin from Wyoming lived with us, another friend lived with us during his divorce, and many others for extended periods of time."

Throughout the years, Susan would "catch" Jerry in secret benevolence, and she asked him once, "Why do you *do* these things for people you don't even *know?*" He looked at her, half-embarrassed, and finally said, "Sue, I just kind of let God work through me."

She was surprised; he had never seemed all that religious to her, but then Jerry was always coming up with surprises.

Although her first priority was Jerry, Susan had never given up her plan to finish college; she had just a year to go. Although he would have preferred to have her stay at home—he made plenty of money—Jerry saw how much her education meant to Susan, and he encouraged her to keep going to school. She had never been that fascinated with marketing as a career; it was something she had drifted into. Nevertheless, Susan kept taking marketing classes, but Jerry could see she was bored. He laughed at the idea that she was taking business classes. Business savvy was as easy for him as breathing. He picked up one of her textbooks, read the title on the spine, and said, "Oh, anybody can write that book. *I* didn't finish college and *I* could write it."

Jerry gave Susan advice from his own experience: "Find something that you would choose to do as a hobby—and then study that. Think of the thing you like to do best, and do that."

Susan laughed and said she knew what she enjoyed the most—buying clothes.

"Then study that," Jerry replied.

Susan signed up for classes at the Fashion Institute in San Francisco, going to school two or three days a week. She was always studying, and Jerry seemed to be traveling constantly. Surprisingly, he didn't resent her dedication to school. Actually, he bent over backwards to be sure she kept up her grades.

"One time," she says, "Jerry had to go to Florida on business, and I went with him—but I had a test in a few days. He flew me back to San Francisco so I wouldn't miss it. Then I found out that he had arranged for his mom and my mom, who were great friends, to meet me in San Francisco after my test. It was a total surprise to me. All three of us went to Fort Lauderdale, and Jerry surprised us all by taking us on a SeaEscape cruise to the Bahamas and to Shreveport."

Then they went to Miami. Jerry took Susan, his mother, and her mother out to dinner in an elegant restaurant that had a dance floor. The air conditioning vent was close to Susan, and she was getting chilly in her bare-shouldered dress. Jerry called the waiter over to ask him to close the vent. With a flourish, the waiter whipped the pink table-cloth off a nearby table and wrapped it around Susan's shoulders.

"My formal was burgundy and my mom said the pink tablecloth matched perfectly," Susan recalled. "Jerry grabbed my hand and asked me to dance—tablecloth and all. I felt like a queen. If we ever got married, I knew I wanted pink and burgundy for my wedding colors."

Susan tried to join Jerry on most of his trips—she often went to Texas with him to pick out the palm tree seedlings—but she was always loaded down with a type-writer and homework. He didn't mind. He wanted her to be as happy with her work as he was with his.

Susan soon had a job as a sales clerk in a retail clothing shop. She never thought of it as a career. She possessed neither the drive nor the obsession to succeed that Jerry did. "I did have a couple of jobs, but it wasn't as though I had high aspirations to conquer the world," she said. "One time I was working, and Jerry came in and asked, 'How long are you going to have to stay here tonight?' And I realized that I didn't want to be there until nine. I wanted to be with Jerry, so I quit on the spot and we left together."

In the end, Susan quit six different jobs, all of them expendable because she preferred to be with Jerry. *He* was her chosen career. He never asked her to leave a job, nor did he admonish her when she did. She was a woman who thoroughly enjoyed making a home—more than any job. It wasn't trendy to aspire to be a housewife in the 1980s, but Susan Hannah marched to the beat of her own drummer. Although she didn't say so aloud, her heartfelt ambition was to be Mrs. Jerry Lee Harris and to have his babies. After three failures, she knew he was skittish about marriage, and she kept her wish to herself.

Jerry Harris never did anything halfway. After they finished their cooking lessons, he had remodeled the kitchen in their Fremont home so that it became a gourmet's paradise. Their home was a far cry from the sparsely furnished bachelor pad it had been. Jerry bought all the special pans and tools needed by a first-class chef, and he and Susan entertained often, cooking everything themselves.

"That was a hobby we had together," Susan remembered, "and it was really fun—having people over to dinner."

Susan was immersed in an entirely new lifestyle. Such a short time ago she had been living in a little apartment with no phone and attending a state-funded college in southern Oregon. Now she lived in Jerry's wonderful house and spent weekends on his sixty-five-foot yacht, the *Tiffany*.

The *Tiffany* was a luxurious floating second home. It had a complete kitchen, a spacious dining area, and a carpeted living room with expensive furniture and wonderful "Jerry" touches that included a golden dolphin statue and a crystal chandelier. The yacht could sleep more friends than most people have, and the deck was sprinkled with sunbathers every weekend. The bridge and its instruments looked like those of a jet plane but Jerry sat at the wheel confidently. For a little boy who had once helped his dad trap furs and a young man who had slaved in the intense heat of a steel mill, the *Tiffany* represented achievement, success, and elegant living. Jerry was never happier than when he was captain of his own ship.

* * *

Jerry's daughter, the real Tiffany, was ten years old when Susan first met her. She was a pretty girl with curly auburn hair, brown eyes, and freckles. The two got along well from the beginning, and Tiffany was always welcome on the yacht or in her dad's home.

Jerry's teenage son, Mike, was slower to accept Susan. He spent more time with Jerry's parents, Faye and Jim Harris, than he did with his father. The Harrises had raised four boys, and they missed having a teenager around the house. Mike filled an empty spot for them.

The longer she was with Jerry, the more impressed Susan was. He was basically a good man who was deeply concerned about other people. His drive to succeed in business was mitigated by his sentimental heart. He usually managed to involve his close friends in his charitable schemes. Since Christmastime 1977, Jerry had delighted in being an anonymous benefactor to destitute families. Faye Marcil, his ex-wife, recalled how Jerry had bought $7,000 worth of stereos, televisions, and toys one Christmas Eve and had them delivered to needy families. "I think he always had a desire to have other people's dreams come true," she said, "to give people a reason to believe in themselves."

Jerry had met his closest friend, Steve King, when he provided backup tapes for Steve's singing act. Tall and handsome, Steve was a talented singer who shared Jerry's dreams. Jerry had expanded Tiffany Studios and become a record producer whose albums came out under the Peak Records label. He released *Prelude,* an album of Steve's songs, recorded, of course, at Tiffany Studios.

"Jerry L. Harris, president, Peak Records" wrote the cover copy on the back of the album: "Every now and then a performer comes along who breaks a few rules, sets some new trends and gives musical entertainment a breath of fresh air! Such is the case with Steve E. King. The fact that Steve and I have become good friends in no way affects my professional judgment of new and exciting talent. In these recordings, you will hear the same energy that Steve generates live on stage."

In his role as a record producer, Jerry posed for the photo on the back of the album. In a fedora, he resembled Sinatra more than Presley. Steve wore a Travolta-like white suit with a bare chest and gold necklace. Dated today, the outfit was in style at the time.

Steve worked as an Elvis impersonator to make a living. So he and Jerry also had that in common. Both of them could mimic Elvis absolutely, and together they sounded like a pure Presley duet.

Steve King's album didn't sell that well, but the men remained close friends. Jerry persuaded Steve to play Santa one year. King delivered clothing, toys, a television set, and hundreds of dollars' worth of food to a San Lorenzo, California, firefighter who had been injured in a terrible fire and was permanently disabled. He had seven children who still believed in Santa. "It was beautiful," King recalled. "It was the best Christmas of my entire life."

Every year after that, the fireman's family was visited by the "secret Santa," who made sure they had a wonderful Christmas. They had no idea who their secret benefactor was. "Jerry went all out," Susan said. "He would go shopping himself and . . . buy a television set for the parents, gifts for all the kids—bicycles and stereos. We would have a wrapping party. On Christmas Eve, when Jerry took the stuff over, he would dress up—or, for him, *down*—like a deliveryman. They always left their house unlocked, and he'd fill the refrigerator full of food. They started expecting that whoever it was would show up every year. They took their secret benefactor on faith. *This* was Jerry's Christmas."

Jerry had attempted to help a lot of families a few years before by starting a group called Friends Helping Friends, but that hadn't worked out, because other members of the group got less enthusiastic each year. He continued alone to be sure that *his* family never missed a Christmas.

That was a Jerry Harris kind of thing to do, just as it had once been an Elvis Presley kind of thing to give away Cadillacs and houses. Both men loved the spotlight unabashedly; they thrived on attention, and they were given to impetuous gestures of charity. Jerry never claimed not to be flamboyant, but he was quiet about most of his philanthropy. Very few people ever knew how much he gave to people who were down on their luck.

Most people liked Jerry Harris and his easy, natural smile, his bravado, his ebullience, his tightwire walk of a life. If they didn't, Jerry always shrugged it off. "If you can't take a joke," he would say, "hell with you." That was the only swearword he used. Although the world he moved in was often rough, he deplored profanity. He had to be quick on his feet and work like any three men to keep his many businesses booming. Bankers liked his financial statement. They liked the profits he could generate. He could get a loan over the phone—on just his signature, when he had time to come down and sign a note.

Other people viewed Jerry Harris less kindly, however. A Union City steel executive who had known Jerry for twenty years commented, "He pursued goals ruthlessly. He had to step on somebody's toes."

And step on toes Jerry did. He took chances and leveraged one business against another. What some men called confidence, others called cockiness. His charisma made less charming men envious. His decisions were not always sound, but when he failed, he simply picked up his marbles and moved on.

When the palm tree business began crying out for more land, Jerry looked to a man he had counted as a friend and whom he could trust completely—a banker named Ben Burk.* Burk had loaned Jerry money innumerable times; Jerry had always paid it back. It was Burk's bank, in fact, that had financed Jerry's yacht. When Jerry told him that he needed to expand his growing space, Burk suggested that he consider buying property that was being foreclosed. In fact, Burk knew of some land near San Diego that would be ideal for growing the palm seedlings.

Jerry bought the land, which included an avocado orchard and a good large house with a tile roof. Susan's aunt and uncle moved in. It seemed like a great solution for everyone.

On Burk's advice, Jerry also bought a gas station and a

San Diego company called Tool Bin,* which rented out heavy construction equipment. The company was currently having a rough time, but Burk thought it could be a winner, and Jerry trusted Burk's business sense.

"Okay," Jerry said half jokingly, "I'll buy it if you'll manage it for me."

Burk took him up on it, moved south to San Diego, and became the manager of the Tool Bin rental company. It had sounded like such a promising company when Burk described it, but in truth, it was mortally flawed, and some wondered whether Ben Burk knew that. Even so, Burk went on Jerry Harris's payroll at $90,000 a year. Tool Bin was too far away for Jerry to check on it in person very often, but he didn't worry because Ben was on the scene taking care of things.

Jerry was an entrepreneur who took tremendous risks in business, but he considered himself a good judge of investment opportunities. The trouble was that he operated on instinct and was way off the mark with Ben Burk.

"I knew immediately that something was wrong," Molly Clemente recalled, when the bottom fell out of the San Diego business. "My husband and I had just come back from our vacation in Mexico. There Jerry was at the airport with my kids, and he looked awful."

Molly knew Jerry so well that she could tell he was trying to be cheerful for her sake. "He told me he had just found out that the business was in real trouble. . . . He was really concerned. Jerry didn't get too upset about things and money [but] it was the principle of the thing. He had trusted Ben too much; he had become a really good friend."

Despite its continuing losses, Jerry Harris held on to Tool Bin and brought in a new manager. Still, the company limped along, never approaching the success Burk had promised.

On top of that, the San Diego weather proved unsuitable for growing seedling palms, and the land Ben Burk had touted so highly lay fallow, another reminder that Jerry's trusted friend had let him down.

Jerry knew he had to find a suitable place for his forest of half-grown trees. With the next staging, the bigger pots would burst the greenhouse walls of Tiffany Plant Rentals.

With no other choice, he bought a nursery that was in foreclosure in Lodi, California—much closer to home—and set about restoring it to give his crowded crop more room to grow.

He got the Lodi nursery up and going, only to realize that he could never keep ahead of the burgeoning crop. He couldn't buy back all the mature trees, nor could he find enough outlets to sell them on a retail market.

"By now," Molly Clemente said, "we've got millions. And there was no way he was going to get rid of all those palm trees—even if he sold them at a penny apiece!"

Steve Bonilla, the titular head of Sun State Tropicals, seemed untroubled by the problems of the palm tree business. He counted on Jerry to solve them. Molly didn't like Bonilla, whom she considered plain lazy, but she saw that Jerry felt sorry for him long after other people had thrown their hands up at his ineptness. Jerry always gave people more slack than the average man, and he was infinitely patient with Steven Bonilla, even when Steve insisted on changing the palm tree operation into something that smelled crooked.

Finally, however, in the mid-1980s, Jerry Harris got out of the nursery-investment business. The initial concept had been a good idea, but he realized he had come to a point where he was barely breaking even despite the money coming in. He was carrying most of the cost and almost all of the worry.

Al Jennings and Steve Bonilla stayed with the business and brought in new partners. Jerry didn't care if he never saw a palm tree again, but the nursery operation would one day come back to haunt him.

Susan didn't want to see Jerry completely abandon his interest in growing things, and they held on to the original Tiffany's Plant Rentals. There was something special about the humid floral-and-earth smell of the greenhouses that made Jerry happy and gave him a few hours' downtime from the rest of his life.

"He loved working in the dirt," Susan said. "We spent many hours digging in the dirt together, alone in the greenhouses, and I liked that, too. Jerry had a green thumb, and he could make anything grow. He would mess with plants to the point where I thought they would die from abuse, and then they would snap back and be much more beautiful than before."

The original nursery was precious to Jerry; perhaps it gave him a sense of security. Other businesses would come and go, but Jerry didn't sell Tiffany's until the fall of 1987. Even then, he missed it.

But like the shoemaker's children who went barefoot, the yard on Chaparral Street was a wasteland. "We had the worst yard in town," Susan said. "I tried to pull weeds occasionally, but it needed constant attention—which it didn't get. The only time Jerry went all out was when my parents came down from Oregon. He hired workers from the nursery to redecorate with fresh plants, gardeners to pull all the weeds, a cleaning company to steam-clean the carpets, a housekeeper to polish everything, and he bought a new bed for the guest room. It was chaotic. I don't know why he always wanted to impress my folks—they wouldn't have cared. I think he wanted them to know that he was taking good care of me."

Susan and Jerry traveled back and forth between Oregon and California often. When her younger sister, Julie, was married, Jerry brought friends to provide the entertainment for the ceremony. In addition to that, "He had Tim Lee, the captain and mechanic of our yacht, and his wife, Lynn, drive up in a truck with sound equipment and plants from the nursery and cases and cases of wine—not the *good* stuff," Susan said. "He bought them tickets to Hawaii for their honeymoon. . . . When my younger brother was married, Jerry found out there was no entertainment, so he found a local band to play. Jerry sang at so many events. He was really popular in my family. Family friends of my parents were having a wedding anniversary once, and Jerry drove up especially to sing for them at their reception."

One of Susan's favorite stories about their trips to Oregon—if not *the* favorite—still made her giggle. She and Jerry had made yet another trip north, this time to visit his brother Jim. Jim had instructed them to meet him at his girlfriend's house. They had never met the girlfriend, who lived far out on some back road in southern Oregon. They found the house, parked Jerry's bright red Ferrari in the driveway, and knocked on the door—but no one answered. Jerry knew Jim and figured he had gone somewhere and would be back in a few minutes.

"The door was unlocked, so we just went inside," Susan remembered. "It was a very hot summer afternoon, and we were dying of thirst, so we opened the refrigerator, and there was a six-pack of beer. We each took one, drank it, and waited for Jim. Well, one thing led to another, and the next thing . . ." Susan looked down. "Well, we got carried away on the pool table. The house didn't have any air conditioning . . . so we decided to take a shower in the master bedroom—a long shower. We got dressed and *still* no Jim. We finished the rest of the beers, and then we left that house, went to my Mom's. Jim called and said, 'Where *are* you two? We've been waiting for *hours!*'"

Jerry and Susan had whiled away the afternoon in a complete stranger's house. "I always wondered what those people thought when they got home," Susan laughed. "Missing beer, wet towels in the bathroom, and my hair bow on the pool table."

3

Despite his misfortunes Jerry Harris wasn't soured on the concept of starting new businesses. He continued to look for new opportunities. Actually, he had long since become bored with raising palm trees for tax shelters and he had always enjoyed the challenge of launching another new enterprise far more than he did the day-to-day management of his companies; he became disenchanted quickly with details and repetitive tasks.

Susan saw that and made it a point to understand the inner workings of all of Jerry's far-flung ventures. Susan was always a great deal more than she seemed to be. It was true that she was the beautiful girl on Jerry's arm, but she was also highly intelligent and she understood marketing and how businesses were run. Most people who saw them together didn't realize that Susan wasn't just window dressing for Jerry. Because he had always attracted lovely women, people made the mistake of thinking Susan was only Jerry's current girl.

She didn't mind, though. Susan was the quiet one, and Jerry was the flamboyant one. She was perfectly happy to let him do the talking while she sat beside him. With her remarkable gift for reading people, she could quickly spot someone who was attempting to use Jerry.

"He always told me how much he appreciated me," Susan recalled. "We would be driving someplace and he would tell me, 'Sue, the only reason I can succeed in my goals is because you're beside me. I can count on you—always. I don't need to do anything but concentrate on business, because I trust you.'"

And then he would grab her and give her a big kiss. A day didn't go by when Jerry didn't tell Susan how much he loved her and needed her.

Jerry talked to Susan about the possibility of their going into the nightclub business in the San Francisco area. He envisioned unique clubs that would be evocative of the fifties and would appeal not only to those who collected Elvis, Ricky Nelson, and Buddy Holly records but also to kids in their twenties. It would take seed money and hard work, but that had never stopped Jerry Harris.

Seeing the enthusiasm in his eyes, Susan nodded. His real interest was music and rock and roll. He was a child of the fifties, and even though he was nearing middle age, Jerry was an insatiable fan of the music of his teen years. He was never happier than when he was producing albums or making new backup tapes—unless it was when he clapped a fedora on his head and gazed at a nightclub audience from a high stool while he sang onstage. As Jerry ticked off the good points about owning vintage-inspired nightclubs, Susan could see that he had already made up his mind.

Jerry liked to have Susan with him even when he was just doing paperwork. And she went to every meeting she could—with his banker, his accountant. "Our personal life was so entwined with business. The creation of our clubs happened during meals and in the car driving somewhere. Jerry had to travel to Monterey and San Diego and Lodi. I usually went with him. I wasn't involved in the conversations. Jerry knew what he was doing, and he was good at it. I was like a mouse in the corner; I only gave my opinions when we were alone," she said. "It was easy to learn about people when I just listened. I used to remind him of who was who at parties and what the wives had to say about their husbands. If a man had integrity in his personal life, he would certainly have it in business."

In early 1983, Jerry found a place that looked as though it would work as a jumping-off spot. It was a large restaurant on Mission Boulevard in Hayward. It was called Frenchy's, and it operated as a restaurant only during the day and then became a nightclub after the dinner hour until 2:00 A.M. It attracted a fairly rough crowd—not Jerry's type. He figured he could cut down on the undesirable patrons by enforcing a dress code.

Frenchy's was the first of Jerry and Susan's high-energy clubs. The crowds loved the 1950s music. They did a huge business for about eight months, bringing in a thousand people a night. Steve Bonilla noted that and went to the club one day to talk to Jerry. He explained that he knew the bar business well—he'd inherited a bar when his father died.

"Jerry gave Steve a job managing Frenchy's in the evenings," Molly Clemente said. "It only lasted about a month or five weeks."

Molly seemed as bemused by the unlikely friendship between Jerry and Steve Bonilla as did everyone who knew them. Everything Steve set his hand to turned to ashes, but Jerry still felt responsible for helping him. Predictably, Steve managed to disrupt the formerly pleasant relationships among the members of Frenchy's staff.

"The people who worked there were ready to quit," Molly said. "Steve just didn't have the personality to work with all those people. People didn't like him."

Jerry was easing gradually into the nightclub business, and Frenchy's did not remain his only club for long. In July he purchased a place in Fremont known as the Penthouse Lounge. He ran the Penthouse Lounge, and he saw what worked and what didn't. He was beginning to formulate improvisations on his theme, but he needed time—and monetary backing—to develop his ideas into what he knew they could become. Jerry was the idea man and the owner of the clubs, the man credited for creating the concepts and whose personality drew the crowds in. All he had to do was *be* there, sitting at the bar, talking to his customers. He didn't do hands-on management; he always had a manager in place for the day-to-day operations of all of his businesses, including the nightclubs.

Steve King dropped in when he could. Jerry heartily supported Steve's singing career, and the two remained fast friends in the way some friendships transcend a business relationship. There were others who were friends simply because business interests brought them into Jerry's world.

As Jerry's nightclubs blossomed in the Bay Area, both Steves were part of Jerry and Susan's social life. Susan liked Steve King; she merely accepted Steve Bonilla. When he came along on the Tiffany weekend yacht outings wearing swim trunks, Susan thought he was the hairiest man she had ever seen, covered as he was with dark fur all over his body. She had to admit that wasn't his fault, but she giggled to Jerry that all the hair was going off his head and onto his back.

Susan had been put off by Bonilla the first time she met him. "He showed up at our house one night for dinner," she recalled. "I don't know if Jerry had invited him or not, but if he did, he hadn't told me."

Steve Bonilla deferred to Jerry in a way that seemed false, and he ignored Susan completely as if she weren't even in the room. But Bonilla had apparently admired her husband ever since their school days. He seemed to want to emulate Jerry in every way he could, and he had almost begged Jerry to let him invest money in the nightclubs. But Jerry wasn't a man who worked with partners. Susan was his only partner and he liked it that way.

Susan learned that Steven Bonilla was the only son of Ella Bonilla, whose family had monetary resources that appeared to be bottomless. Ella also had a teenage daughter who was afflicted with cerebral palsy. While Ella's daughter got most of her personal attention, she funded Steve in his endless pursuit of a career that would bring him respect and wealth. From the time he was a child, all Steve had to do was tell Ella that he wanted something, and she would move heaven and earth to get it for him.

When Steve approached Ella Bonilla and told her that he wanted to be part of the Penthouse Lounge, she made Jerry Harris an offer that was hard to refuse: she would lend him money for his nightclubs, with no strings attached; all she asked was that he give Steve a job.

It seemed like found money. Jerry knew he could easily pay it back. He got along well with Steve Bonilla, but then, Jerry got along with almost everyone. After the problems at Frenchy's, very few people would have let Bonilla come back aboard. He grated on most people's nerves.

Steve Bonilla and Jerry Harris were unlike each other in temperament. Where Jerry was like catnip for women, Steve was quiet and sullen. Jerry Harris was a leader, a visionary, and Steve Bonilla was a bandwagon-jumper with a murky past, eager to be part of what Jerry had begun. Nevertheless, Bonilla began working as Jerry Harris's assistant. John Jacques, head executive of Jerry's clubs, rather bitterly described them as a classic honcho-sidekick team. "Jerry had to be the star," Jacques said. "Steve told him how good he was."

"I was nice to Steve," Susan says. "But only . . . because I tried to be nice to everyone. If Jerry wanted Steve to be in our home, I was polite to Steve out of respect to Jerry. He treated me like a little blond housewife who didn't know anything about anything."

She wasn't the first woman to dislike some of her man's friends. Susan had to smile sometimes at the way Steve Bonilla openly copied Jerry. Jerry had a head of thick hair, but he loved to collect hats. He had skipper's caps, straw sombreros, and cowboy hats, but his favorites were the soft fedoras he often wore in the evening. Soon Steve Bonilla was collecting hats, too.

"One time Jerry bought us several exotic birds," Susan says. "We had about eight of them, including a big macaw. I guess I wasn't surprised when Steve Bonilla announced that he was buying some rare birds, too."

Some of Steve Bonilla's personal and business relationships made him a less than desirable sidekick. Even his ex-wives remembered him with rancor. Ginger* Bonilla, his second ex-wife, said, "Steve attached himself to Jerry because of [Jerry's] success." It might have been the bitter complaints of a disgruntled ex-wife: Ginger and Steve had waged a vicious child custody battle. One day she would describe her ex-husband as a man of uncontrollable temper who had physically assaulted her.

Jerry didn't know about this; he actually felt kind of sorry for Steve, who wanted so badly to *be* somebody and to live an exciting life where he was big honcho. But all of Ella Bonilla's money couldn't change the fact that Steve had the personality and imagination of a stump. Success had always eluded Steve Bonilla, who had never held a job or kept a relationship together for long. A good many of his problems may well have been of his own making.

Jerry knew about some of Bonilla's almost comic mishaps; others he would never learn about. In 1978, Steve had bought Independent Caterers, a lunch-truck supply firm. An arson fire destroyed his business a month later. That was why he had a corporation but no business to run when he walked into Tiffany Plant Rentals a few years later.

Steve Bonilla and Jerry Harris worked together in the Penthouse Lounge for a year. Steve was on site more than Jerry, but Jerry called all the shots. At one point, Jerry discovered that $1,000 was missing from the safe. If there was one thing he hated, it was a thief. He suggested to Steve that everyone take a polygraph test, but Bonilla demurred. He assured Jerry he would take care of the problem. He never discovered the culprit, but there were no more thefts, so Jerry let it go.

After a year, Jerry saw that the club didn't have what he wanted. It wasn't *his*—not really. It was still the Penthouse Lounge, the same place that had been there on State Street in Fremont for fifteen years. Jerry could see in his mind the restaurant he wanted. More space and more glitz. In October 1984 he sold the Penthouse Lounge to two couples at a profit, repaid Ella Bonilla, and looked around for a location where he could carry out his vision.

At this point Steve Bonilla went into the cookie business. He called his product Kelly's Cookies. "He wanted to be the next Mrs. Fields," Susan recalled, "but his cookies were *green*—great big greasy green cookies!"

Even though Ella Bonilla invested $250,000 in Kelly's Cookies, her son's venture got off the ground with all the impetus of his other enterprises, which meant Bonilla would probably be out of business almost before he began. Jerry and Susan looked at his product and took pity on him. Bonilla asked Susan if she would help him launch his product at a convention for new business franchises in Las Vegas. Jerry winked at her, and she said she would. "I stood there and passed out big green cookies to people who walked by," Susan said. "Kelly's cookies."

Jerry and Susan took their most adventuresome cruise on the *Tiffany* in 1983—to Mexico. They docked at Huntington Beach for three months while preparing for the trip. The entire project lasted six months, although they flew back to the Bay Area periodically. During the first leg of the trip, Jerry invited his mother, his parents' best friends, Steve Bonilla and one of his ex-wives, and three or four other couples. They took two weeks cruising to Cabo San Lucas.

They stopped at a small coastal village one night to take on fuel. When it grew dark, they watched movies on laser disc, a phenomenon that fascinated a dozen Mexicans who worked in a mill in the town. One by one, the men gathered outside the *Tiffany* and watched the magical machine that was showing Michael Jackson's new video. Jerry noticed them and invited them all to come inside. They were hesitant until Jerry insisted, gave them each a beer, and found places for them to sit.

"For them, it was like going to the movies," Susan remembered. "For Jerry, it was one more way to make new friends."

The Mexico cruise would have a profound effect on Susan, although it would take her years to understand how much.

Jerry was biding his time. He still owned Frenchy's, which was holding its own, and his original nursery and recording studio. Then he took back the Penthouse Lounge because he felt sorry for the two couples who had purchased it from him. They were not doing well running it.

"They ran it for about a year," Susan says. "Jerry took it back. . . . He forgave their note because he didn't want them to lose their houses. They had put their houses up for collateral. . . . This was in October 1985."

That year, 1985, was one of the most eventful years of Jerry Harris's life. He sensed that Susan was not really happy being his live-in girlfriend. He had fallen in love with her because she was an old-fashioned girl, and despite the life they lived together with yachts and fabulous vacations and the nightclub world, she was still that girl. She wanted to marry him. And Jerry, who had sworn off marriage forever, was surprised to realize that he wanted to marry her, too.

Jerry asked Steven King to be his best man. As his best friend, King was the natural choice. His brothers had stood up for him at his earlier weddings, but now Jerry told Susan he was going to ask Steve Bonilla to be in the wedding party, explaining that it would make Bonilla happy to be asked. Bonilla wouldn't have been Susan's choice, but she nodded. She was joyously making wedding plans, and it seemed like a small thing for Jerry to ask.

Around Christmastime 1984, just weeks before the wedding, Jerry and Susan invited his family, her family, Susan's best friend, Steve Bonilla, and Ella Bonilla to dinner.

Susan cooked for the crowd of almost two dozen people, and everyone seemed to be having a great time. But then Susan was taken off guard when Bonilla pulled her aside and hissed, "Listen, just because you're going to be Jerry's wife doesn't mean you're going to be involved in his business dealings. Stay out!"

Susan stared at him, startled. She wondered what he was talking about. She had always been involved in Jerry's businesses—they were part of Jerry's life, and Steve Bonilla had no right to warn her away. He wasn't even a partner. Why, she wondered, did Steve feel so threatened by her new position in Jerry's life?

Theresa Susan Hannah and Jerry Lee Harris had a wonderful wedding on January 12, 1985. It remains, on videotape, a testimony of sound and film to two elated people about to embark on married life. Before the tape of the wedding itself, a half-hour interview with the bride- and groom-to-be captures how they were then. Obviously in love, Jerry grins at the camera and teases Susan about how she "trapped" him. She is shy but beaming with happiness. A dozen years later it is almost painful to see the images flicker across the screen.

Once Jerry decided to marry Susan, he went all the way. He had provided the floral displays for so many other people's weddings. This time it was his own. The Church of the Nazarene and the reception looked like a garden. The colors were burgundy and pink, a tribute to the night in Miami when Susan had worn a pink tablecloth around her shoulders and Jerry waltzed her around the dance floor. Jerry's cousin, a minister in the church, performed the ceremony. Steve King was his best man, and Steve Bonilla was a groomsman. Susan's sisters stood up for her. The wedding party left the church and headed in limousines for a lavish dinner reception at Frenchy's.

They were as happy as it was possible to be, the groom in his white tux jacket and the bride in a picture hat with a veil and an exquisite wedding dress with a long train. Their parents, Jim and Faye Harris and Pete and Mary Jo Hannah, joined the rest of the wedding party at the head table. After dinner, the bride and groom danced and sang with their guests until nearly dawn.

Jerry sang "their" song to Sue: "I Can't Help Falling in Love with You." He grinned happily, aware that the man who was never going to get married again had capitulated.

The two Steves, King and Bonilla, smiled for the cameras as they whirled their girlfriends around the floor. Everyone seemed to have been rooting secretly for Susan to get this lifelong commitment from Jerry. His mother, Faye, looked into the videocamera and made a typical mother's statement, "Susan is very, very lucky to find a husband as wonderful and successful as Jerry."

Susan Hannah Harris felt exactly the same way.

Typical of Jerry Harris, he was collecting charitable donations at his own wedding reception. He had learned of a young girl who needed an operation to restore her hearing. After the first three rounds of drinks, he started "charging" but explained that the money was going toward the operation. By the end of the evening, he had thousands of dollars, and the child got her surgery.

4

Just as he had survived the bullet in his gut when he was thirteen, Jerry Harris's almost eerie good luck had seen him through any number of other narrow scrapes. He seemed impervious to harm. He barely noticed the surgical scar that seemed to bisect his abdomen. He was a daredevil who drove fast, powerful cars and risked his neck as casually as he risked financial loss. Before Susan met Jerry, he had raced Corvettes. He was fearless behind the wheel. In one aspect, he was like a naughty little boy: he didn't have a driver's license.

"Jerry lost his license in 1960, and he never bothered to get another one. So he wasn't in the computer system. He got tickets for not having a license and for speeding, and I went promptly and paid them for him," Susan said. "He was outrageous, but it was a game with him. Once the tickets were paid, the authorities weren't looking for him. All those years, and he never had a driver's license."

Sometimes Jerry scared Susan, although he always believed he was perfectly safe. Her photo album was full of shots of Jerry pretending to leap off cliffs or hanging over the side of his yacht while Susan stood by nervously. Although he was almost twenty years older than she was, he sometimes acted like a teenager. She had never known anyone who enjoyed life as much as Jerry did or who took so many chances.

On one of their cruises, they moored the *Tiffany* in almost exactly the same spot—near Avalon on Catalina Island—where Natalie Wood had drowned at Thanksgiving time 1981. While trying to tie a dinghy to *Splendor,* the yacht that she and her husband, Robert Wagner, owned, the actress had fallen into the deep water. In an eerie replay, Jerry tried to step from the *Tiffany's* dinghy, slipped, fell into the water, and yelled, "Hey, Sue!"

"I didn't hear him," Susan remembered. "The waves were so loud. He was trying to step onto the deck of the *Tiffany* from the dinghy, and he slipped between the two. He dislocated his shoulder, but he managed to get back on the dinghy. He'd been yelling for a long time, and I didn't even hear him calling to me. . . . We understood why no one heard Natalie Wood. The sound carried so oddly on the ocean that you thought it was coming from the wrong direction. And sometimes you heard nothing but the wind."

Jerry Harris took chances on the road as well as on the ocean. He drove like a bat out of hell, always well above the speed limit. His cars all had powerful engines, and they were the kind that attracted the squinty-eyed stares of police officers. Ralph Springer, an Oregon State Trooper, once clocked Jerry in his red Ferrari at 103 miles an hour through Springer's patrol sector near Medford.

"He shook his head and let Jerry go," Susan said,

laughing. "He told Jerry he didn't see anything in the book about flying too low. He warned Jerry never to drive that way again in his district.

"Jerry loved that story, and he never forgot that trooper." Susan shook her head. "Jerry was just a total risk-taker."

Jerry's good fortune stayed with him as he moved into his forties. And then, just when he and Susan had married and she could see a real future ahead for them, she almost lost him. In 1985 Jerry invited his dad and Susan's father to accompany him on a fishing trip to Alaska. Pete Hannah had long since accepted Jerry as a son and forgiven him for spiriting Susan away from Oregon. The three men had a great time batching it in Alaska.

But that fishing trip almost ended tragically. Jerry had walked away from the others to check out the terrain. He stepped onto a sandbar, which suddenly began to sink. He had thought he was near a slough that was filled with water and mud. In reality, it was quicksand. Laughing at first, Jerry came close to panic as he sank slowly but inexorably. The more he tried to get out, the faster he sank. He was in the sucking sand up to his shoulders, totally helpless, when Susan's dad spotted him.

Pete Hannah was always a very strong man, toughened by many years as a millwright, but that day he showed more agility than he could have believed possible. Adrenaline and desperation gave him speed and power as he broke a long branch off a tree and leaped across floating logs toward where Jerry was rapidly disappearing. Pete held the limb out far enough for Jerry to grab it, but by this time, Jerry's head had vanished and only his arm protruded from the quicksand, waving blindly. Miraculously, he made contact with the branch and Pete fought the deadly suction of the quicksand until he finally managed to pull Jerry out. Jim Harris lost his right boot in the deadly pit as the older men waded in just far enough to get Jerry to the edge of the quicksand. They threw a blanket around him and dried his clothes and parka over a bonfire.

Jerry, being Jerry, made a joke out of the incident, but the thought of how close he had come to sinking beneath the sand gave Susan the shivers. Her father could never even speak about it; it was Jerry who praised Pete's almost superhuman effort to save him. "I guess he must like me, after all," Jerry laughed to Susan.

"There was a bond between them after that," Susan said. "Dad saved Jerry's life, and it brought them a lot closer."

Pete Hannah had been far more frightened than Jerry, who continued to seek out danger. He was walking alone on that same Alaskan trip when a huge grizzly bear reared up in his path, towering many feet above him. He was enthusiastic as he told Sue about it later. "He was magnificent. I just stood still, and he didn't touch me."

After that, Susan remembered that Jerry was intrigued with bears. "He was just fascinated by bears. He came home, and he wanted to go to the bookstore. He bought every book they had on bears. It never occurred to him that he might have been eaten alive—or maybe it did—and he wanted to know more about them."

Jerry had always believed that the more you knew about your opponent, the better off you were—in a fight or in a business deal. And usually he did know who he was dealing with.

Jerry Harris was ready to accelerate his move into the nightclub business. He had met a man named Gilbert Konqui, a multitalented native of France. Konqui was a brilliant interior designer. In 1974 he'd designed a club in Vancouver, British Columbia. The club, called Pharaohs, was an instantaneous success. Bearded and handsome, Konqui was soon a design consultant to hundreds of nightclubs in North America and Europe.

Jerry knew what he wanted in terms of concept and ambience. He visualized that he and Konqui would work as a team to create clubs the like of which the south Bay Area had never seen.

Jerry closed down his first club, Frenchy's, temporarily in mid-1985 while he and Konqui worked to metamorphose it into a nightspot to be known as Shakers. In the space of a few months, Shakers opened as a high-energy, high-volume club catering to a crowd in their early twenties. There was a disc jockey who played Top 40 music, and Shakers did turn-away business, especially on weekends. In a matter of weeks, it was doing four times the business that Frenchy's had done.

In fact, business was so good that there was a problem finding enough parking space for its patrons. A hotel next door had an arrangement with a tow-truck company. So many of his customers' cars had been towed away for several nights in a row that Shakers' management team called Jerry at home. He tried initially to deal reasonably with the towing company, but they insisted that if his customers wanted their cars, they would have to pay the hefty tow fee.

Jerry Harris was not a fighter by nature, and he never lost his temper. But he had a point beyond which he could not be pushed. He would take on a couple of men at a time—that was how his nose had been broken three times. With his customers standing angrily behind him, he eyed their car keys, which were hanging on a board in the towing company's office. Then he leaped over the counter, grabbed the keys, and tossed them to the owners, who wasted no time getting out of the lot. Enraged, the towing yard's owner shut the gates behind them, and chased Jerry to his Bronco.

Harris could be stubborn when he felt he was in the right. His customers had managed to drive their cars away, but the tow operator leaped onto Jerry's Bronco to stop Jerry from crashing through the gate. Jerry floored his accelerator, and the Bronco ended up wedged between the gate and a steel pole, its entire right side crumpled in.

The police came and surveyed the situation, but Jerry didn't get a ticket and there were no more impounded cars.

"Jerry was the hero for a couple of nights," Susan remembered. But he was embarrassed that he had "lost it." Losing his temper was out of character for him.

When Jerry forgave the note signed by the two couples who had bought the Penthouse Lounge, he got the ailing club back. Now he looked at the place in a whole new light. With Gil Konqui, he planned to create a nightclub that embodied all of his favorite things.

The concept of the new club was entirely Jerry's. He

would call the place the Hot Rod Cafe, and it would evoke the spirit of the fifties. Jerry Harris let his memory and imagination run free. Konqui nodded, reading his mind. Together they designed a club ablaze with neon, mirrors, and bright colors. A 1927 Ford hot rod sat parked on the black-and-white checkered floor. There was a 1953 jukebox and genuine gas pumps. One of the lights alone cost $8,000; it had been used in the Steve Martin movie, *The Man With Two Brains,* and it swirled with pink neon gas.

The murals featured Marilyn Monroe, a beach with blue skies, 1950s convertibles, and vintage hamburger stands. Glittering mirrored balls high above the dance floor cast circling lights on the dancers, reminding patrons of their high school proms. Here everyone could be seventeen again, if only for a few hours. There were ice-cream tables and chairs, and a replica of the Columbia space shuttle was suspended overhead. For Jerry Harris, it was a wonderland. Sure, he hoped to see the place turn a profit—but, more than that, the Hot Rod Club was to be a re-creation, a super replica, of the spots where he'd hung out in his teens.

On one occasion Jerry actually hauled sand into the Hot Rod so that the black-and-white tile floor resembled a real beach.

There was an unemployment office across the street from the first Hot Rod club, and when Jerry needed painters, he walked over and approached a couple of men who seemed to be unlikely candidates. He could have afforded to hire a subcontractor, but the men waiting there day after day for any kind of a job had always gotten to him. The new painters turned out to be dedicated and good workmen, and Jerry hired them full-time to do various construction jobs.

The Hot Rod opened in Fremont on December 13, 1985. The cover charge was a modest four dollars, but customers had to be twenty-one to get in, and those who arrived in jeans and T-shirts never made it past the door. This club was designed to be nostalgic—but definitely high-class. Hamburgers, french fries, and "exotic sandwiches" were prepared at the Old General Store and Company next door. Sometimes Susan made the sandwiches.

The club was a smash. Jerry had gambled, sinking

$150,000 into the old Penthouse Lounge. And his gamble paid off. His new club got write-ups in local papers and was featured in industry magazines. He was already designing more Hot Rod clubs in his head. Jerry told reporters he expected to recoup his investment in six months, just as he had done with Shakers. He explained that he would open Hot Rod Cafes in San Jose, San Mateo, Pleasanton, and Walnut Creek.

"How could it miss?" he asked rhetorically, waving his arm at the first Hot Rod Cafe.

Indeed, 1985 was a halcyon year for the Jerry Harrises. They were married, Jerry had three booming nightclubs, and they enjoyed a wonderful getaway almost every weekend on the *Tiffany*, which was as big as most houses.

Susan went everywhere with Jerry, and she knew all the details of their business endeavors. He was having fun doing what he had always advised her to do: "Find a hobby that you like, something you're really interested in, and make a career out of it."

Susan felt much more secure now than she ever had before. When she first moved to California to be Jerry's girl, she had eyed the women who clustered around him warily. She wondered why he had chosen her and worried that he might tire of her. But as the years passed and he remained as devoted as ever, she relaxed. She knew how much Jerry loved her; he showed it in many ways—the flowers, the gifts, the way he couldn't seem to go more than an hour or two without calling her, and the way he held her hand, as if they were new lovers.

Susan had long since come to realize that Jerry never looked at another woman with anything more than a normal appreciation for beauty. He was a monogamous man. Although he left the house in the early morning hours and often didn't get back until midnight, Susan never doubted that he was working. Jerry loved to work; it was part of him, and because that was the way it was, it was a part of Susan too.

Susan missed Jerry when he was gone all day. Even if he was busy and hadn't much time to talk to her, she still liked to be close to him and watch the way his face changed as he talked. "And he smelled wonderful." Susan laughed, remembering. "He had cologne and soap and aftershave, and they all matched. I never met a man who smelled as good as Jerry."

Susan often showed up to surprise him and have lunch or supper with him. Sometimes she tried to lure him home early.

"I would go down to the office and get Jerry to come home so he could eat dinner," Susan remembered. "Usually he would be on the phone with his feet on the desk, throwing wads of paper into the wastebasket. He would smile when I walked in and give me that nod that meant 'I'm almost ready.' I realize now that I didn't comprehend the tremendous amount of stress he must have carried— not until the time I sat at his desk myself. He shielded me from the world in the way he presented it to me. He never said anything bad about *anyone*."

And Jerry was, at heart, a family man. He loved Susan's family as well as his own, and he was never happier than when he was surrounded by a crowd of relatives. Every trip they took would have been a total-family junket if Jerry had had his way.

Susan and Jerry saw Steve King a lot, but Steve Bonilla wasn't around much that year. They had seen little of him since their wedding, and assumed that he was still busy with Kelly's Cookies. Susan certainly didn't miss him, but Jerry wondered once in a while if Bonilla was doing all right.

Couples lined up to pay the cover charge at the Hot Rod Cafe and join the crowd on the black-and-white tile floor to dance once more to the songs of the fifties. On weekends Jerry brought in up-and-coming comedians. The place was fun for its patrons and it was fun for Jerry and Susan.

The first year, Jerry and Susan netted a half million dollars *after* expenses from the Hot Rod.

Jerry Harris was a workaholic who was blessed—or cursed—with an innovative business sense. True, he had to be nimble to keep all his enterprises in motion like so many juggler's plates revolving atop sticks. If one slowed down and started to wobble, Jerry raced to get it spinning again. He used money where it was needed most, then deftly paid off debts in a breathtaking last-minute rush. He had made a tremendous amount of money, but he usually owed a tremendous amount, too. That didn't seem to bother him, though; it was only an interesting challenge to be met.

With two clubs booming, Jerry looked around for a third. Typically, he tried a different concept this time, even though he intended to build more Hot Rod Cafes. On Stevens Creek Boulevard in Cupertino, near San Jose, he found a location that appealed to him. This time he studied the demographics of the local population and asked Gilbert Konqui to design something that would appeal to a clientele that was a little older and more upwardly mobile.

"That club was primarily for people in the computer industry," Susan said. It was in the Silicon Valley, where thousands of people were employed in designing and building computers.

While he was involved in opening this latest nightclub, Jerry Harris took on another financial burden. His father, Jim, owned a company on Blackie Road in Castroville called SteelFab, which manufactured iron rebars used in construction. In mid-1987, Jim Harris had a stroke. He would recover, but he would never be the vigorous man he had been. Jerry was touched when Steve Bonilla had a huge floral arrangement delivered to his father's hospital room.

Jerry saw that SteelFab was more than his father could handle. The rebar plant came complete with a debt of $800,000, but Jerry took it on anyway. He had always been the son who assumed family responsibility, and he didn't think twice about taking pressure off his dad. If he couldn't turn the company into a moneymaking proposition, he figured he could sell it and keep his parents' credit intact.

SteelFab was just one more plate for Jerry to juggle.

Susan and Jerry decided to call their new club in Cupertino the Baritz, a slightly different spelling of the name of one of the fanciest Cadillacs ever made. Jerry figured nobody in San Jose would know how to spell Biarritz, and the two names were pronounced more or less the same and evoked the same image of wealth and upscale entertainment.

Jerry went to his bankers for financing. If at all possible, he wanted to be the sole owner of Baritz. The banks had been delighted with the Hot Rod clubs' showing, and they agreed to a substantial loan of several hundred thousand dollars on the Baritz project.

Construction costs spiraled, however, with Jerry and Gilbert Konqui both coming up with flamboyant but expensive touches for the upscale club. When Jerry went back to the bankers, they shook their heads; they had to put a cap on the loan.

While they were preparing to launch Baritz, Ella Bonilla and several of her relatives invited Susan and Jerry to have dinner at Bobby McGee's restaurant. As delicately as she could, Ella explained that Steve's cookie business had failed miserably. Green cookies hadn't had the same impact on consumers that Mrs. Fields chocolate-chip cookies had. Yes, they had enjoyed a flurry of business around Saint Patrick's Day, but after that, Steve's cookie empire went into a downward spiral. Susan and Jerry listened, trying not to smile. They could have predicted this disaster from the first day, but Ella seemed dead serious about what had happened to her son—and to her money.

After her huge losses in Kelly's Cookies, Ella Bonilla was hesitant to put any more of the family money into Steven's hands. He just didn't seem to handle it well. (Jerry pinched Susan under the table to keep her from laughing.) However, Ella said, if Steven were to invest with Jerry, she could feel confident that it would be a solid thing. She asked to be part of Baritz—with her son as the middleman. She would arrange things so that Steven had money—or, rather, access to money, if he was assured of an investment with Jerry and Susan's club.

Ella Bonilla was eager, in fact, to invest $232,000 in Baritz. If Jerry was willing, she hinted that she might funnel even more money into Baritz later. It would be in the form of loans to her son, Steven, who would be required to sign notes promising to pay his mother back.

Ella's offer was difficult for Jerry to refuse. The amount she offered was just about what he needed to finish Baritz. Jerry had a heavy load of financial responsibilities, and the Bonillas were begging to invest money. Of course, they wanted another job for Steve, but Jerry didn't mind that. He could work with Steve; he felt he understood Steve.

Jerry signed a note indicating that he owed Ella Bonilla $160,000, and Steve invested the money from his mother in Baritz. He was not a partner; Jerry made that clear. Steve would be an investor only.

Ella Bonilla bought her only son jobs much the way the rich mother of a grade school kid might buy him friends with spending money and parties and fancy toys. Steve Bonilla wasn't the first guy anyone would invite to a party or choose for a best friend, but Jerry got along with everyone, and besides, he wouldn't actually have to spend much time working with Steve.

Steve came by the house one day in a tearing hurry when Jerry wasn't at home. He said that they only had an hour to get in on the drawing for a liquor license from Alcoholic Beverage Control (ABC). Usually liquor licenses cost $40,000, but there were drawings where each of fourteen winners in Santa Clara County could purchase a bargain liquor license for only $6,000. Not surprisingly, a number of people wanted one. Fifty restaurant owners would draw lots to see who would get them. Steve Bonilla, one of Steve's aunts, Susan Harris, and a girlfriend who happened to be visiting all wrote checks to ABC. Those who didn't win the liquor lottery would get their money back. Susan didn't even have time to tell Jerry they were going to try for one, but she knew he would be delighted if she got one. They all put their names in the hat to quadruple their chance of getting a liquor license for Baritz.

Steve's name came up first. To Susan's surprise, Bonilla murmured that he didn't think he could get a liquor license in his name. Susan was aware that Jerry preferred that the license not be in Steve's name—unless that was the only way to do it. Luckily, Susan's name was the next one drawn, so she became the titular owner of Baritz's liquor license.

Later, when Susan asked Jerry why Steve Bonilla couldn't get a liquor license, he shrugged. Steve was an odd duck sometimes; Jerry often hadn't seen him for several years at a stretch. He had little knowledge and even less interest in Bonilla's peregrinations. Jerry knew he had been married a couple of times, but Steve didn't talk much about that. He was a good father, and that was enough for Jerry. Mostly, Jerry was eager to see Baritz become a reality.

Steve, however, would not let go of the notion that he should be a full partner in Baritz. Jerry resisted, but Steve wore away at him like rainwater dripping on a rock. The two men played racquetball most mornings, and Steve always had a new reason why it would only be fair to him to bring him into Baritz as a full partner.

Jerry made no bones about the fact that he was never going to give Steve control of any of his clubs, and he said so to Steve, often in front of other people. Molly Clemente recalled hearing Jerry tell Steve, "Ever since Frenchy's, I will never let you have control of my clubs. You just don't know how to handle people, Steve. You want to be a limited partner, that's fine, and that's the way it's going to be."

Finally, on March 23, 1987, Jerry and Steve walked into Jerry's office early one morning. Jerry handed Molly Clemente a sheet of paper. She could tell he was a little irritated. "Molly," Jerry said, "I want you to type something. Steve feels he needs something to protect himself in case something happens to me."

Molly looked at Jerry doubtfully, but he told her to go ahead and type. The ensuing document said that Steven Bonilla would become a 40 percent *limited* partner in Baritz in 1989.

Letter of Understanding Agreement
Regarding Business Known as Baritz,
Located at 5580 Stevens Creek Blvd.
Cupertino, California, 95014

It is understood by all parties that because of regulations required by Alcoholic Beverage Control that Steven Bonilla will be unable to be a legal partner until January 1989. So as an interim agreement, it is agreed that Steven Bonilla's interest in Baritz is 40% of ownership of assets, liabilities and income.

This agreement will act temporarily until further documentation can be put together by attorneys.

It is understood that $40,000 would be capital of money invested by Steven Bonilla—borrowed from Ella Bonilla. In addition, there are two notes due Ella Bonilla; one in the sum of $72,000, payable in 12 months. The second being $120,000. Due in five years.

Jerry L. Harris 3-23-87
T. Susan Hannah Harris 3-23-87
Steven W. Bonilla 3-23-87
Molly Clemente 3-23-87

Bonilla was the only one who had signed with a triumphant flourish, confident that he had just joined the big time. He knew so little about business and contracts that he was apparently oblivious to the meaning of the wording. He was getting 40 percent of the *liabilities* as well as the profits, and he still would have no real partnership interest until 1989. But Steve wanted Baritz more than either Jerry or Susan realized, and he had jammed his foot tightly in the door.

It was Jerry's intention to repay the $232,000 to the Bonilla family as quickly as possible. Steve would get $5,000 a month on the $40,000 he had borrowed from his mother so he could buy into Baritz, but Jerry was careful not to promise Bonilla any continuing role as a working partner in the club. Jerry had put too much into the project—know-how, imagination, concept—not to mention a great deal of his own money. The entire tab for renovating the Cupertino club came to over $800,000. Two banks in San Diego county loaned Jerry a million dollars in

1987, and it was Jerry who was responsible for paying it back; Steve was basically using "play money" his mother had given him.

Given the way in which Steve Bonilla had antagonized the staff at Frenchy's, Jerry didn't want him to be the general manager of Baritz. Still, he could find some kind of a job for him, something where Steve would feel important. Jerry still believed that one day Steve would get a grip and be a competent businessman, but he doubted he would ever have the tact and discipline needed to work with people. Jerry's beneficence didn't go so far as to allow Steve to take a major role in his new club.

That seemed to be all right with Bonilla, at least at first. But it wasn't long before he was once again urging Jerry to sign an agreement with him that would make them partners in Baritz forever. He was forever leaving papers on Molly Clemente's desk and asking her to be sure that Jerry signed them. Molly showed them to Jerry, but he only rolled his eyes and grinned; he wouldn't sign them. Susan was Jerry's only true partner in Baritz—forever. Together they had visited the site almost daily and been thrilled to see it come together.

Just as Jerry and Susan had predicted, Baritz was a huge success. Gilbert Konqui had come up with a design that featured a neon rain forest and waterfalls with little streams running through the club. The club had a champagne bar, several other bars, and a lavish complimentary ten-course caviar buffet. That happy hour buffet alone cost $10,000 a month.

"When a club initially opens," Susan recalled, "it takes a little while for it to get on its feet—until the business builds . . . but in just a couple of months, we had lines all around the building."

Susan recalled that computer company employees and other upper-middle-class people in the San Jose area embraced Baritz gladly. It soon became *the* club to patronize. It opened in March 1987, showed gross sales of $145,000 in April, with a loss of $5,000, which she and Jerry had expected, and bounced back in May. They had gross sales of over $200,000 and a profit of $24,000. Under corporate guidelines, JLH Enterprises, Jerry and Susan's corporation, was to receive 5 percent of sales. By August, profits from Baritz were up to $41,000.

Jerry was steadily chipping away at his notes to the Bonillas. At the rate Baritz was growing, he would be able to pay them back with a handsome profit. In the meantime, Steve had a job, and Jerry looked the other way when he heard that Steve was impressing people by announcing that he was "the owner" of Baritz.

Jerry was reinvesting his share of Baritz's profits—in the Hot Rod Cafe chain. He was about to open up a huge new Hot Rod in Alameda.

Susan recalled one of Steve Bonilla's visits to their home on Chaparral Drive in Fremont around this time. She had rarely, if ever, seen Jerry annoyed with Bonilla, but on this occasion he was angry. "Steve was . . . talking about Baritz and how he wanted Jerry to put a double-decker parking lot there because there wasn't enough room for all the cars, and what he should do with the building next door. And that he should put another Hot Rod there. And he was just going on and on."

Susan saw Jerry's chin set and an icy glaze cover his blue eyes. "Jerry stopped him and said, 'You have nothing to do with the Hot Rod Cafes. These are *my* businesses. Stay out of my business.' And Steve stormed out and left."

Shocked, Susan watched Bonilla leave. Jerry told her not to worry about it. Steven Bonilla's temper tantrum didn't bother Jerry for long. He still went out of his way, Susan recalls, to help the little man out. Although Steve set Susan's teeth on edge, she didn't say anything, figuring Jerry had his reasons. Jerry was always doing things for the underdog and Steven Bonilla's overweening lack of charm, social graces, and likability made him a genuine underdog when it came to business, and yet Jerry seemed to feel responsible for him.

She guessed Steve was like the bums, the Mexican mill workers, the stranded travelers, and all the other people in trouble whom Jerry felt compelled to help.

Steve Bonilla was the embodiment of a nerd, and Jerry admitted that he felt sorry for him. "One time," Susan recalled, "Jerry came home and said, 'Sue, Steve's on his way over, and he's wearing a toupee. You be sure that you don't laugh and don't make fun of him.' I complimented Steve, but that toupee was *bad*. It was done in a big pompadour. I think it was a cheap one."

Susan and Jerry had been married for a year and a half, and to Susan's delight, Jerry was beginning to waver in his determination not to have any more children. He loved the two he had, but he had warned her that he didn't intend to start a new young family now that he was in his forties. He regretted that he hadn't spent as much time as he might have with Mike and Tiffany. He was up to his ears in business commitments, and he was twenty years older than he had been as a first-time father. But when he looked at Susan, Jerry softened. He loved her so much, and she wanted to have his children. There was really nothing in the world that Jerry wouldn't give Susan if she really wanted it.

But first they had yet another nightclub to unveil: the second Hot Rod. If the flagship club in the chain, the Fremont Hot Rod Cafe, had drawn attention, the Alameda Hot Rod Diner elevated their publicity into blazing headlines. The Hot Rods were Jerry's favorites. Beginning with the old Pacific Fresh Building in Alameda, Jerry and Gil Konqui had conceived and built a club that was both glitzy and posh. The decor was hot pink and orange. A Ford roadster with burnished "pipes" and flames painted along its doors hung upside down from the ceiling, and a meticulously restored pink 1959 Cadillac was parked between two of the club's "quilted metal" pillars. There were more of the props that Jerry Harris's customers had come to expect: jukeboxes, gasoline pumps, a biplane flying overhead, gold records, and, as a tribute to the man who had always inspired Jerry, a huge photograph of Elvis Presley.

Harris and Konqui had scouted the world for interesting icons of the fifties. A double-decker bus from London stood, if somewhat improbably, in the middle of the Hot Rod

Diner. Getting it in hadn't been easy; they'd had to dig a huge trough outside so that the tall bus would clear the building's roof going in. But there it sat in Alameda, California, with its destination placard changing from "Blaufield 97" to "Hemsby 75."

Opening night at the Hot Rod Diner was memorable. One of the most famous radio personalities of rock and roll, Wolfman Jack himself, was the first disc jockey to spin records on the state-of-the-art sound system. Flashbulbs went off as press and patrons alike commemorated this moment. Jerry and Susan posed with Wolfman Jack, and the opening-night party went on into the wee hours.

Susan and Jerry Harris were thrilled. In less than five years, they had opened four thriving nightspots: Shakers, two Hot Rods, and Baritz. They had clubs for every age bracket and every pocketbook, and they were wonderful nightclubs, with people anxiously waiting to get in week after week.

Jerry could now jump up onto any stage he chose and belt out songs—if he had the time. Those in the crowd who had never heard him before always thought they were hearing one of Elvis Presley's recordings. And then, seeing that it was Jerry singing, they stopped, transfixed at how much he sounded like Elvis. It was almost eerie at first, the way the room always grew quiet while Jerry's voice soared and broke with emotion. Susan collected tape after tape of Jerry singing, as if she could never have enough of his voice.

Susan knew the real Jerry behind the handsome man on stage, behind the businessman, She knew he was never happier than when he was the anonymous benefactor behind Steve King's Santa Claus. She knew his family meant more to him than any amount of money. And yet it sometimes seemed to her that they were running faster and faster toward . . . what?

Still, they were together; he admired her grasp of the businesses they had begun, and she never got tired of hearing him talk about his dreams. It never even crossed her mind anymore to be jealous of other women. If she was jealous of anything, it would be the Hot Rod clubs. But she knew she had to get used to this "mistress" of Jerry's; he intended to string Hot Rods across the United States.

Jerry always wore a suit and tie. A friend who was an executive in a computer plant, and who wore jeans to work, asked him about it once.

"I wear suits to show others respect," Jerry replied, and he was completely serious. As creative and irreverent as he could be, he had a conventional streak that surprised people who knew him. When one of their tropical birds bit Susan and she swore, Jerry bawled her out for swearing before he looked at the bite on her finger.

Still, Jerry Harris was not above pulling a fast one, more for the adventure of it than to save money. Because he was always scouting out new locations for clubs now, he flew often. He had a cellular phone, and he got a kick out of calling Susan from the plane to tell her where to pick him up. On one trip to Arizona, she and several of his employees went with him. When they returned to the San Jose Airport, they realized that despite the half-dozen vehicles they owned, they didn't have one to drive home in.

"Molly had dropped us off at the airport," Susan said. "We were going to bum a ride from someone when I remembered that we'd left the Honda in the parking lot of a hotel nearby the previous week so we wouldn't have to pay for parking in the airport. We took the shuttle to the hotel to get the Honda, and then Jerry remembered that he had left the Porsche in the short-term parking lot in the San Francisco Airport. It had been there for about a month, and that parking was really expensive.

"We drove to the San Francisco Airport parking lot and I talked to the attendant about the weather so he would remember me. We found the Porsche and it had marks all over it from being there so long. So we wiped off all the marks, and I gave Jerry the ticket I'd just gotten, and he drove out and paid for one hour. I waited a little while and then I drove out in the Honda and told the guy that I'd lost my ticket, and *I* only paid for an hour because he remembered me. We drove home in separate vehicles, and [later we] laughed about our little scheme. . . . It wasn't very honest, but we enjoyed the challenge of seeing if we could do it."

It seems incredible that anyone could forget where he had parked a car—especially a Porsche—for a month, but most people don't have as many vehicles as Jerry Harris did. He collected cars the way most people collect sports equipment.

Jerry and Susan ate out a lot, but their dinners were seldom solitary. All the local restaurant owners knew Jerry, and they would inevitably pull up a chair and ask his advice about some problem they were having. "He fixed sound systems everywhere we went," Susan said. "I didn't mind too much. It was just that he ruined so many silk shirts crawling around behind dirty electronic equipment."

Well into the third year of their marriage, Sue and Jerry Harris were having a wonderful time, despite Jerry's balancing act with his own debts and his family's obligations. There were only a few sour notes. Steve Bonilla was one of them.

Now that he was back in their lives, Susan realized that she still resented Bonilla, not just because he treated her in a caustic, patronizing way but also for Jerry's sake. She thought Steve was edging too much into Jerry's spotlight. "There were times," she recalls, "when Steve actually pretended to *be* Jerry. He had this fakey smooth facade, although he was really kind of nerdy."

He wanted people to think he was the owner of the clubs that were actually Jerry's. Steve affected an air of importance. He had owned the first portable phone Susan had ever seen. It was an unwieldy device with a heavy battery, and he carried it in its own special briefcase. The briefcase seemed to be attached to him permanently, and he used the portable phone to impress women. He even talked Jerry into getting a cellular phone.

One time some members of Susan's family went to see Shakers. One of her aunts, Judy Boyd, who was an Albany, California, police sergeant, spoke with a dark complexioned man who appeared to be the host. "Steve didn't know who my aunt was," Susan said. "And he introduced himself as the owner of Shakers. . . . Steve had absolutely no financial interest in Shakers.

"I always felt that Steve wanted to *be* Jerry Harris, but he was so far away from being anything like Jerry. Jerry was charismatic and outgoing and positive. . . . Jerry always felt sorry for Steve, no matter how irritating he was. Jerry would tell me that Steve had kids and that he took his kids places."

Jerry found this an admirable quality. Too often he'd gotten so involved in work that he hadn't given his own children as much time as he meant to. As he did in everyone, he looked for things in Steve Bonilla to praise.

Finding them wasn't always easy.

5

Susan and Jerry had lived in his house on Chaparral in Fremont for six years. They had been married for two and a half years. By mid-1987 their business interests were growing so rapidly that only a man with Jerry's daring would even have attempted to manage them all. He was as balanced and deft as a tightrope walker, and he thrived on taking risks. Without Jerry, the enterprises would all come tumbling down. With him, they were on their way to huge corporate profits.

Jerry was a showman and a conspicuous consumer. He and Susan had more vehicles than they could possibly drive: Jerry had two red Ferraris, two Porsches, one Excalibur, a little Honda sedan, besides his leased Mercedes and the Bronco. "Then we had a vintage white Cadillac limo," Susan recalled, "and sometimes I'd drive him around in that. He also had a pink Cadillac 1957 limo that he had customized. He'd had it cut in half and extended three feet. It was all upholstered in white leather. They used it later in Los Angeles in movies." When all the vehicles were parked at home, Susan thought the place looked as if they were giving a party.

Jerry's love of luxury extended to jewelry, too. His wedding ring was made of gold nuggets, and he wore a solid gold tiger ring on his other hand; its eyes were diamonds and emeralds, and it had a ruby tongue. He almost always wore a chain around his neck made of gold nuggets too.

Jerry, who had once toiled in a steel mill and helped his father in the woods, was now a wine connoisseur and collector. He built a temperature-controlled wine cellar in the Chaparral Street house and invested more than $30,000 in rare wines. He sometimes went to wine auctions to bid on wines for the owners of upscale restaurants who appreciated his knowledge. As a representative of the posh Papillon restaurant, he once bought a bottle of 1971 red Rhône for $900 and spent $53,150 for 396 other bottles of rare wine.

Jerry compared buying rare wines to collecting stamps. "I used to think an expensive bottle of wine was just buying a name," he once said, "but the feeling you get from a fine wine—the after-feeling—it's incredible. People get blown away at spending a lot of money for a bottle of wine, but the same person will spend $500 on a golf trip somewhere. It's where your priorities are."

When Susan and Jerry went out to eat, they usually took their own wine, and Jerry always offered the waiters a taste. "Once we went to a wine tasting with the owner of the Silver Oak winery, and everyone was talking in wine lingo," Susan remembered. "Aroma and ambience and body and fancy terms. Jerry would just smile and say, 'Either you like it or you don't.' During wine tastings, he could distinguish what he was drinking, even to the year. He knew a lot about wine, but he never bragged. We had several of our own wine tastings at the house. I knew how well Jerry liked someone by what bottle he brought out of our cellar." She smiled. "He liked *me* the best."

Jerry's favorite wine was not particularly expensive; he drank Silver Oak Cabernet. He kidded Susan once: "When I die and I'm in my coffin, Sue, I want you to promise me you'll put a bottle of Silver Oak in one hand and wineglass in the other and a smile on my face."

She turned pale. "Don't even say that."

"Honey," Jerry said, reaching for her hand, "I was only kidding. It's just that that way, when people feel bad and they come up and look at me, they'll start laughing."

"Okay, I promise."

By 1987, Jerry had made up his mind to concentrate on the Hot Rod franchise idea. He held the trademark for the entire state of California for his Hot Rod concept. He had no doubt that within five years he would go nationwide.

He sold Shakers; the restaurant he had purchased in Hayward for $238,000 in 1984 was assessed at nearly $1 million only three years later. Baritz was in good hands with the staff he had in place there—for the moment. He planned to sell the glitzy San Jose club in the foreseeable future, when he was certain that he could return Ella Bonilla's investment to her. He'd never expected to hold on to Baritz long enough for Steve to become a full partner. The Hot Rods were more fun, and they had Jerry's imprint.

Sandy Harris, one of Jerry's brothers, was the closest thing he had to a confidant. He knew Jerry was concerned in the late summer of 1987 about Agro-Serve, although he had almost completely divested himself of his interest in that enterprise. Jerry talked to Sandy of his misgivings about the palm seedling operation.

Steve Bonilla had moved in to oversee the tree business. Jerry told Sandy that he had gradually become concerned that Steve was planning to turn the palm program into a pyramid scheme, where the early investors would be paid off with new investors' money.

Jerry had made an error in judgment with Agro-Serve. When he began Tiffany's Plant Rentals, Jerry had put it in his sister's name. By then he'd had three marriages and a few encounters with the IRS. For eight years he had no business ventures in his own name. Although the businesses were truly his, the only way he could take any profit out was to "borrow" it. That technique worked on paper and in actuality, it was only slightly tricky, and it wasn't against the law.

When Steve Bonilla came into Agro-Serve, he had a corporate license for Independent Caterers, which was soon amended to Independent Caterers DBA (doing business as) Sun State Tropicals. Sun State Tropicals accepted investments from palm tree growers. Much of this money rightfully belonged to Jerry Harris, who was doing all the work in the greenhouses. But the way the books were set up, the only way Jerry could get his money out was to borrow it, just as he had borrowed it from the corporation in his sister's name. Although Steven Bonilla was merely a figurehead who did precious little actual work, on paper he looked good. And, worse, Jerry Harris's financial statement showed that he *owed* Independent Caterers $1.2 million. In truth, he owed Steven Bonilla's catering firm nothing.

Still, it was a dangerous paper tiger.

Pyramid schemes were not the kind of enterprise that Jerry Harris wanted to be involved in. With Bonilla apparently trying to move in that direction, Jerry wanted out of the whole palm seedling business. He sold the last of his interest in his nurseries in September 1987, and he moved the recording equipment from Tiffany's Productions to his house. His music reverted to being only a hobby, as it once had been.

Although 1987 was a good year for Susan and Jerry, it brought some problems that seemed almost insurmountable, even to Jerry Harris. Because of his entanglement with Agro-Serve, he was being investigated by the criminal division of the Internal Revenue Service. Jerry had washed his hands of Agro-Serve, but not soon enough. When two official-looking men in suits came to the house on Chaparral Street, Jerry showed them into his office.

"Jerry never closed his office door," Susan said, "but *they* did, and it made me mad."

After an hour Susan opened the door and brought in a plate of food for Jerry. In an act that was brazen for her, she told the IRS agents it was their dinnertime and asked them to leave. Surprisingly, they did.

Jerry had never hidden anything from Susan; in this case, he had been trying to protect her. He *was* worried about the legality of the tax-shelter aspect of Agro-Serve. He had opted out of it once it looked like Steve Bonilla was changing the original concept into a pyramid scheme, but he knew his name had been connected with Agro-Serve for years, and the entanglement was threatening to blow up in his face. He took Susan out to dinner, and they talked about the problem.

"Sue, if it comes to it, would you leave the country with me—just disappear?" Jerry asked.

She stared at him for a long time. "No, Jerry. Even for you, I couldn't leave my family. I couldn't do that to them. It would be hard, but if you had to go without me, I think I could accept that."

Jerry stared down at the table between them, and when he looked up, he was grinning.

"He never again mentioned the possibility of his having to vanish," Susan said. "As it was, it turned out all right. Everything was quite legal. The IRS finished their investigation and they went away."

With the success of their nightclubs and with an almost unspoken decision to have a baby, Susan and Jerry went looking for a bigger house. Susan was a little concerned because most of their money was already invested in the clubs, but Jerry said they could afford to buy a new house. As unusual as it was, Jerry and Susan were genuinely fond not only of their own mothers—but of each other's. "We knew that women usually outlive men," Susan explained, "and we both kind of planned on taking care of our moms so they wouldn't be alone."

It was Jerry's idea to find a house where both of their mothers could live if they were widowed. "We'll put them at opposite ends of the house," he joked.

Jerry and Susan looked in Alameda and Contra Costa Counties, wanting to stay close to Jerry's family and to his business interests. They found the house they wanted in Danville. It was more than a house. It was a showplace situated among other showplaces. It was located in Blackhawk, a prime community. A number of celebrities, most of them sports figures, lived in Blackhawk. John Madden, coach of the Oakland Raiders and later a sports commentator and author, had a house there. Baseball's bad boy, Billy Martin, who had managed the Yankees and the Oakland A's, lived in Blackhawk, as did Chris Mullen, a basketball star with the Golden State Warriors, and A's outfielder, José Conseco. It was the "in" neighborhood in the Danville–Walnut Creek–Pleasanton area.

Multimillionaire real estate baron and sports entrepreneur Ken Behring had purchased acreage in the Blackhawk area near Danville and rezoned it for custom homes that would sell for over a million dollars apiece. (With that project finished, Behring had headed off to Washington State, where he purchased the Seattle Seahawks and was attempting to zone Cascade Mountain foothills areas for a project similar to the Blackhawk project until the environmentalists blocked him.)

Each home in Behring's Blackhawk Properties was different; there was not the slightest hint of a subdivision. It was a gated community that no one could enter without checking in with uniformed guards. This was an area where CEOs and major executives lived, and the moment Jerry Harris saw Blackhawk, he knew that this was where he wanted to live. The home at 3158 Blackhawk Meadow Drive had an asking price of $1,295,000. It had been designed for Ken Behring Jr. as his personal home.

Susan and Jerry pored over the brochure: "A stylish Mediterranean home with a tranquil creekside, golf course setting. This awe-inspiring estate offers six unique bedroom suites, six and a half baths, plus an enchanting game room perfect for a billiards table and fitness gym, all in approximately 6,200 square feet. The master suite hosts a splendid fireplace, adjacent private retreat with a balcony, and a marble bath complete with sauna and whirlpool tub. Extensive . . . granite, tile, and detailed wall finishes add to the splendor of this one-of-a-kind masterpiece."

There was a pond stocked with huge goldfish (koi) and the house sat near the eighth hole of the golf course, where sycamore trees would cast shade during the hot summer.

Susan and Jerry had been looking for a place big enough for their families to visit for more than overnight, and Jerry liked the idea that every one of the six bedrooms had its own bathroom. His folks could visit, and so could Susan's. It was perfect for them now, and it would be ideal for the changes the years ahead would bring. Susan, who had always felt that she was "running [her] own bed-and-breakfast" on Chaparral Street, agreed with him. The house wouldn't be just for them; it would be for everyone they loved, too.

When Jerry told his dad about it, though, Jim Harris looked at the brochure and stared at Jerry as if he'd taken leave of his senses. His dad figured Jerry already had a perfectly good house. What did he need with a debt the size this house would produce? Jim had grown up during the Great Depression and had just gone through business reverses. Although Jerry had taken over his ailing steel business, Jim Harris still worried. He had a pretty good idea of how strapped Jerry was for cash flow, and he couldn't fathom Jerry's need to live in an exclusive neighborhood and to give Susan a house in the best part of Danville. Susan wasn't like that; she would have been happy in a trailer with Jerry.

Susan, however, understood why Jerry wanted the house. He had the clubs and his other businesses, but this great rambling pink house would be their permanent home, their special place. It would mean more to them than the yacht, their condo in Hawaii, and even their clubs. In a way, it would be the first real home of their marriage, the first home they would come to as a married couple. She had moved into his house in Fremont when it was *his* house; this would be *their* house.

Jim quit arguing with his son. So far, Jerry had done

everything he'd set out to do. Who was to say that buying the house on Blackhawk Meadow Drive wasn't exactly the right step for him?

Steve Bonilla, meanwhile, continued to introduce himself as "the owner" of Jerry's clubs to people he wanted to impress. Jerry knew Bonilla did that, but he shrugged it off and continued to accept Steve as one of the burdens he carried. His stubborn loyalty to Bonilla far transcended the fact that Ella Bonilla had loaned him money; Jerry knew he would be paying her back soon. He always told Susan that Steve was harmless, if annoying, and that it didn't hurt to let him share the spotlight a little if it made him feel more important.

Somewhere along the line, Steve Bonilla had become a licensed Realtor, but Jerry knew Steve hadn't been very successful at it. To Susan's horror, Jerry announced that he wanted to throw a little business Steve Bonilla's way. They had a house to sell. They might as well let Steve take a crack at marketing it.

Susan had long since become used to the idea that Steve was just one of the many people Jerry carried on his back—half friends, half burdens. She just rolled her eyes when Jerry said he was going to let Steve list their house on Chaparral Street.

"Look," Jerry said. "It can't hurt. I'll let him have thirty days to sell it. If he can't sell it in thirty days, we can go ahead and list it with someone else."

It would take some doing to get their Fremont house ready for sale. True to form, Jerry had been impatient when he had remodeled the house; he'd put some additions on without bothering to get permits from the city of Fremont. The improvements conformed to Fremont construction codes, but Jerry still had to get permits before they could get any sale through escrow and qualify the house for title insurance. Jerry didn't have time to jump through all those hoops. He figured that Steve could take care of all of that and earn a commission, too.

Surprisingly, Steve Bonilla did find a buyer for the

Harrises' home in Fremont. Jerry and Susan had listed it at $450,000, and it sold for $400,000. Susan and Jerry had more than enough equity in the Fremont house to make the quarter-million-dollar down payment on the pink mansion on Blackhawk Meadow Drive. The sale had to *close* on the Chaparral Drive house, however, before they would have that money. Then they could get a mortgage loan of $900,000 to pay for the Blackhawk house.

During that period in late summer of 1987, Jerry Harris was leveraged up to his ears. His cash flow was completely tied up in his nightclubs and in trying to salvage his father's business. At the moment he didn't have enough to pay the closing fees on the Blackhawk house.

Worried about losing his commission on two sales, Steve Bonilla came up with what seemed to be a reasonable solution. He would lend Jerry $8,000 on a short-term basis so that the Fremont house could close, and then, like dominoes tumbling, the Blackhawk home would be Jerry's. Jerry would repay him $2,000 a week, and the remainder of Bonilla's commissions would come soon after.

"But Steve's check bounced," Susan recalled. "The escrow on the Blackhawk house couldn't close, and each day we waited to get into that house, it was costing us money. . . . [The situation] was very stressful."

For the first time, Jerry was completely enraged with Steve Bonilla. With Susan standing beside him, Jerry called him and she heard him arguing about the bounced check. Jerry was furious as he shouted at Steve for letting him believe the $8,000 check was good.

Eventually everything worked out. The Fremont house sale closed, and Susan and Jerry moved into their mammoth dream house in Danville on October 1, 1987.

Jerry was making inroads into his tangle of business responsibilities. The established clubs were more than carrying their own weight, and it looked as if the new clubs would open on schedule. Even so, he needed to sell SteelFab before he could breathe easy.

About two weeks after they moved in, Susan carried the phone with the longest cord out onto the deck. It was a beautiful night, and she saw that the harvest moon was a golden orb against the sky. She experienced one of those rare moments of serenity, when everything in her life was in sync. She breathed in the sweet evening fragrance and knew she would be able to summon up the memory of this particular night as long as she lived. She called her sister, Julie, to share her happiness. "I am so lucky," she said. "I have everything I could ever have wished for. It almost scares me because I'm so happy."

Jim Harris saw a change in his son during that fall of 1987. Jerry was not quite himself, although it would have taken someone who knew him really well to detect the subtle difference. He had always thrived under business pressures that would have given most men ulcers. He was an upbeat, happy man for whom depression was completely alien. Jerry was the Harris brother who always took care of his family, with financial help and with good advice. But now Jim Harris watched his son and worried. "He was quiet too much," he said. "It just wasn't like him. He was concerned about our welfare and had long talks with his brothers. He told them they would have to look after themselves more."

On the face of it, that wasn't so unusual. Everyone had counted on Jerry to make business decisions and to provide financial backup. He had always been there, but he had never before been responsible for *three* nightclubs, two more about to be built, *and* his father's obligations. If he was trying to urge his family to take greater command of their own affairs, that was understandable. What worried Jim most was his somber demeanor. As his father said, that just wasn't like him. Jerry Harris was a man who almost always had a smile on his face.

Susan saw the change, too, but she wasn't that worried. "Jerry was leveraged to the hilt," she remembered. "He *was* stressed, but he could handle it. Things were beginning to come together once we got into our house."

And they were. Jerry realized that he had to sell SteelFab, and he was looking for a buyer. By the third week in October, he told his brother Sandy he thought he had found one.

6

That October of 1987 was the height of the halcyon autumn in the San Francisco area. Almost all of the annuals from the summer just past were still blooming, although the eucalyptus leaves were drying into brittle curls that rattled along the ground when the autumn wind blew. The sky was still bright blue. Fog had begun to creep in only at the edges of the day, morning and evening. It might have been summer, but there was a certain sense in the air that it no longer was.

Susan was excited that she and Jerry were in their new house, even though she hadn't made much headway at decorating it. It was so big, and she wanted it to be just right. Their old furniture didn't begin to fill up the spacious rooms, but she moved it around, trying to make it look less adrift in the wide rooms with soaring ceilings. It would be Thanksgiving in no time, and then Jerry would be gearing up for his Santa Claus surprise projects. She doubted that she could have everything done in time.

But that didn't matter; they were home now—home for good.

On Monday, October 19, Jerry Harris did something that was truly uncharacteristic of him—he took the day off from work. He and Susan spent that day together in the new house.

"We tried out the steam bath-shower," Susan recalled. "I remember we sat there side by side and I couldn't see Jerry's face because of the steam. We talked for hours, probably more than we'd ever just sat down and talked. I could hear

73

Jerry's voice clearly in the clouds of steam, and he said, 'Sue, if anything ever happens to me, I want you to take care of my mother and Tiffany.'"

"Of course. Of course I will—*would*," she murmured, surprised. Jerry wasn't given to premonitions of doom.

He changed the subject and spoke of the new clubs. He had always shared his philosophy of business with Susan and his plans for his clubs. Now he summed them all up, as if he wanted to make sure she understood.

If a perfect day existed, that Monday was it. They went out for dinner that evening. "We were driving along, and Jerry gave me that look that a husband gives his wife that says, 'I love you,'" Susan said. "And then he reached out and grabbed me and pulled me close beside him. I loved him so much, and that was a special moment when I knew he really, really loved me."

Jerry didn't require much sleep, and he was invariably up before the sun rose. On Tuesday he was going to drive to Monterey and to the SteelFab plant in Castroville. He had asked Susan several times the day before to go with him, but she kept saying no—she had too many things to do to get settled in the new house.

Jerry was usually dressed and gone long before anyone else along Blackhawk Meadow Drive, and that Tuesday, October 20, was no different. Because he was driving alone to Monterey, he didn't expect Susan to get up when he did, at 4:30 A.M., but she woke anyway and watched while he got dressed. He dressed in the dark so he wouldn't disturb her, and she could barely see him or what he was wearing. She noted idly that he seemed to have on one of his brown sports jackets. He leaned over and gave her a good-bye kiss. Susan rolled over and went back to sleep, knowing he would call later.

"I didn't see his face," she recalled. "I hope that I hugged him, but I can't remember."

Within fifteen minutes of waking up Jerry was gone. He took his favorite car, the 1982 Mercedes 380 SL convertible, which was a pale yellow that became just a light blur in the darkness before dawn. After easing past the gate guard, he drove down Blackhawk Road until he hit the 680 freeway south, where he picked up speed. He had to be at SteelFab by 6:00 A.M.

Jerry was still at the SteelFab plant in Castroville in the late afternoon. He always told Susan where he was going so that she could reach him at his office, their nightclubs, or any of his other businesses. In between, it was easy for her to get in touch with her husband: he had a portable phone years before cell phones became commonplace. The number was 555-7322. It was a number that would be emblazoned in Susan's memory.

As it happened, Susan talked to Jerry six times on October 20. She was trying to get their fishpond working, and she called to ask him how to start the aerator pump. Later, when Jerry called her at 4:30 P.M., Susan asked him what his dinner plans were. He said he was just leaving the SteelFab plant and heading home. Sheepishly, he admitted he hadn't eaten all day. He was about seventy miles south of the pink house in Danville, and the way Jerry drove, he would be home by 6:00. He would eat when he arrived.

Susan wasn't concerned when six o'clock came and went and there was no sign of Jerry. He was always getting detoured by something or someone. She *was* concerned about his stomach, though; she thought he should have regular meals instead of grabbing fast food along the way. Today he hadn't had anything but a cup of coffee. He was going to have an ulcer if he didn't start taking care of himself.

Jerry called again at 8:30 that Tuesday evening.

"Okay, what are you doing now?" Susan asked, a smile in her voice.

"Just finished having drinks with Steve at the South 40," he said cheerfully. "I'm almost in Pleasanton."

Jerry told Susan that he was following Steve Bonilla, who was leading him to a small business park in Pleasanton.

"Why?" Susan asked, surprised. They didn't need another office. Jerry had just about decided to use one of the rooms in the new house for his office. "Isn't it strange that you're looking at an office building this late at night?" She looked outside and saw that darkness had closed in, shutting out her view of the hill behind their house. While she waited for Jerry to answer, she saw that the shadows of the trees had blended into the night. Jerry had left in the darkness and he would be coming home in the darkness.

"Yeah," Jerry agreed. "It is kind of strange, but Steve was so persistent."

Well, that was nothing new. Steve always seemed to have some wild idea for Jerry's business, and Steve was nothing if not persistent. Susan thought Jerry sounded a little tired, and she knew he had to be hungry. She also knew that it drove Jerry nuts when Steve got pushy about expanding the businesses; he had been really angry about Bonilla's suggestion that he build a huge parking lot next to the Hot Rod Cafe.

"Have you had anything to eat yet?" She realized she was nagging—but somebody had to do it.

"No," Jerry said. "I haven't had time. I'm going to go back to Fremont, to the Hot Rod, and I'll be home later."

"Who are you meeting there?"

"Konqui."

That would mean that Jerry was meeting not only Gilbert Konqui but several other people as well. The Hot Rod clubs were going so well that Jerry had options on property in Concord and Dublin, California. These would be huge clubs, like the Alameda Hot Rod Diner.

"They were going to be even crazier," Susan said later, "with moats in them and a sailboat."

While she and Jerry talked, Susan could hear a familiar banging or a knocking sound. It was the engine of the Mercedes missing. She had taken the car to a gas station a few days before, but the attendant hadn't known what was wrong—and hadn't wanted to work on a classic Mercedes.

Jerry said the engine had been knocking quite a bit, and they agreed that they would have to get it fixed. They talked easily for almost ten minutes as Jerry drove along. And then he said, "The traffic's getting bad. I'd better get off the phone."

Susan told Jerry she'd be waiting up for him. She heard the click as he hung up his portable phone. Since he was meeting Gil Konqui, Susan knew he probably wouldn't be home until after the club closed at 2:00 A.M. She had gone grocery shopping, but she hadn't needed to, after all. She turned off the stove in her huge new gourmet kitchen.

Jerry would be eating a hamburger and fries again instead of her carefully planned balanced meal.

The house suddenly seemed very empty. Lonely.

7

Susan didn't wait up for Jerry on the night of October 20. She realized that Jerry and Gilbert Konqui and the others working on the two new nightclubs would probably talk into the wee hours. After a day of unpacking, working on the fishpond, and doing housework, she was tired.

She went to bed, expecting to be wakened by the sweep of headlights from the yellow Mercedes across her bedroom wall through the undraped windows. Jerry wasn't predictable, but he was dependable. He would be home in his own good time.

Susan Harris slept soundly until four-thirty in the morning. When she woke, she was surprised that Jerry had managed to come to bed without awakening her. She rolled over and saw that his side of the bed was empty, the covers as smooth as they had been when she went to bed. Her eyes widened and she was fully awake. Jerry *never* stayed away overnight. For all of his jokes and flirting, he was the most faithful man Susan had ever known. They had been together for more than six years, and he had never stayed out all night unless she knew exactly where he was. She picked up the phone next to her bed, half expecting the line to be dead.

He should have called, and nothing would have stopped him unless the lines were down. She was that sure of her husband. But the line hummed its perfectly normal tone.

She called out Jerry's name, knowing somehow that he wouldn't answer. Jerry had such a presence about him that she always knew when he was around. The house was dark and far too quiet.

Where *was* Jerry?

Susan moved through all the rooms of the new house. She didn't call Jerry's name again; she wanted to discover him and have her nightmare go away. He could be sleeping on the couch, taking a shower, even out back looking at the fishpond. It was unthinkable that he shouldn't be there. She looked out at the driveway. The Mercedes convertible wasn't there, nor was it in the six-and-a-half-car garage. Susan was worried, almost panicked, but she tried to suppress her anxiety. Who could she call at four-thirty in the morning? Gilbert Konqui wouldn't appreciate being awakened, nor would Steve King or Steve Bonilla, and she didn't want to scare Jerry's family.

Susan berated herself silently for being an alarmist. Jerry probably wasn't the only husband in the Bay Area who had stayed out all night. There had to be a hundred different reasons why he hadn't made it home before dawn. She started listing them in her head: Jerry had had car trouble or too much to drink or an accident—please God, a *minor* accident. Maybe the meeting was still going on, and he hadn't wanted to wake her up to tell her, or perhaps his father had had another stroke, or . . .

Susan wasn't doing a very good job of convincing herself that there was a logical reason Jerry wasn't home. They were so close that if he felt something, *she* did too. And now she felt sheer dread. She was frightened.

Susan knew her mother got up at five-thirty to make coffee for her father, and she forced herself to wait until then to call.

"Jerry didn't come home last night, Mom," Susan blurted.

"Oh, Susie," Mary Jo Hannah said, "Jerry will be home. He probably just got involved in something."

ce was very calm, but he was puzzled when
him for more details. "What do you mean?" he
d.

took him to show him an office building?"
teve said. "In Pleasanton. *Why?*"

oo upset to explain to Steve Bonilla that Jerry
hat he hadn't shown up in either Alameda or
meet Gilbert. Susan was trying to get some facts
ld trace Jerry's steps. If he hadn't met Gilbert
at meant that he must have had an accident
leasanton and Fremont. Gil was sure Jerry had
from his car, but he wasn't sure where Jerry's car
time.

" Susan asked, "where did Jerry go after you
the office in Pleasanton?"

't know. Jerry went one way, and I went the other."
Bonilla said he hadn't watched Jerry drive off. The
ilding was located on Stoneridge Drive in Pleasan-
Jerry had come there to see it. That was all Bonilla
erry had driven off after their meeting. Steve had no
here he was headed.

n Harris felt that Steve was being evasive with her. If
w some secret about Jerry—even one that she might
joy hearing—she needed to know. But Steve couldn't
er. He was adamant that he hadn't even seen Jerry
away from the office building.

an called Jerry's secretary, Molly Clemente, at the
of JLH Enterprises in Fremont and told her that Jerry
missing. Molly was shocked. Susan asked her to call
Bonilla and see if she could find out anything more
she had. Molly did, but Bonilla told her the same thing
told Susan: he had no idea where Jerry was going when
eft the business park in Pleasanton.

Both Susan and Gil Konqui had talked to Jerry around
ht-thirty on the Tuesday night he vanished. When she
led Jerry's brother Sandy, she learned that he had talked
Jerry twenty minutes later. "I talked to Jerry on his
obile phone at about ten minutes to nine," Sandy said.
That was good. Susan felt that she was piecing together a

"I'm afraid he's been in an accident, Mom." Susan's teeth
chattered with fear. "You know Jerry always comes home."

Mary Jo did know that, but she tried to offer reasons why
Jerry had varied his pattern—just this one time. She could
only manage reasons that Susan had already thought of—
and dismissed.

Susan tried to believe in what her mother was saying, but
it did no good. If it had been any other man, she could have
clung to her mother's words, but that was what scared her
the most: Jerry was Jerry; he wasn't any other man. In six
years he had *always* come home to her, even though it was
often late.

The sun cast only a pale wash of light over the hills when
Susan started calling hospitals, jails, police departments,
methodically describing Jerry and his yellow Mercedes over
and over again to every department from San Francisco on
down to Monterey. She tried to picture Jerry's route on his
way home the night before. He would have left the Hot Rod
Diner in Alameda, headed east through Orinda and Walnut
Creek, and then driven seven miles south to Danville. He
might have even taken a shortcut and come up winding
Dougherty Road from the south. It wasn't far, and Jerry
knew every freeway, highway, and country road in Contra
Costa and Alameda Counties so well he could practically
drive them blindfolded.

Frightened as she was, Susan struggled to think ration-
ally. She would concentrate on alerting every possible
agency along the route from Alameda to Danville. If Jerry
had been in an accident, it would probably have happened
somewhere within that area. He might be unconscious in a
hospital—or even in jail, if he'd had too many drinks and
driven as fast as he usually did.

She didn't want to think that he might be in a morgue.
Susan refused to let her mind go there.

Something was keeping Jerry from coming home, but try
as she might, Susan could not identify the source of her
terror. She had awakened and been seized by a presenti-
ment of doom almost immediately. In her own heart and
mind, she knew at 4:30 A.M. on the first morning that he was
missing, but adults could not be classified as missing

persons for at least twenty-four hours. Police detectives had learned long ago that any number of adults simply vanish for reasons of their own. Most of them soon changed their minds and came home. The standard twenty-four-hour-rule saved a lot of police work. It didn't do any good at all for Susan to demand that Jerry be declared officially missing from the start. Police shook their heads and explained patiently that, if he wasn't home by Thursday morning, they would reclassify his case.

Susan searched her memory for someone who might have wanted to hurt Jerry. She couldn't think of anyone. There were a few people with whom he had business differences, but those were only mild disagreements. His exit from Agro-Serve wasn't exactly amicable, but neither was it personal. She could think of nothing at all that might have inspired rage. Almost everybody loved Jerry. He was easygoing and generous and fun to be around. He wasn't the kind of man who made enemies. But he was a soft touch— for hitchhikers, for people who were down on their luck. She thought of all the times he had stopped to help women whose cars had broken down beside the road. Maybe he'd walked into a trap set by someone who saw his Mercedes and his jewelry. Jerry always thought he was invincible. He could have pulled out a roll of bills to help someone and been rewarded by a blow on the head. She could envision that happening. But that was the *only* kind of foul play Susan could imagine.

In truth, she had no idea at all what had happened to keep Jerry away. When the police asked her why she was so frantic, she only shook her head. She didn't know. It was a feeling. She had nothing concrete to tell them.

Susan called everyone she could think of who might know where Jerry was. She called all of his businesses, his parents, his brothers and sister, and every friend the two of them had. She made careful notes of what everyone said. Writing things down kept her on some kind of track; it kept her from screaming.

She reached Gil Konqui, who said he had arranged for Jerry to meet with him and the management team from

P. J. Montgomery's i͟ meeting for Jerry. The the Hot Rod in Alameda P.M., he'd said he had to office building. According you guys in about forty m you at the Hot Rod in Fre͟

That threw Susan's cal͟ headed for the Hod Rod Alameda.

"But Jerry never showed up *"What?"*

"He didn't get there. So we

Her heart convulsed when G͟ gone to the meeting at the Hot R͟ him, especially since the meeting chain of Hot Rods. Of all his club best and saw them as the foundatic all over America. Jerry often sched the same time slot, and he was us͟ *missed* a meeting. He had virtually Porsche once when someone rear-grabbed a cab immediately so he wo up at a meeting. If he was shaken up b͟ could tell.

Hurriedly, Susan called Steve Bonill͟ had talked to Jerry, he was following some office building in Pleasanton. Th͟ been fairly early in the evening, and Jer͟ had plans after that. She was sure that the meet Konqui, but maybe she'd misunderst͟

Steve Bonilla was currently living with hi͟ Bonilla's house, and Susan reached him th͟ on that Wednesday morning.

"Steve," she began, "have you seen Jerry?͟

"Why?" Bonilla answered, surprised.

"Well, weren't you with him last night?"

"Yes, at the South 40 for drinks. *Why*, Susa͟

"Then what happened?" she persisted.

trail, and she listened as Sandy related his conversation with his older brother.

Sandy Harris had called Jerry and found that his brother was in a great mood. They discussed the very strong possibility that Jerry had found a buyer for the SteelFab plant. Sandy knew that obligation was hanging heavy over Jerry's head and that he would be relieved to be rid of it. Sandy remembered Jerry telling him he'd had drinks with Steve Bonilla and that Steve was leading him to a spot in Pleasanton so he could check out an office building. Well, that fit. That was what Jerry had told her too.

"All of a sudden," Sandy told Susan, "Jerry got irritated about something. He said 'Damn!' or some swearword. He said he would get together with me today to continue our discussion."

Sandy said his phone rang a minute or so later, but when he answered, no one spoke. He heard the caller disconnect. Susan realized suddenly that Jerry's conversation with his brother was the last traceable contact he'd had with anyone. When she checked with the mobile phone company to verify charges, she found the call that Sandy had made to Jerry at 8:51 P.M. She also found that Jerry had attempted to call Sandy back on his mobile phone but that the call had disconnected in less than a minute. *Why?* Why had Jerry hung up so suddenly? And why hadn't he tried again to call Sandy back?

And, knowing Jerry's aversion to swearing, she wondered what had made him angry enough to say "Damn!" into his cell phone.

That first day passed with agonizing slowness. Susan was afraid that Jerry's car was in a ravine somewhere, that he was injured and trapped in the wreckage and needed her to come and find him. But she had no idea where to start looking. That evening, Ken Hansen, a Contra Costa deputy, got special permission from his sergeant to help Susan look for her husband. Even though he couldn't make a report yet, Hansen took pity on Susan and showed up at her house, offering to help her search for Jerry on his own time.

"He wasn't officially on duty, and he couldn't look for Jerry until twenty-four hours had passed," Susan recalled, "but he came and picked me up and drove with me along this back road, Dougherty Road, down to Hopyard Road. It was a very windy, very scary road. We had always been so in tune with each other that I heard Jerry's voice in my head, saying 'Sue, find me!' and I was saying back, 'Please Jerry, hang on. I'm almost there.' I believed that I could find him. I just had to put all my energy into it. I was so scared that I would find him dead."

It was anguishing for Susan as the sheriff's deputy drove slowly along the road, shining his spotlight far down into the canyons, looking for the glint of a vehicle or the reflection of glass. Susan told herself she would have to be strong if they found Jerry. The most likely explanation was that his car *was* down there someplace. Part of her wanted to find him; part of her prayed he wasn't in a ravine in a crushed car.

They didn't find him.

The sun came up on Thursday, the world started up again, but Jerry didn't come home. At least Susan could now report his disappearance to the Contra Costa Sheriff's Office. Deputy Hansen took her report. Jerry was now officially a missing person: case number 87-26571. Susan couldn't give the authorities much information beyond a precise description of her husband and the fact that, as far as she knew, Jerry had last been seen on Hopyard Road in Pleasanton. He was five feet nine or ten and weighed 180 pounds; he had bright blue eyes and short brown hair.

The hardest part for Susan was relating all of Jerry's scars and individual characteristics; she knew that they would be most helpful if someone found him dead. But she shook that thought away, and continued to give as much information as she could. Jerry's most distinguishing mark was the eight-inch scar on the right side of his abdomen from the shooting when he was a kid. He also had a quarter-sized bruise-colored scar on his buttocks. He had once broken his right leg, and there would be X-rays available of that. He wore glasses for reading, and he smoked a pipe. He always wore his gold-nugget wedding ring and, on his other hand, the tiger ring with emerald eyes and a ruby tongue. He'd had a lot of dental work done over the years, and his bottom teeth were capped.

Hansen typed in "Victim missing over twenty-four hours under suspicious circumstances. Victim and victim's vehicle entered into the system: M270331002."

Detective Linda Agresta was the lead Contra Costa County investigator. She was in her mid-thirties, a tall, beautiful blonde who was unfailingly kind to Susan. She did everything she could to help in the search. Even so, Susan also hired a private detective firm: Rand Investigation—Randy Ontiveros and Francie Koehler.

Not satisfied even with that, Susan organized her own search party. She was very efficient; she had become an automaton who could keep from going to pieces only if she was doing something. "I had all this adrenaline that made me hyperaware of everything going on around me," Susan said, remembering the terribly lucid state she was in.

"I hired a helicopter to search where cars and people couldn't go, I sent people to all the BART [Bay Area Rapid Transit] parking lots to look for Jerry's car. I called all the airports I could find. I even had someone I knew in L.A. check out the LAX airport."

Susan wanted to get as many people looking for Jerry as she could. She knew that, within the month, a large payment would be due on his leased Mercedes. "I told the leasing company that Jerry had taken off in their Mercedes," she said, "because I knew they would immediately start looking for him too."

Susan's sister, Julie, was already close by; she had come down from Oregon to work for Jerry, and she hurried to the big pink house in Blackhawk. Mary Jo Hannah arrived from Medford, prepared to stay for however long she was needed. The two families set up a command post in Susan and Jerry's house. They tried to help, and they tried to get Susan to sleep and to eat. But she couldn't; she would lose fifteen pounds from an already slim frame in the first week alone.

"I was on the phone all the time," she remembered. "I was on the phone so much that my ear was actually raw and throbbing. I kept thinking that the next call would help find Jerry. I couldn't stop just because I was tired." Somehow, she felt that if she slept, Jerry would be lost forever; if she stopped to eat, she would miss doing something vital to save him.

She was not the Susan Harris she had been a few days before, willing to stay happily in the background, a little shy, a listener rather than a talker. She had become a woman on fire. Friends and acquaintances called to ask about Jerry, to say how sorry they were that he was missing. "It infuriated me," she said. "They were taking up my time and hogging the line. I would say, 'Get off the phone!'"

It did not seem possible that a man as alive and vibrant and powerful as Jerry Harris could simply have vanished from the face of the earth. He had always been bigger than life, the strongest man Susan had ever known. He could break your heart when he sang, and he could make you laugh. If you were poor or hungry, he would be there to help you out.

But not anymore. By October 20 something or someone had been scaring the hell out of Jerry Harris. Susan realized that now; that was why Jerry had kept in even closer touch than usual with her and Sandy.

Neither Sandy nor Susan nor Jerry used drugs, and while Jerry might have cut creative corners in his businesses, he would not have allowed anything illegal to go on—that is, if he'd had control over what was going on.

What was happening had to be some kind of mistake or sick joke. Susan felt that Jerry would turn into their driveway any moment with a perfectly reasonable explanation of why he hadn't been home for a week. She could not bear to entertain the thought that he might *never* come home. They had been married only two and a half years, and they had moved into their dream house just three weeks before. No, Jerry was coming back.

She didn't know what was keeping him away—but she knew he would come back to her. "I had to believe that he was alive," she said. "If I gave up hope, it meant he was dead, and it was my job to keep people believing in him and keep them motivated so they would keep looking for him. If

I let them convince me that Jerry was dead, then he *would* be," she explained. "I felt as if I was the only one who could save him, and if I gave up, he would be lost forever."

Susan was walking through the worst nightmare of her life. Everything was unreal. Listening to Jerry's tapes helped a little. One of the songs he sang seemed to speak her thoughts:

"What now my love? Now that you've left me. How can I live through another day? . . . Once I could see. Once I could feel. Now I am numb. I've become unreal. . . ."

8

Gerald B. "Duke" Diedrich had served as a special agent for the Federal Bureau of Investigation for nineteen years, assigned at various times to Washington, D.C., Minneapolis, and the Oakland–San Francisco area. He had once been a lieutenant in the U.S. Navy, a flight officer assigned to the USS *Saratoga* during the Vietnam War. In addition to flying, he had coordinated legal and court-martial matters for all the personnel of Fighter Squadron 31.

As an FBI agent, Diedrich had worked as a hostage negotiator, police instructor, expert photographer, undercover agent, and media relations representative, but his expertise was in abductions and kidnappings. While it would be callous to say he enjoyed his work, he *did* relish the challenge and the chance to understand the psychopathology that spurred a kidnapper to commit one of the most cowardly and heartrending crimes on the books. Diedrich was good at what he did, and early on he had developed a certain sixth sense about the scenarios behind the sudden disappearances of human beings.

Because of his knowledge Diedrich served as a consultant to the National Center for Missing and Exploited Children, and he was occasionally loaned out to other law enforcement agencies. In 1985–1986, he worked for six months with the huge Green River Killer Task Force in Seattle. (The abductions and murders of more than four dozen young women have never been solved despite the concerted efforts of city, county, state, and federal investigators.)

But the Bay Area was Duke Diedrich's bailiwick. When asked to describe himself, he usually grinned and said, "Look for a combination of Robert Redford and Danny DeVito."

In truth, Diedrich was not quite as handsome as Redford and considerably taller than DeVito, but he was something of a joker; it was not unusual for Diedrich to put his friends on. He didn't fit the stereotype of an FBI agent, and that attribute had stood him in good stead during his years with the Bureau.

In October of 1987, when Jerry Harris vanished, Duke Diedrich was assigned to the Concord, California, regional office. On October 23, the Friday after Harris drove away from his home on Blackhawk Drive in Danville—into seeming oblivion—Duke Diedrich received a call in his office at the Concord FBI headquarters. An assistant district attorney in Santa Clara County, two counties south of Danville, was calling at the request of Sandy Harris, Jerry's brother. The assistant D.A., a good friend of Sandy's, wanted Duke to look into the odd disappearance of Sandy's older brother.

Diedrich listened to the circumstances of Jerry Harris's vanishing, but he wasn't particularly impressed—at least, not at first. He explained that it did not sound like a typical kidnapping. "There's no evidence of an abduction or . . . murder," Diedrich said. If it was, it was no slam-dunk kidnapping. "For all we know, the guy may have left of his own accord," he said.

And that was true. There was apparently no ransom note, no sign of a struggle, no bloodstains or bullet casings, no suspicious phone calls, and no car. Diedrich couldn't justify asking for an FBI investigation. But the more he thought about it, the more he felt hinky about the sudden disappearance of Jerry Harris. Diedrich's own unease was only exacerbated when Sandy and his friend from the D.A.'s office kept hounding him with phone calls. The way Jerry had vanished was just too suspicious. At length, Diedrich agreed to go to Harris's home in the Blackhawk district the next day, a Saturday.

Susan Harris and Duke Diedrich happened to be neighbors, although neither realized it until Jerry disappeared. They both lived in the Blackhawk district of Contra Costa County near Danville, California, but Duke's home was not as lavish as the Harris mansion. Their being neighbors was only a coincidence; Diedrich had never even heard of Jerry and Susan before October 1987.

"I went out to Blackhawk Drive that Saturday," Diedrich recalled, "and I go up to this fabulous house and find at least eleven people waiting to talk to me—Jerry Harris's family. And Susan Harris's family. People who worked with Jerry. And Susan, his wife. It wasn't the optimum interview situation."

Given a choice, investigators like to talk with witnesses one at a time. It's almost impossible to talk to a roomful of emotional people, all bursting with opinions and fears, and come away with an organized, cogent version of a possible crime. Still, Diedrich stayed and listened, gradually forming in his mind a picture of the man who had been gone for four days. He knew the patterns in a walkaway and in an abduction, and Jerry Harris did not sound like a walkaway. The people who had gathered to talk to Duke quite obviously adored this husband, son, brother, and father, whom they had lost. Harris sounded like a family man as well as a successful businessman. He also sounded like a damned nice guy.

Diedrich was particularly impressed with the slender young woman who was Jerry Harris's wife. She was quite beautiful, although terribly thin and she had huge purple hollows beneath her eyes. He found her incredibly strong and resolute, a woman who would not allow herself the luxury of breaking down. "Once in a while, she lost it a little," he said. "When she was trying to describe to me what kind of man Jerry was, what made him special, but most of the time she was remarkably calm. I liked her. My heart went out to her because, whoever this guy was, it was obvious that she loved him tremendously."

Besides, Duke was a pushover for a lady in trouble—and Susan Harris was in a lot of trouble. Diedrich listened for hours to remembrances, suspicions, theories and arguments from the people whose lives had revolved around Jerry Harris. He came away convinced that he might well have become involved in a kidnapping case.

For the FBI to enter a local jurisdiction's case, the Bureau must have cause to believe that there has been either an abduction or a murder for hire with interstate aspects, or local authorities must ask for assistance. Duke Diedrich could not substantiate either of the first two possibilities with physical evidence. Still, he felt in his gut that what had happened to Jerry Harris fell into one of those categories.

On Monday morning, October 27, Diedrich went in to see his boss, Dick Held, agent in charge of the Concord FBI office.

"Dick," Diedrich said, "I can't tell you exactly why, but I smell foul play in this Harris disappearance. I'd like to open a case on it. I want to start working it."

Held knew that Diedrich had an unerring sense when something was wrong, and he gave him the go-ahead to attempt to find out what had happened to Jerry Lee Harris.

From that point on, Susan Harris had a staunch ally, a friend, someone she could talk to when she grew close to a breaking point. Duke Diedrich truly believed that something had happened to Jerry, and he was going to help her find him. They usually met at least once a week, and Susan called Duke every other day. Most days he had nothing to tell her. There were also times when he knew things that he could not tell her.

The disappearance of Jerry Lee Harris proved to be one of the cases that Duke Diedrich would never forget. Years later, every detail would spring to his mind as clearly as if it had happened only the day before.

Initially, there were many things for him to learn about Jerry's life, a more complicated and fascinating life than most. And in Susan Harris, Duke Diedrich met one of the most determined women he had ever known. When Susan went to bed on the night of October 20, she had been living a life any woman would have envied. Before daylight, however, she was plunged into a horror story. Although she looked fragile, she was tough. Neither she nor the FBI agent who befriended her had any idea how strong she was going to have to be in the years ahead.

Halloween was coming, and neighbors were putting out jack-o'-lanterns, ghosts, and witch figures. Susan Harris's days and nights were full of unreality, and the Halloween decorations made it worse, somehow, although their effect on her was subliminal. She was so involved in her obsessive search that she scarcely acknowledged they were there. It would be years before Susan Harris could accept Halloween for what it was and not as a reminder of a macabre time in her life.

When there had been no sign of Jerry for ten days, the family went public with a plea for information. They offered a $25,000 reward for Jerry's safe return or for information that would lead to his abductors and a conviction. Papers in the Bay Area printed the FBI's twenty-four-hour number.

However, FBI spokesman Charles Latting denied that the Bureau was officially working the case. He told reporters, "There have been no ransom demands. There's no indication at this point that any foul play is involved. He's just missing.

"We wait until they find a car or the person or a demand—until there is some strong indication of foul play. Otherwise, it's just a local police matter."

In reality, of course, Duke Diedrich had had an open case on Jerry Harris for over a week, but Duke was just as happy that the publicized FBI position was one of watching and waiting.

Sandy Harris, acting as the family's spokesman, faced the media cameras and vehemently denied that Jerry had left willingly. "His businesses are probably bringing in $10 million annually. How could he be turned off by something like that? He just bought himself a $1.5 million home, and his businesses are pumping out cash. . . . Why would somebody who worked his tail off to get all that just drive away and forget it? It doesn't make sense."

October 31, Halloween, was a terrible day. Later on, looking back through the stack of newspaper clippings she had saved, Susan realized that it was on Halloween that she and the Harris family had decided to go public with the news of Jerry's disappearance. He had been gone for eleven days. Eleven days with no word from Jerry. Susan knew he couldn't have had more than eighty dollars in cash with him when he left, and he hadn't used any of his credit cards. They had called everyone they could think of who had even a tangential relationship to Jerry and come up with nothing at all.

On Halloween it seemed that Jerry's picture was on the front page of every newspaper in the Bay Area. The San Francisco papers and the San Jose *Mercury News* ran headlines: "Nightclub Owner Vanishes: Relatives Fear He's Been Abducted."

Mary Jo Hannah was worried about Susan, and she tried to act as a buffer between her daughter and the press as they moved into Jerry's office after the public announcement that he was missing. She needn't have worried; Susan Harris barely saw the microphones stuck in front of her face or heard the questions called out to her. She had always been polite and considerate, but courtesy didn't seem to matter any longer. She knew she had to get the news about Jerry before the public if she wanted help in finding him, but she hated the reporters who seemed about to suffocate her. They didn't care about Jerry. They were looking for a story for the five-o'clock news.

"How do you feel now that your husband's missing?" a young female reporter from Channel 2 shouted.

"Get the hell out of my face," Susan snapped, knocking the microphone aside. "Get out of my way." Where was it written that the worried wife had to pose for close-ups? But then she felt terrible. Jerry hated swearing, especially from her, and he would never have been so rude.

Sometimes she shocked herself with her behavior, but she had no time or energy for niceties anymore. She wanted the focus on Jerry, not on how she felt. How did they *expect* her to feel?

Sandy moved in to answer questions. Asked about family problems, Sandy Harris shook his head. There were none. Jerry Lee Harris was the last man in California to want to run away. He'd had a life that anyone would envy.

He'd had it made.

9

When weeks passed with no sign of Jerry Harris or of his very distinctive car, Susan chose to believe that this was a sign that he was alive. If he was dead, his body would have been found. If someone had stolen the pale yellow Mercedes convertible, it would have been spotted. It wasn't a run-of-the-mill car.

Hundreds of posters were displayed all over the Bay Area with photographs of Jerry and of his car:

MISSING

JERRY LEE HARRIS
   White male, 5'10", 180 lbs
   Brown hair, blue eyes
   Date of birth: 06-01-42
   Missing since October 20, 1987
   From the Pleasanton-Fremont Area

REWARD

Please be on the lookout for this vehicle:

1982 Mercedes Benz
    380 SL Coupe
    Pale yellow (buff)
    Dark brown soft top
    Car license # 2AIGO62
    VIN# WDBBA45A9CB018339

Contact Detective Agresta
Contra Costa Sheriff Investigations
Phone 415-555-4580
Case # SO 87-26571

Nothing about Jerry's disappearance was going to be easy to figure out. He was missing, but from which police jurisdiction? In the end, the Contra Costa Sheriff's Office in Martinez claimed jurisdiction. Captain Russ Pitkin said, "We're in communication with the FBI. He [Jerry Harris] lives in our area, but was last seen in Pleasanton, Alameda County." Charles Latting, the FBI spokesman, continued to say only that the Bureau was "aware of the case."

In an era of burgeoning computer communication and widespread television news, it surely wasn't possible for anyone as well known as Jerry Harris simply to vanish. He knew thousands of people.

Susan struggled to find plausible—or even slightly implausible—reasons why Jerry would not have contacted her if he was alive. She had read about college professors and brain surgeons who simply buckled under stress and walked away from their lives to mingle with street people on skid row. Jerry had been under tremendous stress, and it *had* begun to show during the weeks before he disappeared. His father and brothers had even commented on it. He was trying to manage his own businesses, run his dad's steel plant, and build two new clubs, not to mention the financial burden of the new house. Susan felt guilty now that she had gone along so enthusiastically with buying the Blackhawk mansion. Maybe that had been the final straw for Jerry.

Maybe he had just taken time out from his life. She remembered how they had talked in the steam bath the day before he disappeared, how Jerry had made her promise that she would look after his mother and his daughter if anything happened to him. He had told her to go to his attorney for help if he was "gone."

"When I thought of how he had gone over all his business plans with me and asked me to take care of Faye and Tiffany," Susan said, "I wondered if he might have been preparing me for something—if he had been planning to go away. I even wondered if maybe Jerry had amnesia," she recalled, her voice trembling with remembered fear. "I know it sounds [like a] soap opera, but people *do* suffer from amnesia."

Her family and friends watched Susan closely, afraid that her frail spirit couldn't keep going. She insisted upon going into the clubs and Jerry's office and overseeing his businesses. "I knew he would be so mad at me if he came back and found out I'd let the businesses go downhill."

Jerry had told her to go to his attorney for help, but when she contacted the man, he seemed nervous. "He told me he had no idea what Jerry might have meant. He didn't have anything to tell me."

One day Susan pretended that she had to go to a meeting in San Francisco. She didn't have a meeting; she planned to walk slowly down the city's meanest streets and gaze into the faces of the men who gathered there. She remembered how she and Jerry had gone to San Francisco once to buy her Christmas present.

"Jerry went up to one of the street guys—testing him, maybe—and asked him, 'Hey, do you have a quarter? I really need to make a phone call.' The man started to reach into his pocket—that was all Jerry had to see. He handed the man a wad of money and wished him merry Christmas."

Now Susan hoped against hope that Jerry might be there. She didn't care if he had no money or if they lost all their nightclubs and their big pink house. She only wanted to find her husband. She went to San Francisco, and she looked at the men lined up for meals at the missions and at those who hunkered down against the walls of crumbling buildings. But she didn't find Jerry.

There were more memories in the city than she had expected to find. She gazed at the Bay Bridge and remembered another of Jerry's "hero days." She had been driving when they approached the tollgate. She stopped to pay the toll, and then Jerry told her to speed up and catch the car ahead of them, which, she realized, had no driver. Then she saw a tiny little old Mexican woman chasing the car.

"She wasn't doing very well," Susan remembered. "She was quite a ways behind it. I sped up and Jerry jumped out and got into that car and stepped on the brakes and put it into Park. He jogged back to the woman, and she was crying and saying 'Gracias, gracias' in Spanish. I guess she was so short that she hadn't been able to reach the toll cashier from her seat so she got out with her car in Drive, and it just kept going."

Susan thought of all the people they had helped on freeways at night. Jerry had never been able to leave a woman stranded on the roadside. "He would turn on the light inside the car so that she could see he was with me— another woman—and wouldn't be alarmed. He fixed tires and brought gas. He was very protective of women."

Susan drove home from San Francisco, remembering all the empty faces she had gazed into, wondering if someone was waiting for them someplace.

As Thanksgiving approached, Susan sometimes thought of movies in which runaway husbands completely erased any trail and lived a high life in Europe or on a South Sea island. When that thought crossed her mind, she shook her head hard and made it go away. Susan was ambivalent; she wanted Jerry to be alive, but it hurt so much to think of him with someone else.

She also remembered the conversation that she and Jerry had once—and once only. When he was so worried about the IRS probe, he had asked her if she would go with him if he had to disappear. Would she leave the country with him? She had told him no, she could not do that. He had held her hand and smiled, and never mentioned it again.

Were other things bothering Jerry—things he had never

told her about? Was it possible that he *had* left the country, disappeared without even telling her good-bye? He had always tried to protect her. Maybe he had felt that what she didn't know couldn't get her in trouble. Maybe even his leaving was his way of being sure she was safe.

This was a scenario that Susan found almost impossible to believe in. But it was one that let her continue to believe her husband was alive.

No one who knew Susan Harris had ever realized how tenacious she could be. She had always deferred to Jerry, perfectly content to let him be the decision-maker and the dynamo. But now Jerry was gone, and she would do anything, *anything,* in the name of love to get him back.

Any number of reports were coming in to Linda Agresta about sightings of men who resembled Jerry Harris. Most of them fizzled out. One, however, sounded possible. Someone called Agresta and said that a man who looked just like Jerry had been seen several times in a country-western bar in Jackson, California, a tiny hamlet on the way to Lake Tahoe and Reno. Agresta and Francie Koehler went to Jackson, but they couldn't find the man.

When Linda and Francie told Susan, she decided to go to Jackson and try again. It was a tiny little town with cabins and a rustic, small-town ambience. Susan took an armload of flyers to put up.

"I went into the post office in Jackson," Susan remembered. "And I said, 'My husband is missing. Could I put a flyer on your wall?' The postmistress said, 'Just tack it up there with the rest of them.' I looked at the wall, and there were dozens—scores—of flyers there—all missing people that someone loved. I think that was the first time I realized Jerry wasn't the only missing person. It was just to *me* that he was the only missing person."

Susan had a number of revelations on her trip to Jackson. She passed out flyers as she asked people there if they had seen Jerry. One man studied Jerry's photograph on the flyer and said, "Nope, can't say as I have." Frustrated, Susan showed him a picture of herself, and said, "Have you seen this woman?"

"Nope."

What good was it going to do her to put up Jerry's picture? Maybe most people were like this man—unable to recognize a person who was standing right in front of them? Jerry could have been sitting beside this man in a bar, and he would not have remembered him. Discouraged, she tacked up the rest of her flyers and went home.

Later she learned that Linda and Francie were positive someone had followed them on their trip to Jackson and trailed them around town as they asked people about Jerry Harris. They had managed to snap a picture of the man. When they looked through a book of mug shots, they found him, but his rap sheet didn't reveal anything that linked him to Jerry, and no serious crimes were noted.

"They told me his name was Willie something," Susan remembered. "The name didn't mean anything to me."

She suspected that Steve Bonilla knew more than he was telling her about the last time he'd seen Jerry. She didn't think that he could have hurt Jerry. He would have been a fool to do that, since Jerry was on his way to making Bonilla's fortune. Anyway, Steve wasn't the kind of man who could carry out any project on his own. With Jerry gone, Steve would have to find someone else to attach himself to. Even his mother didn't trust him enough to give him cash—unless he had a winner who would take him on. Steve Bonilla was a piggyback kind of man.

But there was more to it than that. Jerry was one of the few people in the world who actually *liked* Steven Bonilla. He was Steve's friend—probably his best friend. Steve had stood up with them at their wedding, and he was invited to every social function, every cruise, every family dinner. With Jerry gone, Steve probably felt as anchorless as she did.

But still . . . Steve had acted so weird the first time Susan questioned him about the night of October 20. And Duke Diedrich hadn't had much more luck when he attempted to interview Steven Bonilla.

"I'd been told that Bonilla was Jerry Harris's best friend," Diedrich remembered. "I called him repeatedly and asked him to come up to my office in Concord for an interview, but he had a dozen excuses why he couldn't do that. I finally gave him an ultimatum, and he showed up."

Diedrich looked at the sweating, swarthy man slouched across the desk from him. He wondered why a man as dynamic as Jerry Harris had reportedly been would have chosen to befriend a guy like Steven Bonilla. But Susan had explained to him that Jerry felt sorry for Steve. That might have accounted for their association.

The hairs on the back of Diedrich's neck prickled as he took Steven Bonilla's statement and got the same story that everyone else had: "And I never saw Jerry after he looked at the office complex. I didn't even see which direction he was headed when he left."

He was lying. After so many years as an investigator, Diedrich had learned to sense a lie, and he knew the man in front of him was being deliberately evasive. Diedrich knew it with every fiber of his being.

As he remembered his first interview with Steve Bonilla, he sounded surprised. "I never do this," Diedrich said. "I mean, I have *never* done this before or since, but I looked Steven Bonilla right in the eye and I said, 'You did this. Steve, I *know* you did this. And someday I'm going to arrest you for it.'"

"Fuck you," Bonilla spat. "Prove it."

"You prove you didn't do it," Diedrich said flatly. "I've got a polygrapher standing by. We can hook you up right now, and you can walk out of here cleared."

Ron Homer, an expert lie-detector technician, waited. But Steven Bonilla refused to be hooked up to the leads of the polygraph. He stalked out of Duke Diedrich's office.

When she heard that Bonilla wouldn't talk to Duke, Susan decided to give him another try herself. She was sure Steve knew something about Jerry's disappearance, but she wasn't sure what. She felt if Jerry had run off with another woman that Steve would know about it. She wanted to make him tell her.

"I called him," she said. "I was going to appeal to his emotions, and I made myself cry when I called him. That wasn't hard; I hadn't really stopped crying for days."

As distraught as she was, Susan approached Jerry's disappearance in an almost businesslike way. She took notes with the dates and times carefully printed. Even as tears ran down her face, Susan wrote down her conversation with Steve Bonilla.

"Steve, do you know what happened to Jerry?" Susan asked flatly.

"No, I don't," he said earnestly. "Everybody's been asking me, and I don't know any more than what I've said."

"Did I do something?" Susan sobbed. "Is he mad at me?"

"No, no, Susan. He loves you very much."

"I've been calling all the hospitals—everywhere."

"That's a good idea."

"Did Jerry ever talk about going anywhere? Maybe a vacation?"

"Well, you know," Bonilla said, "we talked about going to Tahoe, Reno, Cancun—"

"Okay," she said. "I'll call all the hospitals in Tahoe, Reno and Vegas—"

"*No.* Not Vegas," he interrupted her. "Not Vegas."

"Okay."

"If you need to, call," Bonilla said softly. "You call anytime—even four o'clock in the morning."

Susan hung up, puzzled. Steve Bonilla had always ignored her. She couldn't imagine why he was being so solicitous now. Maybe he felt sorry for her because he knew where Jerry was—and who he was with. But why had Steve sounded so startled when she said she would call hospitals in Las Vegas? Had she hit a nerve?

Susan called hospitals in all the spots Steve had mentioned. She called all those listed for Las Vegas too. None of them had admitted a patient matching Jerry's description.

Susan's days took on a dreadful kind of pattern. She saw to it that the flyers with Jerry's picture on them were in good supply, and she made sure they were posted everywhere. She kept in constant touch with her private investigator, Francie Koehler, and with the volunteers who were searching for Jerry. She had to keep their momentum up. She knew that almost everyone else believed that Jerry was dead. It was easy for the others to lose their enthusiasm for the search. It wasn't as if Jerry was a prime candidate for poster boy of missing persons. He was a grown man, not a helpless child. Susan knew too that a lot of people smiled wickedly and figured that, if Jerry wasn't dead, he had left to enjoy a liaison with another woman.

For weeks Susan had wondered if Jerry was alive and with another woman, and the thought had broken her heart. Now she began to pray that he *had* left her for another woman. She tried to picture him on a beach someplace—maybe Cancun—tanned, laughing. Even if it meant he was with someone else, Susan had almost come to a place where she would rather have Jerry alive and safe than lose him to some dark force that was only a blurry shape in her mind.

Jerry had to be alive. He just had to be.

The still darkness of the night was torture when she was all alone. Sometimes Susan wondered if she had ever really known Jerry. She had been the country hick, a girl who worked in a sawmill, and he had taken her into a world of wealth and glamour and excitement that she could never have imagined. Maybe he *was* tired of her; maybe her days of being half of the perfect couple were over, and she had not even seen the end coming.

She played the tapes of Jerry singing, and the words of his favorite song haunted her: "What Now My Love? Now that you've gone? I'd be a fool to go on and on. . . ."

Maybe she was a fool. Maybe Jerry *had* left her without any good-byes or any regrets.

Susan went to Jerry's office every day now and tried to carry on with business as usual. She went to Baritz and to the Hot Rods to keep an eye on how things were going. It wasn't an easy task for her. Jerry was a natural and she accepted that she wasn't. It took Jerry's hands-on attention, his personality, his charisma, to make his enterprises work. Jerry was a workaholic, but he was also blessed—or cursed—with a magical business sense. There was no way that Susan could manage Jerry's myriad businesses. It was his special touch that made them go. But no one knew where Jerry was, and someone had to step up. Susan served as the conservator of Jerry's estate. She discovered that they owed money to 286 creditors. She spent night after night going over their books to find their assets. Gradually she saw that their financial condition was not as precarious as it seemed at first glance. But it would be touch-and-go for months.

10

The law enforcement agencies working on the Harris case were as baffled as anyone else. They wondered if Jerry Lee Harris, besieged with debt, had taken his own life. No one who had ever known him would go along with that. Jerry Harris wasn't a quitter. Suicide would have been, for him of all people, unthinkable. And, realistically, how could a man commit suicide and manage to completely hide his Mercedes convertible as well as his body?

Susan believed Jerry was out there someplace—alive. The one other person who absolutely refused to believe that Jerry had left on purpose was his brother Sandy. No one could ever convince him that Jerry would run out on his responsibilities. If any one of his businesses or any member of his family was in trouble, Sandy knew that Jerry would have stayed around and worked things out. He wasn't a quitter, and he didn't let people down. "Besides," Sandy told Susan, "he loved you too much to ever leave you."

Jerry's father, Jim Harris, would later ponder a pattern that he could see only in retrospect. He recalled the uncharacteristic way Jerry had behaved that fall. "Everything that we look back on sounds like, since he didn't intend to leave, he realized he might get murdered. I would assume there was a threat made on his life."

But a threat from whom? Unless Jerry *did* have a secret life, there was no one who might have had a reason to kill him.

Steve Bonilla continued to tell police he was as baffled as anyone else. For the dozenth time, he went over his last moments with his friend and business associate. Yes, he had met with Jerry on October 20 to look at offices in the Hacienda Business Park, but then they had driven off in opposite directions. He had no idea where Jerry was going; he had assumed he was going home.

Sandy Harris doubted Steve Bonilla's story. He had seen how Steve intruded himself into Jerry's businesses and how troublesome the Fremont palm seedling business had become. Steve had jumped ship from being Jerry's partner in the palm nursery and suddenly become a partner with two other men. And that, Sandy said, had "forced a situation where my brother had to turn over the business to these people."

Susan Harris was living a life of grief and quiet terror. She didn't want to move out of the house in Blackhawk—that home was the last place she had ever seen Jerry. She knew that she would probably have to leave at some point; she wouldn't be able to make the mortgage payments. But she was going to hang on as long as she could. However, she could not—would not—sleep in the bed she had shared with her husband. For most of the long nights she stared into the darkness, unable to sleep. Finally, she found a kind of solution. "I dragged my blankets into our closet," she remembered. "There were no windows, and it felt safer. Jerry felt closer, somehow. Jerry always smelled so good, and I could smell his aftershave on his jackets. I could sleep there, in the closet, but I always listened for the phone."

Susan's mother moved down from Medford to stay with her. The pink house was too scary to live in alone. There were so many doors to the outside, and many of the windows came down almost to the ground. There was no alarm system; Jerry would have installed one, but he was gone before he had time to do so. Susan couldn't afford to drape the windows now. She listed the house for sale, but she was leery of showing it to strangers.

Susan was glad that there was so much publicity about Jerry, but the address of their home in Blackhawk had appeared in some newspaper articles, and reporters and other inquisitive people drove by. Some of them even came up to the house and peered in the windows. She felt as if she were living in a display window. Didn't people care that she was a human being, a woman who had lost the most important person in the world to her? Apparently not. She and Jerry had become mere curiosities.

Duke Diedrich told her to cover the windows with newspapers. He said she didn't have to be on display, and if she couldn't afford drapes—and he knew she couldn't— newspapers would shut out the world just as well.

Some of the harassment came from *inside* the home she and Jerry had shared. They had eight tropical birds, which they had patiently trained to talk. One of them could mimic Jerry's voice perfectly and another—a big red macaw— sounded just like Susan. It was hard to say which was worse—hearing Jerry's voice from his bird or hearing the macaw calling constantly, "Jer? *Jer?*"

"I had to get rid of the birds. I couldn't stand that."

Short of actually learning that Jerry was dead, that there was no way he could come back to her, Susan couldn't imagine that things could get worse. But they did. She had only begun to understand what raw, abject fear could be.

On November 21, while Susan's father was visiting in Danville, she took him and her mother to Baritz for dinner. It was just after midnight when they returned to the pink house—the last house on the street. The closest streetlight was too far away to cast light on Susan and Jerry's house, and there was a vacant lot across the street. The night was very dark and very quiet.

Susan didn't have the key to the side door of the garage— Jerry had taken it with him that last morning a month before, and they had never had time to have a duplicate made before he vanished.

"I only had the key to the front door, so my dad parked his truck in the driveway," Susan said. "That meant we had to walk out to the curb and go along the street to get to the front of the house."

As they were walking along the street in the dark, a car appeared without warning, seemingly out of nowhere, racing toward them at sixty miles an hour, at least, its headlights blazing. "I heard someone yell as the car went by, but I couldn't make out what they were saying," Susan said.

They had scarce seconds to react. The phantom car almost struck them—coming so close that they felt the whoosh of displaced wind as it whizzed past them. At that moment Susan leaped forward and threw herself on top of Mary Jo, sending her mother sprawling onto the front lawn. She looked around for her dad and saw that he too had managed to jump out of the car's path.

The three of them ran for the front door, and Susan struggled to get the key in the lock with trembling fingers. There was no reason for any car to come down to their end of Blackhawk Meadow Drive, and certainly not at freeway speed. They all knew that whoever was behind the wheel had intended to run over them—and that that someone had been waiting with the car lights off for them to come home. They had escaped death by mere inches.

"My dad was standing on the front doorstep," Susan said. "That car turned around and parked where my dad's truck was. It was almost in our driveway. Whoever it was turned their radio up full blast, and my dad was trying to stare them down."

While Susan tugged at her father's arm to pull him inside, a man stepped out of the car and seemed to stare back at Pete Hannah. All Susan could see was a dark silhouette against the headlights—a faceless man. She shivered.

"I had a bad feeling. I didn't want my dad standing out there, so exposed, such a good target," Susan said. "My mother doesn't drink, but when we all got safely in the house, she poured us each a stiff shot, and we drank it."

They called the police and made a formal complaint, but the police weren't really concerned. They knew how jumpy Susan had been, and they told her it had probably been some kids racing around. Susan knew it wasn't. Why would kids race down a dead-end street?

There was something familiar about the man, but she couldn't put her finger on what it was. Susan had seen only the bulk of a dark figure against the halogen headlights. When someone asked later: "Do you think that could possibly have been Jerry?" Susan was horrified. Jerry would never hurt her. She was absolutely sure of that. But it was eerie, seeing someone but not really seeing him. Who was the man who stood there in the headlights of his car, a shadowy presence that seemed to exude hatred and violence?

Susan called Francie, her P.I., and told her what had happened. There was a long pause at the other end of the line, and she heard Francie take a deep breath.

"You know," Francie said, "I was going to tell you this. I should have. We got a threat through the sheriff's department."

"What threat?"

"They said that if you didn't stop messing around in Jerry's businesses, someone was going to take you out. Someone was going to run you down. What happened to you was *exactly* the way the threat said it would."

"Why didn't you tell me?" Susan breathed.

"I should have. I should have—but it was just another call. There have been so many 51-50s [California police slang for mental cases] that it didn't seem important enough to scare you about it."

That was cold comfort. If so many weird and threatening calls were coming into the sheriff's office that Francie wasn't even telling Susan about them, what else was going on? What other things was Detective Linda Agresta keeping from her? Who else was watching her?

If Susan Harris felt somewhat paranoid, who could blame her? "Up" was no longer up to her, and "down" wasn't down. Black was suddenly white. She looked back at her former life as if it were someone else's. "Everything was wonderful and magical . . . with Jerry," she said. "I was happy. Then everything changed overnight, and my world was dark and ugly without him. . . . I wore those pink-colored lenses that made the world look rosy most of my life. When Jerry disappeared, I saw the world differently, and that broke my heart."

11

Susan was aware that Steve Bonilla was showing up constantly at Baritz and throwing his weight around as if he were the owner. In actuality, he wasn't even slated to become a 40 percent limited partner until 1989, but you couldn't tell that from the way he was acting. She had never liked Steve, she had never trusted him, and now, with Jerry missing, the sight of him set Susan's teeth on edge. He wasn't acting the way a good friend should act; he didn't seem at all concerned about Jerry. He was acting like a vulture settling in to claim for himself whatever was left in the wake of disaster.

Each of Jerry's clubs had its own management team composed of a manager, an assistant manager, and a bookkeeper. Jerry had his secretary, Molly, and his own bookkeeper who kept track of everything. He also had an area manager, John Jacques, who oversaw all three night-club managers. Steve Bonilla had never had access to Jerry's books. He had no official position at all, and his posturing and pretensions shocked Susan. It was as if Steve had finally found his place in the sun. Jerry was gone and Steve was acting as if *he* now owned the Baritz.

Employees began to complain to Susan. Was Mr. Bonilla their new boss? they asked. Again and again Susan said

"No, absolutely not." As far as she was concerned, Jerry was still the boss; she was only filling in until he came back.

Some of the people working in their clubs looked at her with disbelief, and some with pity. A few reassured her that they too believed Jerry would be back. They all agreed on one thing: they did not want to work for Steven Bonilla.

Susan recalled now how Steve had taken her aside at the dinner party she and Jerry gave shortly before their wedding. He had warned her to keep away from Jerry's business interests, and she had been astonished by his vehemence. Now, without Jerry to keep a lid on Steve's ambition, he was seemingly determined to bulldoze right over Susan.

Susan talked to Duke Diedrich about it.

"Put pressure on Bonilla," Duke said flatly.

"How?"

"Cut him off. Don't pay him another dollar. Don't let him into the clubs."

Susan did as Duke said, but she felt a tremendous sense of danger. With every move she made to block Steve from taking over Jerry's spot in Baritz, he became angrier with her.

"He filed a lawsuit," Susan said. "It was a legal document—a restraining order. Basically he was demanding access to all Jerry's books and records."

Jerry had been gone a month, but it seemed to Susan as if he had been missing for a year. Each day started for her with less hope than the day before, but there *was* still hope. Until someone told her that her husband was dead, she would not stop searching for him. Each day ended with exhaustion and despair.

On November 24, 1987, a process server left copies of Steve Bonilla's legal actions at Jerry's Fremont offices. They were orders to show cause, primary injunctions, and temporary restraining orders filed against JLH Enterprises, Susan Harris, and Jerry Lee Harris.

If Steve Bonilla was as good a friend of Jerry's as he had always claimed to be, why would he move legally to make Susan's life even more agonizing than it already was? He obviously wanted control of everything Jerry had built.

"I knew that he always wanted to be like Jerry—to *be* Jerry," Susan said. "And now, with Jerry missing, Steve was ready to step into his shoes. He didn't seem to care about anything but becoming the boss at Baritz."

Whenever she lost faith in her own strength, Susan could count on Duke. She was coordinating her business efforts with the police investigation. She wasn't sure just how Duke felt about Steven Bonilla, beyond his profound distaste for him. Duke had become like family to her, but he didn't betray his thoughts. He stood behind her, though, in urging her to keep the pressure on Bonilla and not give an inch of Jerry's business turf away to him.

Susan had been desperately trying to find an attorney to represent her interests and Jerry's. She had virtually no money, however, and attorneys wanted hefty retainers for what appeared to be a long-drawn-out legal process.

Jerry wasn't the kind of man to have a savings account. He had been plowing the money from the clubs right back into running them. "We had a wicker elephant with a removable head," Susan remembered. "Sometimes we kept a few thousand dollars in there for an emergency. But that was it for savings. Whenever Jerry stuck money somewhere, he always let me know. He did have an awful lot of accounts, but I knew about all of them, and they were pretty low. Jerry believed in making his money work for him. He didn't have life insurance, and he didn't have savings."

Jerry had always told her he was invincible, that he would be around forever. Hadn't he survived bullets and quicksand and nearly drowning? He had teased her when she worried. Why would an invincible man need life insurance?

Susan had always had a household bank account, but her name was not on any of Jerry's business accounts. Now she had to go to court to ask for a receivership so that she would be able to pay for her living expenses while she waited for Jerry to come home.

"That was obtained," she recalled. "Two days later the lawyer who helped me get that died suddenly—just dropped dead. Later we found out he had a heart problem that no one knew about. Next I asked Jerry's personal attorney to represent me. Jerry always said, 'If anything ever happens to me, you go to Tom* and he'll help you.' But Tom refused to get involved. He said he wanted to *live*. . . .

"What did he mean he wanted to *live?* I was beginning to feel as if I was in the middle of a horror novel—that someone *really* was out to get me and anyone who helped me."

It seemed almost as if there were sinister aspects of Jerry's life that Susan had never known about, as if there had always been two scripts for their lives. One was their happy, perfect, exciting life, and the other was bleak and dark and dangerous. Still, Susan never doubted Jerry. Whatever was happening just below the surface, she was still convinced that Jerry was not pulling the strings.

Finally Susan found a lawyer in San Diego who agreed to represent her. She knew she had to find a way to keep Steve Bonilla from sabotaging everything Jerry had built. She had no choice, her attorney advised, but to file for bankruptcy—an emergency Chapter Eleven reorganization. The lawyer explained that bankruptcy law would supersede the California State Court filings that Steve Bonilla had brought against Susan and JLH. If she filed for bankruptcy, Steve would not be able to pore over JLH's books and records.

On December 17, 1987, Susan filed for bankruptcy. Bonilla was livid. Susan was humiliated for herself and for Jerry, but she had no other choice. She listed assets of $3.8 million, including their new home in Blackhawk, a condominium in Hawaii, some property in San Diego, four cars, and Jerry's collection of rare wine. But her house payments were $8,000 a month, and their personal bills had been six times that. Jerry had paid them all easily; Susan could not.

"All the profits of the clubs went into the bankruptcy. I was $5.5 million in debt," Susan recalled. "I paid several different attorneys a total of $600,000. I paid off all the bills."

Steve Bonilla was temporarily frustrated. He responded by filing a lawsuit in Santa Clara County stating that he owned 40 percent of Baritz and that he had just begun to see a return on his investment when Jerry Harris disappeared.

He said that he had invested $150,000 in Baritz and that he was supposed to be receiving $4,000 a week. After Jerry "left," Bonilla said, Jerry's financial holdings began to collapse and his own share of the profits dried up. Bonilla asked that a trustee be appointed to manage what was left of Jerry's estate. Susan Harris fought back, claiming that Jerry had never considered Bonilla a partner. Susan's attorney moved to have Bonilla's suit dismissed on the grounds that it was without merit.

Susan gave orders to bar Steve Bonilla from Baritz. Oddly, Steve announced that he had found three company checks had been made out to Jerry Harris *after* he disappeared. He cited checks on October 27, November 10, and November 24.

Susan hoped it was true.

But Steve's allegations neglected to say if the checks had ever been cashed. He said the mere fact that the checks had been written proved that Jerry was alive and was deliberately staying away.

Even Duke Diedrich had his moments of doubt about Jerry Harris. "Most of the time I wished that I had known Jerry Harris. I'm sure he wasn't perfect, and he might have even been a little devious at times, but from what everybody told me about him, he sounded like a helluva guy. Still, sometimes I wondered if he might have left on purpose. I never told Susan that, but people do funny things."

Diedrich's doubts about Harris didn't last long. Seeing how resolute Susan was, he had to believe in the man she still loved so ferociously. "Susan was the Lone Ranger," Duke said. "I had—and have—the strongest respect for Susan. There aren't many women who could have lived through what she did. And she never once gave up on Jerry."

Had Jerry been in control, in all likelihood his clubs would have continued to turn a profit. Without his personal touch, however, without his presence, they began to sag. Susan did her best, and she held off Steve Bonilla's moves to wrest it all away from her.

Steve Bonilla was not about to relinquish his toehold in Baritz. He had lost his green cookie franchise, he had lost his catering business, and the palm tree tax shelter that he had attempted to turn into a pyramid scheme wasn't working out as he'd planned. But he still believed he could get the restaurants away from Susan easily. He had always regarded her as a dumb little blonde from the tules of Oregon.

If Susan had had any idea of Steven Bonilla's previous plans for women who got between him and money, she might have been even more frightened than she already was. But she didn't know. Jerry hadn't known, either. How much mischief could a short little nerd in a bad toupee be capable of?

Susan still fought to save Jerry's businesses. But most of all—constantly, achingly—she missed Jerry himself. The sight of Christmas lights brought tears to her eyes. She couldn't bear to hear carols sung. She jumped whenever the phone rang or someone knocked on the door. Phones have a number of different tones to their rings, and Susan would never again hear a phone ring with the particular sound of the Blackhawk house phone without feeling a terrible sense of dread mingled with impossible hope. She could almost close her eyes and visualize her husband walking into the front hall, giving her a hug and kiss as he always had, and pulling some brightly wrapped package from behind his back. In her daydreams, Jerry always had a good explanation of why he had been gone almost ten weeks and why he hadn't called her.

Late one night Susan headed home to the big pink house from the Fremont Hot Rod. She always had her car radio set to a rock-and-roll station, deliberately avoiding the slow, sad songs. "Jerry sounded so much like Elvis," she said softly, "and out of the blue they put on an Elvis record. His voice—*Jerry's* voice to me—came on the radio, singing, 'I'll Be Home for Christmas.' I started bawling. It was like—like a message."

Even though they made her cry, Susan played the tapes of Jerry singing, hearing over and over again his voice crack with emotion as he sang the phrase from "Unchained Melody": "Like a river flows to the sea, to the sea, to the open arms of the sea. Lonely rivers cry, 'Wait for me, wait for me. I'll be coming home. Wait for me!' "

For a half-dozen years, Christmas season had meant shopping for Jerry's charities and, especially, for the fire-fighter's family. "The hardest thing I had to do," Susan remembered, "was to call that family and tell them that I didn't think they could have Christmas, that the man who had been their Santa was missing. And I didn't have the money to do it."

It was the bleakest Christmas of Susan Harris's life. She had to come to terms with the unthinkable. Jerry had gone away either because he wanted to go or because something threatened him so much that he *had* to go. Or, worse, Jerry was dead. Her old life, the one she had been so grateful for, had ended so suddenly that it was as if she had run into a cement wall. She had gone through all the phases of grief and shock: denial, bargaining with God, rage, sadness, a terrible kind of curiosity that led her into mental paths that frightened her. She could never get tired enough to really sleep, curled up in Jerry's closet, which still looked as if he had stepped away for only an hour or so. She napped fitfully.

Like almost all women who lose someone they love, Susan looked for signs. Jerry had always worn a heavy gold nugget on a chain, but when she checked, she found that it was still in his jewelry box. Why, on that one vital Tuesday, had he chosen not to wear it? She chose to believe that meant he intended to come back for it. Sometimes Susan willed Jerry to come to her in her dreams and tell her what to do.

"Did he?" someone asked.

"Only once," she said. "Business was falling off at the Hot Rods. In my dream I was sitting on a stool in the club, and Jerry walked in. He said, 'Sue, business is bad because you've changed the music. You have to go back to the old format—to the fifties oldies.' Well, I did what he said in my dream, and people started coming back and we were doing all right again."

By Christmas, Susan Harris hoped devoutly and fervently that Jerry *had* left her. All that mattered to her was that he was out there somewhere, alive, and that he would be coming home to his family. Even if he never came back to *her,* she would rather have Jerry alive, and be without him, than to know that he was dead, gone forever from his children and his family. If he was with another woman, that was okay. She loved him enough to accept that.

She had so little to cling to, now that Jerry had been gone for two months. The fact that Jerry's yellow convertible had never been found was about the only thing that helped Susan believe that Jerry really *was* still alive.

This was the time of year when families got together, when those who had wandered away for their own reasons came home. For Susan, Christmas was an especially significant time. Jerry hadn't come home for Thanksgiving. But Christmas was Jerry's big holiday; his Christmas surprises for poor families had made him happier than almost anything else he did. He would never have let those people down. But Christmas came and went and Jerry did not come home.

Thinner than ever, Susan jumped at ordinary sounds now because she was so afraid. If someone had been able to overpower a man like Jerry, or trick him, and do something terrible to him, that person would have to be very clever and very powerful.

And very cruel.

It was during that December of 1987 that Susan once again invited Duke Diedrich to a gathering at the huge pink house. Duke declined the invitation at first, explaining that he already had plans to have dinner with friends that evening. When Susan pleaded with Duke to come to her home, if only for a little while, he relented and promised to stop by if he could bring his friends along. He could never say no to Susan. He knew that every day that passed was harder on her. If she needed him to show up for a meeting at her house, he would go.

"I took my friends by Susan's house, but I didn't tell them why we were there," Diedrich remembered. "Some of her family was there and some of her husband's family, and we stayed for an hour or so and joined in the discussion.

Everyone was coming up with theories on what could have happened to Jerry . . . and where he might be. It got pretty intense. It was kind of a brainstorming session. When we left, one of my friends turned to me and said, 'I can't believe those people.'

" 'What do you mean?' I said.

" 'This Where's-Jerry game, where we all took part and tried to figure out what happened to Jerry,' my friend said. 'You know, like a Murder Weekend. I can't believe how emotional they got. Listening to them, you'd think Jerry was a real person, someone they knew.' "

Diedrich shifted into high gear as he drove out of Blackhawk and onto the freeway. "He was—is. . . . I guess I should have told you," Diedrich said. "That wasn't a game. And those people have every reason to be emotional. Susan, our hostess, is Jerry's wife, and he's been missing for two months. I'm working the case, and she asked me to be there tonight. A helluva case. Jerry's family and his friends were there to share whatever they knew, or might know, or *didn't* know."

"Oh."

"And by the way, thanks for all your knucklehead ideas about what happened to Jerry," Diedrich said. "Especially the one about his running away with another woman. That helped a lot."

His friends didn't bother asking Duke any more questions; they knew him and realized they had heard all they were going to hear about a man named Jerry Harris, at least for the moment.

Susan was working in the JLH Enterprises office on the afternoon of December 30, organizing year-end books. Her manager at Baritz called to say that Steve Bonilla and a number of other people had barged into the club and would not leave. Susan headed at once to the police department in San Jose; there was a restraining order out barring Bonilla from Baritz. If Steve thought she would simply stand aside and let him take Jerry's club away by force on the eve of the biggest night of the year, Susan was prepared to show him she would not budge.

She arrived at Baritz at seven-thirty that evening and went directly to the office. If she hadn't been so angry and worried, she might have laughed at what she saw there. Steve Bonilla was sitting on the safe, looking for all the world like a glowering crow that was about to hatch an egg. Bonilla's attorney stood nearby.

"What are you doing here?" Susan demanded.

"I am going to stay here until I take all the proceeds from tonight," Bonilla answered.

She stared back at him, amazed. He was serious. She wasn't afraid of him; she felt only a consuming rage. Baritz was Jerry's pride and joy, and Steve was trying to destroy it. "I walked up to him and I held my wedding ring up to his face and I rubbed it—to show him that I wasn't fighting him alone."

It took Susan hours to reach her attorney. In the meantime, she realized that Bonilla had brought about ten people with him, mostly surly-looking men. They were stationed menacingly around Baritz, as if they were going to seize the club by force. Steve was calling them his new management team. It was like a little war, an invasion.

Susan saw that Steve had brought a woman too, a plump woman about thirty-five years old, whom Susan had never seen before. She stared at one man who wore an orange stocking cap. He had heavy-lidded eyes and a thick mustache. He looked directly at her and his face stuck in her memory. As she was about to say something to him, Steve's attorney told the "new management team" to wait outside.

Steve had also brought a locksmith with him who was busy changing every lock in the club.

"I called my locksmith to follow *his* locksmith and change all the locks. They must have changed the locks about three times—each of them—for the whole building."

After hours of fruitless battling, Susan's attorney spoke to the San Jose police, who were standing by. After midnight, Steven Bonilla, his attorney, and his ten goons were escorted from Baritz. They did not take the night's proceeds with them.

Susan didn't care about the money. She knew she would

have wrestled Bonilla herself, if she'd had to, to protect Jerry's club. In her mind, the clubs had *become* Jerry.

She knew the battle was far from over. But Duke had called her the Lone Ranger, and she was. She was physically frail and tired, with a constant ache in the pit of her stomach, but she would keep going.

For Jerry.

Baritz and both Hot Rods had huge crowds on New Year's Eve 1987. The disc jockeys kept playing "Auld Lang Syne" over and over. The year had begun wonderfully for Susan and Jerry, but now she was alone. She wondered what 1988 would bring, and she wondered if she could face it, whatever it would be.

PART TWO

January 1988

12

On Sunday, January 10, 1988, Deputy Bruce Cote of the Washoe County, Nevada, Sheriff's Office was working second watch. He patrolled the vast desert and canyons northeast of Reno and Sparks where Pyramid Lake lay in the wasteland like a huge sparkling jewel. There weren't many towns—only Nixon, Sutcliffe, and Pyramid. State Road 445 ran north from U.S. 80 out of Sparks and connected with 446 and 447, which edged the lake and then looped back down to 80. The Pyramid Lake Indian Reservation occupied the desert north of the lake. In January, it was a lonely patrol. He was a good twenty-five miles from the neon lights of Reno when he arrived at his destination. He might just as well have been driving on the surface of the moon.

The sheriff's radio had dispatched Cote to the Pyramid Lake Store on the Indian reservation. It was two o'clock in the afternoon when Cote arrived to talk to Charles Gardner, 50, of Reno. Gardner said he had been four-wheeling in the Quail Canyon area just south of the Indian reservation. He parked his vehicle about a mile west of 445 and began walking in the desert, sweeping the ground with his eyes as he pursued his hobby of rock collecting. Runoff from recent heavy rains had left gullies in the hillside and forced things up from just below the surface. He was hoping to find a thunder egg—a geode that was dull on the outside but full of magnificent crystal formations when it was split—or some other unusual rock formation.

Gardner was about seventy-five feet from his four-wheeler when he came across a gaping hole that looked as if it had been dug by a pack of coyotes. After working his way through the sagebrush to the muddy incline that had caught his interest, he moved closer and looked into the hole. He could not immediately identify what he saw, but he felt gooseflesh on his arms. It looked to him as if he was staring at a human hand protruding from the ground.

"There was something in there," he told Cote. "A body, I think. I didn't look real close—don't know if it's a man or a woman, or human, for that matter."

Washoe County Lieutenant Ernie Jesch and Detective Donald Means arrived at the isolated store and accompanied Cote and Gardner back to the desert. They drove in Jesch's vehicle in a northeasterly direction just off 445 about a mile until they came to a draw in the hills. From there they proceeded on foot. It was nearing three o'clock in the afternoon, and a high wind buffeted the men and almost knocked them off their feet as they headed across the desert. The air smelled like snow.

Clouds lowered overhead as they marked their path with wooden stakes and bright orange plastic flags that read "Crime Scene: Do Not Enter." The flags, caught by the wind, whistled as they struggled against the stakes that bound them to earth.

The first thing the investigators noted was a pair of human hands protruding from the earth in almost a supplicating gesture that cried, "Come and find me." One arm and a leg showed above the dirt, and there was no question that this was indeed the remains of a human being. The leg was skeletonized, ravaged by animals. The arm, however, was intact and was still clothed in what appeared to be a brown leather jacket.

Because it looked as if a heavy snow was about to fall, Don Means called for the search-and-rescue team immediately to search the area around the grave. Sergeant Muhle and Sergeant Glen Barnes arrived shortly and began a search while Dave Billau took photographs.

Washoe County had a prescribed procedure for handling

death scenes. They had no idea at this point if they were dealing with a natural or accidental death, or a homicide. But like all superior law enforcement agencies, they would assume that this was a homicide and work backward from there. The scene was turned over to detectives, and the area was cordoned off. Bruce Cote closed State Road 445 and began a crime scene log. Those entering the area would be listed, the time they arrived noted, and their purpose there explained.

Whatever had happened had clearly occurred weeks—perhaps even months—earlier. Scores of individuals might have traversed this area in the interim. But from this point on, until a complete crime scene investigation was finished, every soul arriving would be listed. Cote took down the names of three men who drove by. They seemed nervous and had no explanation for being there beyond their decision to take a drive up from their homes in Sparks.

The searchers fought against sundown as they located certain preliminary items: shreds of cloth mixed with dirt, the severed pocket of a pair of trousers, three folded bills—a one-dollar bill, a five, and a ten. There was a penny inside one bill.

It had begun—this investigation of a lonely death. Statistics say that only 10 percent of unattended, suspicious deaths actually turn out to be homicides, but there is always that 10 percent chance. Detectives and medical examiners ask silent questions of the corpses that come to them without warning, without identification, and often without a known cause of death.

"Who are you?"

"When were you hurt, or when did you become ill?"

"When did you die?"

"Where did you get hurt and where did you die?"

"Was yours a violent death or a natural death?"

"What was the manner of your death? Did you destroy yourself, did you have an accident, or did someone kill you?"

"If someone did kill you, who was it?"

A sense of kinship develops between the person who has died and the detectives and forensic experts who seek answers to these questions. The investigators never become inured to violent death, but they learn to look at a skeleton or a decomposed body as a human being who once lived and breathed, who had a life someplace, who might have been loved by someone—someone who waited. In their search to solve the crime of homicide, they almost always come to know the victim as well as anyone they know in life.

At 3:00 P.M., out there in Quail Canyon, Lieutenant Jesch asked the search-and-rescue units to conduct an extended search of the area around the buried body. They had precious few hours until dark, and the detectives would not disturb the body itself until dawn. They dared not risk missing some vital piece of physical evidence. Deputies remained at the site until well after the sun went down. The detectives would begin their investigation again at sunrise.

The SAR unit found nothing much of note before sunset. They did find a weathered .38 caliber bullet casing. Could it be connected to the body in the grave? Maybe. Or it might have been left there by someone shooting at coyotes or tin cans in the desert.

They found an old Marlboro cigarette pack, weathered and misshapen. As they worked, the wind howled like a dozen banshees. It was cold and miserable out there on the desert. Deputy Jim Spain guarded the grave site. He was relieved by Detective F. W. Devine, who arrived at 7:55 P.M. to protect the scene. Devine was spelled at 4:15 A.M. by Detective Larry Canfield and Deputy Ross Rytting. Whatever the wind, the coyotes, the rain, and the snow had not already blown, washed, or carried away from the crime scene was now sacrosanct. The body was covered with a tarp to protect it from inclement weather. Somehow, some way, the Washoe County sheriff's investigators were going to find out who this person was and how he or she had come to be left in the desert near Pyramid Lake.

They knew full well that their task was not going to be an easy one.

* * *

At 9:45 A.M. the next day Washoe County Sergeant Carl Muhle, Detective Means, Washoe County Coroner Vernon McCarty, criminalists Ed Shipp and Dave Billau began the tedious process of exhuming the body. They started by using their hands to remove the loose soil at the head and foot of the makeshift grave. Occasionally they had to break up the soil with small sticks so that they could brush it away with their hands or a whisk broom. When they had uncovered the body enough, they cautiously used shovels, taking care not to disturb the body itself. After more than three hours, the investigators finally removed the body and placed it in a body bag.

Don Means and Ed Shipp continued digging another foot down into the site. Every particle of soil removed from the grave was sifted through a quarter-inch screen. During this process, they found several pieces of cloth and a blue button. The only item of note found in the sifting process was part of a fifty-dollar bill that Don Means unearthed. It appeared to have been chewed along one edge. The victim was wearing only one shoe, and no wallet was found.

Besieged by Reno reporters, Washoe County Sheriff Glen Barnes told the press that the body in the desert was so badly decomposed that he could not give them a cause of death or even speculate on whether the person was male or female. He refused to say if the body was clothed or if his deputies had found any evidence at the scene. Reporters were not allowed past the barriers set up by Barnes's staff.

On Tuesday morning, January 12, Dr. Dennis Mackey, a forensic pathologist from the Washoe County Medical Center, prepared to do a postmortem examination of the nameless corpse. Standing by were Coroner McCarty, Deputy Coroner Barry Moskowitz, Rich Burger, a criminalist from the Washoe County Crime Lab, and Deputy Ed Shipp.

Mackey determined that the body was that of a white male estimated to be between thirty-five and forty-five years old with light brown hair shot with gray. He was five feet nine or ten and had a medium build.

The unknown victim had been expensively clothed, and each garment was removed and noted: medium brown Aero brand shoes, size 8½; beige socks; tan John Alexander slacks; a long-sleeved white dress shirt; Nordstrom briefs, size 34; a brown suede jacket with a zipper front and black trim, Piel De Becerro label; and a brown leather belt with a buckle.

There were no rings, but there was one item on the body that might help identify him—a metal chain with a medallion of some kind on it. Because it was too caked with dirt to see what it was, the medallion was placed in a sonic cleaner. Now they could see that the chain was woven of gold mesh and the medallion was an 1891 Indian head penny encased in a yellow metal bezel.

Deputy Shipp, who was bagging and labeling the clothing, noticed a clump of wet wadded-up paper in the left breast pocket of the jacket. Shipp could make out some faint writing but he couldn't read it. Later he hand carried the paper to criminalist Floyd Whiting in the crime lab to see if Whiting could enhance what was written there.

The left leg, which had been exposed to the elements and animals, was denuded of flesh. The stomach was missing, so there would be no way of examining its contents. As Mackey probed carefully, he found a .22 short slug embedded in the right lower abdomen very close to the spine. Oddly, the bullet seemed far older than it should have been had it been fired within the last few months.

"It looks as if this bullet has been here for a long time," Mackey said. "Years, maybe." He pointed to the area and explained why he felt that way. There was no hemorrhaging, and a linear scar was visible on the lower right abdomen just below the belt line—a long-healed scar several inches long.

The bullet was retrieved and bagged into evidence. In further examination of the exterior of the body, Mackey noted a piece of duct tape about an inch long clinging to the back of the head. This was the only duct tape they found, and it too was bagged and labeled.

The body was washed, and as the dirt sluiced away, it was apparent that the only sure way to identify this lost man would be by dental charts or by fingerprints, and the latter were iffy because of the advanced decomposition. There

13

All of the legal delaying tactics available to her, [g] to the pink house in Blackhawk, just as she held [y]'s nightclubs. She kept the same phone number [f]elt a lilt of hope when she heard the telephone [as] easier to keep the house than it was to keep the [s] and Baritz afloat. She knew that Steve Bonilla [them], and so did some investors from Texas—tall [w]earing boots who spoke in rumbling voices and [ ] her like a girl.

[e]y thought I was a patsy," Susan remembered. "They [in] and sat down at a booth with me and said, 'Little [t]his is way more than you can handle here. You're not [ ] to last two months.' I told them, 'I'll last *six* months,' [ ] sent them away. Keeping the clubs going was part of [b]elief system that Jerry was coming home—that I had [h]old things together for him."

[S]usan knew that employees at the Hot Rods and Baritz [a]nd her short-tempered and complained about her. She [k]new she *was* short-tempered. Everything seemed to be [up]hill. One night someone rammed a car into the Hot Rod [C]afe in Fremont. The vehicle didn't go all the way through, [b]ut it did tremendous damage, and she had to shut the club [d]own until she could get repairs done.

"Someone was calling the state and local offices and putting in complaints, too," Susan said, "mostly about Baritz. . . . The Alcohol Beverage Control Office, the vice squad, the fire department, the health department. I was getting one inspection after another. I had no violations, but

were no tattoos, no anomalies, nothing that would stamp this man as remarkably different from a million other males.

Dr. Mackey shook his head as he performed a further internal examination. He found nothing to indicate cause of death. Foul play certainly seemed indicated, however. The body had been buried—probably completely buried at one time, before the roving coyotes found it—and the desert more than a mile from State Road 445 was not one where a man could hike easily. There had been no vehicles around. Whoever this man was, he had not gone out to Pyramid Lake on his own. Someone had taken him there, either while he was still alive or after he'd been killed somewhere else.

But where?

The first order of business was to contact law enforcement agencies in Nevada and neighboring states to see if they had missing persons who matched the description of the un-named victim. The National Crime Information Center (NCIC) computers also had listings of missing persons. But all Washoe County could offer was a rough description of the man, dental X-rays, a list of the clothing and the me-dallion taken from the body during autopsy.

Tom Moots handled missing persons reports for the Nevada Division of Investigation, and Mike Kelley did the same for the California Department of Justice. Each of them had scores of missing adults in their files. They began to cull out "possibles."

The question was how many middle-aged white males in expensive clothing, wearing an Indian penny medallion were they statistically likely to find?

Not surprisingly, Washoe County's Detective Don Means received any number of calls and Teletypes concerning men who had walked away from their usual haunts. Some—like a Battle Mountain, Nevada, man who had left on Jan-uary 1—hadn't been gone long enough. A Los Angeles man sounded good—until Means checked and found that he had returned home, alive and well, and no one had bothered to notify police.

Some of the missing males who sounded close enough to the Pyramid Lake victim warranted sending out his dental charts for comparison. But there were no matches. One Sparks woman insisted that it had to be her cousin, whom she described as a "street person." But her cousin had a full upper denture, and the desert victim had his own teeth. He had taken care of his teeth, and a number of expensive dental procedures were evident, including gold crowns and a three-tooth bridge. Somewhere, there was a dentist who would recognize this work.

Barring that, there were ways to raise fingerprints, even when decomposition was advanced. The fingers are removed from the body and soaked in solution to soften them so that layers of skin slip off like gloves. Fingerprints—each one unique in the world to its owner—go deep into the layers of the skin. The particular loops, whorls, and arches that had been part of this unknown man were his alone and could be traced deep below the surface. At the time, the Automated Fingerprint Identification System (AFIS), the computerized system that can identify anyone who has ever been fingerprinted, was not in general use. Still, if the Washoe County investigators could find a set of fingerprints to compare to those they had meticulously retrieved from their John Doe, they might be able to identify him absolutely.

The Washoe County detectives were also inundated with reports on missing men who came nowhere near the description of the man with the penny medallion. Some were ridiculous, such as was the man with long black hair, who was six feet four, and weighed 275 pounds.

A fresh murder is relatively easy to solve, compared to one that is months old. Detectives have a "rule of forty-eight." If a homicide is not solved within forty-eight hours, the chance that it will be diminishes in direct proportion to the amount of time that passes. Whoever left their victim in a barren desert grave had done so months before. The killer or killers could well be on the other side of the world by now.

Washoe County authorities were hampered in their ef-

forts to do a wid
snow on the gro
was able to send
Team, the Hasty
Mounted Posse ou
radius. Deputy Karl
for items of evidentia

At the end of a long
evidence as possibly hav
found that made the inve
A Nevada license plate tur
the grave. It had some blac
Smith of the University of
Department was an expert in
Detective Don Means marked
where the body had been four
metal objects. Both men walke
hours on their hands and knees r
itself.

They found a single penny a few
the grave. A single ordinary penny.

Don Means found several remnant
of newspaper dated March 16, 1987,
geology book. Deputy Rusty Snyder fou
tape, which proved to be too weathered

A crime scene or a body site always ho
tion, but it also holds items that are of n
problem going in is that no detective ever
which, and so each one is painstakingly bagg
as if it were solid gold.

On the night of the mammoth search, Don
with weary fingers: "Investigation continues."

it was obvious that someone was trying to shut me down. It was just constant harassment."

Jerry had been gone for almost four months with no word, no sign, and not one sighting of his yellow Mercedes convertible. But still Susan Harris kept going. "Jerry's word was so dependable. He got loans without even a signature. His reputation was important to him. I had to honor his promises, so I was trying to keep the clubs alive. I guess it kept me alive too. I would walk into the Hot Rod in Alameda, and I smelled the food, and I heard Elvis singing. I could feel Jerry's presence, as if I could turn around quickly and see him standing there, winking at me. Keeping the clubs alive would keep Jerry alive."

Susan herself felt ravaged. She trembled all the time and once commented to her mother that she didn't know why. Her mother looked at her, amazed that she couldn't identify what she was afraid of. "She made me draw a picture where I was a big circle, and then I drew all the little circles of people who were coming after me—at least it seemed they were. Some of them wore sheepskins, so I couldn't tell that they were enemies. Then I realized that, while Jerry was gone, I felt like a wounded lamb with wolves eating on me. . . . Waiting for him was the worst part of all. I was afraid he was being tortured, that he needed me, and I couldn't find him."

FBI agent Duke Diedrich and Susan had lunch together once a week, and she spelled out for him the latest theory she had come up with. He never discouraged her or tried to persuade her to let go of her frail hope. He could see that it would have been of no use anyway. Duke was like a big brother, someone she could trust in a world where she had come to trust so few people. He urged her to keep leaning on Steve Bonilla, never to give an inch. And she didn't. With each new step in the bankruptcy procedure—such a complicated legal entanglement—Susan made sure that Duke had copies of all the documents.

Susan loved her aunt Judy Boyd, but Judy was a sergeant with the Albany, California, Police Department and Susan's uncle Mel Boyd, Judy's husband, was a lieutenant. Judy was a realist; she had learned to be in her job. She knew that the odds were that Jerry Harris was dead and that he probably had been dead for a long time. After weighing the situation carefully in her mind, she felt she had to prepare Susan for what Judy felt was inevitable.

Susan didn't want to hear it. She became angry with her aunt whenever Judy tried to bring up the possibility that Jerry was not coming back. It didn't cause a real rift between them; Judy understood.

Almost three hundred miles away from Pleasanton and Blackhawk and all the places where Jerry Harris had spent the greater part of his life, the body found in the shallow grave lay unidentified in the Washoe County medical examiner's vault. To the detectives working his case, it almost seemed that he was meant to be found. Had it not been for torrential winter rains that January of 1988, the body would have remained buried too deep in the earth for even coyotes to catch a scent of it. The desert near Pyramid Lake is one of the loneliest spots in America. Geographically, the Pyramid Lake Indian Reservation is only thirty miles from the bright lights of Reno, but in its essence it is a world away; the topography might as well be on the moon. The presence of a body in that area was not so unusual; Washoe County detectives knew that certain transactions which took place in the glare of the bright lights of Reno sometimes resulted in bodies being interred in the desert. But this time they could find no tracks to follow back to Reno.

With only two weeks checked off on the new calendar, the discovery of the nameless man near the huge lake made him Washoe County's fourth homicide victim in 1988. Two victims had been found in Reno motels—a forty-nine-year-old woman stabbed to death in the Tombstone Territory Motel and a Washington State man dead of unknown causes in a North Sierra Street motel. Chris Apostol, a Reno pharmacist had been shot by burglars who broke into his home. The sheriff's investigators found no connections at all among the four, but the violent crime picture in their county for 1988 didn't look encouraging.

At length, as Detective Don Means worked his way through the computer postings on missing males in the thirteen western states, he came to the name Jerry Lee Harris. He read that Harris had been missing from the Contra Costa–Alameda County region south of San Francisco since late October. Harris's general description matched the Washoe County's John Doe. Routinely, Means sent for Harris's dental charts and fingerprint records, just as he had sent for dozens of records for other missing men from the western states.

It took almost a month for the FBI to verify the identity of the body found near Pyramid Lake. The Bureau accomplished that by matching the fingerprints gleaned from the unknown body with those of Jerry Lee Harris absolutely.

Jerry Harris would never go home again.

Valentine's Day came, but Susan heard no more news of Jerry than she had known the night he failed to come home, or on Thanksgiving, Christmas, or her wedding anniversary on January 12. Although she no longer really believed in miracles, she held on to her conviction that Jerry was alive. But somehow, on Sunday night, February 14, Susan could not sleep. The weekends passed too slowly for her now and gave her too much time to think. She paced past the tall windows in the sprawling pink house, staring out at the darkness. She felt as if she could no longer bear not knowing. "I was up all night," Susan said. "I can remember pleading, 'God, please give me an answer.'"

Susan broke her pattern the next morning; she didn't go into the office to work. She talked to her aunt Judy, who was even more vehement than she had been before. Judy Boyd had tried to warn her over the past four months to prepare for the worst. Susan had figuratively plugged her ears, but Judy's words had clung to the synapses of Susan's brain, taunting her.

"It was a weird day, February 16th. That day," Susan remembered, "Judy said, 'I think he's dead, Susan. They may never find his body. You just have to accept it and go on with your life.'"

For the first time, Susan listened, feeling a pall of tragic acceptance descend upon her shoulders.

A little after 11:00 A.M. that Tuesday morning, Susan saw

a car pull into her driveway. Detective Linda Agresta of the Contra County Sheriff's Office and Francie Koehler, Susan's private investigator, got out and walked too slowly toward the door. Susan didn't want to open it. Once she did, she knew she could never shut it and go back to where she had been.

"When you find out the worst," Susan recalled, "it isn't your family who tells you—it isn't someone you're really close to—it's strangers. They come and tell you the most terrible things."

Linda Agresta had drawn the assignment that all cops hate the most: the task of telling Susan Harris that her husband was dead. In shock, Susan didn't want to believe it. She wanted to find loopholes so that it wouldn't have to be Jerry.

"How do you know?" she said stubbornly. "I want to see him."

Linda shook her head and explained softly that wouldn't be possible.

"How do you know for sure?" Susan asked again, unable to picture Jerry so far away all these months, so far away in a desert she had never heard of. She could hear Linda talking, explaining that the identification was positive.

Linda explained about the fingerprints. She told Susan that the fingers were sometimes the last thing to decompose and that the criminalists had been able to remove the top layer of skin from his fingertips and make fingerprints by rolling the underlying skin on porous paper. The prints from the body had absolutely matched Jerry's known fingerprints.

It was all so ugly and grisly, worse than anything Susan had imagined. She began to cry. "I was bawling," she said. "And my mother was there and she hugged me. Within two minutes Duke called."

Susan sat up straighter and took the phone. "Are you going to get them, Duke?" she demanded.

There was a long silence on the other end of the line. Susan could hear Duke Diedrich take a deep breath. She knew him, and she knew he never promised anything he could not deliver. She estimated that the silence lasted two minutes. In actuality, it was probably closer to twenty seconds. She heard him clear his throat.

"Yes . . . yes, I am going to get them," he said firmly.

"Do you promise me?"

"Yes. Yes, I promise you, Susan. I'll get them."

Susan finally accepted the truth that she had dreaded for so long. She went into the master bedroom she had shared with Jerry and shut the door behind her. For twenty-four hours she sat in Jerry's closet where his clothes still hung. He wasn't coming back. There was no longer any point in making up excuses for him or keeping people looking for him. He had been found.

And he was dead.

When she came out of her bedroom, she was a different woman. She wasn't yet thirty, and she was a widow. She had redirected her purpose in life. She would not rest until she found whoever had murdered Jerry and seen him punished.

Duke Diedrich had been working the case of Jerry Harris's disappearance since the beginning, along with Telford Terry of the Contra Costa County Sheriff's Department and Pleasanton police Captain Gary Tollefson. They now knew that it had been eminently correct for the FBI to have been involved in Harris's disappearance. He *had* been taken across a state line. They didn't know yet where he had been killed. Traditionally, when many law enforcement agencies are involved in a homicide probe, the department left with the burden of finding the killer or killers is the one in whose jurisdiction the actual murder took place.

But how could they know? Four months had passed. No pathologist could say now exactly when—or, by deductive reasoning, *where*—Jerry Harris had died. Despite diligent searches, Jerry's yellow convertible was still missing. It might be in Pyramid Lake, or it might be in the San Francisco Bay or at the foot of some cliff, hidden in a deep canyon.

From Contra Costa County to Washoe County to the FBI offices in both California and Nevada, there was consensus: Jerry Harris had been murdered. He hadn't buried himself in the desert. No one knew whether he was kidnapped and killed where he was found—or murdered first and then transported to Pyramid Lake. And so they all remained involved.

The mysterious disappearance and murder of Jerry Lee Harris was just a case to most of the investigators—but it was more than that for Duke Diedrich. Any good detective will tell you that if the investigators allow themselves to become emotionally involved in a murder case, they are asking for trouble. All good detectives care—that is what makes them good, but they have to maintain a delicate balance between caring and becoming consumed. They have to leave their work at the office. Most investigators don't even tell their wives what cases they're involved in. "I asked my husband once why I have to read about what he's doing in the papers," a homicide detective's wife confided. "He told me that if he sold insurance, he wouldn't come home and tell me about every policy."

Diedrich's special area of expertise was kidnapping—perhaps the most heartbreaking of crimes—and he should have become desensitized over the years. It might have been because Susan Harris was his neighbor that she touched his heart—and that of his wife, Lois. Or maybe it happened because she was just a pretty, skinny kid in her twenties who'd had the rug of her life pulled out from under her but who still kept on stubbornly fighting: the Lone Ranger. Most of all, Duke knew he had to find out who had killed Jerry—because he had promised her. He'd been a damn fool to do that, but once he'd done it, he had to come through.

In the meantime, Duke and Lois Diedrich took Susan bowling, and invited her over for dinner with their friends. Gradually she became "family," and they were like family to her—but Duke couldn't yet give her the thing she wanted most. Answers.

It would take the considerable skill of the best investigators in three states almost a year from the night Jerry Harris vanished to gather enough probable cause to arrest suspects in Jerry's murder. When they did, there would be shock waves.

14

Since Jerry Harris's body had been found in Washoe County, Nevada, that jurisdiction would be responsible for the murder investigation. But while California papers clamored for details, Washoe County detectives were giving out very little information.

Sergeant Jim Lopey of Washoe County headed the investigation into Jerry Harris's murder. Tall and lean, Detective Lopey was the epitome of the western detective. He reminded his California counterparts of Sam McCloud, the character actor Dennis Weaver had played in his series about a country detective who had big-city smarts. Lopey was pleasant to reporters, but he would say only that Harris had been dead "for some time." He refused to give any details at all about what an autopsy might have revealed. "We're playing catch-up," he said. "We've got investigators in the Bay Area now who are attempting to find out who Harris's associates were and who was involved with him in his business."

Sheriff Vincent G. Swinney commented that the body had been buried along what used to be a fence line: "It was a purposely dug grave. It was relatively deep for that type of makeshift grave."

Susan Harris had by now accepted that Jerry was dead. A long time later she looked back upon those first weeks when she had to realign her thinking. She had no longer been able to tell herself that he was coming back. Only in retrospect could she see that the most devastating period had been the four months when she didn't know where Jerry was. "In a way—and this sounds awful, I know—it was almost easier to know that he was dead," she said slowly.

As she prepared for Jerry's funeral services, Susan remembered the promise he'd extracted from her not that long before. She couldn't have the open casket he'd stipulated, and she couldn't put a smile on his face, but despite the horrified look from the funeral director, Susan saw to it that a bottle of Silver Oak Cabernet was slipped into Jerry's coffin.

"Jerry was always on the go, always late," Susan mused. "We used to joke about that, too, and tell him, 'You'll even be late for your own funeral.' And he was, too."

The funeral, on February 20, 1988, in Medford was tense. Several of the men attending carried guns, because it was now clear that someone was after Susan. When the incidents involving cars and phone calls were viewed all together, it was obvious that someone wanted her dead. She didn't know why, nor did the police.

Only afterward did Susan realize that the man who had called Jerry his best friend had not even come to his funeral. Steve Bonilla was conspicuous by his absence.

By late February 1988 it seemed likely that Jerry Harris had been killed in Pleasanton. Lieutenant (now Captain) Gary Tollefson of the Pleasanton Police Department admitted that he just didn't have enough manpower to do justice to an investigation that promised to be unlike anything his department had encountered before. There were already links to Nevada and southern California, and it looked as if Harris's murderer might have had accomplices in other states.

A kind of Jerry Harris Task Force was set up. Tollefson and Detective Mark Allen would represent the Pleasanton Police Department. There would be four special agents from the FBI: Duke Diedrich, of course, and three men from the San Jose FBI office: Tom Westin, who was an expert in surreptitious taping and filming, and Joe Chiaramonte and Quentin Smith, who were organized crime experts and would look into the palm tree business. The Alameda County District Attorney's Office had a Special Operations unit that paired assistant district attorneys with skilled investigators in major cases like unsolved homicides and officer-involved shootings. The Harris probe was fortunate indeed to draw Assistant District Attorney Jon Goodfellow and his investigator, John Whitson, for their team. And of course Sergeant Jim Lopey and his investigators from Washoe County were also on the task force. From time to time, detectives from other departments as well as uniformed personnel would join this core team.

Turf wars are not unknown in high-profile homicide investigations, but there was to be none of that with the Harris team. The detectives and the Alameda County D.A.'s men all worked in remarkable harmony, and they speak highly of one another, even today.

Most important, they made a formidable army as they followed the trail back through the four months of not knowing to the night Jerry Harris had vanished. Something terrible had happened to him that night, and they all were quite sure they knew who had set the killing plan in motion.

Now they had to prove it.

Law enforcement agencies between Reno and Pleasanton had been asked to search for Jerry Harris's yellow Mercedes convertible. It had been found on February 23, 1988. The Mercedes was located in the long-term parking lot at the Sacramento Metropolitan Airport. Ironically, it had somehow been overlooked by attendants checking for overtime parkers in the airport. In contrast to the Porsche that Jerry had left at the San Francisco Airport for a month a few years before, only to find its windshield almost obscured with tickets, there was only one parking ticket on the windshield of the yellow Mercedes. That dusty slip of paper indicated that the Mercedes had been in the Sacramento airport lot since October 20–21, the night that Jerry disappeared.

Four months. How could it be that no one had found the Mercedes in four months? It was a fluke—a disastrous fluke in the search for Jerry Harris.

Detective Bob White of the Sacramento County Sheriff's

Office commented, "If you wanted to make it look like somebody left town, what would you do? Park their car at the airport."

But no one had found Jerry's car until after they had found his body, so that red herring hadn't worked. For someone headed for Reno, the obvious route would have been eastbound along Interstate 80, right through the heart of Sacramento. That raised a question: had Jerry driven his convertible to the airport and then joined someone headed east?

Hardly likely. Jerry Harris had never gone anyplace—until October 20—without calling Susan to say where he was headed. If he was alive when his car was parked at the Sacramento Airport, it seemed certain that he was not the one making the decisions about where he would go next.

Sergeant Jim Lopey dispatched two Washoe County investigators, Detectives Leonard Iljana and Dave Butko, to the San Francisco area.

One of the first people they wanted to question was Susan Harris. That was standard operating procedure. They quickly determined that Jerry Harris had died without a will, which meant that everything he owned would go to his widow. One of the strongest canons in homicide investigation is that detectives must look first at those closest to the victim. The vast majority of murders are not random and motiveless, and it follows that there is usually a connection between the victim and the killer—some link leading to their family, friends, or business associates.

No one had been closer to Jerry Lee Harris than his widow, Susan. On the face of it, it looked as though she had inherited millions of dollars in homes, clubs, cars, and an almost priceless wine collection. She was eighteen years younger than the victim. In a mystery novel and, in this instance, in real life, Susan was the prime suspect. The Nevada detectives didn't know that there was nothing for her to inherit. There was insurance, yes, but that money would go to the bank, not to her. Without Jerry, Susan would be worse than penniless: she owed $2 million more than she and Jerry owned.

Iljana and Butko questioned Susan for hours. She was surprised at first, then nervous. She realized that they suspected *her* of killing Jerry. "They didn't seem to comprehend that underneath it all, there was this huge, huge debt," she said. "I realized later it was like the good guy--bad guy routine, but they put me under so much stress that if I'd done *anything,* I would have confessed. Finally, Duke came in and rescued me.

"By then," she recalled, "I started feeling like I *was* responsible for what happened to Jerry. Before he went to SteelFab, the day before [he disappeared], he said, 'Hey, Sue, why don't you come with me?' And usually I was always with him. But we had just moved into the house, and I had so much unpacking to do. I didn't want to sit down there at SteelFab."

Susan Harris was rapidly eliminated as a murder suspect, but the intense questioning had exacerbated her guilt about not having gone with Jerry the day he disappeared, and the feeling that she had somehow failed him never really left her.

Working with California detectives and Duke Diedrich of the FBI's Concord office, the Nevada investigators were about to find things about Steven Bonilla's life that Jerry and Susan Harris had never known—things they had never even suspected.

Jerry Harris had been a man of the world, at ease in nightclubs and comfortable in many, many different levels of society. Although he loved to play mischievous tricks on authority figures—like his refusal to get a driver's license and his predilection for putting his businesses in his siblings' names—he had never done a truly dishonest thing in his life, and he had never knowingly hurt another human being. To him, Steven Bonilla had always been an awkward, pitiable man looking for success even though he wasn't very intelligent and had no charisma. Steve was just a guy with a bad business sense and lousy luck with women. But to Jerry, Steve was also a good father, and that had always given him several favorable points in Jerry's mind. No matter what goof-ups Steve managed to pull, Jerry had always eventually left the door open for him. Nobody but Jerry himself had ever been able to understand why.

Jerry's attempts to bring Bonilla along in his business ventures had not stopped him from needling Bonilla from time to time. Had Steve resented Jerry's teasing? "Sometimes Jerry would put Bonilla down right in front of other people," a Baritz manager commented. Steve had taken it, but perhaps he seethed beneath the surface.

Now Jerry was dead, and detectives were going over the life of Steven Bonilla with a magnifying glass. Was he just a loser and a mama's boy? Or was he something more?

Steve Bonilla had never seemed in the least concerned by Duke Diedrich's promise to arrest him, or if he was jittery, he didn't betray it. Of course, he was unaware that his entire life was being held up to the light. Bonilla escalated his fight to wrest control of Jerry's businesses from Susan. He sought a full accounting of the limited partnership he had with Jerry from October 1986 to the present. He demanded a financial settlement along with punitive damages and legal costs if it was found that the Harris estate owed him money. His lawsuit asked the court to terminate Susan Harris's control over Baritz. Bonilla said he had been barred from the club and denied access to its books and accounts, and that he had not received his share of profits. Further, Bonilla said that Jerry Harris had made more than $159,293 in "unauthorized distributions" to himself and to other Harris-controlled businesses. "I just want what's owed me," Bonilla said. "I want my day in court."

Duke Diedrich devoutly hoped that Bonilla would have his day in court. He wasn't sure why he felt so hinky about Steven Bonilla. If he'd had anything to do with Jerry's murder, he was bluffing hard—publicly declaring himself a victim of an unscrupulous partner. As he had with Diedrich, Bonilla refused to submit himself to questioning by the Washoe County detectives.

That could wait. The investigative team was busy filling in the blank spaces in Steve Bonilla's biography. He was the older of two children. His younger sister—by eight years—

suffered from cerebral palsy. His parents, Ella and Primo Bonilla, had amassed a small fortune operating nightclubs and owning ranches and retail businesses.

Bonilla's diminutive size had made him a good candidate for flight school when he was in the service, and he had a pilot's license, although he had served as a navigator in the service. He had been married at least twice, and his former wives were not nearly as full of praise for him as Jerry Harris's were for their ex-husband. The investigators had difficulty locating his first wife, Flora,* but they interviewed Ginger, the second Mrs. Bonilla, on March 4, 1988.

Thirty-eight-year-old Ginger Bonilla was currently living in southern California and working for a bank. She was a bubbly woman with a loud laugh. Knowing that Bonilla was barely five feet five, the investigators were a little startled to find that Ginger was five-ten. Even in flat heels she would have towered over the little man. She was big-boned but not fat, attractive but not beautiful.

Ginger Bonilla said she had been the manager of an apartment complex when she met Steve in 1978. "I decided to seek part-time employment in the evening," she said. "I had bartending experience, so I applied at [Steven Bonilla's] cocktail lounge in Cupertino, the Fox and Hounds, and I was hired."

Steve Bonilla hired her, and they started dating. They were married in January 1979. Steve told her that he had owned a business called Independent Caterers but that it had burned down in February 1978, six months before they met. His partner in that enterprise was a man named Tip Blume.* Blume and Bonilla were so simpatico that after Bonilla divorced his first wife, Flora, Blume married her. Ginger Bonilla said that Tip Blume often picked up and delivered Steve's two daughters from his first marriage for visitation.

The second Mrs. Steven Bonilla was a font of information about her ex-husband, some of which Bonilla had told her and some that she had observed firsthand.

She said that Steve had admitted to her that his catering business had not exactly gone up in flames by accident. "He [said] he participated in having a small fire started . . . it wasn't to get as large as it did. The thing just got out of control."

Ginger Bonilla didn't think that Steve had actually lit any matches himself. She said he got some friends to do the actual torch work. "Steve had told me they were biker-type people. . . . Steve's very money hungry, and he needed money for something. . . . He was planning on collecting some insurance."

Bonilla had purchased the Fox and Hounds soon after he received his insurance settlement, causing detectives to wonder if he had used the insurance money to buy the lounge. Ginger didn't think so. She thought Steve had borrowed money from his father, Primo. Although Primo was a carpenter and Steve's mother, Ella, had worked as a clerk for JC Penney, Ginger said they had a great deal of money because they were very hardworking and frugal. She was vague at first about any other money sources they might have tapped into.

"Well, they might have had a ranch," Ginger Bonilla said, "And they still owned another cocktail lounge called the Rumpus Room in Mountain View."

She said that Primo Bonilla had purchased a fifteen-acre ranch for Steve in Watsonville and the Rumpus Room was doing well—until Primo was diagnosed with terminal brain cancer in early 1980. Primo Bonilla died in May 1980, a month after Ginger gave birth to Steve's son. Steve was forced to sell the Rumpus Room that year after a bitter financial settlement battle with his first wife, Flora. He had hated Flora after that. He didn't mind her leaving him for another man; he was angry because she took more of his money with her than he thought she deserved. He had become convinced that Flora and Tip Blume were cheating him out of what was his.

Bonilla's relationship with Ginger Bonilla was mercurial too. Almost before the honeymoon was over, Steve's second wife was appalled to find that he had a vicious temper. Their first year of marriage was happy—at least between fights. By the time Ginger really understood Steve's dark side, she had given birth to their son. The lower his fortunes sank, the meaner he got, and Ginger told detectives that she spent more time away from Steve that year than she did with him. After his two dozen catering trucks burned, and after he had to sell the Rumpus Room and the Fox and Hounds, he worked for about a year as the comptroller for a truck rental franchise in San Jose.

"I left him in the first part of June 1980," Ginger said, "and I was back and forth between my home down here [in the Los Angeles area] with my parents, and *our* home in San Jose for about a year. Then I went back north in June of 1981."

Ginger Bonilla reconciled with Steve the same month that Susan Hannah met and fell in love with Jerry Harris.

The Washoe County detectives were intrigued. The Steve Bonilla they had heard about was a coward and a wimp— even laughable when he inadvertently wore his cheap toupee backwards. They knew Bonilla was money-driven, but from what they had gleaned, he wasn't very effective. Their victim Jerry Harris had apparently been Bonilla's only real friend and his sole champion.

The detectives asked Ginger Bonilla why she had left Steve shortly after their son was born in 1980.

She said she was forced to leave because Steve was "totally out of control."

"What do you mean?" Leonard Iljana asked.

"Umm, well, he was becoming irrational. He had his mother's home robbed. . . . Shortly before I left him, *ours* was robbed twice."

"What do you mean, *he had* the home robbed?"

"His mother, his sister, Steve, and I had the baby at the ranch one evening. We had been there all day working, and toward the end of the evening we were all driving back to Mountain View—you're talking about an hour and a half drive. I had a new baby, and I was very tired. I just wanted to get to the house, put the baby to bed, and go to sleep. Steve said, 'No, you're gonna go have dinner with us.' I said, 'I'm not hungry. I'm tired.' I was getting sick from all of this. At our house, he grabs me by the throat and puts me against the wall and he said, 'You are *going* to dinner with us or I'm going to—'"

Ginger said that had scared her, and she went meekly

along to a restaurant with Steve's family. "We had dinner, went to his mother's house. As we pulled up, Steve jumped out of his car real fast and ran up the walk to the front door and ran in—that is not usual for him. Then he comes running out, and he says, 'We've been robbed!' And I looked at him and said, 'Jesus Christ, what are you doing now?' And he says, 'You shut up and don't say anything.'

"When I asked him about it later, he said there were things he needed."

"Like what?" Iljana asked.

"[Like] what was stolen," she said, shrugging her shoulders. "Nothing in the house was messed up. Drawers weren't pulled out. Nothing. There was a safe stolen that was in his parents' bedroom—in the closet behind things—and they had taken a piece of carpet and drug [sic] it out, and all his father's rifles and guns were gone."

"What was in the safe?"

"I've been told by Ella about the collection of coins and there was—I know—$10,000 cash in there."

Ginger Bonilla said that Steve had never said exactly who he'd hired to pull the burglary of his own mother's house, but she said he had told her that he had "friends" on his payroll. One had a name like McNicholls, and the other was a man named Gary who, she thought, was a bartender in the San Jose area.

The Washoe County detectives asked Ginger why Steve would have had someone rob his own mother's house. "Why did those particular people go in there and take the safe and the guns?"

"Because [Steve] wanted them [the stolen items], and he couldn't just take them. They belonged to his mother," Ginger said simply. Steve needed money to buy into another nightclub.

"If he wanted to get into this club, wouldn't his mother help him out, like [she did] in the Fox and Hounds and the Rumpus Room?"

Ginger shook her head. "No. Once Primo died, no way. She was real tight. She wouldn't let him have any money. . . . He has since—on many occasions—forced her into giving him money."

"What do you mean by 'forced'?"

"My son witnessed it one day. [Steve] wanted money from her for something, and she said no. He began choking her, and when he let go, she said 'Fine.' My son was about five years old at the time. When he came back home, he told me about it. So this was typical of Steve. Hitting people. Strangling people."

"Was he heavy into alcohol or narcotics?"

She shook her head. "If Steve drank at all, he would drink maybe one very, very light screwdriver—vodka with orange juice," Ginger said. "He did not drink, and he did not take drugs. Oh, I've seen him once—when he was trying to impress a fellow in San Jose—doing cocaine. But he was not well for days after that. He does not do drugs."

"He just a violent type of person?"

"It's his nature, uh-huh. . . . He believes he is a person who can control other people—get people to do what he wants. He manipulates them."

This violent Svengali that Ginger Bonilla was describing hardly sounded like the accommodating toady who had followed Jerry Harris around, mimicking him, stealing scraps of Jerry's glory to paste over his own image.

Ginger's memory was warmed up, and she had other incidents to relate. Steve had paid "McNicholls" and "Gary" to do the "dirty jobs" for him.

"He paid this Gary one night to take his [first] wife out to dinner—so she would be out of the house. Their house is sitting there and they'd built a new home, and in it was a double oven, a microwave oven, built-in sinks and lighting fixtures. He went in, and he himself took those things out of the house. He had the oven installed in his mother's place."

Ginger said she had gone to Ella and told her what Steve had done. "I said, 'I keep telling you these things because he needs help. We've got to help Steve.' All Ella did was remove the oven from her home, the fixtures from our home, and dumped them somewhere . . . and covered them up."

"That was basically another insurance fraud?" Iljana asked.

Ginger shook her head impatiently. "No, no, no. He had

nothing to do with the place the things were stolen from. He took them because he wanted them."

According to Ginger Bonilla, her ex-husband had always taken what he wanted when he wanted it. If someone got in his way, he simply grabbed them by the throat. This, of course, would have to be someone he could overpower—a woman, usually. With male enemies, he called in his paid goons to do the dirty work.

Still, most of Steve Bonilla's most daring capers seemed to involve robbing his own houses, his mother's house, or his ex-wife's house. Would he have had the guts to go up against Jerry Harris? Jerry wasn't an elderly woman or a young mother who had just had a baby. Susan had said Jerry could take on three men and win, even if it meant a broken nose. Moreover, Steve Bonilla had always been in awe of Jerry.

Still, Steven Bonilla was emerging as the one person who had lain among the weeds, waiting his chance to seize the nightclub empire that Jerry Harris had built. Almost from the moment Jerry disappeared, Steve had tormented Susan Harris with his takeover bids, his lawsuits, and his hovering presence at Baritz. Steve Bonilla wanted that club.

And, as Ginger Bonilla said so bluntly, Steve took things simply "because he wanted them."

15

There was a cogent reason why Steven Bonilla had been reluctant to accept a California liquor license application when his name was drawn. He knew that the Alcohol Control Board of California would never give him one.

Steve Bonilla had a record. He'd skated free a good many times because his family wouldn't prosecute him or because he paid some muscle men to do what he didn't have the courage to do himself. But there was at least one time when he got skewered to the wall—not by local law enforcement agencies but by the DEA, the U.S. Drug Enforcement Administration.

Ginger Bonilla nodded and grimaced when the Washoe County investigators asked her if she had ever had occasion to travel to Arizona with Steve. "Yes. That was after Primo's death, and I was living with my folks in southern California. . . . Steve called and he said, 'I'm going to Arizona for a few days. I want you and the baby to fly in and meet me there, and we'll spend a few days together and see what we can work out.' "

This occurred midway through her year-long separation from Bonilla, and Ginger was easily persuaded to give their marriage another try. It sounded romantic, meeting Steve in Arizona for some time alone together. At least, that was what she thought the plan was.

"So I went," she said. "We stayed in a Motel 6 over near Scottsdale, and [Steve] would leave off and on because he was there to see McNicholls and these friends of his. I knew of them and I didn't have any interest in being with any of them. So he went off."

"You're implying something about they might be . . . ah, bad people?" Iljana asked. "Are they connected with the Angels—the Hell's Angels?"

"I don't know that for a fact. . . . McNicholls looked more like a cowboy. He didn't drive a motorcycle. He drove a very old broken down 240 ZX."

Ginger said that McNicholls had friends who rode motorcycles, but she didn't think they were in any organized group.

"Why was Steve hanging around with these shady people?" Iljana asked.

Ginger was nothing if not blunt. "I guess you could call him stupid. I don't know why he continued hanging around with them. I kept thinking he thought that he could use them to get money. . . . I've since found out why he was around them."

"And why was that?"

"They supposedly had a guy who had been in prison who was a chemist. He knew the formula for making whatever this drug was they were going to manufacture. So Steve had brought him to California to stay at our ranch and then Steve had driven to Arizona to pick up the chemicals needed and the equipment. I guess there's some big glass thing he needed from the pharmaceutical company."

Although Steve Bonilla was not a drug user, he had apparently seen a chance to make a lot of money selling illegal drugs to other people. Ginger didn't know what it was they were planning to manufacture, but she thought it was cocaine. She discovered that Steve had scouted out connections in resorts near San Francisco and Tahoe where he could sell what they made.

Her second honeymoon ended in disaster after she realized, too late, that she and the baby had been summoned to Scottsdale to serve as a smoke screen for Steve: they were supposed to look like a lovey-dovey family.

"We'd been there a few days," Ginger Bonilla said, "and one day Steve left, and he came back with a truck full of very bad-smelling chemicals. I said, 'What are *those* for?' and he said, 'These are things I need for out on the ranch, and I can get them cheaper here than I can in California.' That made sense to me."

Steve had suggested that she help him unload the chemicals and put them in the motel room. Then he would take her out to dinner. After a couple of hours' sleep, they would load the chemicals back in the truck and drive to California.

"Did these chemicals have a particular smell?"

"Very, very . . ." Ginger Bonilla wrinkled her nose.

Leonard Iljana asked her to describe the smell. He had seen Steve Bonilla's rap sheet, and he knew that Bonilla had been trying to manufacture methamphetamine. The chemical components of that drug are dangerous and volatile, and they smell like nothing so much as cat urine.

Ginger couldn't quite describe the acrid odor in their

Motel 6 room. "It was kind of a burning, strong smell. God, what could I compare it to? Kerosene? A type of strong odor. I don't know. It irritated my eyes. In fact, I had the room window open. We put them in the room, got in the truck, and went to dinner."

The fact that Steve Bonilla would subject the woman he allegedly loved and his own baby son to the danger of methamphetamine chemicals bespoke his lack of concern for anyone. If meth ingredients don't blow up, they do their damage slowly, leaving anyone exposed to them susceptible to throat and lung cancer.

But it turned out that Steve Bonilla's venture into operating a drug lab was no more successful than any of his other great ideas. "We came back from dinner," Ginger said, "and I was greeted by a man opening the door of my truck and putting a gun to the side of my head. I said, 'What the hell are you doing? Who do you think you are?' and he said, 'I'm a cop.'"

Ginger and Steve were ordered out of the truck, searched for weapons, and placed under arrest. When McNicholls came to his motel room door while the DEA agents were searching it, he too was arrested.

Ginger said she later told her story to a judge. She remembered that he believed her. "He said I was 'leadingly unsophisticated.'"

She was released, but she was terrified because Steve realized that she had given the DEA some information about him. Steve Bonilla's ex-wife shivered as she recalled that incident. "They didn't know that Steve is capable of doing terrible things to people, and when he heard that, he was very angry."

Duke Diedrich always felt a prickling at the back of his neck when he pondered the machinations of Steven Bonilla. He had suspected from day one that Bonilla knew what had happened to Jerry Harris, and he had told him so. Now Diedrich was aware that Bonilla had been better at hiding his criminal history than Duke had given him credit for.

The DEA office in Phoenix, Arizona, had files on the

details of Bonilla's abortive attempt to buy the basics to set up a meth lab. Duke knew by now that Bonilla could be counted on to turn any golden opportunity he was offered into clay. Whether it was green cookies or arson for insurance, Bonilla's fine hand usually ensured a cataclysmic ending.

Charles R. Henderson was the special agent for the DEA who had been principally responsible for bringing Steven Bonilla's fledgling meth lab operation to a sudden halt. Ten chemicals are used to make methamphetamine. (For good reason, I will not list them here.) Along with certain flasks, tubes, filters, and heating devices, these chemicals can produce a large amount of speed with a street value that some have felt was worth the risk of illegal manufacture. Meth labs spring up in mobile homes and motel rooms all over America, polluting the premises with the acrid "cat urine" smell as the dangerous mixture cooks.

Henderson told Diedrich that Steve Bonilla hadn't even made it to the cooking stage. He had blithely gone about all of his preliminary preparation unaware that the eyes of the DEA were fixed right on him.

Not having been born yesterday, DEA agents keep track of interesting purchases at chemical supply firms, particularly when the purchasers come from out of state and buy a precise laundry list of exactly those chemicals and paraphernalia used in the illicit manufacture of methamphetamines.

Charles Henderson and his fellow agents had been watching a Phoenix resident, William Winifred Nichols, who had only a post office box number and no street address. He was thirty-three years old, five feet nine inches tall, and weighed 150 pounds. He had brown hair and brown eyes. This was the man Ginger had called McNicholls or Nick.

More interesting than his physical description was the fact that McNicholls had placed an order in person at Worldwide Chemicals* on July 7, 1980. He said he was ordering a "complete laboratory" for a Mr. John Brown. Interestingly, Nick said that Mr. Brown had placed and received an identical order the year before. Nevertheless

Worldwide Chemicals said they required a $1,000 check to begin processing the large order.

Nichols had left the firm in a yellow Chevrolet Vega, saying he would return with the money. Two days later he called and said that the check was being sent from out of town. The check arrived on July 14, made out on the account of Mr. and Mrs. Steven W. Bonilla of Watsonville, California. Duke Diedrich had to smile at how transparent Bonilla's cover was. He used his own name and address, but he jotted a note on the check: "For the John Brown Account."

When William Nichols mentioned that John Brown's 1980 order was identical to a 1979 order, he made a major tactical error. He alerted an already suspicious chemical company—who, in turn, reported the transaction to the DEA. It sounded very familiar to Charles Henderson. In 1979, Special Agent Henderson had assisted the Phoenix Task Force in a drug case where a John Brown had placed orders for "precursor chemicals" and glassware at Worldwide Chemicals in Tempe, Arizona. This man was later identified as Robert Francis Baldwin.* Baldwin's operation was raided by DEA agents, who seized an operational methamphetamine lab. Baldwin later pled guilty to conspiracy to manufacture methamphetamine. He was currently on the run with an outstanding warrant for his arrest.

The whole Motel 6 operation seemed to have been masterminded by dunces. Bonilla had signed both checks, explaining that he was buying the chemicals and glassware for John Brown, an alias that had resulted in an arrest only the year before. Nichols had compounded the matter by giving the same alias. John Brown didn't exist, but his name was instantly recognizable to both the chemical company and the DEA.

Steve Bonilla and William Winifred Nichols might as well have waved a red flag in the authorities' faces. From July on, they were under constant surveillance by the DEA.

On August 5, 1980, Steven Bonilla paid $1,200 in cash for the balance of an order of chemicals and glassware placed for John Brown. Bonilla said he wished to pick up the chemicals that very afternoon, since he would be leaving town the next day. While he was at the chemical wholesaler, Bonilla had made two long-distance phone calls to a man he identified to the man behind the counter as John Brown. He was overheard discussing which chemicals and glassware he should buy for their "project."

Bonilla didn't know that he was observed by DEA agents when he returned in his 1980 blue Chevrolet truck. When he came back later to pick up his order—accompanied by an unsuspecting Ginger Bonilla—Henderson and DEA Agents Bill Fowler, Philip Bellini, and Bob Dinius followed the blue Chevy back to the Motel 6. The DEA agents watched as the pair unloaded the chemicals and glassware into the motel room. Then they followed Steve Bonilla and his wife to a restaurant in Scottsdale. While the Bonillas ate, Henderson called Assistant U.S. Attorney Billie Rosen and obtained a telephonic search warrant for rooms 120 and 122 of the Motel 6.

When the oblivious Bonillas returned to the room, the DEA agents were waiting for them, and they were both placed under arrest. Ginger really *hadn't* known what was going on, and Steve insisted that he had no idea what was in the boxes in his motel room. He said he only knew that he was going to be contacted by someone—he did not know whom—and told to deliver the boxes to a yet unrevealed location.

Fifteen minutes later, after he had been read his rights under *Miranda,* Bonilla asked Special Agent Bellini if he could talk to him alone. He told Bellini he was willing to tell "the truth," which, predictably, involved blaming someone else. He had suddenly remembered that he was supposed to take the chemicals back to his ranch in Watsonville and deliver them to a handyman named John. He said he didn't know John's last name. "I was only picking this stuff up because John was going to pay me."

"How much?" Bellini asked.

Bonilla wasn't sure of that either. The DEA agent looked a little doubtful. Why had Bonilla agreed to take such a risk without even knowing how much he would be paid? Bonilla brushed that aside. He assured Bellini that he wanted to cooperate with the DEA, but he didn't dare. He was afraid that would place him and his family in danger.

As he had so many times before, Steve Bonilla escaped punishment for the Arizona chemical buys, although it was two years before he was in the clear. A judge ruled that his statements admitting guilt had been made before he had been informed of his rights and were therefore not acceptable in a court of law. With that ruling, the DEA's case against him lost so much punch that it was dropped.

After that, Diedrich reasoned, Steven Bonilla must have believed that he could get away with anything.

Diedrich could well understand now why Steve Bonilla hadn't wanted the Alcohol Beverage Control authorities to check up on him seven years later. He wondered how many other secrets there were in Bonilla's past that he didn't want anyone to know about.

16

As stressful as it was, Susan Harris's long interrogation session with the Nevada detectives *had* brought back the memory of a night shortly before Jerry disappeared. It hadn't seemed important at the time, but in retrospect the evening now seemed fraught with foreboding. Back then it had seemed only odd.

It had happened the Friday before Jerry disappeared— the night of October 16. Jerry and Susan often ate out, and Steve Bonilla made a practice of joining them, whether he had been invited or not. On the surface at least, this particular Friday was no different. Steve often went to the Hot Rod in Fremont to have a drink with Jerry. On October 16, he had invited Jerry to have dinner with him at a nearby Mexican restaurant.

"I spoiled Steve's plans," Susan recalled. "What he didn't reckon on was that I knew Jerry so well that I always knew where to find him. And that night I just appeared at the Hot Rod. Jerry was glad to see me. Steve wasn't. Jerry said, 'Come have dinner with us. We're having Mexican.' And I said, 'Not Mexican again! How about Chinese?'"

That was fine with Jerry, but Steve seemed very upset with the change in plans. That made Susan angry. She had thought to herself, Why does he have to come along all the time?

Jerry and Sue drove to Lum Yuen's, a Chinese restaurant about ten minutes away, and they waited for Steve. He was late. "Steve acted *weird* that night," Susan said. "He just was very stilted in his conversation all through dinner. Usually he was very talkative and hyper, but this particular evening he was calculated about what he said—not talkative. He wasn't giving out a lot of information about things we were asking him about. . . . He was being rather evasive. He kept leaving the table, going to the rest room. It took a long time to eat; we must have stayed in the restaurant until everyone else had left. Afterward Jerry asked me what was the matter with Steve. I didn't know, but I said, 'Well, he's met some new girl in Colorado. Maybe this is the way he gets when he's in love.'"

When the trio had finally left the dining room, Jerry excused himself to go to the rest room, and Steve was left alone with Susan. He seemed nervous, and he was sweating. He held the door for Susan to walk outside, and she was vaguely aware that he kept glancing at a red van that had pulled up next to the restaurant. She couldn't see who was inside.

Then Jerry came out, and he and Sue walked to his car. Then Jerry drove her to her car and followed her home. Later they discussed how strange Steve Bonilla had acted. But they had forgotten about it by the next morning.

Now Susan wondered why Steve had been upset when she changed their restaurant plans and why he kept leaving their table in the Chinese restaurant. He had acted like a man who was listening to some other voice in his head. She wondered if there was a connection between Steve and whoever had been in the red van. Steve had not expected Susan to show up that night, and he *had* expected Jerry to leave the restaurant first. Bonilla had been thrown off stride when Jerry stopped off at the rest room.

Susan suddenly remembered several other times when she had shown up unexpectedly to meet Jerry after work and how Steve had seemed both startled and annoyed. She had always supposed it was because Steve wanted to talk business alone with Jerry. She knew that he didn't like her any better than she liked him, but she had never really thought of Steve Bonilla as a sinister or dangerous man.

She had gone through many lists of possible suspects in Jerry's murder, but she had always dismissed Steve as too much of a klutz and a Caspar Milquetoast to overcome Jerry. She had made Duke Diedrich promise "get *them.*" Was it possible that there had been no "them"? Could Steve Bonilla have killed Jerry? Had he planned to kill Jerry for weeks before he finally did?

Susan laid out this scenario for Duke at one of their weekly lunches. He nodded and listened, but he didn't comment. Sometimes Susan wanted to shake Duke and make him react. He was so good to her, but she knew he kept many secrets from her.

"I know why he [Diedrich] didn't tell me things," Susan admitted. "I have a big mouth. I *cannot* keep a secret, and Duke knew that. There were things he must have wanted to tell me over the years, but he knew me too well. I've forgiven him for all his secrets."

By the spring of 1988, Steven Bonilla had emerged as the prime suspect in Jerry Harris's murder. He felt pressured enough to retain an attorney, but he had no idea how many elite investigators were focused on him: Jon Goodfellow and John Whitson of the Alameda County D.A.'s team;

Duke Diedrich, Tom Westin, Joe Chiaramonte, and Quentin Smith of the FBI; Lieutenant Gary Tollefson and Mark Allen of the Pleasanton Police Department; and Sergeant Jim Lopey's team from Washoe County, Nevada, not to mention all the technicians and patrolmen who worked with those investigators.

Even so, it was one thing to have a prime suspect; it was quite another to have enough probable cause to get an arrest warrant. Bonilla had said from the very beginning—the morning of October 21—that he and Jerry had been together the night before to look at an office complex. No one had seen Jerry alive after he was due to meet Bonilla. That did not mean that Jerry had not driven off from the Hacienda Business Park in Pleasanton and met someone else who became his killer. That was unlikely, given what the FBI and the California and Nevada investigators were uncovering about Bonilla's past and personality, but it *was* possible. To charge the man with murder and expect to get a conviction, they needed more than circumstantial evidence and gut feelings.

It *is* possible to convince a jury with circumstantial evidence only, but it is a dicey thing. Aware that they were tracking a man with a short fuse, a man who routinely turned to assassination plots to wreak his revenge, they wanted to get him off the streets for good. Jon Goodfellow was determined to prove to a jury that Steven Bonilla was guilty of murder *beyond a reasonable doubt*.

Even a cursory look at Steve Bonilla's past legal and illegal activities indicated that he never did anything on his own. He never soiled his hands or took a chance of being either caught or caught short. He had always managed to talk somebody else into doing what he wanted. He was manipulative and persuasive, and he often had money to dangle seductively in front of hired muscle men. Moreover, Bonilla was a small man with no particular athletic ability. Jerry Harris could have taken him easily in a fight.

No, the investigators were convinced that they were looking for at least one man, possibly two, besides Steven

Bonilla. But who were they? Bonilla was not a man who had friends; Jerry Harris had been his best friend, and some said his *only* friend.

Once the public became aware that Jerry Harris had been murdered, some people took potshots at his reputation. Steve Bonilla led the pack gleefully, and his partners in Agro-Serve joined in. They hinted to reporters that Jerry had diverted $2 million of Agro-Serve's money to fund his nightclubs. "Jerry left a very bad situation," Steve Bonilla said. "There seems to be a lot of money missing from that program—in the millions."

Incensed, Jerry's brother Sandy said that Jerry had confided in him a month before his death that the plant program had become a pyramid scheme in which initial investors were being paid off with new investors' money. As soon as the IRS probe had declared the program clean as Jerry Harris had run it, he had been eager to get out. He didn't like the way it began to change once Bonilla became heavily involved. "Jerry told me that he felt he was the fall guy for the seedling program," Sandy said. "My brother said it was a bomb ready to blow up."

Al Jennings quickly dismissed the pyramid notion, blaming any trouble on Jerry's mismanagement: "He was either the slickest con man in the United States or one of the stupidest businessmen I ever ran into."

One of Jerry's former financial managers said that Jerry had a gift for dreaming up ventures but no patience for managing the businesses: "Jerry never paid his bills; he never paid the IRS; he never paid anyone. He robbed one company to pay another."

Those who had been closest to Jerry Harris knew this wasn't true, but it hurt, because Jerry wasn't around to defend himself. He had never been one to keep meticulous books. He was always JLH Enterprises, and he used the assets of one club that was booming to help another that was in trouble. He might have been a CPA's worst nightmare, but he was as honest as the day was long. He was an idea man, creative and dynamic. If he had not been, the Hot

Rods and Baritz would never have happened. Susan knew that Jerry had weathered the IRS investigation and come out just fine, and it galled her to hear Bonilla saying otherwise.

People who knew Steve Bonilla said he'd had one burning ambition since he was a boy—to become a "big wheel" like Jerry Harris. Ginger Bonilla agreed with the theory that Steve had attached himself to Jerry because of Jerry's success. Strangely, however, Bonilla's current business colleagues described him as "quiet, nonconfrontational—a follower, not a leader." One partner in the nearly defunct Agro-Serve said, "Steven doesn't have the balls to do anything to Jerry Harris."

Duke Diedrich didn't believe that for a minute. But he needed more ammunition. He wondered what the quickest way to retrace Bonilla's life would be, and the answer popped into his head: the phone. His connection to his phone was obviously an essential part of Bonilla's life—it was almost an appendage to his body. He carried his heavy portable phone with him wherever he went. The technology of 1987 demanded that cellular phone users step outside to place or receive calls, but they were in use by a few individuals who were willing to pay premium prices.

Duke Diedrich got a federal subpoena for all of Bonilla's phone records—home, car, and office phones—from a few months before Jerry Harris disappeared through January 1988. There were hundreds of calls—mostly in the San Jose–Fremont–Cupertino area. Diedrich soon recognized the numbers that Bonilla routinely called: his attorney, his children, his mother, his girlfriends, and his business partners. When Duke came upon a single call to a number in Elko, Nevada, it stood out from the columns of phone numbers like a bright red beacon. Bonilla had placed the call on October 4, 1987, from someplace in Colorado and charged it to his home phone. It was probably nothing—and yet it fit. Susan had said Bonilla was obsessed with some woman in Colorado in September and October of 1987.

But who was he calling in Elko?

This call had been placed only sixteen days before Jerry Harris vanished. The phone company's records came up with the name of the phone customer in Elko: Jeff Carson Rand.* This was an entirely new name for the investigating team. They had never known Bonilla to be connected with anyone named Rand, and Elko was almost 550 miles from where Jerry lived and worked.

It was a long shot, but Diedrich called the Reno FBI office and asked Special Agent Eric Christensen to check out the man who had received that call. It would be an incredibly lucky thing if Diedrich had happened to find the weak link in Steve Bonilla's tangled web of subterfuge. Christensen said he would find out who Jeff Carson Rand was and why Steve Bonilla had called him in October of 1987. Diedrich didn't really expect this single phone call to elicit much information, but it was worth a try.

On Saint Patrick's Day—March 17, 1988, Eric Christensen and Detective Jim Lopey, who was coordinating the investigation from Washoe County, traveled to the Rand home in Elko. They intended simply to ask what connection, if any, Rand had to a man named Bonilla. A pretty young woman who said she was Jeff Rand's wife answered the door and said her husband was at work. However, when Christensen and Lopey identified themselves and asked her if she knew a man named Steve Bonilla, she nodded. "He's been here to visit my husband, and I think they have done business together."

The two investigators managed to keep their faces bland, even though their hearts were racing.

Jeff Rand's wife said that he worked for Bechtel in the Newmont Gold Mine. The detectives located him at work and asked him if he would accompany them to the Washoe County Sheriff's Office in Reno.

There, they questioned him about any contact he might have had with Steven Bonilla.

"At first, I think I tried to deny everything," Rand recalled. "And then I told them that, yes, I knew Steve Bonilla and had an acquaintance with him through Bill Nichols."

Jeff Rand initially told Lopey and Christensen that he had talked to Bonilla because Nichols had contacted him about setting up a "tiling business" in the Bay Area. Bonilla was going to finance it. Rand said he didn't know anything about a man named Jerry Harris.

Jim Lopey stared hard at Rand. "You know, I think you are involved in this murder. I don't believe you."

After hours of conversation, Rand opened up a bit—but only partially. "I left some details out," he would say later. He did admit that he had made several trips to Alameda County to discuss "business" with Steve Bonilla and Bill Nichols. It was a "tile business."

Rand was very nervous. Nervous? He was scared to death. He was also wrestling with memories so corrosive that they were about to destroy him. It would take a number of interviews and careful questioning by the investigative team, but Jeff Rand gave up a little more information with each interview. In the end, he told everything he knew. Finding him had been akin to finding one particular nugget of gold in the mine where he worked.

The evolution of Rand's connection to Bonilla would prove to be the most important information to turn up yet. Jeff Rand knew what had happened to Jerry Harris. He also knew things about Steven Bonilla that only one other living person knew. And yet even when the tristate investigative team finally believed they had all the answers to the puzzle of what had happened to Jerry Lee Harris, they had to stay quiet for five months before they could move toward an arrest. They were about to embark on one of the most intricate cat-and-mouse games in criminal investigative history.

For Duke Diedrich, that would mean approximately twenty lunches and forty phone calls during which he would have to avoid telling a young woman he had come to regard as family what she wanted to know most. Even though he was doing it for Susan Harris's own safety and to help bring about the successful arrest of her husband's killers, Duke still felt a stab of guilt every time he had to tell Susan a half-truth or steer the conversation completely away from where she was heading.

17

Jeff Carson Rand was thirty years old in 1988. A handsome man with a shock of thick dark hair and an old-fashioned mustache, he stood several inches over six feet and weighed almost 250 pounds. His father, a golf pro, was divorced from his mother. Rand had been a wild kid, but he had been trying to build a stable, honest life with his wife and two children. He had worked as a bouncer in a tavern and as a security officer for the Red Lion Inn. His sheer size had usually been enough to encourage loud and obtrusive patrons to go on their way quietly. On rare occasions, he'd had to resort to a full nelson wrestling hold to force them off the hotel premises. He didn't carry a gun; he was not, at heart, a violent man.

In 1984, before he was thirty, Rand had been working on a building project for a retirement community in Arizona when he broke his back. The injury left him with a permanent disability that precluded his taking jobs requiring a strong back. He got a lump sum payment on his disability claim, but the money didn't last long; he used most of it as a down payment on the house in Elko.

Rand and his wife had a hefty mortgage on their home. In October 1987 he had been out of work and cutting firewood to sell to supplement his part-time job with a bail bondsman. His wife was dealing cards at a gambling casino. While he was trying to keep his house, make his mortgage payments, and find a full-time job, he was ripe for an offer that sounded good.

The investigators asked Rand to go over his history with

Bonilla—and with Bill Nichols, whose name had popped up often in Bonilla's enterprises. It was Nichols who had been arrested with Bonilla by the DEA agents in Arizona years before.

Surprisingly, Jeff Rand said he had known Steve Bonilla for about a dozen years. Then, in the late seventies, when Rand was twenty-one, living with his mother, and working as a bouncer in a bar in Arizona, he met Bill Nichols, who was about ten years older. "At the time, I was a serious drunk," Rand admitted. "I don't have clear memories."

Rand's hazy recollection of that time was that he smoked marijuana and drank alcohol whenever he got the chance. Nichols had watched Rand in a barroom brawl and been mightily impressed with his strength. Serious drunk or not, Rand had been a young Adonis who was formidable in a fight. Nichols had approached him and asked if he was interested in helping him get rid of some "bikers from California."

"He wanted help fighting these bikers," Rand told Jim Lopey and Eric Christensen. He said he got to know Bill Nichols well over the next several months. Nichols was a good drinking buddy and a true raconteur with scores of hilarious and breathtaking adventures to relate.

Although he had once been a high school athletic star, William Winifred Nichols was now a talker, not a fighter; he was six inches shorter than Rand and probably a hundred pounds lighter. He had thinning brown hair, a thick brush of a mustache, and the heavy-lidded eyes of a drinker. Slight but muscular and wiry, he worked sporadically as a stunt man in motion pictures. Nichols had also put on stunt shows and had come close to producing major rock concerts. He had been in the military on and off for over four years and had a couple of courts-martial for being AWOL.

Nichols, who bragged that he had once wrestled a seven-foot bear—and won—was a multitalented man. He collected debts, did dangerous stunts, dabbled in drugs, and was also a bomb maker. He could build a bomb from scratch with nuts and bolts, gunpowder, the soft metal backing from a car mirror, some straps, a few wires, and a trigger device. But it was a point of pride with him that he rarely actually designed a bomb to explode. His bombs *looked* so dangerous that he never actually had to activate one.

Married three times, with nine children and stepchildren by his various wives, Nichols was a consummate ladies' man. He could approach the most beautiful woman at a bar and charm her completely. His charisma drew even men to him—not sexually, of course, but the guy was fun to be around. Nichols's conversation was full of his extraordinary exploits and his plans for foolproof businesses. Even detectives who knew what he was admitted that they liked the guy—until they remembered his vicious side. Charm, intimidation, lies, half-truths, embellishments, and adroit conversation were Bill Nichols's stock-in-trade.

Nichols called himself a collector and said that his career was "collections." He might as well have described himself as a mediator or interceder. "A collector," he once explained to a jury, "is someone who settles disputes between two parties or two people where both parties are criminals or involved in criminal behavior."

Certain criteria had to exist before Bill Nichols would take on an assignment. The criminality of the parties involved was essential. "If I'm going to go make a collection from somebody," he said, "the chances are that I'm going to break a few laws in doing so. So the reason that they would have to be involved in a criminal activity is so that they could not go to the police."

Nichols once said that he was, at his center, a gentle man who deplored having to hurt anyone. "I'm not into punishing people. . . . My aim was to collect. I was not always . . . met with open arms."

With the self-delusion of a true sociopath, Nichols viewed his career as beneficial to mankind, and he regarded the people who hired him as "victims" who had lost their money, their drugs, or other items of value to them. "As I perceived them . . . they were ripped off in a very ugly fashion—*very.*"

His "collection" business spanned twenty years, and

Nichols estimated at the forced end of his career that he had probably successfully "collected" between 125 and 150 times. He had never personally had to kill anyone or even hurt anyone very badly, and he had never been arrested for collecting.

He claimed to be something of a sentimentalist and said his family, spread out as they were, were very important to him. Their importance, however, waxed and waned depending on his situation at any given time.

Jeff Rand said he and Bill Nichols had always gotten along fairly well, but he had never liked Steve Bonilla much. Bonilla had a way of divining just what it took to make a man step over a line that Rand never thought he would cross. He said Bonilla could talk and talk and make his plans sound like a good idea, no matter how far-fetched or repugnant they might be. And Bonilla always had a thick sheaf of bills to use as an inducement.

Jeff Rand was nervous about what Bonilla might do, but he was more afraid of spending the rest of his life in prison, or worse, so he grudgingly agreed to talk to the detectives.

As the days passed, he revealed more and more. He did know about the murder of Jerry Harris, but he insisted that initially he had not known about any plan to cause Harris's death. He believed he was brought to the Bay Area to help intimidate Harris into paying Steve Bonilla some money that he owed him. Years before, Rand had had occasion to do some assignments for Bonilla, but they had all petered out, and he had made money for doing basically nothing.

For Rand, there would be more visits to the sheriff's office in Reno and more meetings with the FBI and with Jon Goodfellow and John Whitson. Rand accompanied Washoe County Lieutenant Ernie Jesch and Sergeant Jim Lopey to the Bay Area and pointed out certain locations to them. In the end, the investigative team would agree that the *only* way they were going to trap Steve Bonilla was through Jeff Rand. Reducing a sentence for one felon in order to catch a much bigger fish is a time-honored practice in prosecuting crimes. It is often galling, but sometimes it has to be done.

Alameda Assistant District Attorney Jon Goodfellow and Lieutenant John Whitson flew to Reno and met with Jeff Rand's attorney. The only hidden card the investigative team held was Jeff Rand. And to get his cooperation in convicting Bonilla and Nichols, they were going to have to work out a plea bargain with him. They knew now that Rand had been present during the last moments of Jerry Harris's life, and he had admitted that he helped to subdue him. Even so, of the three men who had plotted Harris's murder, they suspected that Rand was likely the least involved. He was willing to do whatever was necessary to ensure that he would someday be able to return to Elko, Nevada, and his wife and babies who waited there. Chopping wood suddenly looked a lot better to him than it ever had before.

Goodfellow could not and *would* not give Jeff Rand immunity from prosecution, but he agreed to seek only three years' prison time for Rand if he cooperated in getting enough evidence to prove that Steven Bonilla and Bill Nichols had plotted for more than six months to kill Jerry Harris. These agreements had to be signed by every agency involved; the FBI was the last to sign.

In return for his cooperation Jeff Rand would get nothing beyond the promise of freedom in the not-too-distant future. He would be provided no money, no housing—nothing. He would have to find a way to support himself and his family while he worked undercover. He would be taped, wired, and videotaped in conversation with his co-conspirators. The more he got out of them, the more danger he would face. If the other two members of the murderous triumvirate caught on to his betrayal, Jeff Rand would be as good as dead. Rand knew that.

Of *all* people, he knew that.

When young Jeff Rand met Bill Nichols in that Arizona bar in the late seventies, Nichols confided to him that he and others had been dealing drugs from catering trucks in California in territory claimed by bikers. That was, of course, a dangerous business, but it was profitable if you didn't get killed. During their first meeting, Nichols told Rand that he had a friend who needed a strongman to intimidate his "enemies."

"I thought there was money to be gained," Rand told the detectives investigating Jerry Harris's murder. He was remembering activities that occurred a decade in the past, but the investigators were rapidly learning how Bill Nichols and Steven Bonilla operated and that they had been carrying out their devious pursuits for a long, long time.

When Rand said he had had no intention of becoming involved in anything that might be construed as a murder scheme during the summer of 1979, Nichols had assured him that murder probably wouldn't be necessary. Initially, he needed Rand solely to provide muscle against the bikers.

But somehow things escalated when Steven Bonilla entered the picture. Rand had agreed to help Nichols, but he said he only planned to pretend to cooperate so he could get money to support his drug and alcohol habit. "My intention was to keep drinking."

Rand wasn't sure just when he had met Steve Bonilla the first time, but he recalled that Nichols had introduced him to a high roller from California, probably in 1978. Bonilla drove a flashy car and hinted that he had connections to people in high places who could do Rand some good. When a man with a name like Bonilla said he was "connected," a naive listener like Jeff Rand quickly thought "Mafia," and Bonilla said nothing to dissuade him.

Rand said that Bonilla also seemed to have an inordinate number of enemies and old scores to settle. Bill Nichols helped convince Rand that they could do worse than hook up with Bonilla.

(Although the investigators already knew that Bill Nichols would become Bonilla's accomplice in 1980 in Scottsdale, Arizona, when Bonilla purchased the makings of the meth laboratory, they were also aware that there had been no mention of Jeff Rand in the DEA report of that failed project.)

Jeff Rand said that during his first short period of "employment," in 1978–1979, Bill Nichols began to talk about the necessity of killing people who were in Steve Bonilla's way or who had wronged him. Rand soon learned that, with Steve Bonilla, people were either for him or they were his "enemies."

That sounded familiar to the detectives. Ginger Bonilla had once spoken of Steve's rage and paranoia and of how afraid she was of her ex-husband: "Steve is capable of doing terrible things to people."

And now Jeff Rand's recollections validated Ginger's terror. It wasn't Ginger, however, who became Rand's first scheduled hit in 1979; it was Bonilla's *first* ex-wife, Flora Bonilla Blume. Flora had not only left him, she had cuckolded him by marrying his partner. Flora was a pretty woman, slender and lithe, with auburn hair. And Steve was still burning that she had left him for Tip, and, most of all, because she took his money.

Squinting with the effort of thinking back eight years, Jeff Rand explained what Bonilla wanted him to do. "It was about a catering business that he was involved with somehow," Rand said. "And his wife had left him and married his partner and they had taken the catering business away from him [Bonilla]."

Like most of Steve Bonilla's tales, this one was heavily slanted in his favor. As always, *he* was the victim. Steve had purchased the catering firm, which sold deli-type food from trucks to workers in areas where there were few restaurants. He had purchased it from a man named "Beans" Rinaldi.* Bonilla and Tip Blume planned to run the catering firm together.

Independent Caterers did not last long, however, due to an "unfortunate" fire. Apparently Bonilla had commissioned a smaller fire than he got; virtually every truck in his fleet melted down. He collected insurance on his loss, of course, but no one knew for sure where that money had gone. According to Ginger, Steve had not used it to buy the Fox and Hounds. Rand didn't know anything about any insurance.

Things hadn't been going at all well for Steve in 1979. He had lost Independent Caterers, he still owed a lot of money to Beans Rinaldi for a business that was literally in ashes, and he hadn't held on to the Fox and Hounds or the Rumpus Room, either.

Even though he was newly married to Ginger, Steve Bonilla wasn't happy. He was enraged about losing his taverns and his catering business, not to mention his first wife. Under California law, when an establishment that sells liquor changes ownership, a precise inventory of all alcohol must be made and the two parties must meet, agree to the inventory totals, and then file reports with the Alcohol Control Board. On the night that the new owner of the Fox and Hounds showed up, he was furious to discover that Steve Bonilla had removed every ounce of liquor except some cheap wine. There was a fight—a physical fight—and Steve told Ginger to run. Steve got away unhurt, but Ginger was struck in the head with a heavy bar stool and ended up in the hospital.

It was obvious that being Mrs. Steve Bonilla was not particularly safe. Being an ex–Mrs. Steve Bonilla was even more dangerous.

Bonilla's first wife, and the mother of his two daughters, had indeed married Tip Blume, his ex-partner. In stealing Flora away, Blume made a place for himself at the top of Bonilla's enemies list, though Steve feigned friendship when Tip came to pick up or deliver Bonilla's two daughters, who were then eight and nine. Steve's mask of friendliness was so good that even Ginger didn't understand right away that Tip was an "enemy."

But Ginger soon became privy to some private plans that Steve, Bill Nichols, and a young man named Jeff Rand had for Tip and Flora Blume. Tip was doing well; he had a good job as a printer for the *Sacramento Bee*. In the summer of 1979 he and Flora and Steve's daughters lived in Lake of the Pines, a gated upscale community near Auburn, California, on Interstate 80 midway between Sacramento and Grass Valley.

Steve Bonilla smoldered with resentment when he thought about Blume taking not only his wife but his precious daughters too. He had plans for the Blumes on a weekend when he had visitation rights with his daughters.

As Jeff Rand described the plan to kill Flora Blume, the detectives—even given their understanding of aberrant behavior—shook their heads in amazement. Rand said that Bonilla drove him up to Auburn and gave him a gun, Flora and Tip's address, and specific directions on how to locate it. Bonilla had also told him that Tip worked the night shift at the *Sacramento Bee*.

Rand said he met another of Bonilla's "staff"—a man known only as Ponytail Willie—on what was for Rand the halfhearted mission to assassinate the faithless Flora. After several days of hanging around the Auburn area, however, Rand and Willie could find neither Flora nor her house. He and Willie called Steve Bonilla to tell him that the mission had failed.

Bonilla drove up to meet them, Rand said, and told them, "I've got another job for you. I want you to go to a place called Verdi, just outside Reno."

Bonilla had a map and pointed out Verdi, which sat on the California-Nevada state line.

Jeff Rand and Ponytail were to find a bar owner named Beans Rinaldi in Verdi. Steve said he wanted Rinaldi dead because he was involved in causing Steve to lose his catering business. Bonilla pointed out on the map the address of the bar—the Bar-M—and the location of Rinaldi's home. He wanted Rinaldi "gone." He wanted him shot.

Bonilla had promised to provide the guns to kill Rinaldi, and he drove with Ginger to Reno with the guns secreted in his briefcase. Ginger, who had been told they were going on a vacation, recalled that Steve was away from their room for about ten hours during the evening and night. She didn't know if the guns were in his briefcase when he came back.

For all of Bonilla's elaborate plans, however, Rand and Willie were a most inept duo. They hung around Reno, drinking and smoking marijuana. They were so mellow that they never got around to killing Beans Rinaldi.

Rand figured that wanting the Blumes and Rinaldi dead had been just a wild notion of Bonilla's. But he had not reckoned on Steve's single-mindedness.

Jeff Rand told Jim Lopey and Eric Christensen that later in the summer of 1979 Bonilla complained because not one of the three people he had told Jeff to kill was dead. By then Steve had come up with another way to get rid of Flora Blume. Since Bill Nichols was so adept at building bombs, Bonilla commissioned him to design one to put under the Blumes' sedan. Nichols constructed a bomb at a friend's shop and brought it to the home Bonilla shared with Ginger. Nichols and Bonilla persuaded Rand to travel once more to Auburn. This time he was to attach the bomb to Flora Bonilla Blume's car.

Ginger Bonilla would later verify the existence of the bomb. She had seen it in her very own garage. While Jeff Rand was visiting at her house, she said, Bill Nichols had shown up with a device that did look like a bomb. She had watched out the window as Rand, Nichols, and Steve tried out some kind of plastic ignition devices in their driveway. They were popping like firecrackers.

Ginger described the "bomb thing" as about ten inches long with a bolt at the bottom and long straps. She even remembered what she had cooked for the men's supper that night: "ground beef and mushroom gravy and potatoes and green beans . . . kind of slop, but it was good."

Steve had the plan worked out so that his two young daughters wouldn't be blown up too. It was his weekend for visitation; he would pick them up and deliver them to their grandmother Ella's house in Mountain View.

While Jeff Rand was headed for the Lake of the Pines with the bomb, Steve would be in San Jose. After he dropped his daughters off, he would go to a bar and make sure he was noticed so he would have an alibi for the time of the explosion in Auburn. Bonilla loaned Jeff Rand his Volkswagen van, and Ginger saw him slip the "bomb thing" into the van and drive away, headed for the Blumes' home. She knew that it was meant to kill Steve's first wife, and Ginger's conscience jabbed her. She couldn't sit by and let that happen. She called the police and told them that something awful was about to happen, that people were going to be killed. "But they just kept telling me that they couldn't do anything until something actually happened," she said.

* * *

172

Nine years later, Jeff Rand told Lopey, Christensen, Goodfellow, and Whitson that the device *had* been a bomb. He admitted that he had taken it with him in Bonilla's Volkswagen van. He had found the Blumes' home, crawled over a fence to reach it, and attached the bomb beneath Flora Blume's car. But then he got to thinking about it, and he returned and cut the wires to the battery to make sure the bomb wouldn't go off. "I didn't want to kill this person," he said.

When there was no news of someone dying in a bomb blast in Auburn, California, Steve Bonilla must have wondered what had happened. He didn't dare call Flora for fear of raising suspicions.

On Sunday night, Tip and Flora Blume showed up alive and well to pick up the girls. As Bonilla watched their car drive away, he saw a long wire from the bomb trailing along the ground near the tailpipe. The bomb had not yet detonated.

Although he would later say he was terrified for his children's safety, Steve Bonilla said nothing. Fortunately the bomb never went off. Whether he was worried that the bomb would be discovered or whether he felt a pang of concern that it might blow up while his daughters were in the car, no one will ever know. But he did drive up to the Lake of the Pines himself, climb over the fence, and retrieve the bomb.

Steve called Bill Nichols and said he didn't understand why the device hadn't gone off. Everything had worked so well when they were practicing with the trigger devices in the driveway.

Jeff Rand never admitted to Bonilla that he had cut the wires, disabling the bomb.

The would-be hit men, like the Three Stooges, continued their clumsy crime spree throughout the long summer of 1979. Jeff Rand told the investigators that Steve Bonilla asked him to drive to Chicago to pick up some phencyclidine (PCP), a potent animal tranquilizer. Some marijuana that Steve had bought for resale wasn't any good, and he thought that sprinkling PCP on it would make it salable. PCP was the drug of choice with experimental drug users in

the late seventies, but many users had violent reactions—
some of them fatal—to what was essentially an elephant
tranquilizer.

Steve Bonilla had taken his baby son into a motel room
polluted with methamphetamine ingredients and had
allowed his daughters to ride off in a car containing a bomb
that he believed was likely to explode. He was obviously not
a man whose conscience and concern for others dictated his
plans.

Jeff Rand set off to Chicago to buy PCP, but he only made
it as far as Reno, where his motorcycle broke down. He
returned most of the money Bonilla had paid him.

Disgusted, Bonilla gave up on Rand as a henchman, and
Rand was just as glad. He had never liked the idea of killing
someone, particularly a woman, and he was sure that if he
hung around, Steve Bonilla would soon come up with yet
another murder plot. He wanted no part of it.

In the spring of 1988, Jeff Rand told detectives that he
had heard from neither Bonilla nor Nichols for eight years.
Jeff had met his current wife while he and Ponytail Willie
were hanging around Reno trying to figure out how to kill
Beans Rinaldi, the former owner of Independent Caterers,
in Verdi. As a married man and a father, Rand said he
thought he had grown older and somewhat wiser. But
apparently not wise enough.

On October 4, 1987, when Steve Bonilla phoned Jeff out
of the blue and said he would be passing through Elko in a
day or so and wanted to talk to him about a business
proposition, Rand said he had been vulnerable. He told the
investigators he was desperate for a way to make money. He
was out of work and cutting firewood to sell, and his wife
was dealing blackjack in a casino, but they were barely
making it financially. "I hadn't heard from him in years
when he called me," Rand said.

Bonilla showed up within a day and called Rand's home
at 5:00 A.M. He said he was at the Red Lion in Elko and
wanted to talk. Rand said he met Bonilla in the hotel coffee
shop. After an hour's conversation where Bonilla kept
pulling impressive-looking paperwork out of his briefcase, it
seemed to the temporary woodcutter that Steve had really

made it. He appeared to be a partner in nightclubs, steel foundries, and plant nurseries. "He told me there were massive . . . profits and he wasn't getting his share," Jeff said.

Bonilla wanted Jeff to leave Elko at once, fly to the Bay Area, and talk to Bill Nichols about how to solve the problem. "I remember telling him that I couldn't just leave," Rand told detectives. "I didn't have any money in the bank to just take off. And he agreed to leave five hundred dollars at my home so the bills could be paid while I was gone."

Jeff Rand said he had been puzzled to hear that Bonilla needed to use strong-arm methods to get his share of the profits. "I asked him why he didn't just sue this Jerry Harris. He said that the books were doctored up so much that none of the profits showed."

Finally Jeff had agreed to fly to the Bay Area. Bonilla followed him home so he could leave his car there, and then the two headed for the Reno airport where Bonilla said he would buy Jeff a round-trip ticket to Oakland. Bill Nichols would meet his plane.

Rand didn't lie to the investigators about this incident. He admitted that he knew full well that he was going to California to do something illegal; he just wasn't sure exactly what it was.

All of this had happened very quickly. It was barely seven in the morning when Rand introduced Bonilla to his puzzled wife, told her that he had to go to California for a few days, and threw some clothes in a bag. Steve Bonilla asked if he might brush his teeth and was directed to the bathroom. Leaving his wife with $500 to pay pressing bills, Rand drove off with Steven Bonilla.

Jeff Rand had taken his first step into hell. He had figured he would go to California, talk to Bill Nichols, and fly home. He would be $500 ahead—a heck of a lot more than he could make chopping wood for two days. As he would one day admit to Bonilla's attorney, his original plan was to "shine him on" and see how much money he could get out of him.

During the six-hour drive to Reno, Steve Bonilla talked excitedly about his plans to take over Jerry Harris's businesses. He explained that he had known Harris for "years and years" and that they had been "college chums or something like that."

Bonilla was obviously consumed by rage. His voice was loud and harsh as he painted Jerry Harris as a monstrous man who hadn't even paid Steve the commission on a house he'd sold for him, who had thrown his own sister to the wolves when the IRS came asking about the plant business. Harris would betray anyone to make a buck, according to Bonilla.

"He told me that this business partner of his deserved to die," Jeff Rand said, "and *if* he died, he [Bonilla] would be able to go in and exercise all these options . . . he had for different businesses."

While his Datsun sports car sped toward Reno, climbing and zigzagging through mountain passes to summits nearly 10,000 feet high where the air grew thin and it seemed more like winter than autumn, Bonilla was a talking machine, the saliva bubbling white at the corners of his mouth as he scarcely stopped to take a breath. Jeff Rand listened, saying little, but he must have asked himself why he had joined up once more with this man who had ordered him to bomb his ex-wife.

Bonilla spoke of his romance with a girl in Colorado who needed help with "personal or financial problems" and how he wanted to persuade her to move to the Bay Area. He appeared to be either in love or infatuated with her.

"He also talked . . . about me moving with my family to the Bay Area," Rand said, "and he would be able to buy a house through the company so that I would be working for him and reporting to the IRS a small wage, money that he would be able to get by skimming off the clubs. I would be able to get cash on top of that that I didn't have to report."

Rand told Bonilla he didn't want to leave Elko. He liked it there. His only big problem was that he had a balloon payment of $14,000 due on his house in a year.

"I'll be able to take care of that," Bonilla said confidently. Once Bonilla saw that Jeff Rand was safely on the plane to

Jerry Harris and his wife, Susan, aboard their yacht, the *Tiffany*. (Susan Harris collection)

Jerry and Susan clowning around as she puts suntan lotion on his legs on their yacht. (Susan Harris collection)

The *Tiffany*. (Susan Harris collection)

Jerry Harris in his element at the helm of the *Tiffany*. (Susan Harris collection)

Jerry's father and mother, Jim and Lila "Faye" Harris in the early hardscrabble years. Jerry's disappearance was a precursor to tragedy for the whole family. (Susan Harris collection)

Susan and Jerry adored their parents and planned to take care of them "always." Jerry planned a surprise getaway for the moms and Susan. From left: Mary Jo Hannah, Susan, Jerry, and Faye Harris on the surprise cruise. (Susan Harris collection)

Susan and Jerry Harris. He was a daredevil, always taking chances and scaring her—but he always survived. (Susan Harris collection)

Susan's father, Jim Harris (left), and Pete Hannah, Jerry's father, in Alaska. They are drying Jerry's parka after they pulled him out of quicksand. He had sunk to his nose before they managed to pull him out. (Susan Harris collection)

Steve Bonilla (left), Steve King (center), and Jerry Harris (right) aboard the *Tiffany*. Steve King was Jerry's best friend, and Steve Bonilla *said* he was Jerry's best friend. (Susan Harris collection)

Agro-Serve's palm trees. Jerry grew Sophrytzia palms for resale by investors. (Susan Harris collection)

One of Jerry's first nightclubs: Shaker's Diner was a huge success. (Susan Harris collection)

The concept of the Hot Rod Diners was Jerry's and he had planned to franchise them all over America. They were his most popular clubs. (Susan Harris collection)

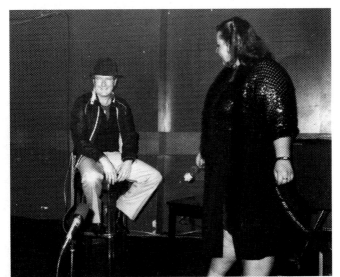

Jerry Harris's bachelor party before his wedding to Susan. He is wearing his favorite fedora. (Susan Harris collection)

Jerry's bachelor party. Steve Bonilla, a member of the wedding party, is at upper right. (Susan Harris collection)

Susan and Jerry's wedding picture. From left: her sister Julie, her sister Kathy, Susan, Jerry, Steve King, Steve Bonilla. (Susan Harris collection)

Steve King—best man and "Jerry's Santa Claus for his secret Christmas"—with Jerry Harris before the wedding. (Susan Harris collection)

Susan and Jerry Harris dance their first dance as a married couple. (Susan Harris collection)

Jerry loved cars and owned enough to fill his own parking lot. He and Susan pose with his Excalibur. (Susan Harris collection)

Susan and Jerry's dream house in Blackhawk.

Lt. John Whitson in his Alameda County D.A.'s office. His investigation helped to convict unlikely suspects who were stalking both Jerry and Susan. (Ann Rule collection)

Inspector Bob Connor of the Alameda County D.A.'s Office—who was in charge of Intelligence for the Oakland, California, Police Department when he unearthed a cruel plot to kill Susan Harris. (Ann Rule collection)

FBI agent Gerald "Duke" Diedrich, whom Susan called her "guardian angel." He kept his promise to bring in the man who had taken her husband away. (Duke Diedrich collection)

William Winifred Nichols, con man, stuntman, ladies' man, and also a man who would do *anything* for money. Jeff Rand, the third felon in the trio of stalkers, cooperated with law enforcement authorities with the understanding that his picture would not be published. It would be akin to signing his death warrant. (Ann Rule collection)

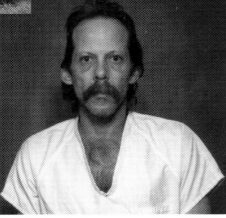

MISSING

JERRY LEE HARRIS

White Male, 5'10", 180 lbs
Brown Hair, Blue Eyes
Date of Birth: 06-01-42

Missing since October 20, 1987
From the Pleasanton - Fremont Area
REWARD

PLEASE BE ON THE LOOK OUT FOR THIS VEHICLE

1982 Mercedes Benz
380 SL Coupe
Pale Yellow (buff)
Dark Brown Soft Top
CA License # **2AIG062**
Vin # WDBBA45A9CB018339

Susan distributed thousands of these flyers after Jerry
vanished. (Susan Harris collection)

MURDER AND THE PROPER HOUSEWIFE

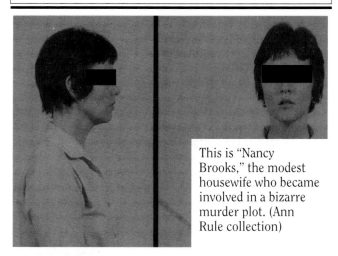

This is "Nancy Brooks," the modest housewife who became involved in a bizarre murder plot. (Ann Rule collection)

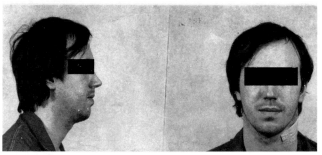

"Bennett LeClerk," who seemed to mesmerize the women in his life. (Ann Rule collection)

MURDER AND THE PROPER HOUSEWIFE

The rear entrance to the Acadia Health Center. Deputies were stationed on the roof of the auto body shop to the left, and Seattle police officer Mike Crist waited at the alley entrance. He faced down a bleeding gunman. Crist won. (Police file photo)

Seattle homicide detective Benny DePalmo, who—with his partner Duane Homan—broke one of the most puzzling cases they had ever encountered. (Ann Rule)

THE MOST DANGEROUS GAME

Detective Doug Englebretson, Snohomish County Sheriff's Office, discovered the identity of the mysterious sniper who stalked two teenagers in the snowy wilderness. (Ann Rule)

The tiny cabins, with a foot of snow on the roofs, where the runaway girls "played house," until fear of a roving monster scared them. (Police file photo)

The Snohomish County Sheriff's Department often has to cope with blizzards and deep snow, as their territory includes mountain foothills.

THE MOST DANGEROUS GAME

The runaways were thrilled that "Al" spent so much time with them and promised to protect them in the snowy woods. He was not who they thought he was. (Police file photo)

Snohomish County sheriff's vehicles parked near the main road. The cabin where Maeve lay injured was far away, in deep snow; the only way to bring her out was with snowmobiles. (Ann Rule collection)

"John Grant," the man who was intent on destroying anyone who kept his estranged wife from him. (Police file photo)

Susan Marsh was trapped on this Welcome mat, with the door locked behind her and a killer with a knife raining blows on her. (Police file photo)

As she fled to get help for her housemates after an hours-long standoff with a wife stalker, Rebecca James didn't realize that she had been stabbed—not once, but many times. She was treated for knife wounds at the University of Washington Hospital in Seattle. (Police file photo)

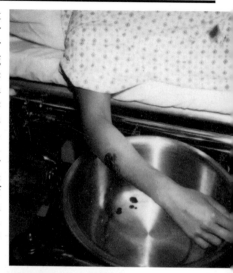

For months Seattle homicide detective Danny Engle tracked John Grant, who continued to threaten his ex-wife, and finally caught him. (Leslie Rule)

THE KILLER WHO NEVER FORGOT . . .
OR FORGAVE

Deputy Ken Trainor, King County Police, was one of the first officers on the scene of the double murder at the Kaarsten home in Kent. (Ann Rule)

The house where Arne Kaarsten's wife and baby were strangled during the night. A neighbor saw someone standing in the living room an hour or more before Kaarsten called for help. The baby's room was to the right of the door; the Kaarsten's two-and-a-half-year-old daughter's room was at the far right. Why did she live and the baby die? (Court photo)

THE KILLER WHO NEVER FORGOT . . .
OR FORGAVE

Lee Yates, who has one of the highest conviction rates in the King County Prosecuting Attorney's Office, behind the wheel of his Porsche in a race at Portland, Oregon's, International Raceway. (Lee Yates collection)

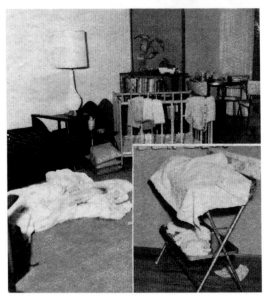

Kaarsten ran to neighbors for help after finding his wife, Judy, strangled under blankets on the floor and seven-month-old daughter Peri Lynn under blankets on the Bathinette (inset). (Court photo)

Oakland, he drove off toward his home. Rand didn't yet realize that he wouldn't see Steve at all during the three days he spent talking to Bill Nichols. As he watched Reno disappear beneath the plane, Jeff Rand pondered the fact that Steve Bonilla hadn't changed much during the eight years since they'd last had dealings. He was still bent on destroying someone who was keeping him from the fortune he thought he deserved.

This time only the target was different. The person who deserved to die was some guy named Jerry Lee Harris.

In Danville, on that Sunday, October 4, 1987, Jerry and Susan Harris were just getting used to living in their wonderful pink mansion, marveling at how great their lives would be once they had unpacked all of the boxes and settled in. They would have a huge housewarming and invite all their relatives and friends.

PART THREE

April 1988

18

All of the devious plotting and stalking had succeeded. Jerry was gone. Six months had passed since Susan and Jerry moved into the wonderful house in Blackhawk. For Susan, the time had passed in a blur of barely healed anguish. In April 1988 it seemed to her that those happy days were years behind her. She had waited in the pink mansion for Jerry to come back for four months. She had held on to her hope for two more months even after she knew he was dead—murdered. There was no reason to stay any longer. This house didn't mean anything now, and she surely couldn't afford it. It only got bigger and emptier with every day that went by. Jerry was gone forever, and she'd had to give their birds away because she couldn't bear to hear them calling "Jer? Jer?" The rooms they had hoped would house their families were empty, except for the one where her mother stayed. Mary Jo Hannah had put her own life on hold for six months so she could be with Susan, but Susan knew it wasn't fair to keep her parents separated any longer. Other people had lives to go to.

It was ironic that Jerry had worried so much about what would happen to their mothers if they were widowed. Susan could hear him teasing her when she asked him what they would do if their mothers both moved in to the Blackhawk house and then didn't get along. "Well, then Sue," he had laughed, "we'll just build them separate mother-in-law wings." But, ironically, it was Susan who was the widow, not Mary Jo or Lila Faye.

Susan didn't want to go back to Oregon, and she couldn't stay in Blackhawk. She rented a condo in San Ramon, a small town just south of Danville, and moved the things that really mattered to her: Jerry's Tiffany lamps, a bronze nude, some impressionistic oil paintings of the boulevards of Paris and crashing surf that they had chosen together. She kept the pecan dining room set, which reminded Susan of all the dinner parties of the past. Her mother wondered if she should cling to things that would be a reminder of happier days, but Susan wanted to keep them. Susan also kept an oak bedroom set that looked as though it was made of bamboo, along with some tall pedestal vases. Almost everything else would have to go. Their yacht, the *Tiffany*, was already gone.

Duke Diedrich's sons helped her pack up and clean the pink house for the new owners. Nobody but Duke's family and her own knew where her new condo was, but oddly, Susan wasn't really frightened any longer. She knew that whoever had killed Jerry was still out there, but she didn't know for sure who it was. She felt that *she* was no threat to Jerry's killer. If she was in danger, Duke would tell her. He wasn't telling her much, but he would protect her; she was absolutely sure of that.

Susan Harris's biggest worry was what she was going to do with her leftover life. She had so many years to live without Jerry.

19

While Susan Harris struggled to find a reason to go on, the attempts to get enough evidence to bring Jerry's killers to trial were being choreographed to be as foolproof as possible. Jeff Rand would be working on the other side of the law now, albeit without salary or benefits beyond a free pass to avoid the gas chamber, which, all things considered, was a powerful incentive. He had agreed to be wired and to place phone calls to Steven Bonilla and Bill Nichols until they said enough on tape for Jon Goodfellow to present the evidence to a judge and get a warrant for their arrest. No one knew how long that might take.

Jeff Rand had told the investigators that Steve Bonilla described Jerry Harris as a "real jerk" who owed Bonilla "millions of dollars." After the first $500 payment, Steve had eventually paid Rand $2,000 to "intimidate" Jerry into signing his business over to Steve. That, Bonilla said, was only a tiny percentage of what Rand would get when Harris was out of the picture.

Rand said he believed at first that they were only going to scare Jerry Harris into doing what Steve Bonilla wanted. The planned murders in 1979 had never happened, and that had led Rand to believe that this time would be the same. Bonilla had promised him really big money. With his balloon mortgage payment hanging over him, it had been easy for Rand to go along with Bonilla's plans to intimidate Jerry Harris.

"He put me and Bill Nichols up at this Motel 6 in Newark," Rand said.

That was true. Pleasanton Lieutenant Gary Tollefson would spend an entire afternoon sometime later going through "boxes and boxes of receipts" at that motel. "Nichols had rented the room, all right," Tollefson said, "but he registered under the name of *Michols,* and he used a phony address in Salt Lake City one time. Other times he used his own name and brought Rand into the room so they wouldn't have to pay for two people. (One receipt showed that the maids had figured out what had happened and [the management] made them pay for two people." It was ironic that Bonilla was promising them millions but trying to save three dollars a night on a motel room.)

When Rand and Bill Nichols talked over drinks at the Hungry Hunter during Jeff's first visit to the Bay Area, he realized that Steve had progressed far beyond even the murderous jealousy of eight years before. He had become consumed, enveloped, *on fire* with hatred. He wanted everything that Jerry Harris had. According to what Nichols was saying, Bonilla hated Jerry Harris even more than he had hated his faithless wife.

Jeff Rand made three trips to California, and with each one, it became obvious that the planned violence against Jerry Harris was escalating. During most of the time Rand and Nichols spent together in various motels pondering plots to destroy Jerry Harris, they drank—both hard liquor and beer. Bill Nichols confided that he had persuaded Bonilla to bring Rand into the plan. And the plan, frankly, was to kill Jerry Harris. Nichols verified that this Harris had really "screwed over" Bonilla and owed him millions of dollars. Jerry Harris, he said, didn't deserve to live.

But it was clear that Nichols wasn't Bonilla's best friend, either. He laughed as he told Rand that the girl Bonilla had gone to see in Colorado was someone he'd met through an ad. Rand told the detectives that Nichols described it as "one of those 'Send me five dollars and I will send you a nude picture' kind of ads."

Bonilla had seen the woman's photograph in a sleazy magazine, Nichols said, and he had started sending her money. The original five dollars had become twenty dollars and then fifty and finally two hundred or more.

Nichols seemed to have little respect for Steve Bonilla, and Rand said they had laughed at him as they drank in the Y'All Come Back bar. Nichols had called Bonilla a doofus who was too damn stupid to realize that he was being taken by a hooker with a convincing sob story.

Even if Steve was a doofus, Nichols and Rand were quite willing to work for him as long as he had money. He had promised to set Rand up as owner-manager of one of the Hot Rod clubs—"probably the Fremont club." Nichols was slated to be head of security for all the clubs. There would be more than enough money for all of them to live like kings. Bonilla told Nichols that he'd been skimming money from the clubs' profits since they opened.

And there it was. Just like before. Bonilla had always started out by saying he wanted someone intimidated when he really wanted them dead. Despite his rage at them in 1979, Beans Rinaldi and Flora and Tip Blume were still alive, but now there seemed to be a sharper edge to Bonilla's hatred and paranoia as the three men planned a murder in October 1987. Steve appeared to blame Jerry Harris for every loss he had ever suffered in his life. There was no question about it: Steve Bonilla would not be satisfied until Jerry Harris was dead. Jeff Rand and Bill Nichols were to come up with a plan to kill Harris—and then carry it out. It was clear to Jeff Rand that the idea of killing Jerry Harris had been a topic of discussion between Bonilla and Nichols for a long time before they brought him into it.

Steve Bonilla was very confident that he could handle any leftover business problems once Jerry Harris was killed. "The wife has caused some problems," Bonilla admitted in a throwaway remark, but he assured them that he could take care of her. "I remember him saying," Rand recalled, "that once Harris was gone, he would be able to walk right in and take over the business. He also talked about Harris's wife, and how she trusted him and didn't know much about business. I also remember him saying he'd even take her to bed, if that's what it took."

As the investigators had long suspected, Bonilla had lusted after everything in Jerry Harris's life, from his booming nightclubs to his beautiful wife. And, as Bonilla's latest ex-wife had once said, he took whatever he wanted.

Looking at a time line, detectives could see that Jerry Harris had reached out a hand to help Steve Bonilla during the summer of 1979 when he took him into Tiffany's and Agro-Serve. Jerry had had no idea that Steve had spent much of his spare time that summer plotting to kill his ex-wife, her new husband, and Beans Rinaldi, who had sold him Independent Caterers. Molly Clemente, Jerry's fiercely loyal secretary, had disliked Bonilla from the moment she saw him. She had told the Washoe County detectives about Jerry's response to her remarks about Steve: Jerry had just grinned at her and teased, "Well, I don't know if he's Mafia, but he may not be far from it with a name like Bonilla." But when Molly looked alarmed, Jerry had patted her on the shoulder and said, "Naw, he's just an old friend looking around for some kind of a deal."

How different might things have been if Jerry Harris, who liked almost everyone he'd ever met, had been able to see beyond the mask of that seemingly friendly little man?

Goodfellow, Whitson, Tollefson, Allen, Diedrich, Christensen, Lopey, Westin, Chiaramonte, Smith, and the other detectives and technicians who were building this case layer by layer were almost ready to move. Jon Goodfellow instructed Jeff Rand to tell the true story of Jerry Harris's murder in as much detail as he could remember. This would be the foundation of their case; once Rand testified in the preliminary hearing, he could not change his story. There would be a trial, followed by a penalty phase. Rand would have to testify over and over and over again about the night of October 20, 1987, and what happened afterward.

There could be no little lies, no half-truths, no holding back to make himself look good, no fabricating, and no forgetting vital details. The time had come to pour the cement into the footings of this case, *The State of California versus Steven Bonilla and William Winifred Nichols.*

Rand agreed. And he kept his word. But no one knew then how many times he would have to tell the story that he wanted only to forget, or how many years would pass before it was finally over.

Bit by bit, Rand told detectives exactly what had happened to Jerry Lee Harris, a man he had never met before the night of October 20, 1987, a man he didn't meet even then except in a sudden violent encounter.

FBI Special Agent Tom Westin of the San Jose office started the tape recorder rolling and nodded to Jeff Rand. While the investigators questioned him and listened to his answers with deliberately bland faces masking their revulsion, Rand told them of an ambush laced with cruelty and cowardice.

Over the next six and a half years, there would be countless versions of what had happened to the man who considered everyone a friend, but Jeff Rand's story would come closest to the truth. If—and when—ADA Jon Goodfellow got Bill Nichols and Steve Bonilla into a courtroom and on the witness stand for cross-examination, it would be fascinating to hear their versions of the events of the night of October 20, 1987.

Jeff Rand spoke slowly, even ponderously, as if he carried a tremendous weight on his chest. Although it was true that Bill Nichols had originally lured him to the Fremont area of California with offers of money in exchange for intimidating Jerry Harris, Rand had known long before his third and final trip that Jerry was going to be killed. The first time Rand flew in, when Nichols picked him up at the Oakland Airport, Nichols confided that he had been "casing" Jerry but he couldn't find a pattern.

Rand said he saw the problem when he and Bill had tried to follow Jerry for a couple of days. They drove by all of Jerry's haunts—the Hot Rods, the JLH Enterprises office, Lum Yuen's, Baritz—but they didn't spot him. During their surveillance and their liquor-laced murder plotting, Nichols seemed to be laden with cash, which he said Bonilla had given him, and he paid for everything. He showed Rand the weapon he carried: a .22 semiautomatic pistol with a homemade silencer.

The hired killers never seemed able to come up with the

right scenario or the right time to kill Jerry. Nichols had confidently assured Rand that he would identify a pattern in Jerry Harris's movements so they could catch him somewhere along his daily rounds. The problem was that Harris *had* no patterns; he was a dynamo who was here, there, and everywhere and never in the same place at the same time. And he was rarely, if ever, alone. If he wasn't with co-workers, his wife always seemed to be around.

Steve Bonilla had eventually convinced Jeff Rand that Harris was a greedy s.o.b. who deserved to die. That didn't matter to Nichols, who was not concerned with poetic justice. If he had to kill Harris to make a bundle of money, he could do it without a second thought. Bonilla was sure that, this time, he had picked himself a dynamite team of killers. It was only a matter of time until they formulated a plan they could work with.

Jon Goodfellow asked Rand what he and Bill Nichols had discussed on the Monday, Tuesday, and Wednesday they were first together in Alameda County.

On Wednesday, October 7, the third day: "Once again, I think we drove by looking at the Hot Rod Cafe and looking for the Mercedes and discussing different ways that it would be possible to get close to Jerry Harris, different ways to kill him, and different places to get rid of the body."

"What kinds of things were discussed?" Goodfellow asked.

"All sorts of stuff. Shooting him as he went in or out of the office. . . . Trying to find him—just trying to find someplace where it would be secluded, where you could shoot him and drag him off and get rid of the body, or shoot him and leave him lie, or grab him and take him somewhere, and just all sorts of different things."

None of the "things" worked out. Frustrated, Nichols and Rand flew home on October 8, but Bonilla summoned them back on Monday, October 12. He picked Jeff Rand up at the airport in his Datsun 280Z. Bonilla had rented a red van for them to drive during this, their second attempt to abduct and kill Jerry Harris. Bonilla was growing disenchanted with the incompetence of his hit men. "He was saying that he couldn't wait any longer," Rand said, "that he was running out of money. This *had to happen,* and we couldn't find any way to get ahold of him, so he was going to have to bring him [Jerry Harris] to us in order for us to get him and kill him."

The two potential assassins waited in an alley next to a Chinese restaurant in their fire-engine red rented van on October 16. Bonilla was to have dinner with Jerry and then lead him to them.

"We tried to catch Harris at his Hot Rod Cafe that night, but we failed," Rand told the detectives. "Then Bonilla delivered him all right at this Chinese restaurant in Fremont. But there was too much traffic, and besides, his wife was with him."

Again they were thwarted, this time by the presence of the woman Rand correctly assumed to be Jerry's wife. She had been very pretty, tall, and slender, and she had walked out of the restaurant with Bonilla. So that attempt had failed too.

Susan Harris had wondered about Steve Bonilla's weird behavior on the night of October 16—the night she, Jerry, and Steve went to Lum Yuen's for dinner. She had glimpsed the red van outside the restaurant that night. But she had no idea what Steve had planned; her presence had given her husband four more days to live.

Rand said they were better prepared the second week. They had gloves from the Big 5 store so they wouldn't leave prints. They had gone to a hardware store, and Nichols had purchased duct tape and a drop cloth. "He attempted to purchase tear gas or Mace and couldn't in the state of California. . . . I remember him asking me to buy it in Nevada."

Once more Jeff Rand headed back to Elko, this time driving Bonilla's 280Z to save airfare. He had barely arrived home when he had a call from Bill Nichols to be back in Fremont on Monday, October 19. "He said that he wanted me to bring a uniform shirt that I had from working as a security guard. . . . He said, 'Don't worry about the other thing—I already got it.' . . . He had bought Mace in Arizona while he was home."

On Monday afternoon Jeff Rand met Bill Nichols in the bar of the Hungry Hunter in Pleasanton, and they had a number of drinks. They checked in and out of the Motel 6 and into the EZ-8 Motel. They went to a restaurant and waited until Steve Bonilla drove up in a white rental car. The time had come to discuss their final plans to eliminate Jerry Harris.

Bill Nichols would have a beeper so that Bonilla could signal him to call back. Bonilla assured them that he would deliver Jerry Harris the following evening—on the pretext of wanting him to look at the new Hacienda Business Park in Pleasanton. Jeff was to wear his security uniform shirt and drive the pickup truck; Nichols was to dress in a shirt, tie, and jacket and pretend to be a real estate agent. Bonilla wanted them to wait for his signal near the business complex. When he alerted them, they were to move to the rear of the Hacienda Business Park so that he could lead Jerry to them to be sacrificed.

After Bonilla left, Bill Nichols showed Rand a pair of handcuffs and said, "Steve isn't totally worthless—he came up with these."

There were many details that none of them had thought of; Steve Bonilla was in a tearing hurry to see Jerry dead, and Jeff Rand and Bill Nichols had rarely had a completely sober moment during their three trips to the Bay Area. But Bonilla had decreed it was time. It was October 20, 1987.

Rand and Nichols played shuffleboard and drank, then ate dinner at Maestro's in Pleasanton, biding their time before they finally carried out the murder plans they had bollixed up together.

It was dark when Nichols's beeper sounded and he went to a phone to call Bonilla's cell phone. Bonilla said that he was heading their way and Jerry was following him. The nervous duo headed for the business park. Rand estimated that they waited about thirty minutes for the two-car caravan to arrive.

As Bonilla and Jerry Harris drove into the front parking lot, Nichols met them with his best Realtor's smile and asked them to follow him around to the back of the

Hacienda Business Park because he "only had keys to the rear entrance."

Rand, dressed in his security uniform, waited in the shadows in Ella Bonilla's newly painted brown Chevy pickup, which had a canopy over the bed.

According to their plan, Rand would wait until he saw Bonilla's Monte Carlo and Jerry's Mercedes parked in the rear lot. Then he would drive the pickup behind their vehicles and start writing down license numbers as if he was merely doing his job. He looked up to see that Nichols had led Bonilla and Harris to the back of the building. Harris appeared to be talking on the phone in his car.

When the detectives and prosecutor heard this, they nodded slightly. They knew that Susan and her brother-in-law, Sandy, had spoken to Jerry on his cell phone shortly after eight-thirty that night. So they were, as they had long suspected, the last people on earth to hear his voice before he met his killers. Jerry had not left Susan, nor had he been kidnapped. He had followed a friend he trusted—Steven Bonilla—into the area at the rear of the Hacienda office complex. Perhaps he realized that he was in trouble shortly after he drove into the dimly lit parking lot.

Something must have seemed off-kilter to Jerry, perhaps when Jeff Rand pulled up behind his parked car and wrote down his license number. Maybe he simply thought he was getting a ticket when he muttered "Damn" into his car phone before the line went dead. At any rate, it was at this point that Jerry ended his conversation with his brother.

When Jerry looked around, he must have realized that Steve Bonilla had brought backup muscle and had lied to him about looking at offices, but he got out of the pickup truck. Jerry may have been angry but not yet afraid. He probably tried to call Sandy back to let him know that things looked suspicious. Only forty-three seconds had passed since he had talked to Sandy. But someone almost certainly snatched the cell phone out of Jerry's hand and broke the connection. In the last moments of his life, Jerry sensed danger and tried to let his brother know.

Too late.

According to Jeff Rand, Bill Nichols confronted Jerry and sprayed Mace in his face. Rand said that Nichols then commanded him to grab Jerry in a full nelson wrestling hold. Blinded and choking, Jerry still tried to fight back. Rand said he heard two "smacks" as Nichols struck Harris, and then Rand fell to the ground on top of Jerry.

The attackers cuffed Jerry's hands behind his back, and Rand and Nichols carried him struggling and coughing to the tailgate of the pickup truck. Jerry was still alive at that point, but he had no chance of fighting off the men who had ambushed him.

"We forced him into the back of the truck, and I held him as Bill Nichols wrapped duct tape around his head," Rand said. They then wrapped Harris in the plastic drop cloth and jammed his body into a plywood utility box in the bed of the truck.

Even months later, Jeff Rand still seemed incredulous that all the plotting and planning had actually culminated in murder. Somehow he had expected the usual last-minute reprieve. But this time there was none. Panicked by what had turned out to be far worse than intimidation, Rand did as Nichols said.

He was not sure if Harris was dead, but he didn't see how he could be alive after being choked by Mace and having duct tape wrapped around and around his head as if he were a mummy.

Although he never lifted a hand to help kill Jerry Harris, Steve Bonilla was there to watch. He had hated Jerry Harris so much that he'd ordered him to be killed and then had observed his suffering. He had not, however, wanted to muss up his thinning hair or get blood on his own hands. Once he was assured that Jerry was helpless, Bonilla drove away. He didn't want to risk being caught in a caravan of vehicles, one of which probably carried a dead body.

Rand said they left the white rental car parked near the Hacienda business complex; Bonilla would have to get someone to return it to the rental agency. Rand, in Jerry Harris's yellow Mercedes, followed Nichols, who drove the pickup. They headed east on Interstate 80. Their first stop was to have been the Sacramento airport, but they were so nervous they drove right past it and had to backtrack. Nichols waited at the garage exit while Rand parked the Mercedes there.

They figured that leaving Jerry's car at the airport "would make it appear that he had taken off."

Then the two killers headed for Nevada in Ella Bonilla's truck to search for a burial spot. As disorganized as ever, Nichols and Rand were still planning the details of a murder they had already committed. They considered knocking all of Harris's teeth out or pouring chemicals on his body to "eat away his flesh and bones."

Back at the Hard Rock in Fremont, Gilbert Konqui and the men interested in Jerry's two upcoming Hot Rods were beginning to glance at their watches and wonder why he hadn't shown up for their meeting. Susan Harris, unaware that she had just become a widow, was telling her sister that her life was perfect, that she had never been happier.

Rand and Nichols had not selected a burial spot ahead of time; they figured Nevada was so full of vast isolated desert that it would be easy to find a suitable grave site. They wondered nervously if anyone had spotted Rand parking the yellow Mercedes in the airport lot. Rand told Nichols to relax; he hadn't noticed anyone around.

When they stopped for gas, Jeff suddenly remembered that, during the struggle to subdue Jerry, he had dropped the notebook in which he'd actually written down Jerry's, Steve's, and the white rental car's license numbers. They might as well have left a trail of bread crumbs for the police. Frantic, Bill Nichols called Steve Bonilla, who had just arrived home.

"You gotta go back there," Nichols said. "Jeff dropped his notebook with everybody's license numbers!"

Mightily annoyed, Bonilla drove back to the crime scene. After scrabbling in the dark parking lot, he finally found the incriminating notepad and picked it up. He would have one of his flunkies return the white rental car the next day. No one would ever be able to tell what had occurred there an hour before.

* * *

It was 133 miles from Sacramento to Reno. Silently, Jeff Rand and Bill Nichols drove through increasingly smaller towns as they headed east to the California state line: Auburn (where Bonilla had wanted Rand to blow up Flora Blume), Applegate, Gold Run, Emigrant Gap, Soda Springs. They crossed the state line and rolled into Verdi, where Rand and Ponytail Willie had failed to kill Beans Rinaldi. The ride was almost a rerun of their previous violent games with Steve Bonilla. Almost, but not quite; this time they had a dead man riding with them.

There were no sounds at all from the rear of the truck. They assumed that Jerry Harris was dead, but that was little comfort. What if some state cop stopped them, maybe to pull a narcotics search? They vacillated between fear of being discovered with a body in the truck, which wasn't even theirs, and a pervasive fatigue that made their limbs and eyes heavy. It was difficult to stay awake. If Nichols fell asleep at the wheel and they ran into a ditch, that would bring the cops too. The adrenaline in their systems fought with the liquor they had imbibed.

Rand recalled that once they reached Nevada, they pulled off Highway 80 and traveled along a two-lane road. It was pitch dark, and they couldn't really see where they were going. For all they knew, they could end up digging in somebody's ranch. Then they realized they *couldn't* dig: they hadn't brought a shovel. They had filled the back of the pickup truck with fishing poles and camping gear so they would have a good excuse for their trip, but they hadn't thought of a shovel.

"I know a place where we can buy one in the morning," Nichols said. They headed into Reno and parked the truck outside the Peppermill Inn while they took a nap, confident that the canopy would hide their silent cargo.

When they woke, Rand said Nichols was antsy because they'd had the body in the truck too long. They bought a shovel as soon as the hardware store opened. They had first decided to bury Jerry Harris's body in a dump near Reno, but they abandoned that plan when they saw a man walking his dog there. In their haste to leave the dump, the pickup got stuck. Jeff had jammed his foot on the accelerator, driving it deeper into the loam and garbage. Finally Bill Nichols had managed to get them out of the soft soil by alternately putting the truck into low and then reverse. The man with the dog had gotten a really good look at them by that time.

There were so many people who had seen them, it appeared, so many chances of being caught—but they weren't.

They headed north toward Pyramid Lake and finally decided the barren land up near the Indian Reservation looked like a safe place. "I started digging the hole," Rand said, and the investigators could see that he was reliving the experience. "Bill started unwrapping Harris."

Jeff Rand said he became ill when he saw Jerry Harris's face. It hadn't been so difficult for him when their victim was wrapped up like a mummy. In the gray daylight, however, he had to acknowledge that they had killed a man.

"Then I . . . I helped Bill pull Harris out of the truck," Rand said slowly. "I took the ring off of his hand, and then we threw his body in the grave."

They covered Jerry's body with dirt, and Nichols drove the truck over the grave to pack the sandy soil down tightly—one more stupid move in a stupid murder plot. If they had been followed or if the grave site had been discovered before weather blew the topsoil away, the tire prints could have been matched microscopically to Ella Bonilla's truck. But no one saw them as they pulled away. Luck continued to ride with them.

They had 289 miles to go to Elko, but they breathed a little easier as they headed east to Rand's home. They discussed what to do with Jerry Harris's ring.

"You want one of them diamonds for your wife?" Nichols had offered.

Rand, sickened, shook his head. He didn't want anything to remind him of what they had done. He told detectives he didn't know what had happened to Harris's wedding ring. The last time he saw it, Nichols had it.

Rand had helped commit a brutal murder, but he said

that he was just hoping to "sucker them for more money. . . . I was thinking that nothing would ever materialize out of their plans." He thought there would be no murder—right up until October 20, 1987, when he realized that he would have to go through with it.

Once they got to Elko, Bill Nichols dropped Jeff Rand off, stopping only to call his wife and ask her to meet him in Reno. Then he headed off, assuring Jeff he would get rid of any evidence left in the truck.

Even as her husband's killers headed toward Elko, Nevada, Susan Harris became aware that something was terribly wrong. She was probably talking to Steve Bonilla at about the time the murderers were driving his mother's truck again and again over Jerry's grave.

And Bonilla was calm, sounding only slightly surprised when she told him that Jerry had not come home the night before.

"Steve," Susan asked, "where did Jerry go after you looked at the office in Pleasanton?"

"I don't know. Jerry went one way, and I went the other."

That part was true. Steve had driven rapidly away from the Hacienda complex, gleeful that his henchmen had carried out the murder he had planned for so long. And Jerry had been transported in the opposite direction. Bonilla had been supremely confident that no one would ever connect him to the quick, brutal attack behind the office building.

In his mind, he was already home free. If he'd been a superstitious man, he might have considered it a bad omen that he had to drive all the way back to Pleasanton and crawl on the ground looking for telltale evidence the killers had left behind.

20

If a jury could hear of the machinations that Jeff Rand described to the investigators, Steve Bonilla and Bill Nichols stood a good chance of being strapped in a chair in the windowed room where California death row inmates met their final punishment, and of hearing the deadly *sizzzzzz* as the cyanide "egg" hit the sulfuric acid beneath the chair.

Jeff Rand had recounted some ridiculously clumsy cloak-and-dagger activities as he and Bill Nichols spent their days at the Super Eight motel or the Hungry Hunter restaurant and the Y'All Come Back saloon, plotting how to kill Jerry Harris and deciding where they should dump his body. "We talked about the possibility of shooting him as he left his office and leaving him there," Rand had said. "I didn't think it was a good plan. . . . We talked about dumping him in a canyon."

Alone later, Duke Diedrich read the transcript of Jeff Rand's confession. He rubbed his eyes as he stared out at the dark night beyond his office window. Susan had been right about that night at Lum Yuen's. She and Jerry had driven home to Blackhawk and never known how close they had come. If the murderers had been just a little more trigger-happy, Susan could have died too.

One thing niggled at Diedrich's mind: the name Willie. Where had he heard it before?

Then he remembered: Detective Linda Agresta had followed up a possible sighting of Jerry Harris over by Lake Tahoe and had written a report about some guy tailing her and Francie Koehler. They had gotten a name on him.

It was Willie. Duke wondered if it was Ponytail Willie. Bonilla consistently employed the same men to do his dirty work for him: Nichols, Rand, some guy named Gary, and Ponytail Willie. It chilled Diedrich to think that Bonilla might have someone following Susan and her private investigator. Bonilla, after all, had every reason to want Susan taken out; her sheer courage and stubbornness were blocking him from getting his greedy hands on the empire Jerry had left behind. And Duke knew that Susan would never buckle under to Bonilla, even if she had to fight him in court until she was a little old lady. She would keep Jerry's clubs going if she had to work seven days a week to prevent Bonilla from taking over.

Duke couldn't tell Susan any of his fears. Not yet—and maybe not ever. He felt once again the sense of "If only—" that he sometimes did in cases where killers just missed getting caught. Jerry and Susan Harris had lived out their last four days together in their brand-new house, oblivious of the fact that Jerry's "best friend" and real estate agent had been trying to find a way to kill him for six months. Even as he oversaw the closing of Jerry's house sale, Steve had been discussing murder theories with Bill Nichols and Jeff Rand.

Maybe that was why Bonilla hadn't been worried that the $8,000 check he'd written in a loan to Jerry was going to bounce. If things had gone as Bonilla and Nichols planned, Jerry would never have had an opportunity to cash that check. But he *had* cashed it, and it *had* bounced, and he'd been absolutely furious with Steve Bonilla. His rage must have affected Bonilla like pouring gasoline on hot coals.

From what Duke could determine, Steve Bonilla had never seen *any* project through to the finish—until this one. When Jerry Harris disappeared four nights after the aborted abduction on October 16, Steve Bonilla had finally carried something off. He had managed to destroy the one man who had been his friend for years, the one man who had put up with all his petty games.

Diedrich smiled grimly. Yes, and the one man who might actually have made Bonilla's fortune.

21

If Jeff Rand was telling the truth—and the investigative team believed that he was, at least in essential areas—Steven Bonilla had arranged to have his best friend killed, and he had managed to carry it off without leaving any physical evidence that would lead back to him. The original klutz had hired two *more* awkward—and drunken—fumble-fingers, and they had all gotten lucky, up to a point. As impossible as it might seem to a layman, Bonilla and Nichols stood a good chance of avoiding arrest unless Jeff Rand cooperated as a prescient witness—a witness who was on the scene at the actual killing. He had agreed to cooperate, but his testimony alone might not impress a jury. Testifying that he had been part of the plan to kill Jerry Harris would be tantamount to admitting he was a murderer who was turning on his fellow murderers to get a reduced sentence. Why shouldn't he lie to save his own skin? He was a co-conspirator—not the most credible of witnesses—and a prime target for a defense attorney. And so the Harris investigative team kept working to establish motive, means, and opportunity for the three suspects. They needed the whole package.

Jon Goodfellow warned that unless Rand was a good enough actor to fool Bonilla and Nichols into blurting out guilty knowledge onto a tape, they still had a dicey case.

Ideally, they wanted Steven Bonilla and Bill Nichols to make statements on tape that would tie them irretrievably to Jerry Harris's murder. The D.A.'s men knew that Bonilla hadn't even been willing to take a lie-detector test when Duke Diedrich offered him a chance to clear himself a few days after Harris vanished. Now that he believed he had gotten away with murder, he wasn't going to take a chance of being taped by someone wearing a wire.

Goodfellow, and his investigator, John Whitson, knew what they needed, and they moved cautiously ahead. Jeff Rand said that Jerry Harris was killed at the Hacienda Business Park. That kept the jurisdiction in the hands of the Pleasanton police and the Alameda County District Attorney's Office. The FBI would continue to be involved because of the interstate aspects of the murder.

Gary Tollefson said that after Rand revealed that Harris had been killed in Pleasanton, his city, his detectives avoided questioning anyone even marginally close to Steve Bonilla or Bill Nichols. They had to be very careful not to alert Steven Bonilla to the fact that the primary investigation had been moved back to Pleasanton. The more firmly Steve believed he was in the clear, the better the police would like it.

They wanted Steven Bonilla, who was living with his mother, zipping around town in his sports car, and acting as if he had no worries. Tollefson's team was tracking him *very* cautiously, so he was unaware that the Pleasanton police knew exactly where he was most of the time.

The police also wanted Bill Nichols, who had left his home in Mesa, Arizona, and appeared to be living near Steve Bonilla between trips to southern California.

Every lawman involved was extremely careful not to alert Bonilla and Nichols to the fact that Rand was talking. Rand's statement-confession would be kept under wraps for five months.

Even though Duke had not told her in so many words, Susan Harris knew that Steven Bonilla had killed Jerry. She had gone through many emotions in the previous six months—loss, hope, despair, shock, mourning, and a sharp grief that she thought she could not bear—and she had finally come to a dull acceptance of what she could not change. But rage now burned in Susan hotter than she could ever have imagined. She hated Steven Bonilla with a white-hot hatred that burned away any trace of fear for her own safety.

Susan was completely alone in the condominium in San Ramon. She had not lived alone since she'd left Oregon seven years before with all her belongings packed in her five suitcases, headed for her new life with Jerry Harris. Nobody except her family and Duke Diedrich knew where she lived. Although she wasn't afraid, she had a heightened awareness of her surroundings, and she now owned a gun, a .357 Magnum.

"I wasn't used to the sounds of the new condo," Susan remembered. "If someone walked up the steps to another condo, it sounded as if they were coming up to mine. It took a long time before I recognized the normal sounds, and I think I was constantly on the alert."

But she wasn't afraid. "I knew Steve Bonilla was free to go anywhere he wanted. I hate to think of this now, but I used to sit in my condo with my gun loaded and aimed at the door. Part of me wanted him to try to get in so I could shoot him."

Susan worked hard enough so she could hope to sleep at night. She *had* to work hard. She was running three night-clubs, two of which had been launched shortly before Jerry vanished. The Hot Rod Alameda was only a year old back then, and Baritz only six months. Jerry had taught her that the life span of most nightclubs was only three to five years, and she wanted to make them last as long as possible for Jerry's sake.

That meant fifteen-hour workdays for Susan. She discovered that most of the 120 club employees didn't even have job descriptions, and many didn't know whom they were supposed to report to. "One day I called a meeting," Susan said. "I put on a toy fireman's hat to illustrate my point when I said, 'I'm so busy putting out fires that we're not getting anything accomplished. Only the emergency room deals with life and death. And we are running nightclubs here. Let's hammer out our job descriptions."

Nobody who worked for Jerry had ever seen Susan as an executive type, but she proved she could do it. She studied the books and realized that she had to make $100,000 a month to break even. After that, whatever money came in was profit. Some months she made a profit and some she didn't, but all three of the clubs began to pick up. Soon they were grossing $700,000 a month. "But I had so many bills to pay," she said. "My hand got cramps from writing checks."

The bankruptcy she'd had to file was a sword hanging over her head. In the next five years she faced 120 lawsuits and she settled them all. She paid so many attorneys that she lost count. "I paid everyone off," she remembered. "The attorneys were paid first and then all secured creditors, and then as much as I could pay on the unsecured creditors."

This was hard for Susan. Because she had no credit record, she had to pay six months' rent in advance on any place she wanted to rent. It was almost impossible for her to rent a car.

One of Jerry's ex-partners at Agro-Serve owned the building Baritz was in. There had always been a parking shortage there. He offered her three possible solutions, all of which would have been prohibitively expensive. "I turned them all down," she said, "and started valet parking at Baritz."

But Baritz had a short lease, and the club was a headache. Someone was still calling in complaints to the fire department, the health department, the liquor board, and every other inspecting agency in the area. Worn down finally, Susan sold Baritz at a break-even figure and concentrated on the two Hot Rods—one in Fremont and one in Alameda. These were the clubs that Jerry loved; they were to have been the basis for a nationwide franchise—if he had lived.

"I hoped to be able to keep the Fremont Hot Rod," Susan said later, almost wistfully.

If she didn't fall asleep over the books in the office, only *hols:* No. Uh-uh.

nd: Well, why don't you get to a phone that
an talk to?

chols: The thing to do is call me over the
end and give me a time and a number.

nd: Man . . . you know this is kinda bull-

chols: You know, just do it collect. You
v—might as well play it safe.

nd: Why can't you talk to me now? Man, I
na know what the hell's goin' on.

ichols: 'Cause I'm soaking wet. I just got out
he shower. I got here about an hour ago. If
're gonna be [there] a couple of days, then
t gives me time to go ahead and get my stuff
anged down there.

Rand: Well, how about later this evening?

Vichols: You just want to hear some comfort
ws? Is that what you're saying?

Rand: Well, I wanna know what's going on. You
ow, I wanna know exactly what he's told
erybody—you know, Bonilla's told them—
d I wanna know what the cops know.

Nichols: Wait! Before you say too much—

Rand: I wanna know where I stand.

Nichols: You're fine. You got no problems what-
oever. None.

nd asked Nichols if he could get to a phone by 10:30,
Nichols grudgingly agreed. "But you know I need about
h hours with you to give you the whole rundown," he
Rand. "I'm serious. That's why I thought you were
ing here."

Rand: I don't want to come down there without knowing what kind of a situation I'm walking into. . . . You guys kinda kept me in the dark
here, and I want to know exactly what's going
on.

Nichols: Well, all right. It's in a hold; every-

---

to be awakened when the early morning cleaning crew came
in, Susan left alone late at night, walking to her truck in the
dark parking lot. "I wasn't afraid," she recalled. "I suppose
someone could have jumped me, but I never thought about
it. I didn't have anyone to walk with me. All I did was work.
And when I got home, I was tired enough to sleep."

She was keeping Jerry's clubs going. She was trying, in her
own way, to vindicate him. The headlines after his body was
found had seared themselves into her brain. People had
been eager to see him as an organized crime figure or as a
participant in a pyramid scheme. "It's like a woman who's
been raped," Susan said. *"She* gets blamed somehow, even
though she has no fault at all. When your husband gets
murdered, people act as if it's *his* fault, and you are
connected to it, as though he had to have been engaged in
some kind of criminal activity."

It was hard for Susan to make friends because of the
public perception of Jerry's activities. "I met one girl in the
beauty parlor near Jerry's office," she said. "We did become
friends, but she told me later that her mother didn't want
her to have anything to do with me. She said that her
mother told her I had killed my husband and I ran nightclubs, so she should avoid me."

Susan moved in a strange world where everything that
had once been washed with sunshine was suddenly shad-
owed in black. She was making money, paying off debts,
fighting in court to keep Steve Bonilla from gleaning one
single penny from Jerry's estate, getting up to go to work,
and coming home to sleep. And sometimes she sat facing
her door with a loaded gun, waiting for footsteps to come up
the stairs so she could shoot the person who had destroyed
her sunshine world.

She was not yet thirty.

Susan talked to Duke Diedrich often, and he assured her
that the investigation was moving along well—but slowly.
He offered nothing more.

Steven Bonilla had actually paid Jeff Rand less than
$2,000 to help kill Jerry Harris. He had promised Jeff a
share in the Fremont Hot Rod and a lot more money, but he

had reneged on his promises to Jeff and Bill Nichols. Since his mother would no longer lend him money and he had none of his own, Bonilla had no way to pay his hit men. Susan Harris had legally blocked every move Bonilla made to take over Jerry's nightclubs. Moreover, he was barred from both Hot Rods and Baritz, and he could no longer skim money from the proceeds. Bonilla was skilled, however, at persuasion and manipulation, and he had been able to convince Rand and Bill Nichols that the mother lode waited just ahead. At least he was able to hold them at bay for several months.

Duke Diedrich and his fellow FBI agents, along with Gary Tollefson and Mark Allen of the Pleasanton Police Department and Jon Goodfellow and John Whitson of the Alameda D.A.'s office, wanted Rand to get Bonilla and Nichols to discuss the murder of Jerry Harris—for the record, on tape. This would involve very delicate and sophisticated surveillance and audio equipment.

They chose a tantalizing hook for Rand to start with: the fact that Jeff Rand needed money desperately. That would alarm Nichols and Bonilla because Rand would imply that he might have to go to the authorities if money was not forthcoming. It was true that Rand needed money. The investigators and prosecutors would not pay his living expenses. He had to find pickup construction work and still be available almost daily to place calls to Bonilla and Nichols.

Rand's calls to his two partners in murder began in April of 1988. They had come together in a cruel scheme, and there was no loyalty among them. Each man was now looking out for his own interests. Jeff Rand was wired with a recording device that picked up every word and every angry intake of breath that came over the phone line. Initially Rand had far more luck getting Nichols to talk than he did Bonilla. Steve had been suspicious of others for most of his life, and he now had every reason to be paranoid. He was apparently using Nichols as a buffer between himself and Rand.

On April 21, 1988, Jeff Rand placed a call to Bill Nichols's rented home in Mountain View at 9:23 P.M. It was

a collect call, as most of Rand's would be. The conversation wa might be expected of a dialogue be committed a murder together.

> Nichols: Hello
> Rand: Hey, what's up?
> Nichols: How you doin'?
> Rand: Oh, all right.

Rand made small talk about getting on his Jeep. Then he asked Nichols

> Nichols: Well, I'm here. How s here?
> Rand: I don't know. I've got so work. It's payin' off here.

For a time Nichols and his wife liv Bonilla had rented for them. In almost that Rand had with him, Bill Nichols su come to where he was—that they could some money. Rand felt—and so did th that his life wouldn't be worth much if Bonilla pinpointed his location. He was li constantly on the move. The last place he close to either one of them. He continuall saying that he had steady work where he w hard up for cash he had to stay on h apparently bought that explanation, altho always asked Jeff Rand to go to another phor they continued any conversation.

April 21, 1988
> Nichols: Well, that's better than what here 'cause I was just gonna say let's hea
> Rand: What you got goin' on down so
> Nichols: Well, no, it's more—not wo maybe.
> Rand: Can you talk on this phone?

thing's in a hold from the procedure. Steve's being looked at real hard for having something to do with this poor bastard's demise. As far as what affiliation we have with him, we're not involved.

Rand: Well, you know every time I see a cop behind me, I get antsy, man.

Nichols: Listen to me. Listen to me real careful. You and I didn't know anything of Steve's business. We weren't involved in any of his business. The only thing we had to do with him—are you *listening* to me?—was the construction, the tile. Nobody wants to talk to us 'cause we—Just because we know him doesn't mean we're guilty of anything, okay? But *he's* being looked at like he had something to do with this. Meanwhile he has been tied up in court with this guy's wife—or widow or whatever you call her—and he's probably going to be tied up for a good six months. . . . That will all be straightened out, you know, him putting any money into our *tile business*. We got six months before we can even get anything out of him. And he's just a nervous wreck these days. I don't even like being around him anymore. And I don't want anybody thinking I even knew any of these people that were involved in this other situation he had.

Rand: Who else is involved?

Nichols: I don't know.

Rand: Who else knows about it?

Nichols: You know, everybody in town knows that— They've spread it all over the papers that Steve was the business partner of this guy.

The countless future conversations between Jeff Rand and Bill Nichols would be repetitive in content. Nichols tried to lure Rand to where he was living, assuring him he could explain how he planned to deal with Steve Bonilla and to get the money he and Rand had coming to them.

And Rand kept stalling, eliciting a bit more information with each call. Always, always, the FBI, the Alameda County D.A.'s Office, and dozens of detectives either listened in or heard the tapes. They didn't want to rush an arrest; they were waiting until they had sufficient evidence.

Bill Nichols wasn't at all hesitant about talking on the phone with Rand, but he *was* nervous about which phone lines they used. Six months after Jerry Harris's murder, Nichols seemed enraged because Bonilla hadn't come through with any of his promises. He had not unrolled the red carpet into Jerry Harris's clubs, and Nichols was as hard up for cash as he had been before.

William Winifred Nichols played a tough guy on the phone, and he talked on and on as the tape rolled. He said he had no fear of Steve Bonilla, and vowed to kill him if he caused any problems. "I'll off anybody who gets in the way," he promised Jeff Rand. "I'm getting *my* money."

He wasn't afraid that the police would look at him just because he'd once been involved in a drug lab with Steve Bonilla. Nichols laughed at that notion. The lab deal was a long time ago. That didn't mean he had anything to do with Bonilla in 1987. He bragged that the police had ruled him out in Harris's murder. He had made up false receipts to prove that he was working in Arizona on the night Jerry Harris was killed. "The police bought it—all the way."

True to his promise, Bill Nichols left his home and moved to a pay phone at ten o'clock on the night of April 21. Jeff Rand told him he had moved to a motel room and gave him the extension number. He was still in an FBI office in Carson City, Nevada, but Nichols didn't know that. Nichols promised to call Rand back.

He did call back and he explained the situation to Rand: "Listen, what I'm doing when I change all these phones and everything—all I'm doing is just taking precautions."

"If they don't know nothing about us," Rand challenged, "how come you got to take off [head for southern California] and be so—"

"No," Bill Nichols interrupted. "They already checked my background. They already checked my basic alibi. They pulled all the records on anything they knew. Okay? And they checked out my end and it came up clean."

"I thought you had some," Rand said. "Didn't you tell me you went to prison in Arizona or something?"

"They checked out who Steve knew. . . . Your name has never— You're not even existing in this thing. So you got no worries whatsoever. But you don't want to be here in this town [Mountain View]. There ain't nothing to do here. See, I came up here a couple of months ago because I've been up here off and on the whole time. And it looked like we were gonna close it all out and everything was gonna be fine."

"What do you mean 'close it out'?" Rand asked.

"Get it all. Take possession [of Jerry Harris's clubs] and all that kind of shit. And it's just been one fiasco in court after another."

Jeff Rand asked for more specifics about what Steve Bonilla had told detectives when they first approached him after Jerry's death.

"They asked him some questions," Nichols said easily. "He told them where he was and this type of shit. And then the next day they come back again and they said, 'Will you take a lie-detector test or go under hypnosis?' And he said, 'Hey, fuck you. Talk to my lawyer from now on.' So he hasn't talked to them other than that. A month later the FBI came back, and they told him right to his face, 'We know you did it. We know this was—was a pro hit. We're going to find him [Jerry Harris] sooner or later, and we know you're behind it. You had something to do with setting him up.' And since then they've backed off."

Duke Diedrich, listening to the tape later, nodded. That was almost exactly what he had said to Steven Bonilla back in October, two days after Jerry vanished.

Jeff Rand plunged ahead: "Well, what about when they found where we buried him there in the Nevada desert?"

"Okay, okay," Nichols said nervously.

"You didn't bury him deep 'cause he got found."

"Well, Jeff, don't say that—just in case somebody's listening. . . . I know what you're talking about so don't say anything directly."

"All right."

"And if he wouldn't have been found, Steve would've had to maybe wait years. So that worked out good that he was [found]. Thank God. Otherwise Steve would have been tied up for years on a missing persons deal. There was some loophole in some kind of contract on this deal. That his wife got. So it was a good thing that he was found. And you know, as far as him dying—nobody knows how he died."

"Well," Rand blurted, "you know, you smothered this dude and you got no money. I mean, I get a lousy two hundred dollars sent to me. He's got enough money for attorneys, but can you come up with two hundred bucks?"

"None of us have any money at this point."

Nichols actually seemed glad that Harris's body had been found. He thought that it would speed up payment of the money Bonilla owed them. Nichols's thinking was oddly skewed. By his bizarre reasoning, Jerry Harris had not been smothered for nothing. Nichols figured they would get more money now than they had ever imagined. Bonilla would be worried and want to placate them because *he* was the link to Harris—not them. Bonilla would be afraid of *them*— afraid that they might betray him.

Nichols said he wasn't worried in the least that Bonilla would ever finger them. He couldn't do a thing without implicating himself. "What is he going to do? Put *himself* in the gas chamber?"

But there was no real indication that Bonilla would ever get any money from the death of Jerry Harris, and Jeff Rand asked Bill Nichols, "Well, then, what the hell did you smother him for—for *free?*"

"Hell," Nichols said with exasperation, "I just got through saying, why are you saying these things on the phone?"

"Oh—I'm sorry. I just got kind of upset here."

"Hey, you think *you're* upset? I've already whipped his ass."

"What do you mean?"

"I've whipped Steve's fucking ass."

"You mean you beat him up?"

"Yeah," Nichols said. "I slapped him around, 'cause I was trying to get money for myself as well as you. I've been trying to get you money for four fucking months sent up there to you."

". . . Well are you guys still getting along after you beat him up?"

"Yeah," Nichols said, "but you know, as soon as this is wrapped up, we will get our money. I have seen all the court papers. I stay right on top of what's going on. There is no money right now. We will get our money. Steve will get his money. There is a lot more than we thought."

"Well, just how much are you talking about?"

". . . I already told him that he owes you at least fifty."

"Fifty?"

"Grand. At least."

"Well, what's your cut?"

"I haven't even gave him my number yet. But I'm so pissed off 'cause [since] I've been up here, I've blown ten grand. Now we sold our house and moved up here and now I'm broke. That's why I'm getting out of here. I got to go make a living."

Nichols put sixty cents into the pay phone at the operator's request. He had good news for Jeff Rand: "This time the ex-wife and Steve are talking about negotiating."

He assured Rand that no one knew who would split Jerry's money—no one but Nichols himself, his wife, Rand, and Bonilla. And then Bill Nichols used up the rest of his sixty cents to denigrate Bonilla as a mama's boy whose mother was paying his attorneys—just as she had always paid.

"You know he hasn't worked a fucking day since this happened? I take that back—he's probably worked a week, total. But he hasn't done shit. All he does is just cry on my shoulder about how worried he is about *this,* how upset he is about *that,* 'cause *this* didn't go through or *that* didn't go through or the courts keep changing. He thought this girl [Susan Harris] was gonna be such a pushover. Fuck. She's fighting him tooth and nail. . . . He's gonna win a certain amount," Nichols said, changing his tack once more.

"They've already conceded that. But she's holding him up. She's gonna hold him up as long as possible. She's not as dumb as he said she was."

Bill Nichols was a superlative talker; he could lie in a most convincing manner. He sounded almost sincere when he said he was fighting Bonilla to get money for Rand. Most of what he said was a mixture of rhetoric and bullshit, but he spoke the honest truth when he said that Susan Harris was not nearly as dumb as Steve Bonilla had said she was. And she was no pushover. She had dug in her heels and by sheer force of will, she was driving Jerry's killers to distraction. Better yet, her stubborn refusal to buckle under was making the three conspirators turn on one another.

Steve Bonilla and Bill Nichols, of course, did not know that Jeff Rand had turned on them and that all their scurrying around to cover their tracks, like rats hiding their nesting spot, had been done far too late. Susan Harris was beating them in court, and the men and women investigating Jerry Harris's murder were listening in on their frenzied plots.

22

Duke Diedrich was spending 50 percent of his time on the Jerry Harris case. "The hardest part of the whole case for me," he said later, "was that period of time—more than a year—when I knew everything about how Jerry had died and about who was trying to kill Susan, but I couldn't tell her."

And Diedrich *did* believe that someone was trying to kill Susan Harris. He had never bought the assumption that the car that almost hit Susan and her parents the previous November had been driven by some show-off teenage driver. He was convinced that someone had meant to run over Susan and that the driver hadn't cared if he took her parents with her. Duke was also sure that Susan had come very close to being abducted along with Jerry. That had almost happened on October 16 at Lum Yuen's. By then Bonilla had been getting desperate to take Jerry Harris out.

If Jerry had not followed Steve Bonilla to Pleasanton on the night of October 20, Bonilla might well have arranged to have both Harrises killed in the next try. Now Susan was defying Bonilla, and Steve Bonilla had a notoriously short fuse when someone came between him and money.

But just when the trail to Bonilla had started to get red hot, Diedrich had to pull out of working full-time on the Jerry Harris case for a while. Six-year-old Amber Schwartz was kidnapped from in front of her home in Pinole, California, at four o'clock in the afternoon of June 4, 1988. Amber was the daughter of Bernie Schwartz, a policeman who had been shot and killed in the line of duty as he pursued a homicide suspect. She was a pretty little girl who had been left somewhat deaf after she was hit by a car. For this reason, her mother and stepfather kept a closer eye on her.

June 4 was a warm day, and Kim Schwartz, Amber's mother, had all the windows open. Amber was jumping rope on the sidewalk. Kim checked frequently to see what Amber was doing. But when Amber's stepfather left on his motorcycle, he didn't see her. He assumed she was in the backyard with her brother.

But she wasn't. She was gone.

Amber and her family lived on a hill above a grade school. There was a creek at the foot of the hill, and the school play yard lay beyond the creek. "They instituted a search at 6:00 P.M., and they looked for Amber until midnight," Diedrich recalled. "They found no trace of her. But—oddly—the next morning they found her socks in the school yard. They hadn't been there the night before. Someone had deliberately come back and left them there."

Since Diedrich was the FBI's kidnap expert in the Bay

Area, he spent days and nights in the frustrating search for Amber Schwartz. It seemed to him that he had gone over the whereabouts of every known pedophile in northern California, including one who spent his nights—and days—in cemeteries. "We spent a lot of time following a character we called Graveyard Gus* who spent many hours 'talking' to the graves of children, some of whom had been victims of kidnappings."

Despite their routine and not-so-routine investigative techniques, Diedrich, his fellow agents, and Pinole policemen never found Amber Schwartz. Her disappearance remains as baffling in 1997 as it was on that warm June day in 1988.

Diedrich worried about Susan Harris while he was caught up in the Schwartz kidnapping case. He called to check on her as often as he could. He tested the waters with Susan to see how much he could tell her.

"He asked me once if I could keep a secret—*really* keep a secret," Susan said, "and I told him the truth—I always told Duke the truth. I said, 'Duke, you know me. I'd want to—but then I'd tell my mom, and then I'd probably tell my whole family.'"

Diedrich now knew that Steve Bonilla had once arranged to plant a bomb under his ex-wife's car and had then let his own children ride away in it. The thought chilled his blood. At that point Bonilla had no longer wanted anything from Flora Blume. *That* murder-for-hire attempt appeared to have been solely in reprisal.

But Susan was different. She held the purse strings to the Hot Rods and the money from Baritz; her legal maneuvers were holding Bonilla's takeover at bay. Rand and Nichols were hounding Steve, demanding money and the share of the clubs he'd promised them. Nichols was doing it on his own behalf, and Rand, of course, was doing it for the investigation team. More than that, Bonilla wanted the money he believed was due *him*. And one 110 pound woman, Susan Harris, was the obstacle between him and money.

When Duke heard that Jeff Rand said the word "bomb"

in his statement about Faye Blume, he had driven at once to Susan Harris's condo in San Ramon. "All I had left was a four-wheel-drive Bronco," Susan said. "The other cars were gone. I couldn't afford to drive a Ferrari or a Mercedes or any of the cars Jerry and I owned once, and, besides, they didn't fit with the life I had. Duke came over and went down to where I had the Bronco parked. He crawled around underneath and checked under the hood.

"When I asked him what he was looking for, he just said, 'Bombs.' That was all. He didn't explain. I guess he didn't have to. He said he hadn't found any."

She was too numb to be afraid. Susan Harris was living her life on autopilot. She went to work and she came home. Only someone who has been under constant emotional siege—or in actual warfare—can understand her state of mind. She had been a target for so long that it felt normal to her. She didn't plan for a future; she lived one day at a time.

"Duke was my hero, my protector, my big brother," she recalled. "He always seemed to know what was going on with me. I can't tell you the times he called at just the right time. He was looking after me. He asked me if I knew how to lose somebody in traffic if I needed to. I didn't, so he took me out and showed me. I got pretty good at zipping into side streets and alleys."

One morning Diedrich dropped by Susan's condo and brought the police chief of San Ramon with him. "I thought they were just visiting," Susan recalled. "I thought he just happened to have this other guy with him. I found out later that Duke was really showing the chief where I lived so that the San Ramon police could get to my condo in a hurry if they had to."

And there was a time very soon when Diedrich feared for Susan's safety. He received a call from her San Diego bankruptcy attorney. "I've been trying to get Susan for hours," he told Diedrich, "and all I get is a busy signal."

Duke tried Susan's unlisted number, and he too heard only the monotonous *bleat-bleat* of a tied-up line. He called the San Ramon police and asked for an immediate check on the welfare of Susan Harris.

"I saw all these police cars pull up," Susan said, "and I wondered what was going on. I watched them out my window—and then I heard them at *my* door. I didn't even know my phone was out of order. I had to use the police phone to call Duke and tell him I was okay."

Meanwhile Pleasanton Lieutenant Gary Tollefson's men were monitoring the comings-and-goings of Steven Bonilla, but they couldn't watch him all the time without arousing his suspicion. They wanted him to believe that the law enforcement agencies in the Alameda–Contra Costa County area were no longer even vaguely interested in him. If and when an arrest came down, it had to be a complete surprise.

During the summer of 1988, all the action in the case was going on behind the scenes, but everyone in Susan's world was growing more frightened. "My San Diego attorney had a concealed weapons permit," she said. "I realized that suddenly all my friends were carrying guns."

Although Duke Diedrich knew he couldn't tell Susan about Jeff Rand or about the trap that was about to clamp down on Steve Bonilla and Bill Nichols, he realized he had to tell someone close to her. Mel and Judy Boyd, Susan's aunt and uncle, were police officers; they would understand the fragile structure of the investigation. One false word might alert Bonilla, and he could rabbit on them. The investigators were so close to getting their arrest warrant. They needed only a few phrases on a tape—phrases that would link the two suspects irrevocably to Jerry Harris's murder. No one knew for sure when that would happen.

The Boyds had been vocal in demanding proof that Susan was safe, and they wanted to know what was going on. Finally Duke Diedrich met with Judy and Mel Boyd in a Chilli's restaurant in Concord. "I told them we knew why, where, and how, and that we were almost ready to make an arrest. They were worried that Susan might still be in danger, and I told them I thought she was safe—and even safer if she didn't know. They were dying to know more, but they didn't ask—and they didn't tell Susan."

23

Lawmen were moving Rand constantly during the spring and summer of 1988 so that his claim that he was calling from different phones all the time would fit. Sometimes he was in FBI offices in Carson City or Reno, Nevada, sometimes he called from Truckee or Santa Clara, California, and he used several phones elsewhere.

Nichols was almost as peripatetic. His home was in Mesa, Arizona, but he was seldom there. He had some major moneymaking schemes planned for the southern California area. One involved repairing and selling expensive used cars, and another was his own twist on the old television show *The Millionaire*. Nichols told Rand that there was a lot of money to be made by locating lost heirs.

The investigators listening to the tapes shook their heads and grinned—Nichols was *good*. Had he chosen to live a straight life, he would have made a dynamite salesman. They could understand why he was so successful with women despite his droopy eyes and skinny build. He could make people believe just about anything.

Just about.

Jeff Rand voiced his concern that he and Nichols might have left physical evidence at the site of Jerry's murder or near his desert grave. "What about the Mercedes or the truck?" he asked Nichols. "You know I lost a little Swiss Army pocket knife. Did you find it in— That was Bonilla's truck, right?"

"Yeah."

"Can you check in there? 'Cause my prints are all over that knife."

"I threw it away."

"You threw what away?"

"Your little knife."

"You found it?"

"I threw everything out of there."

"What about the briefcase?"

"It's gone. Hey, I left *nothing* traceable."

"What about the tarp?"

"Not even that," Nichols said. "I took care of everything."

"What'd you do with it?"

"Burned it."

"And the duct tape?"

"Believe me, you don't have to keep saying the same old words on this line," Nichols said tightly. *"Everything."*

Nichols now tried to convince Jeff Rand that even Bonilla was no longer a suspect. "They're looking at somebody else."

"Well," Rand said doubtfully, "I find that hard to believe."

"They're looking at somebody else this guy fucked over. But the only problem we got is waiting on this court because Bonilla underestimated the cunt. She's fucking smarter than he thought. And she's gonna tie him up. . . . I think it'll come down about August or September."

Steve Bonilla was the biggest item on the investigators' wish list, but he was wary of talking with Jeff Rand.

Rand tried to set up a meeting—or at least a phone call— with Bonilla through Bill Nichols, who had slipped and said that he had talked to Bonilla's lawyer.

"I don't trust Bonilla at all," Rand said.

"Oh, well . . . I don't blame you."

"He won't talk to me. He keeps pushing me off onto you. I feel like he's gonna hang me out there to hold the bag when it all comes down."

"Well, no, he's not, because he has to hang himself in the

first place. . . . Hey," Nichols said, as if he suspected someone was listening to their conversation, *"we* didn't do it."

"Well, you know—you had your chance to talk with
Bonilla all the time, and I really want to talk to this guy. I
want to know what he said," Rand argued.

"Hey," Nichols said, "I'll tell you what. You want to talk
to him? I'll bet you don't talk to him twenty seconds and
you break his neck, and then we won't get anything."

"Get him to a phone that I can talk to him," Rand said.
"I'm serious."

"He won't talk to you. He already told me he wouldn't."

"This is bullshit. . . . Well, what's going to happen in
September? Tell me."

"Well, hopefully by then that's when he can get possession. Because the probate takes ninety days."

"Well, Bonilla can't just slough me off and forget about
me. I want to talk to this guy," Rand said.

Nichols stalled, promising more information in a few
days. He said he needed time to get settled in Los Angeles in
his car resale business. Once he was established, he wanted
Jeff to come down and join him there.

Rand wasn't going for it. "Well, what if Bonilla turns me
or you over?"

"Don't you *understand?"* Nichols momentarily lost his
cool. *"He* goes to the gas chamber if he does. He can't turn
you in without turning himself in."

"You guys have been full of lies from the beginning, and I
just don't know what to believe."

The tape wound on as Nichols pulled out all his stops.
"No. It's not that he's lying, Jeff. It's not lying. It's just that
he gets it so fucked up in his own goddamned head and he's
such a nervous wreck because he's pissed 'cause he ain't got
his money, and that's all it is. He isn't lying. He isn't
screwing us up. He could have had this three months ago—
all done—if he'd done it right in the first place. But he runs
around like a chicken with his head cut off."

Bill Nichols's agenda was clear. He had to pretend he
hated Steve Bonilla, which might not have taken much
acting, in order to convince Jeff Rand that they were on the

same side. He had to keep Jeff calm, so he wouldn't freak out and draw attention to them, and quite possibly he hoped to draw Rand into his world so that, if he *couldn't* control him, he could arrange for Jeff Rand to have a fatal accident.

Most obvious of all, Nichols was clearly under orders from Steve Bonilla to keep Rand away from him. It didn't work; Rand finally wore Nichols down by convincing him that he might do something crazy if he didn't talk to Bonilla himself.

One evening Steve Bonilla picked up his phone and was shocked to hear Rand's voice on the other end.

Rand began his first call by asking casually, "How are things going?"

"Everything's been pretty quiet," Bonilla said furtively.

When Rand said he really needed money, Bonilla explained that Susan Harris had "cut me off from any money from the club. . . . Everybody is under suspicion."

Bonilla said he didn't want to talk on his home phone. "I don't even want to continue this conversation anymore. I don't know who's listening in on these phone calls . . . they can interpret anything I say the wrong way."

"What's the *point* of killing the guy?" Rand asked suddenly.

"Jeff," Bonilla responded, shocked, "what are you *saying?*"

The line went dead. Only Bill Nichols was willing to talk about the mess they were in. Nichols's story continued along the line that he too was frustrated and had grievances to air. As the months passed and he received no money and no interest in Jerry Harris's nightclubs, he told Rand that Bonilla was "an idiot" who had made all the wrong moves in fighting Susan Harris for her dead husband's clubs. "She's foiled all our plans," Nichols said. "This could have been wrapped up months ago. You and I are going to have to straighten him [Bonilla] out when this is all over."

Nichols reassured Jeff Rand that he had nothing to worry about. "They'll never put it together," Nichols said easily. "Nobody's even wondering about you."

Bonilla, however, was another story. Nichols said that the police suspected Bonilla. "They know he did it."

Despite his string of failures in life and in business, Bonilla continued to believe he knew everything about everything. He did not credit the slow-talking Rand with much intelligence. Never in a million years would he have believed that Rand could play both himself and Nichols as skillfully as he did. Day after day, often several times a day, Nichols was accepting collect phone calls from Rand. Bonilla was forced to talk to Rand, too, but his natural paranoia made him hinky about talking on the phone.

Since Bonilla had always chosen motel rooms for his meetings with Jeff Rand and Bill Nichols, the investigators figured that having Rand set up meetings with Bonilla and Nichols in motels would work. But Bonilla would not meet Jeff Rand in a motel to talk.

"Oh, we tried," Diedrich said, "but Bonilla was afraid. Tom Westin supervised the placement of TV monitors and cameras in motel rooms, but Bonilla never showed. He was afraid that Jeff was trying to kill *him*. He was also suspicious that Jeff was going to snitch on him. We were trying to get the face-to-face meetings on film because Bonilla was so nervous about phone lines being tapped."

Steve Bonilla never showed up at the motels where Jeff Rand waited in rooms with cameras and microphones secreted in the walls and mirrors. Still, Steve had no choice but to keep talking to Rand. He felt that Rand was going sour on him, and Bonilla had to try to keep him from doing something stupid. With Rand appearing scared to death that the FBI was about to pounce on him, Bonilla actually went to Elko to discuss the situation with him. He explained that it was now more important than ever to make sure that all of their stories matched—just in case the investigators ever did question them.

Steve Bonilla told Rand—in a taped phone call—that he was to say that Bonilla had originally gotten Rand's name from a mutual friend. "Say I called to ask you if you were interested in becoming involved in the tile business," Steve told him.

"They shouldn't be looking at me at all," Bonilla said confidently. "They should be looking at someone else."

The only way Steve Bonilla would talk to Rand at all now was on pay phones. And it was never just one pay phone; Bonilla and Nichols leapfrogged from pay phone to pay phone until they had convinced themselves that no one could possibly have bugged the phones. It apparently never occurred to them that Rand himself might be bugged.

Nichols and Bonilla wanted Jeff to use the black horse code—a sophomoric code where each letter in the phrase "black horse" stood for a number. That way, he could leave the number of whichever phone booth he was calling from and no one but the trio could break the code. Laboriously they explained it to him as agents listening in stifled their laughter and wrote it all down.

Jeff Rand called Steve Bonilla from Santa Clara, California, and again from Truckee. The calls were, of course, taped. Rand told Bonilla that he was nervous because the FBI had been asking about him in Elko.

That information appeared to stun Bonilla. "You're right," Bonilla said. "We got major problems. I thought everything was starting to quiet down. You better stay out of sight, Jeff," he cautioned. "I can't believe they're in Elko."

Bonilla admitted on Rand's phone tape that he and Bill Nichols had been plotting to kill Jerry Harris for six months before they ever contacted Rand. "We were trying to get all the paperwork straightened out," he said, referring to the nightclubs' records.

"Oh, God," Bonilla burst out. "Nichols has got to talk to you, and you guys have to get all the stories straight! We're going to coordinate everybody's story."

Rand played his part well. He told Bonilla that his life was disintegrating. He had no money beyond what he could pick up from temporary construction jobs. And now, he lied, his wife had left him and taken their children to Seattle. He told Steve Bonilla that he had put everything on the line for him, and here was the damned FBI hanging around his hometown.

Bonilla sounded sympathetic. "I'm sorry," he said. "The

only thing worse [than losing your wife and children] is losing your mother—your father."

But he came back quickly with his *real* concerns. If Rand's wife had left him, she might be a loose cannon. She had been there when Bonilla visited Rand in Elko. She had seen her husband driving Bonilla's car home from California, and she had seen Jeff and Nichols when they drove up after they had left Jerry Harris's body in the desert at Pyramid Lake. "If your wife tells them that," Bonilla warned, "we're in trouble. She can be very dangerous. . . . Jeff, you and Bill were supposed to have all of this covered."

Rand asked Bonilla on tape what *he* had told the police. Bonilla assured him that he had told them only that he showed Jerry an office building someplace in Pleasanton and that they had parted company the evening of October 20. He had his alibi covered; it was up to Rand and Bill Nichols to get their stories synchronized.

The stack of tapes grew.

The spring of 1988 had moved into full hot summer, and even Bill Nichols vacillated. Sometimes he sounded as though he absolutely believed Steve Bonilla's delaying tactics; at other times he was full of distrust. In one call, he tried to convince Rand that the money would be forthcoming. It was just a matter of unraveling all the court hassles that Susan Harris had started, he said. In the next call, he sounded angry because he had received no money.

Rand challenged him. "You trying to tell me you *smothered* this guy and you got *no* money?"

"We'll get our money," Nichols said. "No, no—there'll be more than we thought. Hey, I told Steve I figure he owes you at least fifty thousand. You are a wealthy man. I'm owed a lot of money, and I'm going to get my money. All we got to do is get down the line here. You are completely in the clear. You are sitting pretty."

Actually, Jeff Rand was sitting in the Carson City FBI office while he talked to Bill Nichols in Los Angeles. And Nichols had once again incriminated himself on tape.

* * *

It was amusing to hear Bonilla and Nichols attempting to distance themselves from the omnipresent Jeff Rand. The two little men had needed his muscle when they set out to murder Jerry Harris, but they were frightened of him now. The investigators listening to the tapes could almost *hear* them sweat over the telephone lines. And, finally, even Nichols grew less outspoken. He spoke in cryptic phrases, having been warned, perhaps, by their fearful leader. Even so, Jeff Rand and FBI agents managed to tape three dozen conversations.

Rand had whipped both of his onetime accomplices into a panic. He reminded them often that the FBI had been to Elko and that they were still asking questions about him.

"Is Steve being watched?" Rand asked Nichols in one phone call.

"He's all right," Nichols said. "We didn't do anything wrong." Now Nichols too was trying to smooth everything over with Rand. He told him not to worry at all about the FBI sniffing around Elko, that they were only double-checking, going back over their tracks. "They're not looking that hard for anybody. Believe me, you're going to be compensated for your time."

Nichols warned Rand that it was dangerous for them to talk, even though they switched pay phones frequently. Someone could still listen in. "That's why I never say anything on the phone," he explained.

But he *had* talked over the phone, and he had spilled his guts, all unaware, and it was all on tape, black horse code and all. Diedrich, Tollefson, Goodfellow, and Whitson smiled as they listened to each tape. The net around Steven Bonilla was tightening. And he was weaving most of it with his own words.

On August 9, 1988, Jeff Rand called the number he had for Bill Nichols. Only a recording answered: "You have reached a number that has been disconnected or is no longer in service."

When he kept getting the disconnect message, he called Steve Bonilla, who pretended to be happy to hear from him. "God, I was hoping you'd call," he said.

"What's up?" Rand asked. "I got a couple of disconnected phones."

Bonilla said Nichols had moved. "He's calling me this weekend . . . and I'll have him get ahold of you," Bonilla promised.

"Where's he at?" Rand pressed. "Is he still up there with you?"

"Well, I'll have him talk to you. You just call and give me your file number and time. He'll call me Saturday and then call you Sunday. . . . You know how to use a file number, right?"

"Yeah," Rand said, "the horse."

"Right. Okay. Take care, guy."

"You too."

"All righty."

Jeff called Bonilla at his Capital Real Estate Office, as agreed, but he got only a recording. This time he was sitting beside Agent Eric Christensen at the Reno FBI office. When he called again on August 14, he got the machine again. He left his number, using the black horse code: "This is Jeff. The file number is o-e-l-a-l-a-s-a-k-l. I'll run over and get a bite to eat. I'll be back in about fifteen minutes. I can hang out maybe a half an hour. If I miss you guys, I'll get ahold of you tomorrow or the night after. All right? Try and get back to me."

They did not. Jeff left another coded phone number, o-e-l-o-r-c-s-l-e-b. This time Bonilla called him back and assured him that everything was fine, that Nichols was looking for work in construction, that everything was quiet: "I haven't heard a word. . . . I wanna say to you," he warned, "if those friends of mine [code for the FBI] ever do look you up, they're great kidders and love to buffalo you. . . . They like to talk like they got all the facts—the scoop, the skinny—and make all kind of wheels and deals, but that's what they pulled when they talked to me."

"What do you mean?" Rand asked.

"They just like to imply that they have all this information, [but] they don't."

"Well, have they been bothering you lately?"

"Haven't heard from them for four or five months," Bonilla said easily.

"Oh, yeah?"

"Not since a month after the situation."

Bonilla explained that Nichols was back at "home base," which meant Mesa, Arizona. He was changing his phone number again and listing it under K. Bonilla rather than S. Bonilla.

Steve Bonilla said that the tide was turning in his court hassles with Susan Harris, and he deplored what his attorneys were costing him. (How often had Rand heard that?) "We're going for a real aggressive move for next month," he promised. "I think we're gonna be coming out of it on the fourteenth."

By late August, Steven Bonilla was truly jittery. Rand had told him again and again that the investigators knew too much. He had long phone conversations with Rand about what they should all say if they were questioned by the police or the FBI. "They're gonna push you real hard, and they're gonna ask you some direct questions," he told Rand. "What you don't wanna do is get them into playing games. Don't start playing any fucking games with [them]."

"What do you mean?" Rand asked, playing his usual ingenuous character.

"Well," Bonilla explained, "like there's this guy over here that killed his girlfriend, and they had him pretending he was the guy—and not the guy—and they got the guy so goddamned confused, they said he confessed. And he says, 'Hell, I didn't confess. I didn't even know what I was saying.'"

Bonilla said that his plan was to send Rand to Arizona to hide out with Bill Nichols, but he didn't have the money at the moment. He was so broke he had been reduced to living with his mother. In the same breath, he assured Jeff Rand that the money was about to come through, and he went into explicit detail about how many of Susan's properties were really his.

The calls in mid-September 1988 were more frequent and much longer. Rand talked at length to both Bill Nichols and Steve Bonilla, and the black horse code numbers changed every day. The mother lode did not come through on September 14, and that appeared to break the continually optimistic spirit of the garrulous Bill Nichols. Although he assured Jeff Rand that $2 million was still waiting for them to divide, he sounded halfhearted about it on September 19. He had asked Bonilla to send him $1,600 so he could get a contractor's license.

"You know what he sent?"

"What?" Rand asked.

"A hundred and eighty dollars.... You know who's backing him?"

"No. I have no idea. Who?"

"Well, his mother.... He's real comfortable now. His mommy's wiping his ass. As long as she's wiping his little dick, that's the situation we got.... Now that I'm out of town and you're out of town, then he has no problem. He's sitting there golfing four times a week and mowing the lawn two times a week while me and you do whatever we have to do.... Meanwhile you can go fuck yourself, and I can go fuck myself. If the court has held up this thing, he went home to Mommy."

Nichols was broke. Bonilla was broke. Rand was barely scraping by. All the promises about the riches that would evolve from the murder of Jerry Harris had disappeared like smoke in a hard wind.

If there is no honor among thieves, there is even less among murderers.

Steve Bonilla had given Jeff Rand a last warning. If he was called in for questioning, he must remember to ask for an attorney. Misspeaking, Bonilla instructed, "Just say, 'I want a district attorney' or something." He had meant to say "public defender."

Jon Goodfellow smiled when he heard that particular tape. Jeff Rand already had a district attorney, whether he wanted one or not—Goodfellow himself.

That last phone tape was marked "September 19, 1988, 7:36 P.M."

PART FOUR

September 1988

24

Susan and Jerry Harris had moved into their new home in Blackhawk at the end of September 1987, and Jerry had vanished on October 20. It was now eleven months later. By September 19, 1988, every possible chink in the prosecution's case had been detected and sealed up. The three dozen tapes made by Jeff Rand told the whole story, and someday—soon, Assistant D.A. Jon Goodfellow hoped—a jury would listen to the details of a diabolical plan for murder and the alternately boastful chortlings and worried scurryings of the killers as they tried to evade detection. An arrest warrant was ready.

Two teams of lawmen from the Pleasanton Police Department; Washoe County, Nevada; Mesa, Arizona; the Alameda County D.A.'s Office; and the FBI, were lined up. Their plan was to catch Steven Bonilla and William Winifred Nichols unaware. Even as Bill Nichols and Jeff Rand had taped their last phone call, the arrest teams were preparing their game plans. They met the night of September 19 to coordinate and synchronize the arrests of the two suspects so that neither would have a chance to alert the other. The surreptitious tapes had kept the investigators informed of the day-to-day whereabouts of their quarry. Nichols had gone back home to Mesa, Arizona, to set up a contracting business that would see him through until Bonilla came through with the small fortune he had promised his number one henchman. And Steve Bonilla was indeed living in his mother's home in Mountain View, just south of Palo Alto.

Duke Diedrich and Gary Tollefson would go to Mountain View with the California team. John Whitson, the Alameda County D.A.'s investigator, and Mark Allen of the Pleasanton Police Department would be with local law enforcement officers in Mesa, Arizona.

The arrest team in Mountain View gathered before dawn on that Tuesday morning. Lieutenant Gary Tollefson would make the actual arrest; Ron Parker and Liv Flores from the Pleasanton Police Department were there, as were Special Agents Duke Diedrich and Tom Westin from the FBI, Alameda County Deputy District Attorney Jon Goodfellow, and several Mountain View uniformed officers. The California team would arrive at Ella Bonilla's house before 7:00 A.M. Bonilla, who was not known to be an early riser, would probably be asleep. They had monitored his comings and goings, and they knew that his bronze Datsun 280Z was usually parked on the street outside his mother's home in the early morning hours.

Ella Bonilla lived at 757 Leona Lane in a pleasant but hardly lavish home. With most of her assets devoured by her son's avarice, she lived where she could afford to, and records showed that this had been her home for many years. Of course, she and Primo had owned ranches, too, in the good days before the massive money drain by Steve had begun.

Gary Tollefson and FBI Agent Tom Westin prepared to knock on the front door while Agent Duke Diedrich covered the rear entrance. After a long wait, a sleepy-eyed Steve Bonilla opened the door. He looked as if he'd thrown on some clothes; his fringe of black hair was wild and uncombed. Now he woke up rapidly; he had not expected these visitors. His dark eyes widened as he saw a half-dozen lawmen on his mother's doorstep. He didn't recognize the investigators, although they had been persistent shadows in his world for a long time, watching and waiting just outside his awareness as they sewed new stitches in the net they were now dropping over him.

"Steve Bonilla," Gary Tollefson said, "I have a warrant for your arrest for the murder of Jerry Harris."

Bonilla was instantly in shock. "All the air just went out of him," Tollefson recalled. "He just melted. He never said a word; I just saw the life go out of him. He turned around, and we put the handcuffs on him."

Ella Bonilla and her physically disabled daughter were still asleep. Bonilla's own daughters, in their mid-teens, were in the house too. They clearly loved their father and sobbed as the police handcuffed him. Bonilla's closest female relatives were four more victims of his devious plots.

Steve Bonilla appeared to be the most shocked and furious to see Duke Diedrich, his longtime irritant, among the arresting officers.

"I won't minimize it," Diedrich recalled. "Arresting Bonilla was the thrill of my life. I remember standing in the kitchen with him. He was in handcuffs, and he was very angry. I walked over to him and said, 'Remember, Steve? I told you I'd be back to do this, and here I am.' He didn't say a word." Bonilla just glared at Diedrich.

Duke wanted Susan Harris to hear about the arrest from him. She had exacted a solemn promise from him a few minutes after she learned that her husband had been murdered. Duke had promised her he would get whoever killed Jerry. Now he took some delight in picking up the phone in Bonilla's home and dialing Susan's number as Steve Bonilla glowered at him. "Susan," Duke Diedrich said, "we have just arrested Steven Bonilla for Jerry's murder."

Tollefson hustled Bonilla into a squad car to be transported to the Mountain View Police Department, where Gary Tollefson once again read Bonilla his *Miranda* rights. He attempted to question him, but Bonilla had nothing to say. He had been so busy warning Jeff Rand about the games the police play that he had apparently forgotten that *he* might have to face them again. Bonilla had bragged that he never had anything to say to the police, and he still seemed to be in deep shock. Another of his master plans—perhaps his last—had gone awry. He had begun to believe that he was free and clear of the damnable investigation into Jerry's murder; it must have dawned on him, finally, that *he* had become the quarry who was stalked by police—just as he had stalked his best friend. He was taken to Alameda County's Santa Rita Jail for booking. He would later be moved to the North County Jail in Oakland.

At the same time that the Mountain View team was arresting Bonilla, another arrest was taking place hundreds of miles away. With backup from the Mesa, Arizona, tactical squad, the Alameda County D.A.'s investigator, Lieutenant John Whitson, and Detective Mark Allen of the Pleasanton Police Department were knocking on Bill Nichols's door in Mesa, Arizona, a suburb of Phoenix. Nichols, who had been convinced that he had Jeff Rand in the palm of his hand and had continually assured Jeff that they had nothing to worry about, was taken off guard, just as Bonilla had been. Whitson and Allen took Nichols to the Mesa Police Department for questioning—but he refused to give a statement. He was placed in the Maricopa County jail to await extradition to face murder charges in California.

Nichols was living with his current wife, two teenage daughters, and a young son. Like Bonilla's family, they had to watch as their husband and father was led away in handcuffs.

Steve Bonilla and William Nichols were charged with capital murder—with special circumstances: lying in wait and murder for financial gain. The special circumstances meant that the specter of the gas chamber hung over them. If they knew who had snitched on them, they didn't say.

The Jerry Harris murder story had slipped to the back pages of Bay Area papers, but suddenly it was headline news again.

"Two Held in Club Owner's Slaying—Police Arrest Partner in Mountain View," the *San Jose Mercury-News* announced above a photograph of Jerry. Although reporters clamored for details, the police would tell them little. He was thought to have been killed in Pleasanton, but the news coverage mentioned that officers from myriad jurisdictions had cooperated in the arrest of Jerry Harris's partner Steven Bonilla and a man named William Winifred Nichols in Mesa. It was anyone's guess at this point—at least anyone in the public—what the connection was between Nichols and Harris or if Nichols had even *known* Harris. Pleasanton Police Captain John Severini hinted that there might be more arrests. "The fat lady hasn't sung yet," he said enigmatically.

Since the investigators weren't talking, reporters turned to Jerry's family. None of them seemed surprised to hear that Steve Bonilla had been charged with Jerry's murder. Lila Faye Harris, Jerry's mother, said, "We were pretty certain he did it. He was the last person who saw him [Jerry]." Nevertheless, she seemed confused at the way Bonilla had changed. She recalled that when her husband had a stroke, Steve had sent "the biggest, most gorgeous bouquet. My husband was like a father figure to him." But in the next breath she said that Steve hadn't come to Jerry's funeral or sent flowers or even a sympathy card.

Jerry's brothers expressed rage and a desire "to break [Bonilla's] neck." Duke Diedrich later asked them to tone down their comments to the press.

Susan Harris had never talked to the press. Now, when it seemed that the long hard time might be coming to an end, she released a statement. Her words sounded stilted and nothing like the happy, bubbly woman Jerry had married. The year just past had taken a tremendous toll on her.

Susan named the investigators who had run Bonilla and Nichols to earth and thanked them "for their hard work and dedication to this case. The period following the loss of my husband has been a very difficult stage of adjustment for me. Not only has Jerry's everyday presence been missed, but I miss the enthusiasm for life that Jerry shared with me.

"Although nothing will replace the loss of Jerry for me, I have some consolation that those allegedly responsible for his death are being brought to justice."

Susan's reticence was due in part to the realization that they still had a long trial to go through and in part to the fact that she was moving through her days and nights in deep depression. Jerry was gone forever. She would see that he was avenged—to the degree that she was able—but beyond that, her life loomed ahead bleakly.

Ella Bonilla refused to speak to the press about her son's arrest, but an elderly neighbor woman expressed shock that "such a nice young man as Steven" should be a suspect in a murder. Steve's latest ex-wife, Ginger, gave phone interviews only. "I know it's terrible to be happy about a thing like this. But this is one lady who has been living very frightened since I heard about what happened to Jerry." She said she'd had to leave Santa Clara County because of her ex-husband's threats when the custody battle over their son grew ugly.

While Gary Tollefson was attempting to get a statement from Steve Bonilla, a team of crime scene technicians and detectives moved into Ella Bonilla's home with a search warrant. They recovered a plethora of items that might or might not be helpful in convicting Bonilla of Jerry Harris's murder. They seized piles of financial records relating to Bonilla's business dealings. Among Bonilla's papers, investigators were surprised to find that he had once been a B-52 pilot. He had bragged about a number of things that were not true, but this claim proved to be accurate.

They found nothing in the house that they could link to Jerry's murder, although they'd had only a frail hope that they would, in light of Jeff Rand's recall of how careful they had been to dispose of anything incriminating.

"There was one surprise, though," Gary Tollefson recalled. "When we processed the brown Chevy pickup truck used in the murder, our crime lab technicians were able to raise some indentations on the tailgate. It was Bill Nichols's wife's signature."

Jeff Rand had described a homemade plywood toolbox in the bed of the truck where they had put Jerry Harris, but that was gone. It would have been a rich source of direct physical evidence—but the killers had realized that, too.

"We traced ownership of that truck back to the guy Bonilla bought it from," Tollefson said, "and he described the plywood box, but we never found even a little piece of it."

It didn't really matter. The three dozen surreptitious tapes of conversations between Rand, Nichols, and Bonilla rested safely in a vault, waiting for trial. Neither Bonilla nor Nichols had any idea they existed.

Steve Bonilla appeared in Livermore-Pleasanton-Dublin Municipal Court on September 28 for formal arraignment. He was represented by Attorney Lincoln Mintz. Mintz was a large man with a prepossessing presence and a deep voice. His small client—dressed in bright-colored jail "pajamas" and minus his toupee—didn't look very dangerous, save for his continual glower.

Steven Bonilla pleaded innocent to charges of first-degree murder with special circumstances. He was denied bail and bound over until his next appearance on October 26. Ironically, Bonilla—who always had backup when he was in trouble—had no henchmen beside him. Bill Nichols was fighting extradition from Arizona, and Jeff Rand was nowhere to be seen. The media still had no idea he even existed.

On October 7, Jeff Rand turned himself in to Gary Tollefson of the Pleasanton Police Department and was booked on two counts of accessory to murder and conspiracy to commit murder. He was released on $8,000 bail.

Tollefson would say only that "It was arranged for him to come and turn himself in." He described Rand as a laborer from Nevada, but he refused to say how Rand was involved in Jerry Harris's murder. Asked if there would be further arrests, Tollefson said, "I can't be certain at this time."

Not surprisingly, reporters were frustrated. They interviewed everyone they could find who had ever known Jerry Harris or Steven Bonilla, and they came away with rumors about pyramid schemes, organized crime, and power struggles. They could not know that they were actually dealing with the simplest motive for murder since time began: one man's envy and greed.

In October 1988, Jeff Rand testified in the first of several pretrial hearings and trials. When he described the adventures and misadventures of those who had plotted to murder Jerry Harris, they sounded like nothing so much as a conspiracy of dunces—or a tale of two small-time crooks who had hitched their wagon to a falling star.

The investigators knew that Steven Bonilla had aspired to be as successful as Jerry Harris, while Jeff Rand and Bill Nichols had set their sights on having the kind of life that Steve Bonilla had. To them, Bonilla had seemed like a big man. Both Nichols and Rand had often been unemployed or had worked at low-paying jobs, and both initially believed Bonilla when he told them of his successes. He flashed rolls of bills, drove a bronze Datsun, and bragged about his conquests of beautiful women.

Rand, more than Nichols, had believed that Steve Bonilla was a powerful and wealthy man. Neither man knew going in that Ella Bonilla funded most of her son's projects. In the end, of course, they had both realized that Steve was a mama's boy. Nichols, especially, had spoken derisively of the umbilical cord attachment.

In his own world in California, Bonilla was a hanger-on, an often laughable little man looking for new ways to amass a fortune.

25

Susan Harris lived in her condominium in San Ramon for almost three years. She had moved away from the pink mansion in Blackhawk in the spring of 1988, unaware that the taping of Steven Bonilla's phone calls had begun. No one—least of all Susan—could have known how long it would actually take to bring Bonilla and Bill Nichols to trial.

In November of 1988, Bill Nichols continued to dig his heels in and fight extradition from Arizona to California. He retained an attorney who had represented him before. He understood now what "special circumstances" meant and that he might go to the gas chamber. Whatever his reasons—saving his own skin or, as he claimed, protecting his family—Bill Nichols now wanted to cut a deal with Jon Goodfellow and John Whitson. He wanted a plea bargain that would allow him to plead guilty "and take my punishment." He assured Whitson that he could lead him to the spot where he had buried the handcuffs that had encircled Jerry Harris's wrists.

A somewhat skeptical Whitson made the trip to Arizona three days before Christmas. With a Maricopa County officer along, Whitson was chained to Nichols by waist-wrist manacles. They followed Nichols's directions to a dry riverbed where he said he'd hidden the handcuffs. Whitson and the Maricopa officer dug with shovels for hours, but they found no handcuffs. Whitson wondered if they had ever been there.

Nichols had had thirteen months to come forward and tell police about the "accident" that he said had caused Jerry Harris's death, and it was now too late for his offer to help the investigators. Adding him to the roster of plea bargainers would leave only one defendant: Steve Bonilla.

On January 17, 1989, Nichols was arraigned on charges of murder and lying in wait. His preliminary hearing in the Livermore-Pleasanton-Dublin court was not until the third week of May 1989. Like Steven Bonilla, he maintained his innocence.

But Bill Nichols had not lost his wry sense of humor. When Jon Goodfellow played the FBI tapes of Nichols and Rand discussing Jerry Harris's murder, Nichols's face was a study in mixed emotions. When he heard his own voice saying to Jeff Rand, "God, I hope nobody's listening in on this. As long as they're not listening to this phone conversation, we're fine," Nichols looked at his attorney with an ironic smirk.

When Rand testified in court about how the three dozen tapes were made under the auspices of the FBI, Nichols roared, "I'm not accepting any more collect calls from you, Jeff!" Although Rand did not react, several people in the courtroom laughed.

Both accused killers were arraigned, and their preliminary hearings were finished, but Bill Nichols and Steve Bonilla would not go on trial for Jerry Harris's murder until October 1991—*four years* after Jerry died. California court dockets were crowded, and defense attorneys entered any number of motions that delayed the trial.

Jerry's parents—particularly his mother—wanted to be there in the courtroom when their son's killers went on trial. As fate would have it, they were not.

"It seemed as though Jerry's murder was just the start of so many bad things," Susan said. "While he was missing, his mom was diagnosed with breast cancer. She loved Jerry so much, probably more than anyone in the world."

During a respite in her treatment for the malignancy, a few years after their son was buried, Jim and Faye Harris went on a trip. Jim, after driving for hours, told Faye he was tired, and she offered to trade places with him. They pulled over to the side of the freeway, and Faye got out on the passenger side while Jim stepped out of the driver's seat. At that instant a dump truck with an intoxicated driver at the wheel sideswiped the Harrises' pickup. While Faye watched in horror, the truck dragged Jim and their pickup several hundred feet up the freeway. Faye Harris ran up the road, screaming hysterically. All she found of her husband was his left ring finger, still encircled by the wedding ring she had given him.

Not long after that tragedy, Faye's cancer went into the terminal stage. Without her husband, without the son who had been the center of their lives, Faye didn't have the will to fight. Neither of Jerry's parents lived to see the trial of Bonilla and Nichols.

"I was to be one of the first to testify," Susan said. "But

the defense attorney demanded that I be barred from the courtroom after that. Steve King was there most days, and my aunt Judy and uncle Mel Boyd, but I couldn't go inside the courtroom, except when I was on the witness stand.

"I wasn't even allowed to sit in the courtroom and listen to the trial," Susan said with some bitterness. "Because I was a witness, the defense wanted me out. They didn't want the jurors to watch my reactions. The jurors took a back stairway usually, but I know they saw me occasionally. I don't know if they knew who I was. My picture had never been in the newspapers."

PART FIVE

TRIAL

February 1992

26

Jury selection in Superior Court Judge Benjamin Travis's Alameda County courtroom in Oakland took almost four months, and the trial itself did not start until February 1992.

Jon Goodfellow represented the state, Lincoln Mintz was the defense attorney for Steven Bonilla, and Assistant Public Defenders Howard Harpham and Brian Pori were William Nichols's defense attorneys.

The defense attorneys' first motions were no surprise to savvy court watchers: they asked that potential witnesses be excluded from the courtroom, and they did not want the jury to see photographs of Jerry Harris's body as it appeared when he was found in the Nevada desert. Judge Travis granted the first motion and denied the second. Jon Goodfellow planned to use photographs of Jerry Harris, in life and in death, during his opening statement.

Jon Goodfellow rose to address the jury of eight men and four women for the first time. He had estimated that it would take him almost a day to bring them up to speed on this case, which was so much a part of him now that he could practically have given the details in his sleep. Jerry Harris's life and his business ventures had been complicated, but Goodfellow explained the plant rentals, the nightclubs, and Jerry and Susan's marriage. Goodfellow spent six hours or so helping the jurors understand who Jerry Harris was, who Steve Bonilla was, and who Bill Nichols was. He did a remarkable job.

245

Describing Jerry as a workaholic, Goodfellow did not deny that he had juggled his businesses and used money from one to keep another going. He read aloud the agreements Jerry had signed with Steve Bonilla. "He [Jerry] was borrowing money from whatever source he could, including Steve Bonilla's mother, and Steve really wanted back in. He wanted to be a part. He wanted to ride the train and get in there with Jerry Harris—who was now the big boy, if you will. . . . So now Steve Bonilla has got himself in as a partner to SteelFab, and he got himself in as a limited partner in Baritz."

Goodfellow pointed out that Jerry grew tired of Bonilla's interference. "Jerry Harris, quite frankly, was starting to get fairly successful on his own, and he didn't really need Steve Bonilla hanging on. And at some point he started expressing that to Steve Bonilla: 'I made you a partner in this thing, but you don't have any control.' . . . Steve would go to the Baritz after it opened . . . and he would walk around and tell everybody he was a big owner, and Jerry didn't say anything about that, but Jerry really had the control in terms of what was supposed to happen."

Using a chart, Goodfellow showed the jury where Jerry's clubs and businesses were located. The clubs were pumping out money in 1987, and Bonilla—who apparently didn't understand the difference between gross and net profits—began to feel he was being cheated. Jerry had never intended to make Bonilla a true partner, and he finally grew annoyed and told him so.

Referring to papers found in Ella Bonilla's house in the search after Steve's arrest, Goodfellow gave the jury the motive for Jerry Harris's murder: "Jerry Harris was making it perfectly clear through both his actions and the things he said to Steve Bonilla that although he thought he was going to be involved in *all* of Jerry's now successful businesses, he really wasn't. And that was evidenced by the protracted negotiations regarding the letter that was signed—the letter of understanding—and the fact that Bonilla was . . . trying to get Harris to sign full partnership papers and Harris was ducking him. He didn't want to do that. . . . Steve, if you will, was a wanna-be. He never could quite do it."

Goodfellow stressed that Jerry had always repaid Ella Bonilla, but he had come to a place where his businesses were taking off and he no longer needed Ella's money or the weight of Steve around his neck. "He is making that clear to Steve," Goodfellow told the jurors, "and Steve is not happy."

The tall prosecutor moved on to the last day of Jerry Harris's life, describing how he got up at 4:30 A.M. to go to SteelFab on Blackie Road in Castroville. Goodfellow knew this last day minute-by-minute, and he related it to the fascinated jurors. All the phone calls to Susan, to his brother. The fact that Jerry was following Steve to look at an office complex.

On that evening of October 20, Jerry Harris seemingly vanished from the face of the earth. "On the twenty-first, in the evening, Steve shows up down at the Baritz . . . and he goes in and starts acting like he has got to resolve a problem . . . and he is acting like he is a partner."

Jon Goodfellow moved on to January 10, 1988, using pictures of the grave site near Pyramid Lake, bringing the jurors closer and closer with the photographs until they are gazing at the decomposed body of the man who was once Jerry Harris. Shocked and sickened as all lay people are at the graphic sight of violent death, the jurors paled and swallowed hard.

Skillfully juxtaposing Jerry Harris's fate with the machinations of Steve Bonilla, Goodfellow read aloud a letter that Bonilla had written to the Alcoholic Beverage Control Board, complaining that he had been "manipulated, lied to and defrauded by a person that I considered to be a friend and business associate for over twenty years."

"So," Goodfellow continued, "while the coroner worked up in Reno, Washoe County, trying to identify Jerry Harris's body, Steve Bonilla was still trying to exert control over the Baritz, and one of the ways to do that was to get ahold of the ABC [Alcoholic Beverage Control] and claim there was some impropriety in the way the license was first given, and it was causing business problems for the club at that point."

Judge Travis stopped the prosecutor for the noon break.

He said, as he always would, "Have a good lunch and return at one-thirty." How could they have a good lunch after looking at the photographs of Jerry Harris's body?

When the afternoon session began, Goodfellow wove Bill Nichols and Jeff Rand into the story of what had happened to Jerry Harris. The myriad phone calls among the three conspirators were listed on a giant poster board. Seeing the perfect trail he had left, Bonilla—the man who had never been without a phone at his elbow—must have winced inwardly.

"This card shows a listing of phone calls that were made from various numbers, records that were obtained at some later point in the investigation, showing particular phone numbers of significance and locations where there were calls. This column here"—Goodfellow gestured—"shows the receiving person, and this, this is the destination number."

The charting began in August 1987 and continued to the night Jerry Harris was murdered—and beyond.

Jon Goodfellow described the plotting, the bungled attempts, the cowardly ambush, and the cruel death of Jerry Harris. It seemed then, as it always would, impossible that a timid Svengali and two clumsy, drunk "hit men" could actually have carried off the murder of a man as quick on his feet as Jerry Harris clearly was. But the jurors had seen him in death. They knew it had really happened.

Goodfellow read the agreement signed on April 12, 1988, by Jeff Rand. If he lied in any aspect to law officers or to a jury, after that date, he would be prosecuted to the full extent of the law. If he told the truth and helped to trap his co-conspirators, he would be allowed to plead guilty to conspiracy to commit murder and accessory to murder, and would serve a maximum of three years in prison. The prosecutor explained that Rand was a vital component in arresting Nichols and Bonilla.

"The evidence that they [Washoe County authorities] had was really only against Jeff Rand," Goodfellow said. "There was no evidence to link Bill Nichols or Steve Bonilla to this crime other than the fact that Bill Nichols and Steve Bonilla were together on December 30, 1987, at the Baritz." That was the night Bonilla tried to change the locks on Susan's club. It was also the night that police stopped a car near the Baritz, checked the ID of the occupants, and found one of the passengers to be William Winifred Nichols.

Jon Goodfellow promised the jurors that they would hear tapes of phone calls among the two defendants and Jeff Rand, made over a six-month period. He read selections from two of those calls aloud, and the gist of them left little doubt that Bonilla, Nichols, and Rand had plotted Jerry Harris's murder and then spent the next year trying to evade arrest.

"This wasn't any kind of unintentional killing or anything else," Goodfellow said forcefully. "This was a setup. And it was executed at the behest of Steve Bonilla. He hired these two thugs to do it—Jeff Rand and Bill Nichols. . . . It is very important for you to listen to all the evidence, because it is going to be a puzzle. And every piece of the puzzle is significant. When the puzzle is all done, and when you are ready to take this case, after you have heard all the evidence, it is going to be clear to you that the murder of Jerry Harris was, in fact, planned, thought out, and it was a hit planned by Steve Bonilla and carried out by his pals. It was a hit for money. As simple as that."

The jury left the courtroom at ten minutes to four on this first day of the trial. Susan spent a nervous night; she would be the first witness in the morning.

The next day Jon Goodfellow told the jurors they would hear from the victim's widow, Susan Harris. She did a superb job of remembering the life she had once lived and in recounting the last time she heard her husband's voice. She was not shaken by the long cross-examination by the defense attorneys. She knew what she knew: the truth. It felt cleansing to her finally to be able to speak for Jerry.

And then she was banished to a bench in the hall while the rest of the trial proceeded, even though, in many states, families of murder victims are guaranteed a place in the courtroom, whether they are witnesses for the prosecution or not. "I couldn't hear what they were saying in there about the murder of the most important person in my life," she recalled. "I peeked through the little glass pane in the door and wished I could read lips. I remember the first time I saw the jury. I looked at them—all complete strangers—and I realized that they were going to judge Jerry and me and weigh that against those two men sitting at the defense table. It was weird to comprehend that."

Susan's aunt Judy and Steve King were allowed in the courtroom, however, and they filled her in on what was happening.

At one point in the trial, Susan stopped in the district attorney's office. Before anyone could cover them up, she saw some photographs on a desk. "What are these?" she asked, picking them up.

They were the last pictures ever taken of Jerry. The crime scene pictures. The autopsy pictures.

Her knees buckled, but she took a deep breath. "It's okay," she said. "I'm okay. I wanted to see them, and I'm not sorry."

For the first time in a long time, Susan was not working twelve- to eighteen-hour days. She had finally closed the doors on the Alameda Hot Rod Cafe, also known as Hot Rod Cafe II, at 2203 Mariner Square Loop, at the end of January 1992. Then, only days before she testified, a mysterious fire destroyed the club—on Valentine's Day. Reports that the Hot Rod Cafe was burning came in at 1:30 A.M. Six fire units were dispatched to the scene. They had the fire "tapped"—under control—by 2:30 A.M.

In some ways Susan saw the fire as the irrevocable end of Jerry's dream. His wonderful 1950s memorabilia were reduced to ashes, and the roof came down in several places. Deputy Chief Paul Barneich said that the origin of the fire was under investigation and that his department had asked for help from the arson team of the Bureau of Alcohol, Tobacco and Firearms.

"I was a suspect, of course," Susan said wearily. "I wasn't even surprised this time. I guess I got a little wiser over the years. John Jacques, who had been one of Jerry's top club managers, was working for the fire department by that time. He knew me, and he knew I had nothing to gain from the fire at Hot Rod Alameda. He helped to clear me of any suspicion."

Susan no longer owned the club; she had no insurance on it. It saddened her to see it go. But by this time she was spending her days sitting outside the courtroom where Steven Bonilla and William Nichols were on trial for Jerry's murder.

Arson investigators believed that the fire had started outside a rear door of the club. A police officer reported that he had smelled a flammable liquid at the point of origin. Damage was estimated to be at least $500,000.

Witness after witness agreed that Steve Bonilla's motivation to take Jerry Harris's life was even stronger than his greed. His envy was overweening and malevolent. One man who had known both Bonilla and Harris summed the situation up succinctly: "Everybody liked Jerry, and nobody liked Bonilla. You'd be with Steve for five minutes and you couldn't stand him. Jerry felt sorry for Steve, and he kind of took him under his wing."

Jeff Rand was on the witness stand for more than two weeks. He was free on bail, but he was escorted to the courtroom each day by an FBI agent. He was, as was to be expected, fair game for the defense attorneys. Their clients faced the gas chamber, and Rand had plea-bargained his risk down to three years in prison. And yet his testimony had the ring of truth to it. Both Rand and Jon Goodfellow knew that the tapes were coming. And they knew what was on them—enough incriminating evidence to convict Bonilla and Nichols three times over.

The tapes spoke for themselves. Three dozen surreptitious tapes on which the three men who had planned and carried out Jerry Harris's murder discussed the crime itself in code, worried about when they would come into their huge fortune from his clubs, and tried to make their alibis consistent in case they were questioned by the investigators. It was implicit in the tapes that Jeff Rand would be expendable if he became a loose cannon. Bonilla and Nichols obviously hadn't known that he had already gone over to the other side.

27

The defense attorneys began their case in the first part of April 1992. Steven Bonilla took the witness stand and broke one of the cardinal rules of a defense case. By testifying on direct examination by Lincoln Mintz, Bonilla opened himself up to cross-examination by Jon Goodfellow. He denied that a kidnaping, much less a murder, had been planned. Bonilla said that Jeff Rand had suddenly attacked Jerry Harris—unexpectedly and violently. Rand had sprayed something in Jerry's face.

"I didn't understand what was going on," Bonilla testified, his face a mask of total innocence. "I was a little bit shocked. Jeff and Jerry physically got into it. They made contact, and at that time I left. I turned and went toward my Monte Carlo. . . . It happened so fast. I remember seeing Jeff spray Jerry and I looked back at Bill. I took my eyes off it and how they were entangled. I don't know how to describe it. Things got crazy."

Steve Bonilla reacted as he always had when things got rough: he ran. "I guess I just reacted," he told the jurors. "Whether in fear or not understanding, it was my impulse to get out of there."

He insisted that he had nothing at all to gain from Jerry Harris's death. "That didn't enter my mind."

Still maintaining his puzzled demeanor, Bonilla said he really hadn't known what had happened until he received a phone call from Bill Nichols in the middle of the night. "He let me know there had been an accident. I asked what was the accident, and he didn't want to talk on the phone. . . . I heard Jeff in the background saying, 'Tell him not to say anything about us.' "

Steve Bonilla said he did not call the police that night or later because he was afraid that Rand might harm him or his family.

Piously denying that he would ever have arranged the murder of his friend, Bonilla did admit that he had planned the meeting that led to the "accident" and Jerry's death. He said he had lied to Jerry and told him he wanted to show him office space at the business park. Bonilla testified that there was $100,000 missing from a business account where he was a partner, and he wanted to talk to Jerry about it. He needed the money so he could invest in a tile business with Bill Nichols. He had no idea that Jerry would be roughed up at the meeting. He certainly would never have set him up for a kill.

His position was that Jerry Harris had stolen from him, held back money that was due him. Bonilla claimed that when Bill Nichols pressured him about the money for the tile business and Bonilla explained what the holdup was, Nichols said, "Let me talk to him."

Nichols assured him, Bonilla said, that he could persuade Jerry to pay up. His "collection" talent was the only reason Bill Nichols had flown to San Jose so often.

Lincoln Mintz veered away from Bill Nichols and questioned Steve Bonilla about the woman he wrote to in Denver. It was apparent that Mintz was attempting to show that Bonilla was an easy mark. "How did you establish a friendship with her?" he asked Steve.

"Through correspondence—letter writing."

"Who wrote to who first?"

"I wrote to her first. I wanted to meet somebody from the Midwest."

Mintz had to virtually drag from Bonilla the admission that he had found the woman's address in a "body exchange" magazine. "Okay," Mintz said, "so she was someone who was advertising in a magazine for men to write to her?"

"Yes."

"Over what period of time did you write to her?"

"Year and a half."

Bonilla said that he and Leah had talked on the phone and had established a "personal relationship."

"Did you send her money?"

"Yes, on several occasions."

"How much money did you send, all told?"

There was a long pause as the courtroom quieted. "It's hard to say. The last time I sent her money," Bonilla testified, "was before I went on vacation. I sent her five hundred dollars."

"Why did you go to Colorado?"

"She was having problems at work, financial problems, and wrote me a letter saying that she would like to borrow some money from me. . . . There were problems in her not getting her check at work . . . and there was nobody else she could turn to. If I would lend her the money, she would definitely pay me back. . . . After I sent the money, she called and thanked me. I started getting a guilt complex that maybe that wasn't enough. Maybe she was having a rough time, you know."

Bonilla said that he had planned a hunting trip that fall with Jerry's father, Jim, and some other friends, but he was worried about Leah in Denver. So he had canceled his deer-hunting trip and decided to go to Denver to see if Leah was all right.

"Did you let her know you were coming?"

"No," Bonilla said.

"Was your interest in her romantic?"

"Somewhat, yes." He said they had exchanged photographs. They had discussed Leah's coming to California to live.

"So you figured you would pop in on her?"

". . . I went to Denver."

"Did you see her there?"

"No . . . I went to the address she had given me, and I talked to the lady that lived in that house, who was a friend of hers. She moved in with the lady who was a friend of her mother. She knew the mother from the time when she had lived in Missouri," Bonilla explained ponderously while court watchers stifled smiles. "But she had only gone over there after she had had problems in the apartment. . . . I'm not quite sure if she got kicked out from her girlfriend's or they had stole her money or what happened . . . and I also had the address of this woman's house, which was the last one that she had gone to stay with when she hit bottom."

"Where had you sent the five hundred dollars to?"

"To this address where the woman lived."

"Did you mail a check?"

"Cash."

"You mailed five hundred dollars in cash in a plain brown envelope?" Mintz asked incredulously.

"Yes."

"Why did you do that?"

"I had sent her checks before, but she had no way of cashing checks."

Mintz asked his client if the woman at the house in a Denver suburb might not have been Leah. "Did her voice sound familiar?"

"No. I told her who I was. She knew who I was, exactly. . . . She said, 'I would have more than gladly kept her [Leah] here, but you can see I have a small house. I'm barely making it with my two kids. But I'm sure not going to throw her out in the streets . . . she waited desperately until she got that money from you . . . and she was able to start over again.' And, in fact, I guess a couple of friends talked her into going away that particular week on a camping trip, just to get her mind back straight."

The woman was very concerned about his having come so far, Bonilla testified. "She says, 'You know, where are you staying? Let me see if I can get ahold of her, because she checks in with me.'"

There was a long pause. Finally Jon Goodfellow asked, "Is there a question pending?"

"No," Judge Travis said, "I don't think so."

The courtroom exploded with laughter.

"Did you ever talk to her again?" Mintz asked Steve Bonilla.

"Yes, she called—the next morning."

"Did you get together?"

"No, she was out camping."

"Did you *ever* get together?"

"No . . . she was having a rough time, and she had moved away to Missouri. . . . She moved back with her father. And when she moved back with her father, I never talked to her again."

If Lincoln Mintz had set out to show that Bonilla was gullible, he had succeeded. The little man in the bad toupee had been taken by one of the oldest games around. But that did not mean he hadn't plotted to kill Jerry Harris. He said he had called Jeff Rand on the trip back home only because Bill Nichols wanted him to—to help set up the tile business they were all so anxious to establish in California. All of the meetings, all of the trips that Bill Nichols and Jeff Rand had made to California, all of the attempts to contact Jerry Harris, now had another explanation: Bonilla insisted that he had been in touch with Nichols and Rand solely to start a tile business. Yes, he needed the $100,000 he insisted Jerry Harris owed him—but that was for the tile business too.

And Bill Nichols was simply supposed to *talk* to Jerry, to convince him that it would be wise for him to pay Steve the money. It was almost as if Steve Bonilla had not sat in that very courtroom and heard the thirty-six tapes where his own voice clearly implicated himself in the murder of his "best friend" and of how he planned to take control of everything Jerry had worked for.

When Jon Goodfellow finally had his chance to question the defendant, he referred to Bonilla's claim that he had taken Jerry Harris to the Hacienda Business Park on a ruse, simply to give Bill Nichols a chance to speak to Jerry about the $100,000.

"Okay," Goodfellow said with just the right touch of incredulity in his voice, "so part of the way this was supposed to happen was: Bill Nichols was going to tell Jerry Harris, 'I'm not a real estate agent. You are not here to look at a building. I'm here to talk to you about $100,00 that you owe Steve Bonilla'?"

"That was my assumption," Bonilla murmured.

"And that didn't strike you as odd in any way?"

"I don't know what is normal when you are talking about misappropriation of funds."

"Is that a yes or a no?"

"Yes and no."

"Had you ever talked to anybody that owed you some money in this fashion before?"

"Which fashion are you referring to?" Since Bonilla clearly had no acceptable answers to the prosecutor's questions, he waffled and pretended not to follow Goodfellow's line of thinking.

"That is," Goodfellow said slowly, "take him out to a vacant building and have some friends meet him and talk to him?"

"I don't recall ever doing it before."

Responding to Goodfellow's questions, Bonilla once more testified that he saw Jeff Rand spray something in Jerry Harris's face, but he had said nothing to any of the other three men in the dark parking lot.

"So let me get this straight," Goodfellow said, "your *best* friend is being sprayed in the face with something and you don't *say* anything?"

"That's right."

"Then the next thing that happens is that they are somehow entangled?"

"I have a better recollection today than when I testified the other day. I have thought about it more since then. I guess I kind of blocked it out of my mind."

"Last week you called it an entanglement. I believe you testified you looked over and somehow their bodies were in contact and they were entangled. . . . And then immediately after that, you said you got in your car and left?"

"Yes."

"But today, after having thought about it, you have a more clear recollection of exactly what happened? Tell us what *did* you see?"

"After the spray, I left in the car. The entanglement that I was trying to recall the other day is . . . as I was *pulling out,* Jerry and Jeff were on the ground."

"Okay. So you saw Jeff Rand spraying something in Jerry's face . . . and at that point you turned to go to your car?"

"Yes."

"Because you didn't want to see what was happening. Is that right?"

"I left. I panicked. I don't know. I left."

Bonilla bowed his head as he once more described Jerry Harris as his best friend whom he made no effort to help. He denied that he was crying, but it seemed a token effort at remorse. The last time he had seen Jerry, he was down on the ground with Jeff Rand, a massive man, over him. Bonilla said he went home and went to bed—but he "worried." He testified that when Bill Nichols called to tell him there had been an "accident," he still didn't suspect that his "best friend" was dead, nor did he when Susan called him the next morning. Yes, he had sworn on his father's grave to Jerry's brother that he had no idea where Jerry was. Yes, he might have been mistaken about the address of the office complex that he gave to Sandy Harris and, a few days later, to Duke Diedrich.

Steven Bonilla was not a convincing witness. His denials and explanations sounded patently ridiculous. The man who had seemed dapper and confident at the beginning of Mintz's direct examination mopped sweat from his face as he finally stepped from the witness chair.

On April 16, after two months of testimony, Jon Goodfellow replayed some of the damning phone tapes during his final argument. The prosecutor said the tapes told it all. "This case is not a whodunit," Goodfellow said scathingly, "but a whatisit. It's a classic first-degree murder—a planned, willful, deliberate, premeditated hit. And clearly, from what you heard on the tapes, it was murder for financial gain. Everybody was making money off it."

It was apparent that Jon Goodfellow had spent years committing even the tiniest aspect of Jerry Harris's murder investigation to memory. What separated him from a pedestrian prosecutor was his ability to relate its unfolding in a crystal-clear narrative manner. Sometimes he was folksy; more often he was riveting as he pulled in all the stray threads of a tapestry that led from Jerry Harris's glory days inexorably to the moment he died, choking on Mace and his own vomit, his head swathed in gray duct tape, his hands cuffed—while Steven Bonilla sped from the scene and let his hired killers do his tragic dirty work.

Goodfellow had not missed the defense's attempt to show the killers as stupid bumblers. "What we see in this courtroom is that people do something and they get tripped up and they do get caught, in fact," he said. "So then you have a bunch of defense lawyers saying, 'See how stupid it was? They got caught.'"

Goodfellow admitted that many sophisticated killers were never prosecuted, but he reminded the jurors that even klutzy killers sometimes succeeded. "People thought the plan to kill Abraham Lincoln was a pretty silly plan. Nevertheless, it worked. Going into a theater in front of everybody and jumping down on the stage and running out, breaking your leg. Yeah, maybe it was pretty silly—but it was pretty deadly. That does not equate to a lack of premeditation, a lack of deliberation, a lack of preplanning. Quite the contrary."

In his final arguments, Lincoln Mintz blamed Bill Nichols for Jerry Harris's murder. "There is far more motive for Nichols and Rand to have Jerry Harris dead and Steven Bonilla as the last person to have seen him, than to have Jerry Harris dead at all. There is no way Steven Bonilla can say a word to anyone without burying himself. Nichols and Rand got a sugar daddy by taking out Jerry Harris and having Steven Bonilla on the hook for it."

William Nichols's attorney, Howard Harpham, blamed Jeff Rand for Jerry Harris's murder.

On Wednesday, April 22, 1992, the jury began deliberations. On Thursday afternoon they asked to hear a transcript of Jeff Rand's testimony. The wait was agonizing, particularly when the jury suspended deliberations from Friday through Monday.

On Wednesday, April 29, the jurors asked for more explication of a point made in the trial. Then they returned to their deliberations. It didn't look promising for the prosecution; the jurors had been out far too long.

Finally, on Thursday afternoon, April 30, Foreman Mark Schmoes signaled the judge that they had reached a verdict.

There was a hush in Judge Ben Travis's courtroom, and then Schmoes read the verdicts aloud. The jury had found both defendants guilty of first-degree murder. They also found Bill Nichols and Steve Bonilla guilty of two special circumstances—lying in wait, and committing the murder of Jerry Harris for financial gain. Lincoln Mintz and Howard Harpham asked that the jury be polled. One by one the jurors affirmed their decision by answering "True."

Steven Bonilla had turned pale. He was totally stunned by the verdict.

In this bifurcated trial—a guilt or innocence phase followed by a penalty phase—Steven Bonilla and Bill Nichols now faced the possibility of the death penalty. It was up to the same jury that had just found them guilty to decide their punishment.

Steve King, Jerry's longtime friend—his Santa Claus in the good days—told reporters he was greatly relieved. "Now the healing can begin for those of us who knew Jerry."

Susan left without fanfare. She had nothing to say to reporters. Jerry had been dead for four and a half years: his mother and father were gone, too. She felt numb.

28

The penalty phase of the Bonilla-Nichols trial began on May 18, 1992. When jurors deliberate the question of life or death for convicted defendants, they may be given more information than they received during the first phase of the trial. Now Jon Goodfellow would be allowed to mention "prior bad acts" that Bonilla and Nichols had committed, so that the jury could see that murdering Jerry Harris was not out of character for them.

Steve Bonilla, annoyed with Lincoln Mintz because he had been found guilty of first-degree murder, told Judge Travis that he was dismissing Mintz; he was going to represent himself. Mintz, who may have wanted to be free of Bonilla, nevertheless argued that it was his duty to continue. Judge Travis refused to let Bonilla fire his attorney, ruling that he could not capriciously dismiss legal counsel in an untimely manner in the middle of trial.

They began the process of deciding whether Bonilla and Nichols should live or die. It seemed as if they were finally nearing the end of a marathon run.

Jon Goodfellow described Jerry's phenomenal success in business. Bonilla, on the other hand, had several businesses fail. With money from his mother, Bonilla had invested in Jerry's businesses, but arguments over Baritz had caused dissension between them. "He sees the gold ring out there," Goodfellow said, "and it's going to be taken away from him by Jerry Lee Harris. That is where his plot starts—to murder Jerry Harris."

There in that Alameda Superior Courtroom, Jon Goodfellow once more told the jurors the story of the stalking of Jerry Harris and of the final terrible moments when he fought to breathe as Mace and duct tape shut off his airway. Goodfellow also told them of how Jerry's car was parked at the Sacramento Airport as his killers carried him toward a lonely grave in Nevada.

It was an ugly plot, vicious and clumsy. Jerry Harris was murdered and left in his shallow grave. Only coyotes and torrential rains had exposed him to the surface and drawn the Washoe County detectives.

But, Goodfellow stressed, the murder of Jerry Harris was by no means the first time Steve Bonilla and Bill Nichols had joined up to practice violence. Ten years before they killed Jerry Harris, Bonilla had hired Nichols and Jeff Rand to get rid of his ex-wife and her new husband.

The jurors exchanged glances.

Nichols had designed a bomb, Goodfellow explained, and Rand was supposed to plant it under their car. But

Rand, his conscience nagging him, had dismantled the fuse so that it wouldn't go off.

"Steve Bonilla didn't know the bomb wouldn't go off," Goodfellow said. "He allowed his own daughters to get in that car, thinking that it was about to blow up."

Jeff Rand now testified that he had planted a bomb, built by Bill Nichols, under Flora Bonilla's car. He also told the jury that he and Ponytail Willie were once sent to kill a bar owner in Verdi. He had, in fact, begun getting requests from Bonilla and Nichols to murder people since 1979.

One of the witnesses who testified during the penalty phase was Steve Bonilla's most recent ex-wife, Ginger Bonilla. She had lived with the knowledge that Steve had once tried to bomb the car owned by his *first* ex-wife. He had enjoyed telling Ginger the details. He had not seemed fazed by the knowledge that if the bomb had exploded, his own daughters would probably have been killed along with his ex-wife.

Ginger felt safer now than she ever had, and she told of the time when she believed that she, too, was going to fall victim to Bonilla. She spoke about a time three months after their January 1979 marriage. She had done something to annoy Steve, and he put a gun in her mouth and threatened to pull the trigger. Under cross-examination, Ginger said that she did not call the police because she was still trying to save her new marriage. "I really wasn't one to talk about it," she said. "It was a problem I was trying to solve myself."

She did call authorities, she said, when she discovered that Steve was plotting to kill his first ex-wife, Flora Bonilla Blume, and her new husband. Ginger Bonilla testified that she had been present at a meeting with Steve Bonilla, Jeff Rand, and William Nichols. This was a test run for some blasting caps that Rand was to use when he put the bomb under Flora's car. "They practiced setting them off in the driveway," Ginger said. "I called the police after Jeff left with the bomb," she testified, "but they said there was nothing they could do about it."

Jeff Rand had already told the jury about the aborted

bombing of Flora Bonilla Blume, but Ginger's testimony accentuated the cold-blooded aspect of it.

Character witnesses for Steven Bonilla were difficult to find. Two men he had befriended in the Santa Rita Jail extolled his good qualities. "I was nervous and confused," one man said. "Steve told me everything is not as bad as it seems."

Others said he had urged them to stay off narcotics and to study computers.

A man who had known Bonilla in Fremont described him as "a saint as far as his relationships with his kids."

Rebecca,* Bonilla's sister, admitted that her brother might have been involved in something illegal, but she said he was incapable of killing anyone. Tearfully she said, "He can't even kill a deer, and you think he's going to kill a human person?"

Rebecca, who needed crutches to walk because of her cerebral palsy, said she needed her brother to stay alive. "He can still help me over the phone and give me advice. Ever since he's been in jail, he's still alive, he can continue to do that."

Ella Bonilla took the stand to defend her son. "I know my son. He wouldn't do that," she said.

Steven Bonilla's twenty-year-old daughter, Pamela,* said she "believed with all my heart" that her father had not killed Jerry Harris. She recalled that after Jerry disappeared, her father was very worried about his daughters' safety. "Kit* and I were not allowed to leave the house by ourselves or be in public by ourselves. . . . He thought the same people that came after Jerry might come after us."

It was very sad. These women who loved Steven Bonilla seemed blinded to the truth. They had rearranged stark facts so that they could live with them.

Pamela Bonilla testified that she knew her father had put a bomb under her mother's car in the late 1970s, when Pamela, who often rode in that car, was only seven years old. Her mother had told her, and sometime later, she had asked her father about it. "I believe he said he was very upset at the time," she testified, "and he [said] he wasn't thinking straight. As soon as he knew what he was doing, he took it out."

This was apparently enough explanation for Bonilla's daughter, and she had forgiven him.

William Nichols had daughters too—Lianna,* age twenty-one, and Madonna,* nineteen. He had been divorced from their mother, one of his many wives, and he had not had much of a relationship with his daughters, but now he needed them badly. And they came forward to testify for a father they barely knew. "Of course he can contribute to my life," Madonna said, "just by being alive so I can talk to him, and I'd like to get to know him. I love him very much." She said that he had called and written to her since his arrest for murder. "He's shown great interest in my schooling and personal life. He's just a typical dad."

A typical dad in prison for murder, perhaps. A typical dad who had suddenly realized he had daughters. Madonna—who wanted to be a stuntwoman in the movies, just as her dad had once been a stuntman—said he had written her from jail and sent her drawings and instructions on how to perform stunts. "But it's not just stunts," she said. "I want to see him. I want to come visit him. I need a dad. I never had a chance to be close to him and I want a chance."

Their mother, Damiana,* also testified during this penalty phase—in an attempt to save the life of a man she had once loved. "The Bill Nichols I know, who used to write poetry as a young man, has a lot of things inside him. I believe Bill Nichols is the only one who can bring them [his children] through this."

Oddly, Nichols's two ex-wives fought to save his life, but his current wife did not testify. Perhaps time had dimmed the memories of the dark side of being married to Bill Nichols for the women who came forward to try to save him.

One interesting character witness was a "Hollywood producer" who said he was working with Bill on a movie proposal based on Nichols's involvement in the Harris murder.

Finally the time came to sum up, and final arguments in the penalty phase began.

Lincoln Mintz told the jury that Jon Goodfellow was trying to make them believe that their decision to give his client less than the death penalty would signify their approval of the scheme to murder Jerry Harris.

"Jon Goodfellow would have you believe that Steven Bonilla's entire life is a cesspool of criminality. There is more to his life than that, and it's worthy of being spared."

Goodfellow responded that the jury could well feel sorry for the children of Bonilla and Nichols. "The kids of William Nichols had no choice who their father would be. Rebecca Bonilla comes and cries for her brother. It touched us all . . . but it has nothing to do with Steven Bonilla or William Nichols."

Goodfellow urged the jury to feel sorry also for Jerry Harris's family. "These two defendants have destroyed three families all on their own. They destroyed their own and they destroyed the Harris family."

Tiffany Harris, Jerry's daughter, broke into loud sobs as Jon Goodfellow described her father's murder and burial in the desert.

Goodfellow recalled the times Steve Bonilla had tried to kill one of his ex-wives, had stuck a loaded gun in another ex-wife's mouth, and he spoke of Nichols's violent fights with his wife. "Enough is enough," he warned. "They are going to spin their web and create criminal enterprises in jail or out of jail."

Jon Goodfellow's voice was full of conviction as he told the jury that Steven Bonilla and William Nichols deserved the death penalty for the murder of Jerry Harris. "I submit to you that what these two defendants have done since 1979 has been social anarchy. They have done any damn thing they pleased. And they can't care about the consequences. They don't care if they blow up a car with two or three people in it, with Steve Bonilla's *kids* in it, if it means getting his goals accomplished. Bill Nichols doesn't care about that as long as he is a paid hit man."

Referring to Bonilla's attempt during the penalty phase to be found mentally ill, Goodfellow said, "There is no evidence of that. Steven Bonilla is sick. . . . He may be a sociopath. Bill Nichols may be a sociopath—but they are not *sick*."

Howard Harpham continually reiterated that William Nichols was not "the worst of the worst" and that he could counsel his fellow prisoners—a thought that might give one pause. Harpham cited infamous killers, including Charles Manson, and suggested that they were far worse than Bill Nichols.

One thing worried Jon Goodfellow more than any other; he had seen the way Steve Bonilla could manipulate other people. He reminded the jurors that Bonilla had brought in two fellow inmates from his "pod" to talk about what "a great guy he was in jail with them—gave them extra supplies. Let me suggest something else to you: now he has somebody else on the outside. Does Steve Bonilla need to be in jail or out of jail to hire people to kill?

"Of course not. . . . Are the people in jail, the people who work in the jail, that work in the prison, the other inmates within the general population who are eventually going to get out—is *anybody* safe with him around? 'Mr. Hirer.' He has had a pattern of anybody who crosses him in life he tries to eliminate. Who's next?"

If Bonilla was sentenced to life in prison, Goodfellow suggested, he had nothing whatsoever to lose, no matter what he might do. "Mr. Head-of-All-These-Criminal-Enterprises can sit in jail and pull his strings again."

No, only a death sentence would ensure that Steven Bonilla would not continue to play his murderous games of revenge.

The jury retired to deliberate. It seemed that the long ordeal was almost over. But on Friday, June 26, as the jurors were taking a final vote, writing "life" or "death" on slips of paper, the twelfth man paused. Instead of dropping his slip of paper in the voting box, he crumpled it and dropped it on the floor. He could not vote for the death penalty.

The jury reported that they were deadlocked at eleven to one in favor of the death penalty. Although the jury tried mightily to agree and had asked to deliberate well past their usual adjournment the day before, they could not sway the sole holdout.

Superior Court Judge David Lee, filling in for Judge Ben Travis, who had been called away, declared a mistrial. Jaws gaped. The trial of Steve Bonilla and William Nichols had begun in October 1991 and it had dragged on for eight months, with preliminary motions taking three of those months. The jury had begun hearing evidence in February. It was galling to think that it was not really over yet. It was almost as if they would be trying this case forever, on a treadmill to nowhere.

Bonilla and Nichols *had* been found guilty of murder; only their punishment remained to be decided.

Jon Goodfellow told reporters that he expected that he would have to present much of the evidence from the guilt phase again, including countless hours of taped conversations. The prosecutor hoped he would draw Judge Travis again; that would, hopefully, shorten the retrial.

Susan Harris was beyond shock; it had gone on for so long. While she waited for still another trial for her husband's killers, she filed a civil wrongful death suit against Steven Bonilla. This would effectively tie up any money he had access to. The money didn't matter to her; making Bonilla pay for what he had done to Jerry, and pay where it hurt him most, did.

Tentatively, Susan Harris began to live again. Without Jerry. She remembered Jon Goodfellow's words, though. Sometimes, when it was very dark and she was alone, they came back to her: "They are going to spin their webs and create criminal enterprises in jail or out of jail."

29

Susan's sister, Julie, was divorced in 1992. "I felt so bad for her," Susan said. "I didn't want my sister to be living alone, so I rented a house for both of us in Fremont."

Julie and Susan moved in together. They had every reason to believe that the worst was over. Only the second penalty phase trial lay ahead, and Susan was confident that the next jury would agree on the death penalty for Steven Bonilla. Whatever they decreed, she knew Steve would be locked away for a long, long time—until she was an old woman.

The two sisters looked more like twins—tall and slender and pretty, with long blond hair and blue eyes. They bought bicycles and whizzed around their neighborhood, enjoying the freedom all the more because both their lives had been affected by the threat of violence from Steve Bonilla.

It was May of 1993, and Steven Bonilla and William Nichols had been convicted almost a year before. They faced a retrial on the penalty phase and still might be executed, although the Alameda County courts were so jammed up with felony cases that it was anyone's guess when the second penalty phase might begin. Still, they *were* locked up in the Alameda North County Jail in Oakland, and no longer a danger.

"We had lived in that house for about a year," Susan recalled, "and I'd sold the Fremont Hot Rod about six months before. I hated to do it, but I had to. I had just found a job in sales, selling advertising. I hadn't even started yet."

One evening, Julie and Susan had just come home after riding bikes when there was a knock on the door. They both froze, still cautious after so many years in hiding. No one but really close friends knew their address. Susan looked through the peephole in the door and saw a very well dressed black man standing there.

"I just opened the door," Susan said. "I figured he was selling something, and I didn't want to be rude. I probably opened it *because* he was a black man and I didn't want to act prejudiced."

As she opened the door a few inches, she noticed that the man had both his hands behind his back. "Does Susan Harris live here?" he asked politely.

"No," Susan lied, already feeling a familiar dread creep up the back of her neck.

"Well, according to my information, she owns this house, and she lives here," he said in the same pleasant tone.

"I don't know where you get your information," Susan said, sorry that she had opened the door. *"I* rent this house."

The man stared at her, his expression one of disbelief. She thought that he was probably a process server. Over the past half dozen years she had been served with papers often enough.

"Well," Susan stalled, "I can get you the number of the rental agent. If you tell me what it is you're here for, I'll try to help."

The man just stood there with his hands behind his back, saying nothing. The seconds yawned.

Julie Hannah was watching through the crack in the open door. She was very uneasy; she thought the conversation through the door had gone on much too long. She was poised for action if she had to help Susan fight.

"Then he whipped his hand out," Susan remembered, "and I couldn't see what he had in it. I was trying to get the door closed."

She expected to be shot or to feel a knife plunge into her. There was no time to run—no place to run. Then suddenly a brilliant white light half blinded her.

"He took my picture," she said.

Susan had long since learned to take action and not to accept whatever happened passively. She always kept a notepad and pencil near the door. "Julie was a runner, and she still had her sneakers on from riding bikes. I handed her the pencil and paper and told her, 'Julie, get his license number!' I shouldn't have done that, probably, but I wanted to know who he was and why he wanted a picture of me."

When Julie rushed outside, she saw the stranger already across the street, way ahead of her. "She paced him, hiding behind trees and bushes so he didn't know she was there," Susan said. "It was a huge neighborhood, but there was only one real exit. Julie knew that he would have to leave that way. She cut around and waited at the entrance, hiding behind a bush.

"She got his license number," Susan said. "And then she actually snuck out behind his car in the middle of the street to double-check. She thought he had seen her, and it made her nervous. And she was taking so long that I was scared for her, so I ran out and met her halfway. And she said, 'I *got* it!'"

Susan called the police, fearing that they would think she was paranoid. When the patrolmen showed up, she told them the whole story. When they heard that her husband had been murdered six years earlier and that she had been stalked before, they paid attention. Susan had a perfect description of the photographer, and Julie had committed to memory all of the information about his car.

The man had been so clean-cut. He hadn't looked dangerous when Susan peeked through her door. But something was wrong. Someone wanted to know what she looked like. Instantly she was drawn back into her fear response.

Even with Bonilla and Nichols in jail, it wasn't over yet.

Duke Diedrich and his wife had asked Susan and Julie to go with them to Sunday brunch a few days after the phantom photographer incident. But for some reason Duke called just after it happened. "I don't know how he knew," Susan said, "but he always seemed to know when something was wrong. He just said, 'What's going on?' and I casually said, 'Oh this guy came to the door.'"

tigators came to Susan's house—Bob Connor
and Police Department and Bob Nelson from
Police Department. "I gave them the note and
rmation I had," Susan recalled, "and they said
aced the car. Bob Connor told me all that, and
, 'We can't guarantee your safety.'"

g had it been since anyone had been able to
Susan's safety? Not since Jerry died, she thought.
was no longer something she believed in.

ant John Whitson, the Alameda investigator who
ed with Jon Goodfellow gathering evidence for
illa's and Bill Nichols's trials, had never planned
op. After he left military service during the war in
, his goal was to be an underwater photographer.
ed to Brooks Institute of Photography in Santa
only to learn that some of his college credits
be transferred and he would have to wait two years
. He had a wife to support, so he looked around for
rim job. Somebody suggested that he apply at a
department, and he found himself filling out an
tion in Berkeley. It happens that way sometimes;
reat investigators come from a long familial line of
nd some happen upon a career in police work almost
ident. Before Whitson knew it, he was a patrolman
e Berkeley Police Department. "It was almost like
camp," he remembered, bemused.

worked two years on the street, and then he moved
investigation. "I loved hunting," he said. "Not the kill
uch, but all the planning, the plotting, the steps needed
ack your quarry. And I found that detective work was
that. Edison once said: 'Genius is one percent inspira-
n and ninety-nine percent perspiration,' and I went with
latter. It might take me a long time, but I never quit."
Whitson had worked scores of homicides by the time he
s paired with ADA Jon Goodfellow on the Harris case.
e was in his forties, a darkly handsome man with a
ceptively soft voice, when he fixed his sights on Steven
onilla and company. Jeff Rand had been a real find as a
itness, but "he was a co-conspirator," Whitson com-

Diedrich wasted no time getting in touch with the Alameda County D.A.'s office. They were all concerned; they didn't think she was overreacting. They contacted Sergeant Bob Connor, a member of Oakland's intelligence unit. Connor, who is now with the Alameda County D.A.'s investigative unit, checked out the license plate that Julie Hannah had jotted down. Initially, it wasn't much help. The car had been rented from an agency in Stockton. Someone had taken great pains to hide his or her identity. But Connor, one of the best intelligence men in California, had just begun. He knew the nether side of the law in the Bay Area, the gangs, and the friends of friends. He could talk the language and he was tireless. He would find out who that person was and what the connection to Susan Harris was.

A few days after the camera incident, Susan received a letter. There was no name—just her address on Quail Run Road. "It looked like something you'd see in the movies. I picked up my mail at night, and I was sorting through it and I saw this envelope, and I thought, This is funky. It just looked weird. I opened it up and it was on blue stationery."

The letter had been typed. At first it made no sense because the words all ran together without punctuation or capital letters.

Harrisin1988borrowed25000cojointlywith
    bonillapay net50.000
    duenowbonillawillingtohonordebtunabletodosodue
toadversaryclientclaimsdropcaseallowboniiliato
    paytotaldebtdue100.000orjaspersillthenbrother
    thenyou
    strangethingswillhappensoonest
    oneofoureletcollectingagentshasfoundya
        thistime
            nexttimewhoknows
                        dropbonilla
    releasefunds

Susan stared at it, and suddenly it came into focus. It looked like gobbledygook *until* Susan carefully separated the words and added punctuation. She felt icy sweat despite the warm May day:

Harris in 1988 borrowed $250,000 co-jointly with Bonilla. Pay net $50,000 due now. Bonilla willing to honor debt. Unable to do so due to adversary client claims. Drop case. Allow Boniilia [sic] to pay total debt due: $100,000 or Jasper will. Then brother.

Then you.

Strange things will happen soonest. One of our elet [elite?] collecting agents has found you this time.

Next time—who knows?

Drop Bonilla.

Release funds.

The letter was a threat. If she didn't drop her lawsuits, which kept Steve Bonilla from looting the assets left from Baritz, she would die.

The worst of it for Susan was that she was no longer the *only* target in her family. "I could have handled it myself, I think," she said. "But . . . that letter had mentioned Jasper. My father's name is Everett Jasper Hannah, even though everyone calls him Pete. My grandfather's name is Jasper. But no one knew [that] but our family—and then that letter threatened my brother too. My blood ran cold."

As she read the letter aloud to her sister, Julie, they both remembered that their folks had been having problems with bears. Pete and Mary Jo Hannah lived in a mobile home on the banks of the Rogue River in Oregon. They had told the girls that they had been jolted awake by something that crashed against the side of their trailer at night. They were sure it was a bear, so Pete grabbed his gun and crept outside. He saw a tall, dark figure moving at the back of the mobile home. And then it broke away from the shadows there and disappeared into the woods.

It was probably only a bro[w...] had smiled and thought that J[...] bears—would have liked that. [...] the thing lumber off into the n[...]

Reading the letter and remen[...] against their parents' mobile h[...] denly started to cry. It hadn't [...] someone trying to kill Pete and M[...] both crying, and I called my par[e...] night," Susan said. "I woke them u[...] bear that's trying to get in—it's son[...]

The steadily building stress had [...] Luckily, her parents had cooler hea[...] said, "I'm sure it's only a bear."

Pete Hannah got on the phone. "He[...] We're fine. You take care of you and J[u...] of everything up here in Oregon."

Pete Hannah had watched his daught[e...] and terror and he had developed a tren[...] respect for Susan; he had seen her chang[...] one-year-old girl who fell in love with [...] grieving widow, and then to a very strong[...] managed to hold a crumbling financial e[...] woman who was resolute in demanding[...] husband's murder.

"In the end, my dad and I had a kind [...] ment," Susan said. "I knew he would take ca[...] and my brothers and sisters in Oregon, and he [...] take care of Julie. We couldn't afford the en[...] about each other."

Susan and Julie were about to be sucked [...] terrifying game. But the letter didn't make se[...] Bonilla was in jail, convicted of murder and aw[...] second penalty phase trial, at which he could be s[...] to death. How could he be behind the letter and [...] with a camera? He was mentioned in the letter, bu[...] no secret that Susan had been fighting him in co[...] years. That had been in all the local papers.

mented, "and juries don't usually view a co-conspirator as credible. Sometimes circumstantial evidence, taken cumulatively, *can* convince a jury that the defendant is a killer."

And in the case of Bonilla and Nichols, it had. It was only a matter of time until they both got the death penalty. But now, Whitson was terribly concerned for the safety of Susan Harris and her sister, Julie. Bonilla and Nichols were locked up, yes, but Whitson feared that Jon Goodfellow's prediction that Bonilla could pull strings from *anywhere* had come true. Somebody on the outside had located the young women and was threatening to kill them. Susan's face had never appeared in a newspaper photograph; someone had evidently needed to know what she looked like. Whitson and Connor feared that the photo had been taken because someone needed to know what his target looked like.

Whitson and Bob Connor wanted to set up a twenty-four-hour-a-day stakeout so they could watch over the two young women, but higher-ups in the D.A.'s office vetoed that suggestion. If they set a precedent by using valuable manpower to protect Susan and Julie, the D.A.'s office would have to baby-sit everyone who was frightened of reprisal.

In a case fraught with frustrations, Whitson recalls that his biggest frustration was dealing with a stubborn Susan Harris—and Julie too. He wasn't sure if they were so unyielding because they didn't realize how pervasive the danger was or if they had finally come to a place where no amount of danger could scare them.

The women would not leave their house on Quail Run Road, no matter how often Whitson and Connor warned them that they could be setting themselves up as targets. Bob Connor had been speaking a somber truth when he told Susan that no one could guarantee their safety if they stayed in their home. All the police drive-bys in the world wouldn't guarantee that a killer wasn't waiting for the squad car to disappear around a corner before he struck. Nobody—not Goodfellow or Whitson or Connor, and not Duke Diedrich, either—*nobody* knew who was after Susan. And until they did know, they were unable even to tail a suspect or suspects and keep track of them.

Even though the situation was getting more and more frightening, Susan and Julie were obdurate. They had been through so much in the past half-dozen years. "I thought, I'm not moving again," Susan said. "I have a gun and I know how to use it. I'm staying."

Susan was going to school, she had just found a new job, and she and Julie loved the Fremont house. Neither of them intended to pack up and leave because some unknown enemy was threatening them.

Duke called Susan and told her that she had to get out of the house. He told her that Whitson and Connor weren't exaggerating. He didn't know who was behind this new intimidation, but that didn't matter. It was time to pay attention. Duke insisted that Susan pack up immediately and go into hiding.

"Usually I did what Duke said," Susan recalled. "This time I said no. I was staying put."

At Diedrich's urging, Judy and Mel Boyd, Susan's aunt and uncle, drove from their home in Rodeo, California, to Fremont. "They told us, 'Girls, you're leaving *now.*'" Susan remembered. "And I said, 'We're staying.' So they said, 'Then we're staying too.' And they moved in."

For Susan and Julie, living with their aunt and uncle baby-sitting them was almost as bad as having to move. But the Boyds were cops, and they knew that Julie and Susan were in danger. The letter writer had gloated that "an elit (sic) collector had found them," and the note had warned Susan to drop her court cases involving Bonilla. That was enough for Mel and Judy.

Julie and Susan finally softened their resolve when they saw how frightened John Whitson, Bob Connor, Duke, and the Boyds were for them. They knew that none of them was an alarmist; maybe they *were* in mortal danger. With a last look around the house where they had had so much fun and felt so safe, they capitulated. The threat was worse now, because they didn't know who their enemy was or what he looked like. The next knock on the door might be from someone holding a gun instead of a camera.

"We gave in," Susan said with a sigh. "We grabbed a

couple of sleeping bags and the first clothes we put our hands on. We started living in hotels. We lost all of our freedom, all of the life we'd built."

Although Susan thought the cops were paranoid, their arguments had convinced her. "They told me to get a rented car," she said. "I already knew about checking into places with another name, so I was Susan Smith and Julie was Julie Jones. I guess we weren't very original."

They couldn't stay in just any hotel—they had to stay in *expensive* hotels to be sure that security was tight. "Julie was working at Intel, and that was a security-minded company," Susan said. "We couldn't have people following her, or she might lose her job. I didn't dare even *start* my new job."

Susan's thirty-third birthday was on June 2, Julie's birthday was on June 4, and Jerry would have had his fifty-first birthday on June 1. There was no reason to celebrate; they were moving from one hotel to another, driving a rented car, living under assumed names. They might as well have been in prison. A day or two here, a day or two there. Their clothes, Susan's computer, everything that made them feel as if they were living in a home instead of like Gypsies was back in the house on Quail Run Road—the house where they dared not go.

Sometimes Susan longed to go home to Oregon. "But I couldn't go home. If I did, I would endanger everyone up there. Whoever was following me would follow me up there. I tried to get Julie to stay with a friend, but she said she couldn't leave me. It was odd," Susan said. "I had been through so much, and I thought I could handle anything. I actually felt that Julie was safer with me, that I could take care of her, and we stuck together like glue. We always will have a bond because of what we went through that summer. . . . I knew she would kill for me, and I would kill for her without question," Susan recalled. "Our days in Oregon seemed so far away. We were moving in a world we could never have imagined then."

30

During the early summer of 1993, Julie Hannah and Susan Harris were living their lives on the run. They were tired of hotel rooms, weary from looking over their shoulders constantly, and sick of restaurant food. Even though Susan had the money she had saved from the sale of the Hot Rods—money she had thought would give her a financial cushion for a year at least—they were running out of funds. The rent on the house in Fremont was $2,000 a month, and she had to keep paying it even though she couldn't live there. Her Bronco was still parked in the garage there. She was paying for a life she could not live.

"I kept calling Bob Connor at Oakland Intelligence and saying, 'When are you going to do something?'" Susan recalled. "'How long are we going to have to hide?' And nobody knew. We ended up being in hotels for about two weeks, moving all the time."

Although Connor and John Whitson were making progress in finding the faceless, nameless stalkers who wanted to harm Susan, they couldn't tell her the details of their investigation. Connor had sources deep inside the jail where Steve Bonilla enjoyed the run of his pod. Connor now knew who had issued the order to hit Susan, but he and Whitson were not quite ready to pounce. They could only urge her to stay hidden. She was angry and impatient, and they could not blame her for that—but they feared for her safety.

"Julie and I needed a place to live," Susan remembered.

"We couldn't go back to the house, and I was running out of money, so we got a little apartment in Pleasanton. It was a big enough complex where no one would pay any attention to us."

Susan herself had had enough of being a target, and she was ready to give up and leave California, but her sister had a good job. Susan couldn't leave Julie, so the apartment seemed the only solution. "But we had *nothing*," Susan recalled. "We didn't even have a chair to sit on!"

Her life had changed so much that she could barely remember the wonderful pink mansion in Blackhawk—or the house she and Jerry had fixed up on Chaparral Drive. Was it really true that she and Jerry had once owned a perfectly appointed yacht, or was that just her imagination? Sitting on the carpet in the tiny apartment, she thought it all seemed like a dream.

Again, John Whitson asked for a stakeout in the house on Quail Run. The word was that whoever had tried to get the sisters once was ready to try it again. Even if it took full-time surveillance, Whitson was ready to do it. But the county thought it would cost too many man-hours.

"Everything was falling apart," Susan sighed. "We weren't even allowed to go to our house to get our mail, and we weren't getting it on time. Our credit cards were cut off, our phone at the apartment was turned off because we hadn't paid the bill. Our credit was totally ruined."

Susan and Julie ended up staying in the tiny apartment for eight weeks, some of those weeks without "even a plate or a spoon." Desperate, they were ready to take a chance—against the law enforcement officers' advice. They had to have some of the things that would make their lifestyle more comfortable than camping out, sleeping on the floor, and eating fast food.

With her money running out, Susan returned the rental car she was driving and managed to have her Bronco delivered to her at a safe place. She and Julie were ready to go for it.

"We decided . . . to go back to the house and get our stuff," Susan said. "I had a paper that was due—believe it or not, I was still going to school. I needed my computer. I had my .357, and we decided to take the chance. . . . We didn't tell *anybody* we were going to do it."

Fully aware that a killer might be waiting inside their house—or watching from outside—Julie and Susan headed toward their old neighborhood. Susan explained to Julie that they had to decide exactly what they were going to grab. If they were lucky enough to find the house empty, they would have no guarantee that they weren't being observed. Whoever was after them could be alerted that they were back.

"I figured we had two minutes or less to get in and out. Julie was in the passenger seat, and I said, 'Okay, Julie, this is what you're going to grab, and this is what I'm going to grab'—and I spelled it all out for her. We had a garage door opener, and I could zip into the garage with the Bronco."

Any woman who has ever been ripped from her everyday life will understand their situation. What they needed was prosaic and yet essential. They were running out of underwear; they wanted more than one change of clothes, and they couldn't afford to buy new ones. They had to get the computer. They weren't going to bother with dishes or furniture or any of the other niceties of life.

Although they felt like targets outlined in flashing lights, Susan backed the Bronco into the garage and shut the door. Then she and Julie raced into the house.

Nobody was waiting inside. All they heard was the sound of their own breathing and the echo of their footsteps as they raced from room to room. In less than two minutes they were back in the Bronco.

"I had the gun in one hand, the steering wheel in the other," Susan remembered. "The garage door opened partway, and we were facing the road . . . and then we saw legs—right in front of us. I pointed the gun at the figure and it seemed as though the garage door was opening so slowly. I floored the accelerator and we tore out of there."

Only then did they realize they had almost run over "some poor guy walking his dog." They were horrified that living under siege for so long had made them view everyone as an enemy. They had almost run down an innocent neighbor.

Their world had turned inside out, and they no longer saw it as a safe place. Until the investigators had the evidence they needed, they couldn't move in on the suspects they were shadowing.

After eight weeks in hiding, Susan and Julie could no longer afford to stay in the apartment they'd rented. "I lost so much money on that, on the house on Quail Run—all the deposits, the last month's rent—but I found another little house in Fremont. I rented it under a false name, and I had to pay six months' rent to get in. It was about the end of my money," Susan said, "but Julie had to be close enough to her job to get to work."

This time the sisters moved everything out of the Quail Run house. They sneaked in at night, drew the curtains, and packed everything in boxes by candlelight and flashlight. They had no help; it was just the two of them against whoever might be watching. What they couldn't carry out in one trip, they simply abandoned.

Even living under assumed names in yet another location, they were afraid. If a car parked in front of their house, Susan and Julie panicked. When a fellow student offered to bring over a tape of a lecture that Susan needed, she told him cryptically that he shouldn't knock on her door if he saw a car parked out in front.

"I didn't want to get someone else killed," she said later. "He saw a car out in front, and he didn't stop, but he went to a pay phone and called me. He said there was a man sitting in front of the house. Julie and I had just gotten home, and we immediately thought there was someone in the house with us. I took the gun and went from room to room, checking out closets one by one. I didn't find anyone, but we were still frightened."

They called the police. Bob Connor had told Susan that she could call 911 anytime, give her name, and someone would be out right away. Susan had pared her life down to minutes; time could mean the difference between life and death. She called 911 and gave her name, and she and Julie waited, Susan with her loaded gun drawn. It took eighteen minutes for a patrol car to respond, and Susan was furious and frightened as she waited. Remembering later, and a little ashamed, she recalled that she had left a bitter message on Connor's answering machine, "I just called 911, Bob, and it's taking them too long."

Susan gave Connor a description of the car in front, and of the man inside. "We've waited eighteen minutes," she said tightly to his answering machine. "I just want you to know, in case we're dead when the cops get here, I wanted to leave you a clue about who did it."

This wasn't the real Susan, but she was so frustrated, so tired of running and hiding and being afraid that the next time she opened the door somebody would be standing there with a gun—instead of a camera—aimed at her head.

When the Fremont police arrived, they pulled the man out of the car and patted him down. He was the father of a neighborhood paperboy, waiting to take him home after he finished his route.

Susan sighed. "I guess . . . that is how we had come to think. Everyone was a threat; everyone was suspicious. It changed me for a long time—maybe forever. Having to hide like that made me afraid of people. I couldn't have friends, and no one could really protect me. I just had to be really smart and really careful. I learned to . . . lose a car tailing me. I learned to search a house with a gun. I just wasn't the same person any longer."

At one point, Susan recalled, "Julie talked to the D.A.'s office and said I didn't want to testify in the second penalty trial. John Whitson said they could subpoena me if they had to. I just looked at him and said no one could force me to take that chance again. I was scared for my folks, my sisters, my brothers. . . . I told Duke about it, and he didn't argue with me. He just nodded and said, 'Family is family. Do what you have to do.'"

John Whitson and Jon Goodfellow understood too. But they also knew Susan. They knew she would have the guts to testify again when the time came.

No one will ever know how long Susan and her sister could have gone on living with foreboding and quiet terror. As it turned out, the siege ended on July 29, 1993, when startling charges were filed by Alameda County authorities.

Bay Area newspapers headlined the story but gave only the sparsest of details:

Four Charged in Plot to Kill
Former San Ramon Woman

A Mountain View man already convicted of first-degree murder for the death of nightclub owner Jerry Lee Harris at a Pleasanton business park in 1987 was charged today with conspiring to murder Harris's widow. Stephen [sic] Wayne Bonilla, 45, and three other defendants— including his mother and a reputed hit man for the Black Guerrilla Family prison gang—are charged with a murder-for-hire plot targeting Susan H. Harris, according to Alameda County Senior Deputy District Attorney Bob Platt.

And so, after months in hiding, Susan Harris found out exactly why her protectors had been so afraid for her and why they'd had to tell her they could not guarantee her safety. When the Alameda County D.A.'s men and Duke Diedrich had pleaded with Susan and Julie to leave their Quail Run home, they hadn't been overreacting. It was almost a miracle that the two young women were still alive. Had Diedrich, Whitson, and Connor had their way, they would have sat outside the sisters' bedroom doors with drawn guns. Instead they had worked around the clock many days to build a chargeable case against the man they suspected.

Naturally, the first person John Whitson and Bob Connor looked at when they began their probe into the "cameraman" and the coded death threat letter was Steve Bonilla. But Bonilla wasn't going anywhere. He was safely locked up in the North County Jail in Oakland, awaiting the second penalty phase trial.

Gradually, with the help of a secret witness—to protect his life, his name would never be revealed—the investigators learned that there had indeed been an intricate plot involving a shocking cast of characters.

In order to protect the thirty-one-year-old unnamed informant, I will call him Tiger and describe him no further, except to say he was a member of a Bay Area gang and a prisoner in the same jail where Steven Bonilla was held. He told investigators that he had gotten to know Bonilla when they played chess "through the wall" in their adjoining cells. As he got to know Bonilla, Tiger learned that Bonilla was looking for someone who would eliminate two witnesses against him.

Perhaps Tiger came forward with his story because taking money to have a woman killed bothered him, but he was not averse, of course, to having gun possession charges against him dropped. Whatever his primary reason for snitching on fellow prisoners, he had a horrendous tale to tell.

Through the efforts of Oakland Intelligence Sergeant Bob Connor and D.A. Inspector John Whitson, Bonilla's plan emerged into the daylight. It was an ugly and cruel scenario with a strange and varied cast of characters.

Tiger said he had told Bonilla that the "shot-caller" was a prisoner in an upstairs pod in the jail: Thomas "Totomba" Innsley* who was a "colonel" in a prison gang active in correctional institutions all up and down the West Coast. But it would take money to arrange the hits Bonilla wanted. Tiger, who was allowed out of the pod several times a day, became a courier between Totomba and Bonilla. The word from Totomba was that it would cost $35,000 up front to get rid of the woman; the man would be $50,000. Bonilla said he could pay, but the money would have to come in stages.

Steve Bonilla had not varied his pattern of taking what he wanted, no matter who got hurt. He had explained to Tiger that he had a three-phase plan to carry out. First, he wanted Susan Harris either dead or so frightened that she could no longer be a damaging witness against him in his upcoming death penalty trial. With Susan out of the way, her wrongful death suit against him would also disappear and he would be able to get his hands on funds that were now frozen. Bonilla was prepared to pay the $35,000—with $10,000 down—to get rid of Susan. Second, he wanted a Nevada man known as "Gary" killed. (This Gary was undoubtedly Jeff Rand.) If his funds were freed up because of a successful "first phase," Bonilla would pay $50,000 for Gary's assassination. Bonilla's third aim was to get out of jail and become rich by selling drugs.

Ella Bonilla was devastated at having her only son in jail, with prison and perhaps even the gas chamber awaiting him. Even so, when he begged her for money to carry out a violent attack, she demurred. She had never done anything overtly illegal, although she had covered up secret things that Steve had done. Ella was now seventy years old, her financial assets had long since been diminished by her attempts to help Steven succeed in business, and she had an invalid daughter to care for. She had no one left to help her. But Ella had always been an easy mark for her son's cajoling and his threats. She loved him, and she was both afraid of him and half beguiled by his manipulation. He had stolen from her, and he had let her money slip through his fingers like water. But he was her son. Her *son*.

In the spring of 1993, Steven Bonilla told his mother that she was the only one who could save him from a horrible death in California's gas chamber. He needed $2,000 up front, and later he would need $10,000 more. He had tears in his eyes as he pleaded with Ella, implying that any mother who truly loved the son born of her womb would find a way to help him.

Ella wanted Steven out of jail and safe, but she didn't like the people he was hanging around with in jail. They were common criminals, gang members, and she was afraid of them. As they got out of jail on lesser offenses, many of them came to her house on Leona Lane in Mountain View. They made themselves at home, used her phone, and she suspected they were stealing from her. She was an old woman, and she no longer had the strength to fight back. She begged Steve not to tell these people where she lived, but he just laughed and said she was perfectly safe.

Steve Bonilla wore his mother down. He said he had met a man named Tiger who knew of someone who would frighten Susan Harris so much that she would never testify against him again and she would even drop her suits against him. If necessary, this person could snap his fingers and have Susan Harris killed. Without Susan's interference, Steve whispered, he would be free to come home and take care of Ella and his sister. Together they could build a business empire.

Steve explained that he could not go directly to the hit person; that would make it too easy for the police to trace him. Tiger would be the go-between. He had promised Steve that, for $2,000, he would go to that person and make all the arrangements. "They will never connect anything to me," Bonilla assured his mother, "or to you, of course."

Somehow Ella Bonilla came up with the $12,000 for Tiger. And Tiger did indeed start making phone calls for Totomba (Thomas Innsley). Innsley had been convicted of one charge of attempted murder involving other gang members and was awaiting trial on a second attempted murder charge. Later he accepted the $10,000 down payment for the first phase of Steve's plan. Ella Bonilla made out her check to Innsley's attorney.

The investigators had discovered that when Julie Hannah ran after the car of the man who had taken Susan's picture, she did more to protect her sister than she realized. True, the license number was traced to a car rental agency, but the investigators found that the car had been rented by a young woman named Francine Curtis.* They checked her out and discovered that Curtis was a paralegal who worked in the office of the Oakland attorney who represented Thomas Innsley. Even more interesting, Francine Curtis, known as Big Woman, was Innsley's girlfriend.

It all fit.

Did Innsley and Francine Curtis really plan to murder Susan Harris? Or did the powerful gang member regard Bonilla as a fat pigeon to pluck? Tiger wasn't sure. He knew that Bonilla had already paid another prisoner $5,000 to kill Susan, but that hit man had simply taken the money and disappeared. Innsley had to produce something to prove that he was serious. Perhaps Susan's photograph was that proof? No, Tiger said, the man who had gone to Susan's home was supposed to kidnap her, not just take her picture; Innsley had been very angry that his emissary—known as CeeQ—had messed up so badly.

Obviously the man with the camera had had no trouble locating Susan, even though she and Julie were living under assumed names. Susan had tried to hide by putting everything in her sister Julie's name when she rented the house in Fremont. "I made one mistake," she said. "I registered to vote."

The nicely groomed photographer had been on Susan's porch within days after Innsley put out his orders.

According to the indictment, Ella Bonilla and Francine Curtis had worked together to transfer the funds that would get rid of Susan.

Deputy D.A. Platt said that all four of the people who conspired to murder Susan Harris faced sentences of up to life in prison: Steven Bonilla, Ella Bonilla, Thomas Innsley, and Francine "Big Woman" Curtis.

The news of the arrests was shattering to Susan, but it strengthened her resolve. She had testified against Bonilla twice, and now and she was ready to do it again. All the murder plots in the world would not deter her now. She had come through the fire.

Did she feel safe at last? No. If one plot had gotten through the bars that held Steve Bonilla away from freedom, who still was to say that another would not?

Susan still had lunch with Duke, and she still spent holidays with the Diedrich family. She tried to put on a happy face, but, underneath, she was gripped by a depression that turned her world gray. Her doctor prescribed antidepressants, but she didn't take them. Instead, she waited for the next round, whatever it might be.

31

It was two days after Valentine's Day 1994 when Tiger testified in a preliminary examination in Oakland Municipal Court in exchange for immunity from prosecution in his role in arranging a link between Steven Bonilla and Thomas "Totomba" Innsley.

Tiger recalled that Bonilla had confided in him in the North County Jail that he "hated" Susan Harris because she had tied up all his money in her wrongful death lawsuit and because she planned to testify against him in his upcoming penalty phase retrial.

If Susan could not be "persuaded" to drop her lawsuit, the plan was for four muscular black men to "kidnap her and take her to the ghetto." There her captors were instructed to tear her clothes off and "pour chicken blood on her—just scare her." Susan Harris was to be held captive for three or four days until she was truly terrified for her life.

"If that didn't work," Tiger testified, "then the plan was to kill her."

Tiger testified that Totomba, who was thirty-six years old, said to tell Bonilla he could find someone to do it and that he intended to have Susan Harris killed and "leave no trails." Tiger's personal opinion, however, was that Totomba intended to take Bonilla's money and not threaten or kill anyone.

Francine "Big Woman" Curtis, Totomba's fiancée, testified that she had not seen the plan as a genuine murder plan, but that they could probably kidnap Susan and frighten her enough to make her drop her suit against Bonilla.

Oakland Municipal Court Judge Jack Gifford ruled on March 1, 1994, that there was sufficient evidence to find Bonilla, Totomba, and Francine Curtis guilty of conspiring to kill Susan Harris. Ella Bonilla's case was severed from the others, and no judgment was made on her alleged guilt at that time.

On October 10, 1994, the court procedures began again. Jerry Harris had been dead for almost exactly seven years. Twelve new jurors, who had never heard of Jerry Harris, would be selected. Jon Goodfellow expected jury selection to take several months, and the actual second penalty trial might not begin until the end of the year. Once again Harris's convicted killers were facing the ultimate penalty.

Jon Goodfellow had been angry and frustrated for a long time. He had warned the jurors in the first penalty phase of the danger of allowing Bonilla and Nichols to live. He had predicted that they were dangerous and would continue to concoct wicked plots whether they were inside or outside prison walls. And Bonilla, at least, had proved him right. "While he was convicted of first-degree murder, he was plotting to do it again," Goodfellow said.

Susan Harris had almost died because of Steven Bonilla's contract on her. None of her terror had been necessary. This time around, though, Goodfellow had an even stronger case against Bonilla. His opening statement not only detailed the murder plot against Jerry but also included the contract put out on his widow.

The second day of trial went to the defense attorneys' opening statement. They could not deny that their clients had been convicted of first-degree murder, so they took other approaches in their attempt to save the defendants' lives. Spencer Strellis, who now represented Bonilla, after saying he had been taught "not to speak ill of the dead," proceeded to do just that. He castigated Jerry Harris for running a palm tree business that was a "scam." He also said that Jerry had refused to pay Bonilla his share of profits and had not filed his income tax returns.

Strellis said that Harris had turned to Bonilla often for

loans, and Bonilla's mother had furnished money for those loans. "Like a mule hit too many times, Bonilla began to realize Harris was using him. You have to consider to what extent he was conned and used by his lifelong friend and how that factored into what happened."

Strellis avoided discussing how Bonilla had hired Nichols and Rand to kill Jerry Harris, but he promised to show how many times Jeff Rand's story had changed.

Howard Harpham, Nichols's attorney, said his client was basically a con man who had been stringing Bonilla along and who had never actually intended to kill Jerry Harris. The murder was, if anything, an "accident."

He would call Nichols to the witness stand to explain exactly what had happened the night of October 20, 1987.

Once again Susan Harris took the witness stand. In a steely voice, she denied that Jerry had ever cheated anyone. "Any business investment with Jerry would be a good investment," she said firmly.

Spencer Strellis questioned her about why she had declared bankruptcy after her husband's death. Susan said she blamed herself: "It would be fair to say I was not a businessperson. After Jerry was gone, I was not able to operate the businesses, and that's why they are gone."

Asked about her $20 million wrongful death lawsuit against Bonilla and Nichols, she gazed at her questioner with tears in her eyes. "There wouldn't be enough money in all the world to make up for what they've done," she said. "I am very tired of lawsuits." Susan told the jury that she had already been living in fear when she learned of the death threat against her.

Asked to describe the impact of Jerry's death, she could not speak. "It was heartbreaking," she managed to say before she broke into sobs. But she recovered her equilibrium on redirect and answered Goodfellow's questions about Bonilla. "He expected me to give up without a struggle. He thought I would go to Oregon and behave in a way he had always perceived me—as my timid little self. He never expected that I would fight him for what Jerry had built. But I became like a roaring lion when Jerry disappeared. I filed bankruptcy to stop him [Bonilla]. Chapter Eleven. It took eight years and millions of dollars, but I didn't care. As long as I'm alive, Steve Bonilla will never receive anything."

Bill Nichols took the witness stand in his second penalty phase trial. Public Defender Howard Harpham asked him about the death of Jerry Harris. Nichols said he had never, ever, thought the plan was to *kill* Jerry. He had meant to talk to him—to get Bonilla's $100,000 and, through that, $40,000 for himself to set up a tiling business. When things got rough, they had been "forced" to restrain Jerry and put him in the brown pickup truck.

"Susan Harris believes that her husband was executed," Nichols said sadly. "And there is no way that I could look Jerry Harris in the eyes and tape his head with duct tape and kill him. That didn't happen. There is no way I could do that. I'm not that kind of a person. I know I'm no angel, by a long shot, but I'm not a cold-blooded killer."

Nichols explained how he kept pounding on the side of the truck and shouting to Jerry Harris that they would have him out of there "real soon." He had been horrified twelve hours later when he discovered that Jerry was dead.

"What I did to Jerry Harris's family is unforgivable," Nichols told the jury. "What I did to my own family is unforgivable. I can't bring Jerry Harris back. And every night I go to bed with Jerry Harris and every morning I wake up [and] Jerry Harris is there waiting for me."

Yes, Bill Nichols was asking for mercy. He admitted that. "I don't want you to spare my life for *me* at all. I have nine reasons that I'm real concerned about—my nine kids. I honestly don't believe they can handle it. I will spend the rest of my life in prison. I have four grandparents that all lived to be eighty-five or older, so that means I'm probably going to spend a long time suffering. And I promise you I will mentally flog myself every day if you can just spare my children from what Tiffany Harris had to go through. Please, for that reason only, help me avoid the death penalty."

"I have no other questions," Harpham said.

Jon Goodfellow rose to cross-examine Bill Nichols. "Mr. Nichols, do you have enough Kleenex up there?"

"I hope so."

"Were you crying for yourself, or were you crying for Jerry Harris just now?"

"I was crying for my children."

And then Goodfellow subjected Bill Nichols to a steady rat-ta-tat-tat grilling about his life and his crimes—his "collections," his scams, the women he had left with babies while he moved on to other women, only to leave *them* with babies.

"I think you said that you were always interested in providing for your family," Goodfellow said. "Is that true?"

"Yes."

"After you were arrested for this offense and after you were in custody in Alameda County, did you send a letter to a friend of yours—a film-producer?"

"True."

"And you proposed that [he] engage in a project to make a film about your life. True?"

"It was more about Jerry Harris's life than mine."

Bill Nichols said piously that he had suggested the project to provide for his family—but mostly for Susan Harris.

The case had gone 'round and 'round for too long. They had moved through October 1994, seven years after Bill Nichols and Jeff Rand had left Jerry Harris in a three-foot-deep hole in the desert. Once more, Jon Goodfellow asked a jury to decree the death penalty for Harris's convicted killers.

This time, they complied. The new jury of nine men and three women spent six and half days deliberating before they came back with a recommendation that Steven Wayne Bonilla should die in the gas chamber. At 10:45 A.M. on November 18, the verdict of the jury was signed and filed with Alameda County. Steven Bonilla waits now on death row in San Quentin prison.

The jurors were evenly split over the death penalty for William Winifred Nichols. Nichols was subsequently sentenced to life in prison without parole.

Afterword

Susan Harris has left California and moved to another state. She has changed her name and entered a different phase in her life. October 1997 marked a full decade since her husband was murdered. She is still a beautiful young woman, but she has not remarried. In many ways, Susan is a different person now.

One memory of the happiest time of her life came back to Susan when she felt the lowest. Even as she grieved for Jerry, she remembered that moment. "When we took the *Tiffany* to Mexico, Jerry took me up to the bridge one night, and he said, 'You take over the wheel, Sue. I'm going to bed.' And he did. At first, I was afraid I couldn't do it, and I know the ship was all over the place for a while, but then I set it straight, and it felt good to be in charge, to be responsible for all those people sleeping below. I *could* do it. All by myself."

She didn't know then how much she would have to do all by herself. In 1995, Susan read about the refugees in Bosnia and realized that her problems paled in comparison. Something in that far-off country called out to her. "I wish I could say that I decided to go there to help the refugees," she says regretfully, "but it was more of a personal quest."

Susan traveled to Bosnia—again, all by herself. There she met a priest who helped her find the Catholic faith that had lain fallow for some time. She has made two more trips to Medjargorje and plans to lead pilgrimages there in the future.

Susan has grown strong through adversity—not tough,

but strong. She doubts that she could ever again be a devoted stay-at-home wife, as she was to Jerry Harris. Forced out into the world, she has come to enjoy challenges and even, in some small way, to take chances, as Jerry once did.

Susan will never stop loving Jerry Harris, and she is aware of that. "I took some courses at Saint Mary's College [in Moraga, California] after Jerry died," Susan says. "And one of the economics professors told me that he had lost his young wife after only five years of marriage. He gave me some good advice—something he had had to learn: 'One day you will find a person who will love you *and* accept your first love.' I suppose that is what I'm looking for."

As I began this book, Susan uncorked one of the few remaining bottles of Jerry's favorite Silver Oak Cabernet wine, and we drank a toast to him and to a book that would make him come alive in readers' minds.

Susan's parents, Betty Jo and Pete Hannah, still live on the edge of one of southern Oregon's beautiful wild rivers. They are very proud of all their children.

Susan's sister, Julie, has remarried and recently gave birth to a baby. She and Susan share a bond forged as strong as steel when they lived through months of being stalked and terrorized.

Steve King, Jerry and Susan's best man and Jerry's true best friend, now has five sons and works as a dental technician. Steve was instrumental in arranging for a bronze plaque extolling Jerry's gift for friendship to be installed on a boulder in one of Fremont's parks. He and Susan keep in touch.

Jim and Lila Faye Harris, Jerry's parents, died before they could ever see justice done for their son. Perhaps they know.

Jerry's brothers and sisters are rarely in contact with Susan; the link between them was broken when Jerry died.

Duke Diedrich has retired from the FBI and now is head of security for a large corporation. He still keeps tabs on Susan, who for a long time has been like a member of his family. He still seems to know when she is troubled or frightened.

In the Name of Love

Assistant District Attorney Jon Goodfellow and Inspector John Whitson continue to work together in the Alameda County District Attorney's Office on major felony cases.

Sergeant Bob Connor retired from the intelligence unit of the Oakland Police Department and is now Inspector Bob Connor, an investigator in the Alameda County District Attorney's Office.

Captain Gary Tollefson is in his third decade with the Pleasanton Police Department. He recalls the investigation into Jerry Harris's disappearance and murder as perhaps the most memorable of his long career.

Pleasanton Detective Mark Allen was working patrol a year after he participated in Bill Nichols's arrest in Mesa, Arizona, when he was shot in the neck and almost died. That was the second time Allen had a gun pulled on him with a death threat. He eventually left the police force and worked with Diedrich in industrial security.

Steven Bonilla is on death row at San Quentin.

William Winifred Nichols is serving life in prison.

Jeff Rand served his three years—much of it credit for time served—and returned to Nevada to his wife and children. He has not been in trouble with the law since.

Ella Bonilla is dead. Steven Bonilla's sister remains loyal to her brother.

Thomas "Totomba" Innsley is serving life in prison. The charges against his fiancée, Francine Curtis, and CeeQ, the photographer, in the plot against Susan Harris were dropped. Totomba and CeeQ were already facing lengthy sentences when the conspiracy against Susan was discovered.

Someone else picked up the concept of the Hot Rod Cafes, and there are many of them—but they are not Jerry's. His clubs are all gone—burned, demolished, or replaced by other businesses. Had he lived, I have no doubt that he would have achieved his goal of a nationwide franchise of clubs with a 1950s theme.

Sergeant Ralph Springer of the Oregon State Police, my good friend and longtime editor of *Trooper* magazine, was the officer who once pulled Jerry Harris over for speeding. Long before I ever heard of Jerry Harris, Ralph had told me of the incident involving the gregarious man in the red Porsche. Ralph said he warned the driver that he was risking his life traveling so fast that state police radar could barely track him. "I told him he was flying too low," Ralph recalled. The two men, born four years apart, were very much alike, although they never knew it. Ralph was a risk-taker too, a pilot and a motorcyclist, renowned for his sense of humor. He, like Jerry, was an extremely kind man. Tragically, Ralph Springer was killed in the crash of his light aircraft on September 23, 1995, at the age of forty-eight.

Murder and the Proper Housewife

There are myriad motives for murder, and there are almost as many co-conspirators—would-be killers who have virtually nothing in common but who form fatal alliances. Once their goal is accomplished, those who have seen homicide as the answer to their problems usually go their separate ways. I don't believe I have ever researched an odder partnership than the man and woman who joined up to carry out a hit. Neither was connected with organized crime; neither had much to gain from the murder they joined forces to plan. To this day, I am not sure why they did what they did.

One of them was merely doing a favor for a friend whom she dearly loved; the other fancied himself to be a force larger than life. Somewhere along the line, they both lost touch with reality.

We have all had friends whom we loved so much that we would have risked our money, our serenity, and even our freedom for them. Nancy Brooks* seemed like the last person in the world who would plot to kill another human being. But Nancy felt so sorry for her dearest friend that she did just that. She was quite willing to arrange a murder because she loved her friend.

She came within a millimeter or two of carrying it off.

Nancy Brooks was a California housewife in the early 1960s. She married in an era when young wives strove to emulate the perfect television sitcom mother. Their floors were waxed, their children behaved, and they cooked healthy, nutritious meals. Their homes had orange shag carpeting, avocado-colored kitchen appliances, and daisy-print wallpaper.

Nancy and her husband, an engineer, lived in a large apartment with their son and daughter—the perfect 1960s family. One of their neighbors in the apartment house was a divorced woman, Claire Noonan,* whose son, Bennett, was in his late teens. Nancy and Claire became very good friends, and Bennett was also welcome in the Brooks home. He was a rather odd kid, lanky and gawky with stringy dark hair, who was considered a nerd by some of his contemporaries and just plain weird by others. Nancy was sympathetic when Claire confided that her former husband had been abusive to his stepson. Bennett had suffered so much physical abuse that he had problems with his self-worth and his own identity.

Nancy, a registered nurse, recognized that Bennett needed someone to listen to him, and she was kind to him. Her children adored Bennett, who was an accomplished magician. He would entertain them patiently for hours with amazing feats of magic. He had few social contacts with people his own age, however, and Nancy suspected he was lonely. He probably had a crush on Nancy Brooks who was

299

very pretty and only about a dozen years older than he was. Claire was grateful that the Brookses were so kind to her son.

Both families were transitory residents of California, though, and they soon moved thousands of miles apart. Claire married a physician and moved to Memphis, Tennessee; Nancy Brooks's husband, Cal, got a job in Seattle working for Boeing.

In the mid-1960s the Brookses moved to Bellevue, Washington, a burgeoning bedroom community for Seattle at that time and the best possible place for young Boeing engineers to reside. Neighborhoods with picturesque names like Lake Hills, Robinswood, Phantom Lake, and Bridle Trails sprang up almost overnight. Houses were built close together so that the developers could get the most out of every piece of forest land they had snapped up, and barbecues and kaffeeklatsches were popular social events.

Nancy Brooks had always seen herself as a person who helped others. That was why she had chosen nursing as a career, and that was why she had done her best to help Claire LeClerk Noonan with her problem son, Bennett. It wasn't long, however, before Nancy found a new best friend in Bellevue. She met Rose Stahl* through an interest they shared: they were both animal lovers, and they entered their dogs in local shows. Nancy and Rose raised show-quality poodles, a breed that requires much grooming and care. The women were the same age, thirty-nine, and they had so much in common that they saw each other almost every day and talked on the phone several times a day.

In California, Claire had had problems with Bennett and Nancy had been a godsend to her. Now, in Washington, Nancy was a sympathetic listener as Rose confided the details of her unhappy marriage. Nancy and Cal Brooks appeared to have a solid marriage, and that made Nancy doubly sorry for Rose.

Rose and Art Stahl hadn't been married for very long, and they both had children from previous marriages, so they had a combined family of his-and-hers children, plus they had two baby sons together. But theirs was not a happy union. They had marathon fights over how to deal with their children. Rose resented Art's older children visiting and would not let him discipline her children. Their biggest arguments, however, were over how to spend, or *not* spend—a $780,000 trust fund that belonged to Art.

At the same time, Art had the best and worst of all possible worlds. On one hand, the fortune he had inherited from his father was enough to keep a man of modest needs comfortable for a long time. On the other, he found himself locked in a marriage that was not only destroying his peace of mind but which caused him constant anxiety. Stahl wanted it to last, if only for the children's sake, but nothing he did seemed to please his wife.

Although the interest on his trust fund was more than enough to support his family, Art Stahl chose to work. He was a teaching assistant in the Mechanical Engineering Department of the University of Washington. He was a very intelligent man, and he loved to teach. He also enjoyed the ambience of the University of Washington campus.

At age fifty-two, Art was five feet nine and weighed a trim 150 pounds; he was a dapper man with wavy dark hair, a beard, and a mustache that was waxed at the tips. He chose to dip into his near-million-dollar trust fund only sparingly. Rather, he wanted its interest to accumulate. He and Rose had signed a prenuptial agreement stipulating that she had no access to his inheritance; the only people who could touch it were Art and an attorney in New York. Rose fretted over the luxuries they could be enjoying if Art were less stubborn about their living on his teaching salary. She found him unnecessarily stingy.

There were times, of course, when the Stahl marriage seemed to sail on an even keel. At other times—which were becoming all too frequent—Art Stahl was a beleaguered man. Rose was nothing if not relentless. The children needed money, she needed money for her dog shows, and they needed a nicer house. To preserve even a modicum of peace, Art often gave in to her demands. Whenever he could compromise to glean even a little serenity in his marriage, he tried to do so.

Art Stahl's biggest sacrifice was to send his own teenage daughter to live in a foster home because Rose couldn't get along with her. He regretted having to banish his daughter from his home, and he visited her as often as possible. He was torn between his loyalty and love for her and his belief that his two baby boys from his marriage to Rose needed him more.

At Art's urging, he and Rose spent a lot of time talking to counselors about their problem marriage. He knew that Rose told even the most intimate details of their marriage to her best friend, Nancy Brooks, and got advice from Nancy. Art told *his* secrets to a journal that he had begun to keep. The more miserable he became, the more he spilled out his pain onto the pages of his journal, which was really a sheaf of loose papers filled with longhand notes.

Nancy Brooks seemed to be a sympathetic woman; Art didn't mind that Rose confided in her. Sometimes he too talked to Nancy about the problems in his marriage. But he soon regretted it; he found out that anything he told Nancy soon got back to Rose. It was clear that if Nancy had to choose sides, she would stand firmly behind Rose. Art wondered sometimes what kind of exaggerated complaints Rose was telling Nancy.

Nancy Brooks was not an animated woman, and it was hard to tell what she was thinking. Five feet seven and slender, she carried herself rather stiffly. This was not her fault—Nancy had been in a number of car accidents, which had necessitated three surgeries to fuse vertebrae in her back and neck. She was quite pretty—or would have been if she'd smiled more. She had dark hair, cut short and curling around her cheeks, big brown eyes, and a sweet mouth. Despite her physical problems, Nancy was always on the move, doing something for her children or her husband or her friends.

Nancy Brooks, with her PTA-mother facade, seemed like the last person in the world who would ever become involved in criminal intrigue. She was a wife, mother, friend, and dog trainer. She dressed conservatively, keeping her hemlines well below her knees—no matter what fashion dictated. She wore sensible shoes with Cuban heels, and she often wore dark-rimmed glasses.

As the Stahl marriage continued to come apart at the

seams, Rose Stahl's good friend Nancy was beside her, listening to her complaints about Art and her worries about how she could support her children if Art moved out. The huge trust fund would go away if Art went away. Nancy patted her hand, poured her another cup of tea, and told her there had to be a way to work things out.

Meanwhile, Art's journal of marital misery grew thicker. There were times now when he actually felt afraid of Rose. He decided he could no longer keep his diary in the home they shared, so he locked the thick stack of pages in his desk in his office at the university. Sometimes he felt a little foolish about saving his writings and wondered why he even bothered to keep them. But he *did* keep them. If anything ever happened to him, he would leave some kind of record behind of the shambles his married life had become.

By the middle of 1974, Art Stahl realized that there was no way he and Rose could ever live together in harmony. He wasn't so sure he would live at all if he stayed with Rose. He was not an aggressive man, but Rose was certainly a hostile and aggressive woman. One night in September, he had the temerity to change the channel on their television set. There was a show he wanted to see, but Rose, who was working in the kitchen, was angry that he had switched away from what *she* wanted to see.

According to his diary, Art looked up to see her storming toward him with a butcher knife in her hand. She shouted, "Some night I'm going to stick a knife between your ribs, and you won't know what night it is."

He stared at her, horrified at her rage and convinced she meant what she said. Art Stahl was a prudent man, and he saw that he no longer had a choice. He had tried reasoning and counseling, but now he knew he had to go. On October 3, 1974, he left the family home in Bellevue and moved into an apartment.

It was wrenching to leave his little sons behind. He had always intended to provide for Rose and their children, and he had been in the process of drawing up a will that would leave the principal amount of his trust to Rose, with substantial sums to all of their children—his, hers, and theirs. As it was, if he should die, Rose would take his place

in the trust management. *She* would work with the financial
adviser on the East Coast to decide how the money would
be spent.

Stahl, of course, provided full support for Rose and the
children, even while he maintained a separate residence.

Nancy Brooks and Rose Stahl continued to be best
friends and to hash over the state of Rose's marriage—and
they remained active in dog show circles.

Art Stahl was beginning to build new interests of his own.
He started taking a class in an obscure medical art: reflexology. He enrolled in the evening course offered by the
Experimental College Program at the University of Washington. It was held at a health center a block away from the
north precinct of the Seattle Police Department, and it dealt
with the healing techniques that reflexology offered, the
premise being that all the ills, aches, and pains of the
human body could be made well by the skilled application
of foot massage.

Instead of the needles used in acupuncture, a trained
hand on the right spot of the foot could allegedly cure
almost everything. The once-a-week classes were to continue through November 26.

Whether Art really believed in the benefits of reflexology
or not, it was an interesting concept, and he met new
people. Aside from his classmates in the science of the
human foot, the only others who knew he was studying
reflexology were his estranged wife, Rose, and, through her,
Nancy Brooks, although Art might have mentioned the
classes to a few of his teaching associates at the university.

Nancy Brooks had reestablished her acquaintance with
Bennett LeClerk sometime in 1972. The awkward, nerdy
teenager she had known in California had metamorphosed
into an entirely different person in the decade since she had
befriended him and his mother.

Bennett had called her Bellevue home and asked to speak
to Nancy. At first, she had no idea who he was. He had
changed his last name and was no longer using his mother's
name.

"Oh, I'm sorry," he said smoothly. "You would know me as Claire Noonan's son. I used to do magic tricks for your kids in California."

"Of course," Nancy said. "You're *that* Bennett." It had been a long time, but she invited him to come and visit at the Brookses' home. He came over that very day and stayed for hours, reminiscing. He stayed for supper and long after.

Nancy stared at him, amazed. He had certainly changed. The skinny kid was now six feet two and weighed almost 200 pounds. He was dressed in a well-cut dark business suit. He said he lived in Everett, Washington; he had married a California girl, and they had moved up to Washington State. He told Nancy he had worked for a while as a jailer in the Snohomish County Jail and that he was studying to be a reserve officer.

Bennett had always been a little strange. Although she didn't bring it up, Nancy recalled that he had become upset if he heard about children being physically punished or abused—because he had suffered terribly as a child. He seemed quite urbane now that he was in his late twenties, but she wondered if his early insecurities still gripped him from time to time.

In the series of events that began to unfold in Bellevue, Everett, and Seattle in the mid-1970s, it is well nigh impossible to give complete credence to any of the principal characters' recall. The only way to tell the bizarre story is to give each person's viewpoint, and let the reader judge who was telling the truth—or perhaps came *closest* to the truth.

Nancy Brooks recalled that Bennett LeClerk came to see her frequently, always dressed in a dark business suit. He was not one to drop in for a quick visit; he invariably lingered for hours. He hung around until she was preparing supper for her family, and she felt that she had no choice but to invite him to stay. She began to hint broadly that she had things to do and places to go, but he never took it as a cue for him to leave. His presence became, she said, "intolerable."

At length, Nancy said she considered Bennett a nuisance

and a pest. Her neighbors had begun to ask who he was, and her own children were puzzled about the man who came to their house so often and stayed so long. Apparently her husband was not jealous or suspicious. She never mentioned that he questioned her about the younger man who was becoming a fixture in their home.

Nancy led a busy life with her dogs, her family, and her friends, and she finally told Bennett LeClerk not to visit her again at her house when her husband was away. "My neighbors are talking," she said.

According to Nancy, he became enraged. *"We* know we're doing nothing wrong," he said, "and I don't care what society says!"

But Nancy Brooks said she remained adamant: she would not have him hanging around her house. She said that he had stormed off and never came back to her house—except for one final visit.

Who *was* this reborn Bennett LeClerk?

LeClerk was different things to different people. He had indeed been employed as a jailer in the Snohomish County Jail in Everett, Washington. Members of the sheriff's staff said he always wore green tennis shoes to work and that he liked to bounce off the walls with his feet to demonstrate his agility. He claimed to be a master in kung fu.

Others who met him said he told them that he was fluent in many languages, including Russian, German, Japanese, and Sanskrit. He also said he was a speed reader who could read upside down and backwards faster than most people could read right side up and forward.

He was reportedly a devout Buddhist and considered himself a Buddhist priest.

None of these claims would make him undesirable as a jail guard; it was his attitude that cost him his job. According to fellow jailers, he was dismissed after a number of prisoners complained about his brutality and his propensity for choking them out.

With the demise of his career in law enforcement, Bennett LeClerk opened a business called the Cash Card Company. He apparently did well: he owned a home that would be worth $175,000 in today's real estate market. He was still married to his first wife when he moved a second woman, whom he *also* considered his wife, into the house and began a ménage à trois. His second "wife" had money, and she and LeClerk bought a tavern together. It was called the Iron Horse, and it soon became a thriving operation. In addition to being adept at Sanskrit and kung fu, Bennett made great fried chicken, which the Iron Horse served nightly.

His three-sided marriage lasted until Bennett's first wife gave birth to a son. Soon afterward she took the baby and left him, returning to California.

Bennett LeClerk, once a friendless teenager who put on magic shows for little kids, had become a kind of cult hero, even though his cult was small. Even when he had two "wives" living in his house, he wasn't satisfied; he was an accomplished womanizer, apparently insatiable when it came to conquests of new females.

He had an almost hypnotic effect on women. He met some of them in his various business enterprises, some came to the classes he taught in kung fu, and others attended Buddhist worship services, which he conducted in a shrine he'd had built in the basement of his home. Some said that he had his own little cult in his private shrine and that the religion he practiced was more like witchcraft.

One would think that a man with money, women, and business success would be confident, but Bennett wasn't. He could not bear to have even one of his women leave him or, worse, to have one of his seduction attempts fail. He could not take no for an answer without being plunged into depression.

It is quite possible that he'd had a teenage crush on Nancy Brooks and that he had hoped to seduce her during one of his many lingering visits to her home. If that happened, she never admitted it, and she sent him away, triggering in him a rage and quite probably an obsession. He could not endure rejection in any form.

Image was everything for Bennett LeClerk. He worked hard to create a macho image. He saw himself as a kind of Clint Eastwood figure—in the days when Eastwood was making spaghetti westerns. He affected an outfit that would have been almost laughable if he hadn't taken it so seriously and if he hadn't been such a large and threatening man: black shirt, pants, and boots; a black leather jacket; and a wide-brimmed black hat with a fuchsia band.

At least one woman, Brenda Simms,* a lovely blonde, said that Bennett simply could not believe she didn't want him as a lover. He even insisted that she leave her husband and come to him. She also said that he once forced himself on her. But she nonetheless continued to work with him at the Cash Card Company.

Nancy Brooks knew Bennett LeClerk and Rose Stahl, but they did not know each other. Nancy had met them in entirely different phases of her life. In 1974 all three of them just happened to live in Washington State. Two Bellevue housewives and a businessman–kung fu instructor–Buddhist priest. They sounded like the cast of an experimental theater play.

Early in November 1974, Sara Talbot, a teacher in Everett, Washington, twenty-six miles north of Seattle, was very troubled. After debating what she should do, she decided she had to go to the police, even though she was afraid they would think she was crazy. Finally she approached Officer Donald Rasmussen of the Everett Police Department and haltingly told him an incredible story.

It concerned a man named Bennett LeClerk, who, she said, had once been a jailer in the Snohomish County Jail in Everett. (Rasmussen checked; *that* much was true.) Sara Talbot said that LeClerk was living with his second wife, although he'd never divorced his first.

Sara Talbot said she had met LeClerk during a legitimate business deal. She described him as a very large man who seemed to be a confirmed philanderer. While she had avoided any personal relationship with him, she had observed him coming on to women, and she said he almost mesmerized them with his manipulative manner and his eyes.

She told Rasmussen about the kung fu classes LeClerk taught and about his Buddhist temple. "He can speak many languages," she said. He is an expert in explosives, a Special Forces veteran, and he has an IQ of 170."

If even half of what she was saying was true, she was certainly drawing a picture of an interesting character. Rasmussen explained that he still couldn't see that this Bennett LeClerk had done anything illegal—unless he had, indeed, committed bigamy. He asked Sara Talbot why she was so concerned.

"Because now he says he's been hired to kill someone," she blurted. "He says he's a hit man and that he has to kill two men. The first one's going to be next Tuesday. He says he's doing it as a favor for a friend because the man is a sadist who's cruel to his children. He says he usually gets $5,000 to hit somebody but that he will do this for only $1,000 because his friend asked him to do it."

Now Sara Talbot had Rasmussen's full attention. LeClerk might be a braggart, but no law enforcement officer could look the other way when murder for hire was mentioned.

"I didn't pay too much attention to Bennett the first time he told me this assassin story—he does like to tell grandiose stories," Sara said. "But now I'm frightened. He keeps insisting that I go with him and do the driving. I'm actually beginning to think there's some truth to it."

Sara said she had stopped by the Iron Horse Tavern to pick up some fried chicken and Bennett had said in all seriousness, "What are you doing next Tuesday?"

"I told him that I'd be off work at noon," she said, "and he said, 'Good. You will be with me on my hit next Tuesday.' I actually think he meant it."

Rasmussen conferred with his superiors, and they set up a meeting with Detective Sergeant Don Nelson of the Snohomish County Sheriff's Office. The investigators were in a bind. First of all, they could not arrest this LeClerk before the fact—for something he *might* do. Secondly, Sara Talbot had no idea who the purported murder victim was, so they couldn't warn him or her.

If Sara Talbot refused to go along with Bennett LeClerk's plans and it turned out he *was* serious, he would probably find someone else to aid and abet him, and *that* someone might not contact the police. It was a lot to ask of a woman who was as frightened as Sara appeared to be, but the authorities asked Sara to go along with LeClerk and make him think she was a willing accomplice.

"Do you know where this person is supposed to be killed?" Nelson asked her.

She shook her head. "But I got the impression that it's to be at a community college about ten minutes' drive from downtown Everett," she said. "The only community college that close would have to be Everett Community College."

"You'll have to go along with him," Nelson said. "But *we'll* be along with you."

Sara told the detectives that she was supposed to pick LeClerk up at his home at 6:30 P.M. on Tuesday, November 5. The hit was supposed to take place at 9:30.

As she drove up to LeClerk's home, Everett detectives Thomas Anglin and Truman Hegge, Rasmussen, and Snohomish County detectives Don Nelson, Don Slack, and Dick Taylor waited nearby in unmarked vehicles. They weren't sure in whose jurisdiction the hit was supposed to occur, so both city and county detectives were part of the task force that would follow Sara's car.

Sara Talbot parked in front of the expensive home where Bennett LeClerk lived. He jumped into her blue 1970 Toyota, and she saw that he was dressed in a bizarre costume. He wore an army fatigue jacket and trousers and a black navy watch cap.

He asked her to wait while he finished putting on what appeared to be theatrical makeup. His skin was naturally pale, and he darkened it until he was barely recognizable. To complete his disguise, he glued on a fake mustache and beard.

He had one gun tucked inside his belt at the small of his back, and he showed her where he carried another in his fatigue jacket.

The detectives, who were parked nearby, saw Sara's blue car pull away, and one by one they fell in behind her, often changing places with one another and occasionally passing her car so that it would not become apparent to LeClerk that he was being followed. From time to time one car would turn off on a side street, only to rejoin the covert convoy later.

Almost from the beginning, nothing went as planned. They had expected the blue Toyota to head for Everett Community College. Instead, it gathered speed after it pulled onto the Interstate 5 freeway.

"They're heading for Seattle," someone said on the radio. "They've passed the community college."

Once Sara's car picked up speed, it was quickly swallowed up in traffic. Even she didn't know which of the cars behind her held police, and Bennett seemed perfectly calm. He obviously had no idea that he was being tailed.

They passed Lynnwood, and then Mountlake Terrace. In a few minutes, they would be crossing the northern boundary of Seattle. The Everett detectives radioed Seattle police and informed the dispatcher that a threatened hit was headed into their jurisdiction. They gave their location and asked for backup.

The way Sara was changing lanes told the police that her passenger was giving her directions. Then suddenly they were caught in a traffic jam, and they could no longer see the blue Toyota. For a few heart-stopping minutes the sneaker cars from the north found themselves in a morass of unfamiliar streets along the west side of the University of Washington campus. LeClerk had lots of places in which to get lost here.

The Everett and Snohomish County cars fanned out and, to their vast relief, spotted Sara Talbot's car. She was just parking it, and, although they didn't realize it at the moment, she and the hit man were only two blocks from the north end police precinct in Seattle. The stakeout team had the car in sight again, but where was the hit to take place, and, more important, who was the potential victim?

Seattle Police detectives Gene Birkeland and Doug Fritschy and officers Mike Crist, Jim Devine, and Sergeant Gerald Taylor joined the cops already waiting.

The blue Toyota moved frequently from one parking spot to another, settling for a time near an apartment building and then moving on to a tavern. At one point it drove away from the area entirely and, with a police tail, circled a plush residential area and then came back to what Seattleites call the Wallingford District.

This time the Toyota stayed in one spot. Don Nelson placed two of his deputies—Don Slack and Dick Taylor—on the roof of an automotive shop where they had a bird's-eye view of the area, and the other police personnel found spots where they could watch the activity in the blue car but still be out of sight.

The watching policemen tensed as a tall man wearing fatigues and makeup left Sara Talbot's car, but he only walked back and forth, peered around buildings, and then came back to her car.

He repeated his forays several times during the two hours the officers waited. They were at an impasse. They tensed each time the man got out to prowl the quiet residential streets and alleyways. They couldn't arrest him; there was no reason to. He had committed no crime.

The minutes ticked by, and Nelson reminded everyone by police radio that the hit was supposed to take place at 9:30 P.M. "We decided to confront the man," Nelson recalled. "But that's when he crossed the street and was momentarily out of our view."

Suddenly, at a few minutes after nine, LeClerk left the car again, and things began to happen fast. Once the hit man could no longer see her, Sara Talbot pulled slowly along the street craning her neck until she spotted an Everett officer she knew. "Now!" she mouthed frantically. *The time is now!*

The officer spun around and headed for LeClerk. Mike Crist, a Seattle patrolman, had decided at almost the same instant that they had waited long enough. The men felt as if they were moving through molasses as they ran to catch up with LeClerk.

And then they heard a sound that made their hearts convulse. Before they could reach the tall man in disguise, a single shot echoed in the chill November night. Almost immediately they heard a man's voice screaming, "Help me! Somebody help me!"

Crist dropped to one knee at the exit to the alley where LeClerk had disappeared. Holding his .38 Police Special in both hands, Crist leveled the weapon and pointed it at a tall figure running toward him. Six more shots rang out as Slack and Taylor on the garage roof fired at the fleeing gunman. He slowed but didn't stop.

The man in fatigues was visible to Mike Crist in the yellow glow of a streetlight now. He whirled toward Crist, prepared to shoot it out with him, but Crist never wavered. "Drop your weapon," he ordered, aiming at the gunman's heart.

There were a few tense moments, and then Crist heard the clatter of a gun hitting the pavement. He had not had to fire his weapon. Slack's and Taylor's shots had struck the suspect.

The man, presumed to be Bennett LeClerk, was already wounded in the side of his neck and bleeding profusely. It was difficult to tell if he was seriously injured, but he was still on his feet. He was handcuffed and placed in a police unit to wait for paramedics, as the detectives who had pursued him and the Seattle officers rushed into the alley to check on the man who had screamed.

The target of the assassination plot lay in the alley, terribly wounded. He was conscious, though. He gave his name as Art Stahl. Stahl gasped that he had just walked out of a class on reflexology at the Acadia Health Center. He was in critical condition from a bullet that had pierced his chest at the midpoint of the breastbone and passed through his body, missing his spinal cord by a fraction of an inch. Seattle Fire Department Medic One paramedics rushed to stabilize his condition. When they tore open his shirt, they saw that the shot that hit him was a near-contact wound: the shooter had been standing less than a foot away from Stahl when he fired.

Before they could begin work, however, they had to shoo off members of Stahl's reflexology class, who had removed his shoes and were applying pressure to his feet in an area that they insisted would help heal his chest wound.

The scene was chaos. The gunman was bleeding more heavily than his victim, but Bennett LeClerk was in no danger. Police bullets had merely torn away some of the soft fleshy part of his neck. As a Medic One rig raced Art Stahl to the ER at Harborview Hospital, Sara Talbot sat in her car trembling. She had attempted to pull away from the scene before LeClerk could run back to her car, and Seattle police had arrested her as an accomplice.

"No," the Everett detectives said. "She's with us. She's a police informant." Her handcuffs were removed, and she waited to give a statement.

Bennett LeClerk was taken to the Wallingford Precinct for questioning, complaining all the while about his wound. Deputy Dick Taylor informed him of his rights under *Miranda*, and he admitted orally that he had shot a man named Art because he was "trying to help a friend solve a problem. The best solution was to shoot the person causing the problem."

LeClerk said he had been offered $1,000 to do the shooting, but he hadn't taken it.

"Who asked you to do it?" Taylor asked.

"I can't tell you," LeClerk said. And he refused to put any statement in writing. He said he couldn't answer any more questions because he could feel his throat swelling closed on the inside and he was having trouble breathing.

All questioning stopped—for the moment—and LeClerk too was transported to Group Health Hospital.

The mysterious hit had occurred in the city of Seattle. Seattle homicide detectives Sergeant Bruce Edmonds, Benny DePalmo, and Duane Homan were about to embark on one of the strangest investigations of their careers, and they were starting from scratch.

They retrieved and bagged LeClerk's clothing from the hospital. They found a clump of artificial hair from the beard in his pants pocket, two black leather gloves, a black "Jawa" stick, two rounds of .38 bird shot, and a paper napkin. The napkin was covered with notes and doodles. Among the doodles was a swastika, which—given the crime—was not surprising.

The paper napkin had come from the cocktail lounge of the Holiday Inn in Everett, and on it was written all the vital information a hired killer might need to identify Art Stahl: "52, Art and Rose, L.D. Dogs, $3,000 5'9 150."

On the lower half of the napkin was even more information that indicated that Bennett LeClerk knew exactly where to find his target: "Tuesdays only—Nov. 26, Acadia Health Center, 7–9 p.m. 1220 N. 45th, OTV-940, Black 2-door Dart 70, Bounty Tavern (next to the health center)."

The Seattle detectives knew already that Bennett LeClerk hadn't known Art Stahl even well enough to recognize him by sight. Witnesses who had walked from his reflexology class with him said that the gunman had walked up to him and asked, "Are you Art?" When Stahl said yes the stranger pulled the trigger. The first shot misfired, but the shooter instantly fired again, and Art Stahl fell to the ground and began to scream.

Stahl, who was fighting for his life in the hospital's critical care unit, could not be questioned. His estranged wife, Rose, was home when she was notified that he had been wounded. She told detectives later at the hospital that she was shocked and at a loss to explain the shooting. Yes, they'd been having marital difficulties, but violence had never been involved. She said they had been seeing a counselor and their friend Nancy Brooks, a registered nurse, was also helping them.

As soon as Rose Stahl got word that Art was in the hospital and might be dying, she called Nancy, who rushed over to baby-sit for the Stahl's little boys. She would spend the night at the Stahl home so that Rose could stay at the hospital with Art.

Detectives Benny DePalmo and Duane Homan asked Rose if she knew anyone named Bennett LeClerk, and she shook her head.

"Does your friend Nancy know him?"

"I don't know. . . . I don't think so. She's never mentioned him."

Several seemingly unrelated events occurred the next day, November 6, while Art Stahl remained in the ICU.

Claire Noonan called Nancy Brooks and asked her if she knew anything about Bennett's shooting some man named "Stowe."

"No," Nancy replied.

"Have you seen Bennett lately?"

"Not for a long, long time, Claire," Nancy said, adding that she had no idea what Bennett had been doing and she knew nothing of a man named Stowe being shot. Although her friend from California had misunderstood Stahl's name, Nancy certainly *had* heard of the shooting, but she didn't admit that to Bennett LeClerk's mother.

At this point the Seattle police were working without a number of pieces of vital information. They knew that their victim was a University of Washington instructor, that he had been having trouble in his marriage, and that he had been shot by someone who was apparently a stranger to him. They did *not* know yet that Art Stahl was worth almost a million dollars.

The Seattle Homicide Unit commander, Captain Herb Swindler, received an anonymous call at home that day, however, that filled in a lot of the blank spots. "Stahl's worth a bundle," the voice said. "Nancy Brooks may know something about all of this."

Detectives Duane Homan and Benny DePalmo learned that Art Stahl was out of surgery and awake. He was alert but clearly very frightened. He asked them if the police guard outside his hospital room could be kept there indefinitely. He didn't say who he was afraid of, and the detectives got the idea that he didn't really know. "I don't know who to trust," he said quietly, "but I have confidence in you two. I want to give you something. Hand me my trousers, would you?"

DePalmo got Stahl's trousers from the closet, and the injured man fished in his pocket until he came up with a key ring. He took a small key off the ring and handed it to the detective. "Here, this is for my desk drawer in my office at the university. I have a private journal that I've been keeping there for a year. Get it and read it. Maybe you'll get an idea of why this happened."

They retrieved Stahl's journal from his office and sat down to see if it held any clues to the shooting. As they read the running record of a loveless marriage, the two homicide investigators sympathized with Art Stahl. He'd had good reason to move out of his house. But even though Rose

Stahl had threatened Art with a butcher knife, she wasn't a viable suspect. They could definitely place her at home in Bellevue miles away across a floating bridge from the alley where the shooting occurred.

Rose had a motive for wanting her estranged husband dead; the investigators checked and found that Stahl *was* wealthy, that his $780,000 plus was tied up in a trust, and that if he died before his will was finalized, Rose would become the beneficiary of the trust.

By November 13 Art Stahl was recovering well, although he still wanted a police guard twenty-four hours a day. Homan and DePalmo couldn't really blame him. They had attempted to learn more about his bleak marriage from the couples' friend Nancy Brooks. But she told them she had been in still another automobile accident, which had aggravated her already delicate spine. "I just can't come into Seattle to talk with you," she said. "Could you come here? And I know you won't mind, but I'd feel better if my attorney was present while you were here."

Homan and DePalmo had no problem with that, although it seemed a little peculiar that Nancy Brooks would take such a precaution when she was only an outside witness—someone they hoped knew both Art and Rose Stahl well enough to throw a little light on their investigation.

The two detectives drove to the Brookses' comfortable Bellevue home. They found Nancy to be a tall, somewhat fragile-looking woman, who seemed bemused by the news of Art Stahl's shooting. She told them she knew Bennett LeClerk but did not mention any recent contact with him.

"Did LeClerk know Rose Stahl?" DePalmo asked.

Nancy Brooks shook her head. She didn't think that he knew Rose, but said it was possible because they all raised dogs. "Rose and I raise poodles, but Bennett has German shepherds. I suppose she might have met him at a dog show or something."

Nancy Brooks seemed slightly ill at ease when she spoke about LeClerk, but the detectives could not be certain why; it was almost as if she feared him. But this was a shocking situation, and the woman before them seemed refined and unused to violence. Nancy volunteered that she had last seen Bennett in Everett sometime around the latter part of October. She had gone there to "counsel" him because he was upset, but she hadn't mentioned the visit to her husband.

"Why not?" Homan asked.

"My husband's an engineer," she said, wryly, "and he thinks like one."

While that remark might have gone over the heads of anyone outside the Seattle area, Homan and DePalmo understood. "Boeing engineer jokes" were always making the rounds. The jokes ridiculed engineers for having no imagination and showing no emotion, for wearing pocket protectors full of pens, and for thinking only in mathematical terms.

Homan and DePalmo wondered about the relationship between Nancy Brooks and Bennett LeClerk, and they discussed it as they drove back to town. Were they lovers? It hardly seemed possible. Nancy was eleven or twelve years older than Bennett and had known him since he was a kid. She seemed like the complete housewife, modestly dressed to the point of being prim; it was almost impossible to picture her in a love nest with a man as flamboyant and peculiar as Bennett LeClerk. No, Nancy appeared to be the kind of woman who was always trying to help people—listening to their problems, offering solutions.

Still, there had to be *some* connection. No matter how they tried to reconstruct the events leading up to the shooting, Nancy Brooks was the link—seemingly the only link—between Bennett LeClerk and Art Stahl. The two men had not known each other even by sight, but Nancy knew both of them well.

It would be almost four months later before Bennett LeClerk was ready to give a full statement about the shooting on November 5. His story was so incredible that it was difficult to believe him, and yet it was the only explanation that made any sense.

Bennett LeClerk said he had known Nancy Brooks for many years, ever since he was a teenager in California.

When he moved to Washington and learned that she and her husband lived within thirty miles of him, he had reestablished his friendship with her, and she had become his confidante.

LeClerk told police that Nancy had called him in late October 1974 and asked to meet him in the cocktail lounge of the Holiday Inn in Everett. There Nancy told him how worried she was about a "terrible" situation in her friend Rose's home: Rose's husband was a sadist, a child-beater, and an abuser. This was about the worst thing that Bennett LeClerk could imagine, he said. He himself had a blank space of several years in his memory of his early childhood because he had been physically abused by a stepfather. He deplored the thought that anyone could harm a child, and Nancy was telling him that this guy named Art was making his and Rose's children's lives hell.

"I asked her," LeClerk said, "if divorce wouldn't be the answer to saving the children from this guy, but Nancy said it wouldn't be good enough."

Nancy Brooks was asking him to kill Art so that her friend and the children wouldn't have to be afraid any longer.

"I told her I'd think it over," LeClerk said.

On Halloween, LeClerk and Nancy Brooks had had a second meeting at the Holiday Inn, this time in the parking lot. She seemed distraught and told him that the situation in Rose's home was "deteriorating rapidly" and that he must do "it" as soon as possible. The children were suffering terribly.

He didn't feel comfortable sitting in the hotel parking lot discussing murder, LeClerk said, so he drove Nancy to his own home, where they talked for about two hours, weighing the pros and cons of blasting Art off the face of the earth. There were two little boys in Art and Rose's family, Nancy said—babies really—as well as some older children. Their father made them suffer, she said, very much as Bennett had suffered when he was a child.

LeClerk said Nancy promised to pay him $1,000 if he killed Art, but he said he wouldn't take money from her; the money should come from Rose. "She shouldn't be uninvolved emotionally or morally," he told Nancy. After all, they would be doing it for her and her children.

Nancy had convinced him, finally, that someone had to kill Art—and soon. "I told her I would do it," Bennett said, "probably [the] next Tuesday."

He then asked the woman who had been like an aunt to him, "But what if I get caught?"

"I hadn't thought of that," she reportedly said. "Then I would have to deny everything."

She showed him some small pictures of Art so he would know what his target looked like—but she took them back, LeClerk said.

LeClerk said he had then figured that if he wasn't caught in the first ten minutes after the shooting, he would be home free. Police would not be able to connect him to Art, any more than they could connect two strangers passing on a busy street. He didn't even want to know Art's last name.

Bennett just knew he had to kill him. It had to be done to save the children.

The detectives realized that if their prisoner was telling the truth, Nancy Brooks had been an integral part of this murder for hire. Quite possibly she was the instigator. She was the sole connection between LeClerk and Stahl; she was the only one who knew exactly which buttons to push in the complex mind of Bennett LeClerk; she knew all about his childhood; and she knew that he lost it when he heard about kids being abused.

Once he had agreed to do what Nancy Brooks asked, LeClerk said he began planning. He needed Sara Talbot to drive him to the address Nancy had given him—the place where Art went every Tuesday night. Sara's car wasn't nearly as recognizable as his own fleet of flashy cars. "I planned to find Art's car and clip the ignition wires so he couldn't drive away from that health center," he told the detectives.

He spent Tuesday morning, November 5, looking at houses "because I planned to go into the real estate business with Sara," he explained. "I ate lunch with her. Later I had supper—what little I managed to get down."

He said he owned three complete theatrical makeup kits, and he made himself up to look like a South American revolutionary, with dark makeup, the false facial hair, and the fatigue jacket and pants. "I took two guns with me— one a drop gun [an untraceable gun left at the scene to confuse police] and the attack weapon that I tucked into my belt."

He said he hadn't worn his glasses for fear he might drop them and his prescription would be traced to him. "I'm nearsighted in one eye," LeClerk said, "and farsighted in the other. My night vision in the medium range is poor."

Duane Homan and Benny DePalmo stared at the hit man. He seemed to be living in a fantasy world—with his elaborate makeup—but he was not as clever as he pretended to be. To go out on a murder-for-hire mission half blind without even knowing what his quarry looked like seemed less than clever. And yet this man in front of them was supposed to be a genius.

"I deliberately had no identification on me," LeClerk said, "just that napkin that Nancy gave me at the Holiday Inn on Halloween."

They had arrived near the Acadia Health Center around 7:00 P.M., Bennett unaware, of course, that they were tailed by a caravan of law enforcement officers. "I figured Art would park his car near the Bounty Tavern," he explained. "I found the 1979 Dart and I tried to clip the wires, but it was too dark to find the leads, so I gave up, for fear I might be noticed.

"I asked Sara to move her car several times, and I made several reconnoitering trips around the neighborhood on foot. I saw the alley between the health center and the Bounty Tavern and figured that would be the best place. . . . I would just stand there and wait for Art. Sara would wait for me at the other end of the alley. After the shooting, I was going to take off my makeup as we drove away."

"Why did you leave the area that one time and drive through Windermere?" Homan asked, curious. Windermere is one of Seattle's poshest neighborhoods.

"Oh, that?" LeClerk said. "Well, this woman who worked

for me had relatives there. I told Sara, 'It should be *him* I'm killing.' See, this Brenda left the week before, and she took money from my tavern and left a note. It said, 'Try to understand—this is all I can do. I'll get in touch.'"

(Bennett LeClerk certainly led a complicated life. Two wives, numerous mistresses, and one woman he wanted as a mistress, Brenda Simms, who would one day give detectives a good deal of background on him.)

"Tell us about the shooting," Homan said.

"Well, the class got out a little after nine. I saw the man I'd seen in the photographs Nancy showed me. He was talking to other people in his class. I walked up to him and said, 'Are you Art?' and he said, 'Yes,' and I fired. It was a misfire, and I fired again. But at the last minute, I turned the gun to avoid a fatal shot."

DePalmo and Homan looked at each other. Since Art Stahl had suffered a through-and-through wound to the dead center of his chest, it was hard to believe that Bennett LeClerk had *really* turned his weapon away. You couldn't aim with much more fatal intent than he had.

Bennett LeClerk pleaded guilty to first-degree assault and on March 5, 1975, was sentenced to up to twenty years in prison by Judge William C. Goodloe. Deputy Prosecutor Lee Yates had recommended that LeClerk be sentenced for "up to life" in prison, and Goodloe suggested that the minimum should be the same as the maximum—twenty years. "You are not a contract man flown in from Chicago with a violin case," he said scathingly to LeClerk. "You are a citizen of this state who made a decision that turned to mud."

LeClerk was uncharacteristically humble. "There is no question that my judgment was poor beyond description. The act is repugnant to me and leaves scars I am going to bear for a very long time."

It was a classic sociopath's statement; those with this personality disorder *always* think of events in terms of themselves. While Art Stahl had barely escaped with his life and bore *real* scars on his neck and chest, Bennett LeClerk talked of *his* scars.

LeClerk remained in the King County Jail so that he

could serve as a material witness against another suspect. The investigation, of course, was far from over. That very afternoon after the sentencing of her old friend, Nancy Brooks was arrested.

Detectives Homan and DePalmo obtained a warrant for her arrest on suspicion of conspiracy to commit first-degree murder. They arrived at the Brookses' Bellevue home at 4:17 P.M. Nancy Brooks seemed only a little surprised when she saw the warrant for her arrest. Otherwise, she maintained the same calm demeanor they had always seen. She quickly made arrangements to have her children and her dogs cared for and then walked with the Seattle investigators to their car.

She talked a little with detectives Homan and DePalmo at headquarters.

She told them that Bennett LeClerk had "haunted" her since 1970, remarking, "I don't know why I am even telling you this, because you won't believe me. LeClerk is so *strange* you will think I made it all up."

They knew LeClerk was strange from personal experience with him, but the fact remained that Nancy Brooks was the thread that bound shooter and victim together.

Nancy denied any connection to Art's shooting. She told Homan and DePalmo that she did go to Bennett's house on Halloween and that he had insisted on giving her a "tour" that included even his shower. "I was afraid," she said, "because I kept thinking of that movie, *Psycho*. But I only met him, as I told you before, because he was upset and said he needed to talk to me."

Nancy Brooks was released a few hours later on $10,000 bond. A week later she pleaded innocent to the charges against her.

For three months the Stahl-Brooks-LeClerk case faded from the media. Nothing would be happening, at least on the surface, until Nancy Brooks's trial in June. Chief Criminal Deputy Prosecutor Roy Howson and Deputy Prosecutor Les Yates would represent the state, and Defense Attorney Gerald Bangs would attempt to show that Nancy Brooks had no connection to the near-murder of Art Stahl.

It was ironically fitting, perhaps, that Bennett LeClerk was the first witness for the prosecution. He made a striking figure as he left the jail elevator. His wrists were manacled, but he wore an expensive suit, a crisp white shirt, and a silk tie. His head was shaved, and he had grown a goatee and mustache. (This time, his facial hair was real.)

As he was led toward the courtroom through the marbled corridors of the courthouse, LeClerk passed his would-be victim, Art Stahl, who by now had recovered. Suddenly LeClerk whirled, and the court deputies' hands moved to their guns. They need not have been concerned. LeClerk merely leaned down and presented a very surprised Art Stahl with an expensive book about Buddhist philosophy. He had carried it in one hand, ready for this meeting.

Stahl, bemused, accepted it and thumbed through it as he waited to testify.

As a witness, LeClerk seemed intelligent and responsive, if more than a little eccentric, as he discussed his wives, mistresses, Buddhism, the temple of worship in his basement, and his small collection of *shrakin* (Japanese weapons), which included a *manreiki*, a chain with weights on the end.

"The Imperial Guards used [the chain] on assassins," he explained to the jury, "so that they could disarm them of samurai swords without spilling blood in the palace."

LeClerk spoke of his long friendship with Nancy Brooks and of his revulsion when she told him about a man named Art who was cruel to his children. Nancy had told him that Art was a sadist. He testified that she had finally convinced him that Art would have to die so that the children could be safe.

The jury would have to choose between this flamboyant witness and the prim, sweet-faced woman at the defense table whose skirts hung discreetly below the knee, whose makeup was barely visible, who was a registered nurse, and who had no criminal background at all.

Defense Attorney Bangs hit hard on LeClerk's many affairs and his religious "disciples," but the witness appeared to enjoy jousting with Bangs. He went into minute detail about his Buddhist shrine and the Buddhist symbol—a water dragon, or *miziechi*. He denied that he considered himself the eye of the dragon, or *so-ryugn*.

The words might as well have been Greek, but the man on the stand radiated charisma, and something more— perhaps a thin sheen of madness? Nevertheless, his genius was apparent to the jury and the gallery. No one listening would have denied that.

Nancy Brooks, sitting at the defense table, showed no reaction at all as LeClerk gave his version of the events of the previous fall. He said that his "conscious intent was to kill the man" but that a "subconscious intent" had made him attempt to turn the gun. So, in effect, he had saved Stahl's life.

LeClerk's mother, Claire Noonan, testified that she had called Nancy Brooks as soon as she read about the shooting in the newspapers. That would have been the day after— November 6. She said Nancy claimed to know absolutely nothing about it. Next, Claire had called her son in the hospital, where he was recovering from his neck wound.

"Why did you shoot that man?" she asked, and he replied that he "had done it for a friend of mine."

The witness said the only friend she had in Seattle was Nancy Brooks. "I asked my son if Nancy was the friend, and he said, 'That's right.' "

Art Stahl, the intended victim, was the last witness for the state. He recalled that the "violence" in his marriage had come not from him but from his estranged wife, Rose, who was furious over the way he spent his trust fund. No one except Rose and two friends at the university had known that he attended reflexology class on Tuesday evenings.

Stahl testified that he didn't see the stranger with a gun until a moment before he was shot in the chest. He also said he had filed for divorce from Rose as soon as he was well enough to leave the hospital.

Sara Talbot, the young woman who had driven the hit car, testified for the defense, but not in person: she had been diagnosed with terminal cancer in the months between the crime in November 1974 and the trial in June 1975. Her image appeared in the courtroom on videotape as she recalled the frightening evening she had spent with Bennett

LeClerk. She had been told he had cut his "kill fee" because he was going to shoot a man "for a friend," but she had never heard the name Nancy Brooks.

Rose Stahl testified in support of her close friend Nancy. Rose admitted that she and Art had had a marriage marked by ups and downs, but she denied ever threatening to kill him. She certainly had not offered to pay $1,000 to have him shot. She had never discussed any of her financial problems with Nancy. "My husband would not have approved of that," she said calmly.

Although it is rare for defendants in cases of murder or attempted murder to take the witness stand, Nancy Brooks's attorney evidently felt she would make a good impression on the jury. Dressed modestly, as always, Nancy Brooks squeezed her husband's hand as she rose to defend herself.

She testified in a soft voice, recalling that Bennett LeClerk had come back into her life a few years before. She had met him at a shopping center in 1973 and gone to see his house. She'd met "both his wives." They had confided that they had difficulty deciding who should answer when a caller asked for "Mrs. LeClerk."

Nancy Brooks said that the last time LeClerk had come to her house he'd worn all black and had carried a gun and a syringe full of poison meant, she said, for the husband of one of his mistresses.

Bennett's lengthy visits to the Brookses' Bellevue home had become a nuisance. She said she'd finally had to tell him not to come again because the neighbors were talking, but she said he could phone her. "You're making it up because your husband is jealous," she said LeClerk had raged. "All men are jealous!"

Asked by her attorney to try to remember all her contacts with twenty-eight-year-old Bennett LeClerk, Nancy Brooks said he had called her in the fall of 1973—twenty months before this trial—and he had said that one of his wives was pregnant and the baby was due in January. He thought Nancy might like to come and visit his mother when she came to Washington.

"And the next time?"

"It was probably in May—May of 1974." Nancy Brooks said she was just out of the hospital after having a neck fusion. Bennett was once again calling her and begging her to meet him, asking if he could come over and see her. "I told him he would have to call first—but he never called." She said he was very upset over a woman named Brenda Simms—"the one woman he could really love."

In September 1974, Nancy Brooks said, Bennett called again. He told her he had been drinking saki and taking Valium, Empirin, and codeine for a back injury. He asked her if she wanted to invest in something, and she had said no.

In October he called again, threatening suicide because everyone had deserted him.

"I believed him," she told the jury earnestly. "He was begging for just one hour of my time." She testified that she had agreed to meet him in Everett on October 25 only because he told her he was so depressed that he would kill himself if she refused. "I didn't want his suicide on my conscience."

Bennett wanted her to intercede with Brenda, who was leaving him. Nancy refused, but suggested he get counseling. She mentioned the name of a psychiatrist, she testified, and he became enraged. She then said she had friends who had gone through counseling and that it had helped them a great deal. No, she said, she "thought" she had not mentioned the Stahls by name.

Oddly, though, Bennett had referred to the Stahls as if he knew them.

Nancy Brooks blushed as she said LeClerk "got fresh" and put his hand beneath her blouse during the meeting in the cocktail lounge. After three hours he walked her to her car and threatened her by saying: "I'll run the show. You will meet me again. I know where your daughter rides, and she's beautiful. If you want to keep her face in that condition, you'll meet me."

He also threatened her husband, she testified. "He told me that if he couldn't get him, someone else would."

She had been terrorized by Bennett LeClerk, she told the jury. But had she told her husband—or the police or her attorney? No, she had not. "I was so scared," she explained to Prosecutor Roy Howson.

Asked if LeClerk had scribbled notes on a cocktail napkin during their meeting, she said she could not recall.

Despite her terror, Nancy Brooks said she had met LeClerk again on October 31. This time, she embellished what she had told Duane Homan and Benny DePalmo. They listened, amazed. They had been led to believe her visit to LeClerk's home had happened much earlier and in the presence of his wives.

Now she said that Bennett had forced her from the Holiday Inn to his home at gunpoint. He had shown her his shrine, his shower, and his bedroom. He had subjected her to sadistic teasing, laughing hysterically. He had shown her the Buddha downstairs and told her the orange dragon was modeled after him.

"He wrapped the chain . . . around his arms, legs, waist," she told the jury, "and he did barefoot karate kicks. He threw the chain toward me, and I jumped back and it fell on the floor."

As the jury leaned forward, Nancy Brooks continued her story of her secret visit to the home of a man she claimed to be afraid of. She said he took her into his bedroom and then into the shower, explaining how "sexy" it was. He told her, she said, that he had brought "many women" there. He'd asked her if she could tell what was so special about the shower. When she shook her head in bewilderment, he showed her how he'd had the shower head mounted so that he could direct the spray wherever he wanted it.

Hesitantly, Nancy said that Bennett had pushed her down on the bed and tried to kiss her. She looked beseechingly at her attorney, "Do I have to say it all?"

"Try to paraphrase," he said gently.

"He pushed me on the bed and tried to kiss me. He told me over and over what an exciting lover he was . . . a lot of rubbish like that. He showed me a bottle of cinnamony liquid and put liquid from it on his finger and made me taste it, and he said it was part of his sex rituals."

The defendant insisted that she had not had sex with LeClerk. Finally, she said, he let her go and drove her back to her car. Again she failed to tell her husband of her frightening ordeal.

She was positive that she had never mentioned the Stahls while she was with Bennett. Positive that she had not said a word about Art's being brutal to his children.

She certainly had never contracted to have Art killed.

As Prosecutors Lee Yates and Roy Howson questioned Nancy, there was a hard edge to her answers. The softly modulated voice was gone now. She denied over and over again that she had been a go-between for LeClerk and Rose Stahl, the facilitator of a planned murder. She refused to look at the attorneys for the state as she answered them.

It was a lengthy trial. In his final arguments, Yates pointed out that Washington statutes declared that anyone who "aids, assists, abets, encourages, hires, counsels, induces or procures another to commit a crime is guilty and shall be treated the same as the person who actually commits it."

Yates stressed that Nancy Brooks had known exactly what strings to pull to make LeClerk do what she wanted. She was Rose Stahl's close friend. The women shared every confidence with each other. Nancy Brooks had known about the inheritance and the threatened divorce.

And she had also known just where Art Stahl would be on the night he was shot. She had known all the facts found on the napkin that Bennett LeClerk had carried. Who else would have provided him with the address and the description of the intended victim, right down to his license-plate number?

In the end, Yates asked the most salient questions: "Why Art Stahl? Why would LeClerk shoot Stahl, a man he didn't even know?"

And that was the question that the jury could not answer satisfactorily without finding Nancy guilty. There was no other way to fit the pieces of the puzzle together. Rose didn't know Bennett. Bennett didn't know Art Stahl. But Nancy Brooks knew everyone, and she knew just which buttons to push. The prosecution team didn't deny that Bennett LeClerk was a bizarre man, a man who professed to have great power and strength, but he was also a man who could not stand rejection from women.

Nancy Brooks had known him since he was a disturbed teenager; she knew all his vulnerable places. Whatever her attachment to Rose Stahl was, it was intense. Nancy wanted Rose to be happy—and rich. The only way to facilitate that was for Art to be gone. Really, really gone. When all the circumstantial and physical evidence was evaluated, the only conclusion to be drawn was that Nancy Brooks, the sweet mother and wife, had manipulated eccentric Bennett LeClerk into within a fraction of an inch of outright murder. And she had done all of this as a favor to a friend.

The jury of eight men and four women, after deliberating for less than five hours, found Nancy Brooks guilty of attempted first-degree murder. The penalty for attempted murder was the same as it would have been if the murder plot had succeeded. Judge James Mifflin sentenced Nancy Brooks to up to life in prison.

At this writing, both Nancy Brooks and Bennett LeClerk have served their prison terms and been paroled. They have not come to the attention of Washington State authorities again. Like Nancy and Bennett, Rose Stahl has disappeared from the public eye. Art Stahl recovered completely from his gunshot wound and is alive and well two decades later.

In the end, the argument for the healing powers of reflexology may have been strengthened. Art Stahl received what should have been a fatal—or at least a paralyzing—wound. But immediately after he was shot in the chest, a classmate removed his shoes and massaged the "heart healing" area of his feet. Who is to say that, at least in Stahl's case, it wasn't reflexology that saved his life?

The Most
Dangerous Game

When I was in high school, our English teacher assigned us a short story that has become a classic. "The Most Dangerous Game" was the story of a millionaire whose private island was his personal hunting preserve. It left a lasting impression on me and gave me a view of cruelty and manipulation I had never imagined. Many years later I came across a case that made me remember that troubling story. I have chosen the title of that short story for this Snohomish County, Washington, case. There are many dark similarities between the fictional story and the true case.

The victims in this case were very young and naive, full of the spirit of adventure and in search of a perfect world and perfect love. They were the age that I was in high school, and they had the same innocence. The peace and love and joy of Woodstock was only two years past, and many young people were still captivated by the concept the flower children had embraced: "All you need is love."

The girls in this case had never encountered pure, distilled evil before, and they did not recognize it for what it was until it was too late.

As terrifying as this encounter in a howling blizzard was,

the ending was not as tragic as it seemed destined to be. For those who believe in miracles—or in angels—the astonishing denouement of "The Most Dangerous Game" will only strengthen that belief.

Washington is bisected by the Cascade Mountains. The state is rainy and mild on the Pacific coast and prone to hot dry summers and freezing winters on the eastern side. The mountains themselves often have snowy peaks year round. Skilled highway engineers have cut routes through the mountain passes, so that it is possible to cross the Cascades in all but the wildest of winter storms: White Pass, North Cascades Highway, Snoqualmie Pass, and Stevens Pass. The North Cascades Highway tends to close down for the winter first, and Snoqualmie Pass is the easiest route. Success for those who attempt to cross White Pass and Stevens Pass depends on the depth of the snowdrifts, the threat of avalanches, and the accuracy of weathermen.

None of these routes east from the Washington coast should be chosen by ill-prepared youngsters bent on running away—not in winter. Never in winter.

Maeve Flaherty* was sixteen years old in the winter of 1971. She lived in Seattle with her parents and brothers and sisters. Her father was a doctor, and the family lived in a more-than-comfortable home in one of Seattle's nicest neighborhoods. Maeve was a pretty girl, short and a little plump. She had a pixyish sense of humor, and like many teens in the early seventies, she was caught up in a world where the young were protesting what they saw as the sins of adults. The Chicago Seven, the Beatles with their long hair and their message-filled music, and the National Guard shootings at Kent State were in the news. While their parents were listening to Dinah Shore and Lawrence Welk, teens were buying Janis Joplin, Three Dog Night, and Simon and Garfunkel—music that sounded like cacophony to the older generation. It has always been so, and it always will be, but the youth revolution of the sixties and seventies was stronger and more visible.

Maeve liked to think she was a rebel—but she wasn't, really. She was a dreamer whose fantasies far outweighed her common sense. She was restless—eager to try her own wings. Whenever things didn't go well in her life, Maeve ran. She had run away often enough so that her parents, at their wits' end, considered putting her in a private girls' boarding school. Although they would miss having her at home, they hoped that she would get strict supervision there.

Maeve was adamant that she would not go away to school. She would rather run away than wear a uniform and observe a curfew and go to a stuffy school. She began to formulate a plan. She didn't tell her parents, of course; she needed time to prepare. By February 20, 1971, she was ready to leave. Maeve "triple-dressed"—and then some. She piled on layer after layer of clothes and jeans. That way, she wouldn't have to carry a suitcase, which would certainly have sounded automatic alarm bells.

Maeve wouldn't be running away alone. She had a friend whose views were much like her own. Kari Ivarsen* was eighteen—two years older than Maeve—and had lived away from her family for months. They both felt they were perfectly capable of taking care of themselves. They saw their parents as having morals and rules right out of the Stone Age. They both believed that the world was a good place, that you could trust strangers because all people were good if they were shown love, because love transcended all danger. If they could have, Maeve and Kari would have journeyed to Woodstock in 1969 and participated in that giant muddy love fest where everyone got along wonderfully despite the dire predictions of adults.

Where Maeve was a cute and cuddly girl, Kari was absolutely beautiful. She was slender and graceful with the perfectly symmetrical facial features that made men swivel their heads to look at her. Having already proved she could get by very well without parental supervision, Kari assured Maeve that they would be perfectly fine once they hit the road. They would have fun and interesting adventures, and when they were ready, they would come back home.

The two girls arranged to meet away from Maeve's home. They knew if they were to evade Maeve's parents and the authorities, they had to avoid all their usual hangouts and get out of Seattle as soon as possible. They had saved some money, but not enough to rent a room or an apartment. If they ran out of money for food, they could work as waitresses or dishwashers. Figuring out how to survive would be part of the adventure of their new life.

Someone had told them that there were scores of summer cabins around the Cascade foothills and the isolated lakes in Snohomish County just north of the King County line. Reportedly those cabins sat there empty during the off-season; their owners rarely, if ever, used them in the winter time.

Kari brought it up first: why couldn't they "borrow" a cabin for a while? She envisioned a cozy hideaway with a roaring fire where no one would find them or bother them. They wouldn't really be hurting anything; maybe later they could repay the owners for whatever canned goods or supplies they used. It wouldn't be stealing—not really—since they intended to replace everything.

Neither girl knew anything at all about mountain survival. They figured they would learn as they went along.

One thing about Washington State that its residents appreciate is that they can leave Seattle and be in the mountains in an hour—or on a Pacific Ocean beach in an hour and a half. One can actually stand in the middle of Seattle and see the snowcapped mountains in the distance; tricks of depth perception make them seem close enough to reach out and touch.

Maeve Flaherty and Kari Ivarsen decided to head for those deceptively safe-looking mountains. They had enough money to take a bus twenty-six miles north to Everett, the Snohomish County seat. They knew how to make their way to Stevens Pass from Everett, hitchhiking through the little towns of Monroe, Sultan, and Startup, where Highway 2 began to climb toward the summit of the towering mountain range. They passed through Gold Bar and Index, and then stood beside the highway. They needed to find shelter before dark. Kari and Maeve had no real plans at all after that; that was half the fun—waiting to see what would happen.

The dream sounded good, and they fueled each other's enthusiasm.

Almost three weeks earlier and some eighty or ninety miles south of the hideaway Maeve and Kari sought, a young man had also made plans to run away. But he didn't run away from his parents and the boredom of school. He was escaping from the U.S. Army. He used the name Al, although that wasn't his real name. The less people knew about him, the better he liked it. Al was twenty-one. He had been confident that joining the army would be the answer to all of his problems, but he found the rigors of basic training at Fort Lewis, south of Tacoma, more than he'd bargained for. He didn't like getting up before dawn, he didn't like hikes in the rain, and he didn't like being told what to do every waking moment. Most of all, he didn't like the idea of being shipped to a war in Vietnam.

Another soldier, who was from Washington State, had told Al about the cluster of empty cabins near Index in Snohomish County. He said that lots of the places up there were too deep in the woods to appeal to their city-dwelling owners in the winter. He directed Al toward Stevens Pass in the snowy foothills of the Cascades. From what Al could gather, a lot of people showed up there in the wintertime for reasons of their own.

The deserted cabins would be only the first phase of Al's plan. He had studied maps to find a place where he could cross the Canadian border without a lot of questions from the border patrols. Once free of the United States, he hoped to get on a plane or a boat to Sweden. Reportedly, many American draft dodgers and servicemen like him, who were absent without leave, had taken refuge in Sweden. He had picked up on rumors that an active underground, run by conscientious objectors, would shelter runaways from military service.

Al figured he'd blend in—protective coloration, as it were—in Sweden. He was blond with a crisp wave of hair that fell over his forehead, and he had dark eyes under heavy brows. He was a handsome young man, six feet tall, broad-shouldered, and trim but muscular. He was also outgoing and convincing. People liked him and were drawn to him—especially women, whether they were little old ladies or young girls. All he had to do was grin. If there was rage just beneath his attractive facade—and there was—he hid it completely.

Al hitched a ride north to Seattle and beyond. He visited with some relatives near Everett and then rode with a truck driver through Sultan, Gold Bar, and Startup. He was looking for a place called Mineral City.

The truck driver shook his head. "Never heard of it," he said, "and I've been driving Stevens Pass for years."

That shook Al a little. According to rumor, Mineral City was a ghost town, a regular Shangri-la, with everything a man needed to live. Miners had abandoned the settlement decades before, but the buildings were still there. Al hadn't located it, but he figured it was too small to show up on the map he'd bought at the service station. In truth, there was no such place.

There *was* an area called Garland Mineral Springs, or Garland Hot Springs. It had once been a mecca for those who believed that the minerals in the spring water would cure all manner of physical ills. The springs were fourteen miles east of Index on the Index-Galena Road. The road wound north from Index and then east along the north fork of the Snohomish River and past the Troublesome Creek Campground and the San Juan Campground to Garland Mineral Springs before it meandered tortuously south back to Jack Pass and Highway 2. The road was used mainly by loggers. Garland Mineral Springs, a scene of former grandeur, was now in disarray. Lodges and buildings designed to attract health pilgrims had long since fallen into skeletal ruins.

In summer, the area Al sought was verdant and inviting to experienced hikers who were trail-wise and willing to venture so far from civilized roads. In February, however, it was buried in snowdrifts, and icy tentacles clung to the 100-foot fir limbs and the few buildings that still had roofs. The foothills were over 5,000 feet high here: Troublesome Mountain, Bear Mountain, Frog Mountain. This was no place for amateurs.

It was sometime around February 2 when the tall young man known as Al lowered himself from the cab of the logging truck and headed into the tiny town of Index. Beyond his clean-cut handsomeness, he was not particularly unusual-looking, but there are so few strangers in Index in midwinter that almost any newcomer is noted and remembered. In the summer, things are a bit different; vacationers come and go for a week's hiatus from the city noise in the jerry-built cabins that dot the hills around the village. Strangers are commonplace in Index in August; they stand out in February.

Al had stopped for a beer in an Index tavern and made small talk with the bartender as he drank. The bartender noted that the stranger carried a duffel bag and wore jeans that had been slit up the outside leg seams and then laced together with rawhide. The young man, who said his name was Al, obviously wasn't a complete novice about winter survival; he wore an orange-and-green field jacket, gloves, a scarf, a sweater, and heavy-duty brown boots.

He said he was from California and he carried a map, which he said would lead him to Mineral City. The bartender had never heard of such a place, but he nodded noncommittally. Fantasies are not unheard of in taverns and he had heard a lot of stories in his job. If the stranger thought he was going to find some magic place up in the woods, let him dream.

Some distance out of Index, two young men occupied one of the rustic cabins that were sprinkled through the woods. They had come by it honestly; they paid rent on it every month. The men, known as Handy* and Digger,* were conscientious objectors. By inclination and principle, they were opposed to violence in any form. Because of their pacifist beliefs, they were involved in the underground passage system that smuggled draft evaders into Canada. Although many would find fault with their activities, few would argue that their participation in the underground was for any personal gain. Handy and Digger took risks to help other young men who felt the way they did about war. In return, they received nothing more than the knowledge that they were following their consciences.

The man named Al wandered up the Index-Galena Road to Handy and Digger's cabin a few days later. They gave him a place to sleep, fed him, and listened as he explained that he could not bear to hurt or kill anyone.

"I can't go to Vietnam," he said hoarsely. "I can't shoot someone. I have to get to Canada."

"We'll help you," Digger said. "We'll get you there." He and Handy explained that a lot would depend on the weather. Until they could assure him of safe passage into Canada, they would see that he had enough to eat and a place to stay.

The temperature dropped and the drifts grew deeper, and Al became something of a familiar sight around Index.

A few weeks later, Maeve Flaherty and Kari Ivarsen hitchhiked into Index. They were carrying supplies that they naively believed would see them through the mountain winter: several changes of clothing, a hammer, some nails, matches, and their eye makeup.

The two girls started walking up the Index-Galena Road away from civilization, looking for a cabin where they could settle in for the next few months. But night fell and caught them far from shelter. They managed to find a lean-to where they huddled together for the night, curling up spoon fashion to share their body heat. But it wasn't enough as the night deepened and the temperature plunged lower and lower. In desperation, the girls managed to set fire to the shelter, and the hard wood burned long enough and hot

enough to keep them from freezing. They were grateful to
see a pale sun come up, saving them from what had seemed
like an endless night.

With the resiliency of youth, Kari and Maeve pushed
farther into the woods. Eventually they came to Handy and
Digger's cabin. They could see that someone probably lived
there, although no one was home at the moment. They
found a vacant cabin nearby, and Kari and Maeve used
their hammer to break into it.

They were like little girls playing house. They swept the
floor, started a fire in the fireplace, and prepared to settle in.
Later that day, they met Handy and Digger, their "old
ladies," and Al, their houseguest. Al smiled widely and held
out his hand. Maeve and Kari liked him. He made them
laugh and they thought he was awfully good-looking. After
walking away from Fort Lewis, Al had grown a mustache
and a Vandyke beard, which gave him a rather exotic
appearance. His dark eyes were compelling as he stared at
Kari and Maeve; he seemed fascinated by their story of
running away to find a mountain hideaway.

The two teenagers felt as if the adventures they sought
were beginning. They had met two genuine hippies, their
girlfriends, and Al, who seemed concerned about them and
who was very helpful and attentive.

After Maeve and Kari had spent a few nights in the cabin,
Al came to them and suggested that perhaps the three of
them should move farther into the woods. Handy and
Digger were paying rent for their cabin, but the three of
them were not. "I'm afraid somebody's going to show up to
evict us," Al said worriedly, "or worse. You know, strictly
speaking, we're breaking the law by being here. We could be
in big trouble if they found us."

As the girls listened nervously, Al said he had heard that
police were planning to move into the area and flush out
squatters who didn't belong in the summer cabins. He
would end up in jail, and they might have to go to juvenile
hall. Kari said she was eighteen, but Maeve looked anxious.
Juvenile hall would be even worse than a private girls'
school.

Al had an air of authority about him, and Kari and Maeve

realized that he was probably right about moving deeper into the woods. They had managed to walk into these cabins easily. The police could show up at any time; they weren't really very far from town. After a short discussion, they agreed to pack up and join Al in hiking farther from the highway as soon as he was ready.

They had known Al for several days, but they felt as if they had known him longer. He seemed a lot wiser about the world than they were and Kari and Maeve had come to count on him. It felt safer to have a strong man to look after them. It had been so scary the first night when they had to burn their shelter to survive. With Al leading the way, they wouldn't have to worry about being caught in a snowstorm again.

The trio started out the next morning. The Index-Galena Road grew narrower until it seemed to disappear completely in huge waves of white as they neared the Troublesome Creek area. There they had to break through drifts and wade through waist-deep snow. They were vastly relieved when they finally came to several habitable cabins standing side by side in a narrow clearing that had been hewn from the thick forest. It was almost like seeing a mirage in the desert, but this was real, the little cabins placed improbably in a nearly impenetrable forest of towering fir trees.

The snow on the tiny cabins' roofs was five or six feet deep, and drifts nudged so close to the doorways that they had to scoop the snow away with their hands before they could force the doors open. The cabins were only about ten feet by fifteen feet, and, of course, there was no electricity or running water. Still, with the sun shining down on it, the whole setup looked like a scene from the Swiss Alps. The girls half expected to see Heidi come leaping through the snow.

They would be safe here. The owners wouldn't come to check on their cottages—not with all those snowdrifts they had waded through. And the police couldn't drive this far; the road was drifted over for miles behind them.

Maeve and Kari took one cabin; Al chose one right next door. They filled lamps with coal oil and were delighted to find the cupboards stocked with enough canned food and staples to last them until spring.

Their first few days in the cabins were idyllic. They popped corn, played in the snow, and rearranged the rustic furniture in their cabins. Maeve and Kari felt good about joining up with Al. He was just a nice guy. He hadn't made any sexual overtures. It hadn't taken them long to find out that girls on the run had to expect men to come on to them, but Al wasn't like that. He was kind of like a big brother.

It was lonely way back there in the woods, though, and quieter than they had ever imagined it could be, with no television or radio, only the wind in the trees, a few birds calling, and crashes in the forest when a load of snow slipped off a tree branch high in the air. Maeve and Kari weren't afraid, but they *were* grateful for Al. They were especially thankful for him when they began to hear frightening noises—sounds that they couldn't identify.

One night the three of them were spending an evening in front of the fireplace in the girls' cottage. The coal oil lamps and the fire on the hearth sent flickering shadows on the rough walls, and the wind whistled against the frosted windows. It seemed as if they were the last people alive on the planet. And then suddenly there was a harsh scratching noise against one wall. It sounded as if an animal was trying to claw his way in.

Kari and Maeve had confided to Al that they worried about wolves and coyotes—and bears. Most of all, they were terrified of the Sasquatch—the legendary half-man, half-beast rumored to rove free in among Washington's mountains. There are those who swear they have seen the Sasquatch and his mate. The girls had even seen a blurred photograph that someone took of a creature who walked upright with a face that was half human and with thick, straggly hair sprouting from his body.

"The Sasquatch is ten feet tall," Kari whispered, "and they say he leaves a footprint eighteen inches long. If he wanted to get in, he could."

They listened, their voices hushed, to the scrabbling

sound against the wall. After a while, the scratching stopped, but sitting around the fire wasn't much fun anymore, and the girls didn't feel like laughing at Al's jokes. When Al left to return to his cabin, Maeve and Kari bolted their door and decided to leave the lamps burning all night.

Just as they began to feel a little less frightened, they heard a shout and a cry for help. Shaking, they forced themselves to open the door. They found Al in the snow where he had fallen from a footbridge. He said he didn't think he could walk, so they lifted him and helped him to his cabin. Once they got him there, he didn't seem to be badly hurt, just shaken up. The girls scampered back to their own cabin.

They had scarcely gotten the door bolted when there was a tremendous, violent scratching and clawing against the wall. Whatever was out there had to be huge. They heard a powerful thump, as if something was hurling itself at their fragile cabin in an attempt to break through the wall. When the thumps grew louder, Kari screamed and Maeve sobbed in panic as they ran to Al's cabin, hysterically crying for his protection. But he wasn't there.

They screamed his name for several minutes, afraid to stay on his porch and afraid to go back to their cabin. Finally he came limping up, a dim figure in the dark.

"Where were you?" Kari demanded.

"I was chasing rabbits," he said. "Somebody has to get us some food."

"Did you try to scare us?" Kari asked accusingly.

Al shook his head and looked hurt. "You know me better than that. I wouldn't ever try to frighten you. But maybe you two had better bunk over here tonight just in case there *is* something out there trying to get in."

If they had any qualms about sharing a one-room shack with Al, they needn't have worried. He was a perfect gentleman. He slept in his bunk, and Kari and Maeve curled up in their clothes in the other. There were no more animal sounds, and gradually they all fell asleep.

Still, with the morning light, Kari and Maeve made a decision. Life in the deep woods was not the picnic they had pictured. They were afraid something "out there" was trying to get them. Also, it was still snowing, and they were fearful that the snow would cause their roof to collapse. Then they wouldn't have anything between them and the creatures that came out at night. The sky looked as if another snowstorm was on the way. If they didn't leave now, they might miss their last chance to get through the drifts to the road.

Al tried to talk them out of leaving. They had all been having a great time, he said, and they shouldn't let some branch scraping the cabins in the wind scare them away. "I have a gun," he said.

"Where did you get a gun?" Maeve asked, surprised.

"From this woman who lives down near Index," he said. "She loaned it to me. If anything happens, I can take care of you."

"You can stay if you want to," Kari said, as she stuffed her belongings in her backpack. "We are getting out of here while it's not snowing and it's still daylight."

Maeve nodded. "Come with us, Al," she said. "There *is* something dangerous out in the forest. You heard it last night just as much as we did."

Suddenly even homework seemed okay. Maeve thought longingly of her family's warm house and her own bed.

"I can't change your minds?" Al said with a smile. "Aren't we the Three Musketeers?"

"Nope," Kari said. "We're out of here."

Finally, grudgingly, Al agreed that maybe they *should* go. "But if you're going down to town, I'm going too. I don't want to be up here all alone."

Maeve and Kari didn't have adequate clothing or boots. They put on all five of their shirts and three pairs of jeans. They looked at their cabin for the last time and began to plow through the deep snow, headed for Index. They had almost ten miles to go, and they wanted to be sure they took the right fork in the road so they would head south past Snowslide Gulch and follow the river down to town. Al told them to go ahead. They moved slower than he did, anyway, and he would catch up with them. "I'll just get all my stuff in my duffel bag," he promised. "And I'll be along before you know it."

It was Saturday, February 27, although Kari and Maeve had just about lost track of the days of the week. There was no time up in the forest. No clocks. No radios to remind them. They slogged ahead, already feeling the snow seeping into their shoes.

The girls looked back to see if Al was following them, but they didn't see him as they rounded the first bend in what they hoped was the road. It was hard to tell.

It was midafternoon on Sunday when Handy and Digger heard someone frantically pounding on their door. They opened it to find Al, exhausted and disheveled. He was babbling something about a girl "being hurt" way back in the woods.

"You've got to get help!" he shouted. "She's way up there, and it's really bad. *Really bad.* Call the sheriff—or somebody."

Digger didn't stop to ask questions. He hurried out to where he knew there was a pay phone and called the Snohomish County Sheriff's emergency number.

The dispatcher gave the call to Deputy Allen Halliday who was on patrol in the Index area. He soon got backup from Deputy Frank Young. All the deputies knew was that someone was hurt—"possibly shot"—and the general location of the cabins up near Troublesome Creek Campground. But they realized almost at once that snow and ice prevented them from driving their patrol cars in to aid the injured girl.

Because its boundaries encompass so many perilous areas, Snohomish County has maintained one of the country's top search-and-rescue units for many years. Now Young and Halliday called Inspector C. R. "Bob" Fisher, and he sent Deputies Don Daniels and Bob Korhonen in a four-wheel-drive vehicle that had snowmobiles aboard.

At the same time, Young called Detective D. C. "Doug" Engelbretson at home, where he was on call for the weekend.

"We don't know too much now," Young said, "but there's something strange going on here; maybe you'd better come up, Doug."

Fisher and his crew joined Deputies Young and Halliday. Digger and Hank told the rescue men that they thought a man they knew only as Al and two young women named Kari and Maeve had left several days before to go up the Index-Galena Road almost to Garland Hot Springs.

"I think they must have hiked a long way," Digger said, "maybe eight or ten miles. Al came down and said there was trouble, and one of the girls was injured."

"Where is he?" Fisher asked.

Digger shook his head. "I don't know. He's gone. He was gone when I got back here from phoning you guys."

Fisher's men, who had made almost a thousand rescues since their unit was mobilized, looked in the direction Digger gestured. A road—if it could be called that—extended at least partway through that area. After that they would be searching through a forest so deep in snow that any trail or road would be obliterated. Moreover, it was dark. Fisher had gotten the call at 2:30 P.M. Even though his group had gotten up there in record time, he estimated it might be after six before they could find whatever lay ahead in the black woods.

Halliday, Young, and Engelbretson waited anxiously as the four-wheel vehicle disappeared into the drifts. At Troublesome Creek, Fisher, Daniels, and Korhonen abandoned the rig and moved forward aboard snowmobiles. At one point, their powerful lights played over bright crimson stains in the snow. It didn't look good.

It was 7:50 P.M. when the mobile radio at the base camp crackled. "We have the girls," was the terse message. "Have an ambulance waiting."

Doug Engelbretson, whose area of expertise was homicide investigation, waited anxiously, straining his eyes for the sight of lights coming back down the road from Troublesome Creek. Finally he hurried forward as the search-and-rescue rig emerged from the woods with two passengers on board.

Both were girls, but there was no time for Engelbretson to get much information about what had happened. One girl—the sixteen-year-old, whose name was Maeve Flaherty—was loaded at once into the waiting ambulance, which headed toward Providence Hospital in Everett. Kari Ivarsen, who said she was eighteen, seemed to be in shock but otherwise uninjured. She was taken where she could get warm and have some food.

Doug Engelbretson learned that Maeve Flaherty was alive when she reached Providence Hospital, but that she was in critical condition from a gunshot wound and was undergoing surgery.

Engelbretson waited until Kari Ivarsen was finally able to talk. He assured her that Maeve was alive and receiving expert care, but he did not mention how critical Maeve's condition was. Even though time was of the essence in finding the person who had shot Maeve, Engelbretson could see how delicate Kari's grip on reality was. He questioned her gently about what had happened up there in the deserted woods. As she spoke haltingly, he listened, horrified. Kari Ivarsen spun out a tale of twenty-four hours of shattering terror.

Kari recalled how she and Maeve had planned to walk out of the woods to Index the afternoon before. "Al didn't want us to go, but we were afraid to stay," she said.

"Afraid?" Engelbretson asked.

"The snow—it was so deep—and we thought we might freeze. And there were funny scratching noises on our cabin at night."

Kari said that she and Maeve had put on as many clothes as they could to protect them from the freezing temperatures and had begun the nine-mile hike toward town. "We must have been walking for about an hour and a half when all of a sudden Maeve just fell forward into the snow. She just kind of keeled over.

"She seemed to be kind of out of her head," Kari remembered. "I didn't know what had happened, but I was scared. I started crying and screaming for Al, because I knew he would help us if he was around."

She said that Al was supposed to be following them into town, but he had sent them on ahead. She was relieved when Al heard her screams and caught up with them.

"I saw Al coming, hurrying to help," she said. "But before he got to us, he turned around and fired his rifle at something behind him."

"What was he shooting at?" Doug Engelbretson asked.

"He said there were two men on the ridge who were shooting at us. He shot at them to drive them off," Kari said.

Kari said that she and Al considered trying to get Maeve down to Index for help, but they knew it was too far. Somehow they managed to get her on her feet, and, half-carrying her between them, they finally made it back to the cabin.

Kari closed her eyes, remembering a nightmare. "I remember saying, 'Maeve, you're in shock,' and she said, 'Yes, yes, I've been shot.' And I said, 'No, no: *you're in shock.*' But then I undressed her and I held the flashlight over her back, and I said, 'My god, Maeve, you *have* been shot!'"

Kari said that she and Maeve had been so thankful to have Al there. "He said he had worked for a veterinarian in Kansas," Kari told Engelbretson. "He said that he knew enough about medicine to get the bullet out."

Al had taken complete charge of the situation, according to Kari Ivarsen. "He told me to get clean snow to pack the wound in Maeve's back to kill the pain. Then he took this huge bread knife from the kitchen table, and he cut a large *X* across the wound."

Kari had watched him work over Maeve. He seemed to know what he was doing, but he couldn't find the bullet. She didn't know why they had to take the bullet out right away, but Al said they had to.

"Every time Maeve moaned from the pain, Al packed more snow on the wound to freeze the area," Kari said. "And then he said he needed something sharper," Kari recalled. "He got a piece of glass—"

"Glass?" Engelbretson asked quickly.

"Yes . . . just a piece of broken glass, and he filed it down until it was pretty sharp, and he started probing with that."

Next, Kari said, Al took a broken pool cue and stuck it in the ugly bullet wound, saying he could feel the bullet but that he needed tweezers to get it out.

Kari told Doug Engelbretson that she had begun to sense that something was not right. A growing horror had risen in her, she said, as she watched Al working over Maeve, who was in and out of consciousness at this point.

"He was enjoying it," Kari said.

"What do you mean?"

"Her pain was turning him on," she said. "I realized he wasn't trying to help her—not really. He was enjoying sticking the knife and the glass and that pool cue into her."

With that awful knowledge, Kari said she had begun to wonder who had really shot Maeve. They hadn't seen anyone except Al. They had only his word that snipers were firing at them. Al had a gun, and she had learned that he was behind them all the time they were walking, although they had not heard or seen him. It was as if he was stalking them like deer or rabbits.

Kari said she thought as fast as she could. If she panicked, she knew that neither she nor Maeve would get out of that cabin alive.

"I told him that maybe we'd better let her rest awhile," Kari said. "I told him I would fix her some hot soup, and maybe that would give her some strength."

To her great relief, Al had agreed. Maeve couldn't eat much, but Al stopped trying to operate on her. She tossed and fretted, but occasionally she was able to take a few sips of soup. Kari said she felt a little more confident that Maeve would survive, because she could see very little blood from the wound, except for the irritation Al had caused by probing for the bullet.

"Still," she told Englelbretson, "I was afraid that Maeve might be bleeding internally. I thought about walking down to town by myself to get help, but I couldn't leave Maeve alone in the cabin with Al, and I didn't know if I could find the road in the dark. Besides, if Al really had shot Maeve, what was to stop him from discovering Kari was gone, shooting Maeve again—and then tracking Kari down in the night?"

It was full dark by then, and Kari knew that none of them would be able to get out of the woods until morning. She was frightened that Maeve wouldn't live that long, but she didn't know what she could do to save her.

"I sat up all night, watching over Maeve," Kari said. "I watched Al, too, and it looked as though he was sleeping. His gun was on the other side of the cabin. I wondered if I could reach it before he did if I went for it."

At 7:30 A.M., it began to get light outside. Maeve was still alive, and Al didn't seem to suspect that Kari no longer trusted him. From time to time he said he probably should go for help. When she heard that, hope rose in Kari, but two hours passed and Al made no move to leave.

Finally, at nine-thirty, Al did put on his coat. Kari waited for him to pick up his rifle, but he left it leaning against the wall. He promised to come back with help as soon as he could. Hours passed, with no sound but the crackling of the fire and the wind whistling around the cabins. It was bitter cold, and Kari expected that it would start to snow again at any time.

"Finally I said, 'Maeve, we've got to try to walk out, or we might be here all winter.' And I got her on her feet and dressed, but the minute I got her out the door, she fell down and couldn't move. She said one of her arms didn't have any feeling."

Kari would not leave her friend alone. So the two girls went back into the cabin, which had become their prison. They waited. And waited. And waited.

Kari said she realized that she had been a fool to believe that Al would send help. If he had shot at them—and she believed now that he had—why would he send someone to rescue them?

Kari admitted to Engelbretson that she finally began to panic. Maeve would die up there, and then she might, too. She didn't know where Al was—maybe hiding outside, waiting to play some more of his sick games. Still, she felt she had to do *something*. Another night was coming on, and the icy cold had already begun to creep into every corner of the cabin. No longer thinking clearly herself, Kari said she tried once more to get Maeve on her feet and moving toward Index.

"And then," the pretty girl said, smiling faintly, "we went outside, and the snowmobiles found us."

While Engelbretson awaited word from the hospital, he talked to a young boy who lived near Handy and Digger. The youngster said his mother had loaned Al the .22 rifle. "I got that gun in a trade," the boy said. "It was an Ithaca Model M49 that fired .22s short and longs."

In Providence Hospital, doctors worked desperately over Maeve Flaherty. She needed surgery, but they had to get her strong enough to withstand it. When she was stabilized, they rushed her into the operating room.

Maeve was in surgery for hours. As the surgeon probed, he was astounded to find that only a miracle had kept her alive so far. A .22 caliber bullet had entered her back. If it had traveled in a straight line, it would have pierced her heart. But .22 bullets travel at high speed, and if they hit a bone, they are deflected and their paths altered. This bullet had hit one of Maeve's ribs and changed course. The impact had caused the bullet to "mushroom" before it entered one of her carotid arteries—arteries present on either side of the neck that provide oxygenated blood to the brain. By a freak of fate, the mushroomed bullet had formed a crudely effective plug to prevent hemorrhaging. Had the bullet bisected the carotid artery instead of becoming stuck in it, Maeve Flaherty would have bled to death within three to five minutes.

As it was, the stoppage of blood to the brain on the affected side had acted like a small stroke. This explained why Maeve had complained of a lack of feeling in one arm and hand. Whether it would be permanent could only be determined by time.

Maeve's doctors cautiously predicted she would live—*if* infection or complications didn't develop.

Surgeons wondered why that tiny mushroomed bullet had not been jarred loose during Kari's attempts to walk her friend out of the woods or during the rough snowmobile ride down through the drifts. And they thanked God that Al had not been able to reach it as he tried to remove it. The bullet that almost killed Maeve had also saved her life.

Detective Doug Engelbretson issued a wanted order on a young white male, five feet eleven to six feet tall, twenty-three to twenty-six years of age, with medium blond hair two or three inches long, brown eyes, a three-week growth of beard, and a heavy mustache. The man might be called Al. Kari Ivarsen remembered that he had a scar on his right thumb.

Early Monday morning the investigative team from the Snohomish County Sheriff's Office went back into the wilderness where they had rescued Maeve Flaherty. They found tracks in the snow, all leading toward Index. They found the ridge with the platform where Al had said he'd seen men shooting, but there were no footprints indicating that anyone had been there recently. There had been no snowfall since Maeve was shot, so the unbroken snow on the ridge pretty well wiped out Al's story about snipers.

They did, however, find other tracks—tracks indicating that a lone stalker had trailed the two teenage girls as they headed for town and safety. Someone had moved stealthily along a creek bed just below the road the girls walked on. From time to time the tracks went up the banks of the creek bed, suggesting that the stalker had climbed to a spot where he could take a bead on the road.

Just as a hunter stalks an animal, a man alone had obviously stalked the helpless girls. Evidently he had waited until the opportunity for a perfect shot presented itself. Then he had fired.

Back at the cabin, the sheriff's men found several knives sharp enough to probe for a bullet. Why, then, had Al used a dull bread knife, a piece of glass, and a pool cue?

"This man is a sadist," one investigator said. "He wanted to hurt her as much as possible. If we don't find him, I have a terrible feeling he'll do it again."

Deputy Frank Young, who was fairly new in the department, offered his time—on-duty and off—to Doug Engelbretson. Engelbretson, a former assistant police chief of Snohomish, Washington, and a seventeen-year veteran in law enforcement, was glad to have the help; they had at least twenty-five cabins to check.

It was almost March, and down in Everett, where their offices were, crocuses, daffodils, and pussy willows were budding out, but it was bitter winter in the mountains. Their breath froze and hung in the air as the investigators tromped through the drifts. They questioned every resident they could locate. Some locals had seen the elusive Al, but he had been very careful not to reveal anything at all about his plans or his background.

Doug Engelbretson talked again with Handy and Digger. They, of course, had every reason not to want to talk in any depth with a lawman. But Engelbretson knew they were opposed to violence of any kind.

"This man we're looking for," he began, "isn't the nonviolent type he told you he was. He shot that little girl, and then he operated on her just to hurt her more. I don't think he's the sort of person you want to protect. You think about it. If you can help me, call me at home any time. Leave your first name or don't leave any name at all. I'll know."

Handy and Digger nodded. "We'll see what we can do."

A day later an anonymous informant called Engelbretson. "The man you're looking for is named Daniel Albert Prentice.* He's AWOL from Fort Lewis, and he came from Salem, Oregon, to begin with."

Before Engelbretson could ask more, the phone went dead.

Armed with this information, however, the Snohomish County detective was able to locate Oregon records on Prentice. The suspect was on probation out of Reedsport, Oregon, charged with assault with a deadly weapon. He had apparently managed to hide that fact from army recruiters, but Daniel Albert "Al" Prentice had shown a predilection for violence in the past. Oregon authorities promised to cooperate completely in locating the missing man.

Doug Engelbretson had assured Handy and Digger that

they could trust him, and his word was good. It paid off several days later. He received a phone call at home that spurred him into action.

"Listen," the voice began. "The man you want is being shuttled up to Canada after midnight tonight. He's going out of Redmond on 405 to Bothell and then north to the border at Sumas. We know now that he's not one of us—he wanted to kill that girl—and we won't cover for him. He's yours if you want to stop us along the road."

"What will you be driving?" Engelbretson asked.

"A dark blue Chevy van—license number J78862. There'll be three of us. He'll be the short-haired man in the middle. Me and Digger will be the long-haired hippies."

"Okay," Engelbretson said. "We'll intercept between Everett and Arlington. I won't tell you where—you'll act too nervous if you know. But we'll be all around you."

Engelbretson contacted Detective Sergeant Tom Hart at home in Arlington, and Hart said he would approach Highway 9 from the north. Detective Jerry Cook would come in from the east. A patrol car would approach from the west, and Doug Engelbretson and Frank Young would head toward Arlington from the south.

Sometime before dawn, Hart radioed that he had the van in sight.

"We're moving in," Engelbretson responded. "We should intercept at Frontier Village."

It happened fast. One minute Prentice was relaxed and confident that he was almost free and clear in Canada. The next moment the van was surrounded by Snohomish County sheriff's vehicles, marked and unmarked. Digger and Handy bailed out of either side of their van and out of the line of fire. But the officers didn't have to shoot. Prentice was ordered out and told to lean against the van while he was frisked. He obeyed meekly.

"You're under arrest for first-degree assault with intent to commit murder. I must advise you of your rights," Engelbretson said, and he read Prentice his *Miranda* rights.

"What's it all about?" Prentice asked casually.

"A sixteen-year-old girl," Engelbretson answered tersely.

Prentice gave his name as Frank Fink.

One of the deputies, a man who had not been briefed on all the facts, moved in to arrest the long-haired duo who accompanied the suspect. Digger and Handy looked at Doug Engelbretson, a question unspoken in their eyes.

"They're with us," Engelbretson said. "Just let them move on."

The deputy did as he was told, but he stood shaking his head as Digger and Handy drove off.

At sheriff's headquarters, Engelbretson again informed "Frank Fink" of his rights. The suspect gave a statement, repeating his story of the unknown snipers who had shot at Kari and Maeve.

Engelbretson held up his hand and said quietly, "Dan, you're not telling me the truth. You stalked those girls as if they were deer, didn't you? . . . And then you shot Maeve."

Suddenly Prentice shuddered, drew a deep breath, and blurted, "Yes!"

Although he claimed to have no explanation for why he had attacked the girls who thought he was their friend, he admitted that he had hunted them, stopping from time to time to draw a bead, and then dropping back until he got a better shot. He said that he had shot Maeve through the back because he'd figured the bullet would go right through her heart. If she had died, he planned to shoot Kari dead too.

After the first shot, he said, he came to his senses. He fell to the snow and asked himself why he had done it. Finally he made himself get up and go to them.

Master criminalist George Ishii, who headed the Washington State Police Crime Lab, did ballistics tests on the bullet taken from Maeve Flaherty's neck and the .22 rifle Prentice had abandoned in the cabin. Under a scanning electron microscope, all the lands and grooves matched perfectly.

Daniel Prentice went on trial in Snohomish County Superior Court on August 5, 1971. Deputy Prosecutor David Metcalf presented the almost unbelievable case to a jury of

Prentice's peers. Maeve Flaherty and Kari Ivarsen took the stand to recall the frigid night when their trust in Prentice turned to terror.

The jury quickly returned a verdict of guilty, and on September 17, Prentice was sentenced to twenty-five years in a Washington prison.

Doug Engelbretson had found his man, beginning with only a description and a false name: Al. Amid those endless acres of snowdrifts he had found one of the most dangerous criminals he had ever hunted. Handy and Digger had held the key, and while they had no reason to trust cops, they *had* trusted Doug Engelbretson and he had kept his word to them. They would return to what they did, and the quiet-spoken detective would go back to his work.

Handy and Digger, the conscientious objectors who knew they were placing themselves in jeopardy but felt Prentice was so dangerous they had to take the chance, have long since moved on from Index to an unknown destination. The war in Vietnam that they deplored is over. For a short time, they fought a different kind of violence.

Maeve Flaherty recovered from the bullet wound that almost killed her, but she was left with semiparalysis in one hand and memories of terror that never quite went away. She and Kari had believed in a kind of love that was idyllic but dangerous—a love that included a trusting acceptance of everyone they met. They were ultimately disillusioned by Al. And yet they found the purest, most selfless kind of love in Handy and Digger.

And, I might suggest, in Doug Engelbretson who would not rest until their attacker was safely behind bars.

One question has always haunted me. On the first night that Maeve and Kari heard an animal thrashing and scratching against their cabin, Al was *inside* with them. He could not have made the initial noises they heard, although it was certainly Al who made noise later that night when he said he was hunting rabbits. Who—or what—was outside their cabin? Could it have been the dread Sasquatch who scrabbled at the walls of the girls' cabin that wintry night in February? No one will never know.

The Most Dangerous Game

In retrospect, Maeve Flaherty and Kari Ivarsen came to realize that the monster they tried to escape from was not nearly as dangerous as the one they ran to for protection.

Today Kari and Maeve are women in their forties. Maeve suffered permanent physical damage from her bullet wound; both of them still carry a heavier emotional burden.

How It Feels to Die

In many ways this may be the most unusual case I have ever written about. In a sense, it has an almost happy ending. The victims, by any standard of judgment, should be dead; that they lived is a miracle. Because the crime of murder always ends with death, we cannot really know what the victim suffered or thought about during the final moments before light and sound were blotted out forever. The murder victim is gone by the time I come upon the scene, and I can only imagine what the person's dying was like. People ask me if I have nightmares. Sometimes I do—spurred by just those imaginings.

Once in a while, when a killer confesses in detail, I hear about the murder from his own lips. But I am sure that I am hearing a revisionist version of the crime. The killer provides a sanitized, softer account of the murder. The victim never gets a chance to tell her side of the story.

On July 26, 1979, three young Seattle women came so close to death at the hand of a would-be killer that they actually experienced those awful last thoughts. They believed that they were dying.

Hesitantly, they agreed to tell me about an incident that could have happened to any woman who, to save on rent, shares a house with comparative strangers. I would think many readers have shared rentals too. When I was a twenty-

359

one-year-old policewoman in Seattle, three friends and I
rented a house together. Two of my friends got married before
the lease was up, and so the two of us remaining advertised
for "instant roommates."

If I had not been a policewoman at the time, I would not
have spotted three applicants who were wanted for second-
story burglaries. Luckily, I did recognize them from a wanted
bulletin I had memorized.

But you never know.

The victims in this case took in a new roommate who
seemed perfect. She was easy to get along with, did her share
of the housework, and had a good job. The one thing she did
not tell them was that she was being stalked by a man who
"loved" her too much.

Much too much.

Despite the rumors, it doesn't always rain in Seattle. July 26, 1979, was a stifling hot day. It was Thursday, an ordinary workday, except for the heat. Crime news of interest to Seattleites was being made 3,000 miles away in a Miami courtroom. Ted Bundy had just been found guilty of seven counts against young Florida women, including murder and attempted murder. Within the week, he would be sentenced to die in the electric chair.

Seattle women who lived near the University District where Bundy once prowled were relieved and felt somehow safer. It was almost as if Bundy had been the *only* dangerous man around; knowing he was safely locked up in Florida gave them a false sense of security. And yet, before that July day in Seattle was over, it was to become the most extraordinary afternoon the three victims had ever endured.

Four young working women lived in the 1940s-style brick home in the city's near north end, between the University of Washington and Green Lake. They shared the rent, utilities, and grocery bills. They got along well, and the location of the rental seemed as safe as any could be. The Wallingford Precinct of the Seattle Police Department was only a few blocks away. So was the Seattle Fire Department station with its Medic One crew. Even so, the women living in the brick house never dreamed they would need the services of either department.

They were college graduates who worked at professional

361

jobs, and they were from good, stable families. They were cautious but not paranoid; they took no chances either at work or at home. They never went out with men they'd just met, they locked their house, they locked their cars.

Rebecca James* was a twenty-six-year-old teacher, slender, petite, and dark-haired. Alene Connor,* taller and blond, was a medical technician. Mimi Sloane* was a legal secretary. Rory Booth* was a graduate student in journalism, but Rory is not really part of this story—save for the fact that her decision to leave the communal house and move to California was the first step in setting tragedy in motion.

Sometime in February Rory had told the others that she was moving. Rebecca typed out a card and put it on the bulletin board in the student union at the University of Washington: "Wanted: young woman to share house with three others."

It seemed innocuous enough. That gigantic bulletin board was one of the best ways for people in the U. district to communicate. Sell a car. Get a ride home. Sell anything. Find a roommate. Everybody did it.

"We got a lot of applications," Rebecca recalled. "We arranged to interview the most likely candidates, and we all liked Shelley the best. She was outgoing and vivacious but responsible. She worked for a florist, and she could easily afford her share of the expenses. We never thought to ask her about her personal life. We all kind of went our own way and minded our own business. As long as everybody did her share of the chores, it worked out fine."

Shelley Lee* moved in, and things seemed to be normal. At least for a while.

"But we noticed that Shelley jumped every time the phone rang," Alene said. "One time, the ironing board fell over with a crash, and Shelley just ran and cowered in the corner. She was scared to death. We didn't know why she would react like that."

Shelley Lee had reason to be afraid of a ringing phone or an unexpected loud noise. Although she hadn't told the other girls, she had just escaped from a marriage that had left her teetering on the edge of a complete nervous breakdown. She was i... that her ex-husba... relieved to lose hersel...ving again and again, hoping and hoped he would nev't find her. She had been

John Henry Grant* a.ke with three other women, seemed so attractive and char now. in California. He wasn't that tall as Luis Barande* had was well built and very strong. H...hen she first met him beard, and a mustache. The fact t...worked out, and he approve of him had only made him seeer family didn't She didn't know then about his penchamore interesting. about a background of charges involving p...violence or that stretched back to his teenage years. J...ical attacks Barande never seemed to attack young strong...en like himself; his victims tended to be the elderly—and women. He had also been picked up several times on charges connected with bad checks. But Shelley knew nothing of that when she fell in love with him.

Ironically, Grant's job was in a field that would tend to stamp him as a humanitarian, not a bully. He was a youth counselor and child-care worker. He had been married before and had a small son. When Shelley married him after knowing him a short time, she was blinded with love. Sadly, she would have ample time to regret the day they wed.

Their marriage had barely begun when she found that John was a bully who pushed her around when he didn't have things exactly the way he wanted them. She still loved him, though, and Shelley tried to get counseling. By this time, she was in Seattle, far from her family. Her attempts at marriage counseling were spectacularly unsuccessful. Confronted with Shelley's concerns, Grant not only beat up her minister-counselor but also attacked two neighbors who ran to the counselor's aid, leaving them with multiple cuts and bruises. Shelley looked on in horror and knew she had to go underground if she wanted to escape the same fate.

She barely recognized the man she had married. This drunken, raging man was obsessed with the idea that she belonged to him; he didn't want counseling, and he didn't want interference from anyone. Grant's name quickly became known to the Seattle police. It had taken two Seattle

officers to pin the furiou... ie ground and handcuff
him. Unfortunately, all... f assault were dismissed
when Shelley was afra... fy against him.
John Grant was sti... ng as a youth counselor when
he got into a scuffle ... le with a supermarket manager
after a clerk refuse... ash his check. He had ordered his
small son to pick... groceries and was striding from the
store when the... ager stopped him. Again there was a
fight, and aga... n Grant won.
Grant beh... like a spoiled—and brutal—child when
he did not ... what he wanted. And he still wanted Shelley.
He had n... given her permission to leave him.

Shelle... Lee moved from place to place in Seattle during 1978 a... d early 1979, trying to keep one step ahead of the man who refused to release her, even though their marriage was over. She believed absolutely that he would kill her if he found her.

This was the woman who had moved into the brick house in the Wallingford district. Of course, it didn't take long before her new housemates realized that something was terribly wrong in Shelley's life. They felt sorry for her, but they didn't think her ex-husband would have any impact on their lives.

They hadn't reckoned on the single-mindedness of an obsessed stalker. John Grant had followed Shelley home from work one night and written down her new address. From that and a reverse directory, he got the phone number at the house. He called her continually, and she broke into hysterical tears each time he railed at her over the phone. When he started coming to the house, Shelley went out to him, telling her housemates that she had no choice.

"He'd kill me if I didn't go," she whispered. "He says he *loves* me and he can't let me go."

Her helplessness outraged the other women, and they tried to protect her. When John called, they pretended Shelley wasn't home. When he came over, they made excuses about where she was. They thought they could handle him; they had no emotion invested in him, as Shelley did. He was a punk bully, and they were independent women wh... realize that his rage... extend to them as well... stand for that. They didn't

One day in the middle of... wife was now beginning to house and grew furious when... ohn Grant appeared at the home. He fumed and paced an... ned that Shelley wasn't of hiding her, when in fact she t... sed the other women occasion. Grant demanded cab f... as not home on that Alene, and they quickly gave it to him... om Rebecca and out of the house. They were beginni... ything to get him decision to let Shelley move in. They li... her, but the fallout from her former marriage was spilling ... ver into their lives.

None of the women in the brick home knew about John Grant's violence-laden rap sheet. They knew they despised the man's personality, but they figured that anyone who worked in youth counseling wouldn't really harm anyone. He wanted Shelley back, but she wasn't going back, and sooner or later he would have to accept that and start dating someone else.

By July 26 there were five women living at the house. Susan Marsh,* a slender twenty-nine-year-old investment counselor, was only a temporary tenant. She was waiting for her new apartment to be ready, and the other women had invited her to stay with them in the interim. Susan had never even seen John Grant, but she had been told about him and she had heard Shelley pleading with him on the phone. She felt sorry for Shelley, but her own life was so busy that she had little time to ponder the situation.

Shelley Lee was still at work just before five o'clock on that Thursday afternoon when Rebecca James arrived home. She called out as she unlocked the door, but she wasn't surprised when no one answered; she was usually the first one home. She thumbed through the mail.

It was hot inside the house, so Rebecca opened the heavy front door, but she left the screen door locked. She couldn't have been home more than five minutes when she heard someone coming up the front steps. She moved toward the

front door, a little alarmed that it was John Grant,
heavy. She gasped when ... by—probably one of his
accompanied by a tee... enter.
charges from the coun... ecca said.

"Shelley's not here ... ughly.

"Let me in!" he s..., go away—go away or I'll call the
"No," she said.
police."

The word "...ce" galvanized the muscular man into
action. He tor... it the screen door, demolishing it as if it
were made of ... apier-mâché, and forced his way in.

Rebecca w...s shocked and thought she shouldn't have
sounded so ... nnoyed. But it was hot, and she was tired. And
she was tired of John. "Then I saw the knife in his hand,"
Rebecca remembered. "He held it up against my neck and
told me to shut up. Then he locked the front door."

The tiny woman recalled that she felt conflicting emotions at that point. "I was terrorized into immobility, and
yet I was consumed with outrage that this man could simply
take over my own home and hold me captive. I couldn't
fight him physically; I weigh 102 pounds, and John must
weigh about 180. And he had the knife."

John Grant began to bombard Rebecca with questions
about his ex-wife's sex life, insisting that Shelley was seeing
other men. In fact, she was not. She went to work and came
home to hide from him, but he wouldn't believe Rebecca's
protestations. He dragged her with him as he roamed
around the house.

He focused most of his attention on Shelley's room. He
tore it apart as he went through her personal belongings,
looking for some proof that she loved someone else. There
was nothing to find. Rebecca saw that the teenager he had
brought with him was looking around for things to steal.

John never took the knife blade away from Rebecca's
neck. She knew that just a little more pressure would slide it
into her flesh.

"I knew I had to keep my voice calm," she recalled. "I
knew that I had to keep him from exploding. I knew he
could kill me, and I knew he hated women—all women—

not just Shelley. I don't know how I did it, but I kept talking to him quietly. There was no way to warn the other girls. They were due home shortly, but I couldn't think of any way to stop them from walking in."

She had no hope of getting to the phone and knocking it off the hook; John had ordered the teenager to disconnect the phone and hide the cord in the kitchen drawer.

The two men held Rebecca captive for what seemed like an eternity, although it was really only an hour and a half. Part of her hoped for rescue, but the other dreaded the danger to her housemates if they walked into the powder keg she was living in.

"I heard my roommates coming up the porch steps about five-thirty, and I hoped I could let them know what terrible danger we were in," Rebecca remembered. "But there was nothing I could do to warn them."

Alene Connor and Susan Marsh looked at the closed front door, and they were curious about the mangled screen door, but they were inside before they had time for the broken door to register. They walked into the darkened, suffocatingly hot living room and saw Rebecca sitting on the couch. Then they saw the two men, who were poised as tensely as rattlesnakes about to strike. They glanced at Rebecca's face and saw the warning in her eyes.

"Be quiet," Rebecca told them softly. "He has a knife. Do what he says."

Alene knew what John's presence meant; Susan, on the other hand, had no idea who he was. Alene sat in a chair across from the couch and Susan sat down beside Rebecca. They, too, went through the initial reaction of anger at the way their privacy had been taken over. They saw the trickle of sweat roll down Rebecca's cheek, and wondered at what she must have endured before they got home.

And now all three of them were captive.

Later on, Susan remembered her naïveté. "I didn't know who the man was, but I couldn't believe he would actually try to kill us. I come from an ordinary middle-class background where I played outside, went to school, to college, went to work, got married; things like murder just don't happen to people like us. That's what I thought then. I don't think I'll ever truly recover from my shock and surprise that it *could* happen to people like me."

Susan listened to the angry dialogue between the man with the black beard who held the sharp knife and Alene, who seemed remarkably brave. With a sinking sensation, she realized that this was Shelley's husband, the man Shelley feared so much. She heard him accuse Alene of trying to interfere in his relationship with Shelley, of trying to protect Shelley.

"Then I knew that they weren't just two scruffy-looking strangers," Susan said. "I heard him scream at Alene and I knew who it was."

Susan listened and watched and tried to devise a plan. Rebecca had warned them to be cool, but she couldn't just remain passive. "I kept thinking of the Richard Speck case—all those nursing students in Chicago who died because they were passive, because they didn't even try to fight him. We all sat there, and it got hotter and hotter, and I was afraid we were going to die like the nurses in Chicago if I didn't do something."

She saw that the second man was really only a kid, and that he didn't seem to have a weapon. Instead of being frightened at that point, Susan felt herself growing angry. They were trapped. The other girls might not be home for hours, and if they did come in, what good would that do? It would just be five trapped women instead of three.

"I asked him, 'If you're so interested in your relationship with Shelley, why are you harassing us?' But Rebecca told me to be cool again. I was beginning to feel frightened, to absorb the magnitude of the danger we were in. Still I felt that somehow I could save us if I could just use my mind. That's the deception. And that's what bothers me so much, the realization that there comes a point where your mind can't save you.

"I didn't know what to do, but I knew I couldn't just sit there and be passive. I knew we were going to be lined up and annihilated."

Susan made a choice. She began to reason with John Grant, telling him that she had to call her parents. "They're leaving town and I have to pick up some theater tickets from them. If I don't call them, they'll think something is wrong. Just hook up the phone. You can listen in while I talk to my folks."

The beefy man turned to the teenager and told him to go get the phone cord. But the moment he plugged it into the jack, the phone rang, making everyone in the room jump.

John answered it. It was Alene's boyfriend calling to confirm a date, but John only barked, "No one's home," and slammed the receiver down. He ripped the cord loose again. Concerned, Alene's friend decided to drive over and see what was going on.

Time was running out.

Susan stood up and walked toward the phone, talking softly to her captor, assuring him she wouldn't pull any tricks on him. But John was tired of conversation. He turned to the teenager and said, "Put her out!"

The ticking time bomb exploded.

"They both went after me," Susan recalled, "and hit me in the face with the phone. The next thing I knew I was flying through the air, across the coffee table, finally landing on the couch. John was on top of me, pummeling me with his fists. The boy who was with him panicked and disappeared out the back door. Alene and Rebecca moved instinctively to protect me, to somehow get him off me."

Rebecca, with strength born of desperation, struggled to pull the big man off Susan. Suddenly she felt what she thought was a blow from his fist on her forearm.

"I didn't know he'd stabbed me until I saw the blood spray and realized it was spouting from my arm. He'd stabbed all the way through it," Rebecca said. "I knew then we were hopelessly trapped and I had to try to get help."

Rebecca recalled that she felt as if she were moving through quicksand as she headed for the front door. Getting there seemed to take hours rather than seconds. Just when she needed it to work, the bolt refused to open. Her hands were slippery with her own blood, making it hard to throw the bolt. As she fought it, she felt another blow to her back. Rebecca didn't see the blood spurt from that wound, but Susan did.

"I looked up and this jet of crimson just erupted from Rebecca's back and splashed over the wall. I knew Rebecca had to be gravely injured, but she kept going down the steps and headed toward our neighbors' house, with John following her."

John had temporarily forgotten about Susan—all his attention was focused on the fleeing Rebecca. Alene sat paralyzed with horror.

"I just reacted," Susan remembered. "I had to get John away from Rebecca. I grabbed a cup and threw it at him. I wasn't even trying to hit him; I was trying to distract him. I was standing in the front doorway and I could see Rebecca down on the sidewalk turning a corner with John right behind her—with the knife."

Susan was trapped now, standing on the front porch with no weapon at all to protect herself. The front door had slammed shut and locked behind her. It seemed like a bad dream—but it wasn't.

"I could see that John had turned back and was coming up the steps toward me. I only had time to fold my arms over my breasts before he started hitting me with both fists." One fist was empty; the other held the knife.

"I took about thirty blows—fifteen of them with the knife," Susan said. "I was stabbed in the upper neck, back, and chest. I couldn't even break my fall as I crashed to the porch. It's strange—I was totally conscious, but I was absolutely sure I was dying. Inside, I was saying, This is it. This is the way I'm going to die—and I don't even know this man. I never did anything to him.

"I was utterly terrified for the minute or so it took before I passed out from loss of blood. I could feel the blood gurgling out of the subclavian artery in my neck, but I could do nothing to help myself."

As Susan lay on the front porch with her life draining out of her, Alene was inside, frantically trying to plug the phone into the jack and call for help. Her hands felt as if she had boxing gloves on. She couldn't make the little plastic connector fit into the wall.

And then she heard a footfall behind her and turned in horror. John Grant was back inside, coming for her now.

She saw the knife raised high, plunging toward her face. At the last moment she managed to turn her head away, and the knife sliced into her neck instead.

Alene fainted from the shock. It probably saved her life. Grant stood over her, panting, and decided she was dead. He ran out the back door.

Susan lay as still as death itself on the front porch, the blood pooling beneath her and cascading down the front steps, where it left scalloped crimson stains.

Somehow, despite her wounds, Rebecca had made it to the neighbors' home and gasped out her plea for help. The neighbor's frantic call to 911 brought squad cars and Medic One units racing to the brick house.

When Patrol Officer Jerry Bickell reached the scene, followed by Patrolmen Thomas McCrae and Gerald St. George, the Seattle Fire Department's Aid Car 17 and Medic 16 were already working over the injured women. The police officers began roping off the scene and gathering witnesses. They fully expected that they were dealing with a multiple homicide.

Susan Marsh was not dead, however, and despite the stab wounds in her neck and chest, her mind was still working. "I felt hands lifting me," she recalled, "carrying me down the steps, and out to the parking strip. I felt them cutting my clothing off to see where I'd been stabbed. They were trying to stanch the blood. I could hear a police radio somewhere far off, sirens, and people talking."

The body's own reactions mobilize in the event of catastrophic trauma. Adrenaline is released that blocks off the peripheral blood vessels, trying to save blood for the most essential organs—the heart and the brain. More than that, Susan's own rage may have saved her life. Still, she had an overwhelming desire just to give in to the heavy drowsiness that washed over her. Both her lungs had collapsed; she was being kept alive with an artificial airway through which the paramedics were forcing air—"bagging" her lungs.

"It's strange," she remembered. "You don't feel it when you're stabbed. You feel as if you're being struck forcibly, but the pain doesn't come until later."

Despite the lethargy brought on by shock and massive

blood loss, Susan Marsh was still angry. "I kept thinking that I wouldn't let myself die over something that had nothing to do with me. This man had struck out at me because I was a woman and women are easy targets for men like him.

"I was beginning to be in terrible pain as I lay there on the parking strip. I felt that I probably was going to die, because I knew how badly I'd been injured," Susan said, and she asked herself a silent question: "Had I lived my whole life to end up this way . . . full of knife wounds? I don't know how I did it, but I vowed I wouldn't die!"

Susan was placed gently in an ambulance and rushed to Harborview Medical Center's trauma unit—the best emergency care unit in the Northwest. Alene and Rebecca were taken to nearby hospitals for treatment.

The Homicide Unit of the Seattle Police Department had been alerted in their downtown offices. Detective Sergeant Craig Vandeputte and Detectives Danny Engle and Al Lima left at once for the scene of the attacks. When they saw the huge pool of blood on the welcome mat and the waterfall of blood on the steps descending from the porch, they felt sure they would soon be investigating a homicide. No one could lose so much blood and live.

Inside the house, they found signs of a tremendous struggle. Chairs and plants had been knocked over, and there were droplets and spray patterns of blood all over. The phone cord was disconnected from the baseboard jack, and the phone book, open to the emergency numbers page, was beside it. The pages were also stained with red. Even the kitchen sink was splotched with blood. The detectives took blood samples from each area they found, marking the vials for later identification.

They moved next door to the home of Doug Finch, the neighbor who had come to the girls' aid, and there, too, they found a trail of blood—the blood that Rebecca James had lost in her desperate flight to safety.

"I was outside in the yard," Finch said, "when I heard a commotion and saw a girl next door running toward me. I got Rebecca and tried to help her, and then I called the police."

As the detectives worked, Rob Weeks,* Alene's friend, drove up. He said he had called at five-thirty and talked to a strange male who had barked that no one was home and hung up. "The phone was slammed down and then came off the hook again. I heard noises in the background and the sounds of an argument. Then nothing. I headed over here."

At Harborview Hospital, a team of fifteen doctors worked over Susan Marsh. She remained in surgery for six and a half hours, and every drop of blood in her body had to be replaced. Eleven units were required during that surgery.

She was cruelly bruised over much of her body, the result of her attacker's pummeling fists. Her lungs were collapsed, and the subclavian artery in her left arm was severed completely; there was nothing for the surgeons to do but to tie it off, a technique that would leave that arm permanently weakened. The knife Grant had used on her was six inches long and an inch wide. She had escaped death by mere millimeters. A fraction of an inch in either direction in many of her wounds and she would have died instantly.

"I wasn't really conscious for more than those few seconds when the paramedics were working over me. I didn't wake up until the next day," Susan recalled. "I was on a life-support system to get air into my lungs. I was in intensive care for forty-eight hours."

The doctors had told Sergeant Vandeputte that there was cause for cautious optimism about Susan's condition, "but it could go either way."

Rebecca's arm wound was a through-and-through wound that had narrowly missed the radius and ulna bones and major veins in her forearm. The knife wound in the back of her shoulder had been close too. Pure luck had made the blade plunge into soft tissue instead of vital organs.

Rebecca was able to identify their attacker easily: "It was John Grant, Shelley's ex-husband," she told detectives.

Shelley Lee herself had disappeared, terrified that John would come after her next. She had good reason to be frightened; detectives learned that a man had called her place of employment a few hours before the attack on her housemates. He had demanded to talk to her—even after he was told she wasn't there. Incredibly, the same man called back the day after the knife attack—even as his victims remained hospitalized—and left a message: "Tell Shelley she better see me unless she wants to see more of her friends killed."

John Grant's rage had not been sated by the terrible scene at the brick house in Wallingford. He was out there someplace, still trying to find Shelley. But the Seattle detectives found that he had not shown up for work at the youth center, nor had he returned to the house he shared with several roommates. He had cleared out.

With the help of California authorities, stakeouts were put in place at the homes of his relatives in that state, all of them with negative results. Shelley Lee called Seattle detectives to let them know she was hiding at her parents' home in California. She was aghast and saddened at what had happened to her friends, but she was too afraid to come back to Seattle.

Charges were filed in absentia against John Thomas Grant a.k.a. Tomas Luis Barande on three counts of first-degree assault, with bail set at $50,000. The Seattle police noted that they would extradite him from any of the seven western states. Several photos of Grant-Barande were duplicated on hundreds of bulletins, which were released at once. Detective A. Garcia of the Los Angeles County Homicide Unit arranged to meet the plane carrying the bulletins on Grant-Barande and get them distributed in his area. They drew no hits. The suspect seemed to have vanished completely. Every one of his known haunts was checked frequently, but he had apparently abandoned his past. The investigators wondered if he might not have committed suicide.

They learned he was still alive, however. Grant's housemates said that he had called the house several times since the stabbings, but he would never say where he was. A female friend of the fugitive had already come to Grant's room and cleared out his belongings. Apparently, the man with a grudge against women had managed to maintain his Svengali-like influence over at least one female.

Sergeant Vandeputte's team of detectives checked Grant's

room, but the only things he'd left behind were books, some Hare Krishna texts and pamphlets, a bookcase and a few items of clothing. It seemed obvious he had no intention of coming back.

Although they were clearly frightened of Grant too, one of his housemates volunteered haltingly, "We did get a call from someone—a collect call we wouldn't accept."

"Where was it from?" Craig Vandeputte asked.

"Someplace in Hawaii."

"And then?"

"Well, then, a few minutes later John called back and paid for the call. He told us he was in Hawaii, staying at a Hare Krishna temple. He didn't say what city he was in. He said he's using the name Janada."

Vandeputte immediately relayed the information by Teletype to the Honolulu Police Department and forwarded Grant's photos and fingerprints.

When detectives phoned Shelley Lee at the place where she was hiding, she verified that it would be likely that John would run to Hawaii. "I've seen pictures of him in a Hare Krishna outfit with his head shaved," she said.

But if John Grant was indeed in Hawaii, he had managed to blend in smoothly with his surroundings. Hawaiian detectives could find no trace of him.

The teenager who had accompanied Grant during the bloody siege in the women's home was antagonistic toward police. He told Detective Danny Engle, "I've got fifty witnesses who'll say I was on Rainier Avenue that day. Try to prove anything else." However, he seemed very worried that the victims might be able to identify him. He said he didn't want to be in a lineup.

Engle told the boy that he didn't intend to arrest him at that point. "We don't know yet if you're going to be a witness or a suspect."

And then Engle left the interrogation room to let the kid ponder that for a while. When he returned, he found the teenager more talkative.

"I'm afraid," the youth admitted.

"Afraid of what?"

"Afraid John might get me for talking."

Engle waited.

"I didn't hit any of them," the boy began. "I talked that one lady into putting down the phone. I didn't hit her with it. John went up on the porch first, and then I followed him. I didn't know he was going to hurt them. When that started, I just ran."

Despite her efforts to hide, Shelley Lee had begun to get phone calls from someone who said nothing. She could hear only breathing at the other end of the line, and then someone quietly hung up. A counselor who had worked with Shelley and John at the time of their divorce reported to police that she had received a call from Grant on August 3, telling her he was back in Seattle. "He wanted to know how the girls were and if I knew if there was a warrant out for him."

She promised the detectives she would call them at once if she heard from him again. "One thing I should tell you," the counselor said. "John says he won't be taken alive, but that he still intends to kill Shelley."

John Grant was keeping adroitly one step ahead of detectives. He made phone calls continually—to Shelley's relatives, to counselors, and, silently, to Shelley herself. But he never stayed on the line long enough for a trace to be made on the calls, and he never gave away where he was. Then, near the end of August, one of his friends reported that John had called him from Hawaii. He had asked that his belongings be sold and the money forwarded to him. He gave no address, but said he would call back.

The Seattle detectives felt that Grant had been in Hawaii all along, moving from phone to phone and pretending he was calling from within the continental United States.

But where in Hawaii?

By the beginning of September there were virtually no clues left to go on. Craig Vandeputte and his crew of detectives didn't feel reassured that Grant was no longer a danger. They believed, rather, that he was merely lying back in the weeds and waiting for his ex-wife to come out of hiding. There seemed no forgiveness in him; they were convinced he still wanted to kill her.

None of the injured women had gone back to live in the little brick house that had seemed so safe before; they could not bear to look at the rooms, which held such ghastly memories.

Susan Marsh recalled her slow recovery. "I was in the hospital a long time, and then I was so weak. I relived the incident over and over after I'd regained consciousness. I finally concluded that, if we had it to do over again, we would have reacted the same way. We *acted*," she said. "No one teaches you what to do if your life is threatened like that, but we weren't passive. Fear is completely immobilizing, but the important thing to remember is that you have to act. You have nothing to lose. Rebecca responded by running for help. That was right. *I* acted to try to distract him from her. We all tried to save each other, and we didn't just sit there and let him kill us without a struggle. We could have been like those women in Chicago that Speck killed. John was working himself into a lather, and he was fully prepared to execute all of us."

Although the women's wounds healed, their terror was far from over. Before that hot afternoon in July, only Shelley Lee had lived in fear of a knock on the door; now, with John Grant still at large, all three of the women who had lived in the house with her were afraid of what he might do. They learned that the thirty-three-year-old fugitive had an extensive record showing that he had always vented his rage by bullying those who were smaller and weaker than he was.

If and when he was captured, Rebecca, Susan, and Alene knew that their testimony would be necessary to convict him. He would know that, too, since he was familiar with the judicial system. They wondered how far he might go to prevent them from testifying in court against him.

"John had always beaten the system," Susan said incredulously. "He thought he could go on doing what he felt like forever—and the most he would get was a slap on the wrist or a few years in prison. Yes, we stayed in hiding, but we were adamant that we would press charges all the way."

Beyond their terrible wounds and the emotional trauma that walked with them, the three women had been robbed.

377

Susan Marsh had lost a diamond pendant worth $2,500, and a number of other items were missing when they returned to their house—under police guard—to hurriedly pack their belongings.

While the victims waited to hear that John Grant was in custody, they kept in constant touch with the detectives working the case. It was a kind of lifeline, but it didn't help when night descended or when they were driving and noticed that another car seemed to be following them. They had jobs to go to, and they tried to pick up the remnants of their lives, but they no longer trusted the world they lived in.

By late September—two months after he had slashed three women he didn't even know—John Grant was still free and still calling relatives asking for money. He said he needed $5,000 and he needed an attorney, but he would not say where he was, only that he was watching Shelley's parents' home.

That would mean that Grant was in California. Or would it? This was long before the days of Caller ID, and he was clever enough to get off the line before a trace went through. Detectives suspected that he was employing his usual scare techniques, but they couldn't count on it.

In the end, they caught John Henry Grant a.k.a. Tomas Luis Barande on a fluke. On December 10, 1979, the Seattle Homicide and Assault Unit received word from the Oakland, California, Police Department that a Tomas Barande had been stopped on a routine traffic check because he was driving erratically. As he was arrested for drunk driving and booked, the existing warrant out for him popped up on their computers.

Grant-Barande later attempted suicide in his jail cell and was transferred to a mental health facility in Alameda County. On March 7, 1980, he was extradited to Seattle and booked into the King County Jail to await trial.

His victims' ordeal was far from over, however. Having to face him—first in the pretrial hearing, then at the actual trial—brought back all the terror of the attack.

"John was mouthing profanity at me from the stand," Rebecca James recalled with a shiver. "The judge couldn't see what he was doing. Even knowing John was in custody, it was still so frightening. They kept postponing the trial. First, it was set for May . . . and then June and finally for August. We had to wait so long. The prosecutors were good to us, and so were the detectives, but nobody could really understand what we were going through."

Susan Marsh nodded her head. "Under the judicial system, we're not able to avenge ourselves—we can't settle accounts. We had to rely on the system, and John had always avoided punishments before. We felt as though we really had no control over what would happen. John seemed to feel that he was going to get away with it again, that he would go free or serve only a few years."

John Grant's defense this time around was that he suffered from diminished capacity because of a head injury he'd suffered as a youth. The prosecution soon proved this argument specious by pointing out that the alleged mind-altering head injury did not occur until nine years after his career of violence had begun.

A King County Superior Court jury quickly found John Grant guilty on three counts of attempted murder.

Six weeks later, Judge Warren Chan handed down three consecutive thirty-year sentences. The cocky bully turned pale when he heard the ruling. "He was aghast," Susan said. "He flinched and cried, 'I don't deserve that!' The judge just looked at him and said, 'I beg to differ with you. I don't care to discuss it!' John was finally being punished for hurting people, even though he had been getting away with that kind of behavior for twenty years."

For Susan Marsh, Alene Connor, and Rebecca James, it was finally over. It had taken fourteen months for the wheels of justice to grind along. Their long ordeal was over—but it will never truly be over for any of the three women who were held captive by a pathologically jealous man with a knife. Susan's subclavian artery is permanently severed, and she has lost much of her former robust health. All three still carry deep scars from the knife wounds.

"But it's not the physical damage," Rebecca said vehemently. "It's *our* mental anguish. We've lost trust, we've known such frustration, and we're afraid of the generalized hate that seems to be out there."

"I keep thinking that something like this kind of violence exists in any number of men out there," Susan says softly. "It happened to be John, but I wonder how many more there are. I'm a target. I still feel like a target because I'm a woman, because I have to go outside the safety of my home. I don't know if that will ever change."

Sadly, this feeling of being endangered is not uncommon among crime victims. Even though statistics tell us that lightning rarely strikes twice, a terrifying thought is always present underneath the calm facade victims strive to maintain: *It happened.* And if it happened once, it could happen again.

Susan and Rebecca cope with the fear in their own ways. Rebecca has become an active worker in programs to protect victims' rights. Her involvement helps a little. She can speak out in anger and work to try to make things better. Susan is quieter; she is working through therapy to try to deal with the fragility, the vulnerability that she cannot yet shake.

Shelley Lee was married to John Grant for only five months before she divorced him, only to find he would not let her go. She regained a measure of security, but she never forgot the depths of rage he was capable of.

"I'm sure John came there to kill *me,*" she said. "I don't think he intended to kill my friends, but things just got out of control. Sometimes he doesn't think the way other people do."

Susan Marsh and Rebecca James have this advice for other women: "Never move someone into your home unless you really know her background. Never assume that the odds are with you—that it's always someone else who gets attacked, raped, or even murdered. You have to take care all the time because the one time you forget to be cautious, that might be the time you need to be most alert. And if you ever are attacked, don't be passive. Fight, kick. Scream. If you have to go out, go out fighting. It's the only chance you have."

For Susan, there is another memory—the memory of

lying on the grass in front of her home as paramedics worked frantically to save her life. She wasn't particularly frightened at that point, but she was very tired. It would have been easy for her simply to close her eyes. But she knew instinctively that she was dying—that sleep would not be sleep at all—but death. Somehow she was able to use her mind to keep her body alive. She knows now how it feels to die. She also knows how it feels to live against all odds.

With Washington's sentencing guidelines, John Grant could be released from prison as early as April 1999, or—if his parole hearings do not go well for him—he could serve his full sentence and not be a free man until 2018. As long as he is safely behind bars, his victims will breathe a little easier.

The Killer Who Never Forgot . . . or Forgave

Of all the emotions humans feel, love may be the most confusing—and the easiest to misidentify. Infatuation, possessiveness, sexual attraction, jealousy, and passion have often been mistaken for true love. One of the strangest, saddest, and longest cases I ever covered dealt with a married couple who had separated, reunited, and separated again. Their final "separation" brought one of them into court in a series of trials that seemed endless. I spent two Christmas seasons on the hard benches of a King County Superior Courtroom, taking copious notes.

And so did the defendant in a double murder trial.

And so did the deputy prosecuting attorney.

Every morning we passed a huge Christmas tree in the lobby of the courthouse, but inside the courtroom, there was no holiday season.

The defendant was attractive, charming, and so at ease it seemed impossible that he was on trial for the premeditated murder of two members of his own family.

And yet he was on trial—not just once but twice. If what

the deputy prosecutor said about him was true, love had disintegrated into blind jealousy and then murderous hatred until finally the most innocent victim of all was killed because of an erroneous assumption.

The trials culminated at Christmas, but the case had begun close to another holiday weekend. The tragic story of Jody* and Arne Kaarsten* first made headlines on July 6, 1966, the Wednesday after a long Fourth of July weekend. It was only a little over two weeks past the summer solstice, and the sun rose early in the Northwest that morning. Although dew still clung to the grass, it had been daylight for more than three hours when twenty-three-year-old Arne Kaarsten appeared at his next-door neighbor's house in the suburb of Kent, where the one-story homes were built close together. It was typical sixties mass-produced construction where the same three or four floor plans were repeated in every third or fourth house; only different colored paint and varied landscaping made the homes individual. For the most part, this was a neighborhood of young married couples.

It was a little before 8:00 A.M. when Arne Kaarsten pounded frantically on the kitchen window of Ted Pearce's home. Pearce looked up, startled, to see Kaarsten, dressed in a bathrobe, carrying his two-and-a-half-year-old daughter, Anna.*

"There's something the matter with Jody," Kaarsten gasped.

Pearce took the little girl and handed her to his wife. Then he followed Kaarsten, who was already running back toward his own home. Arne entered his house through the

385

sliding glass doors at the back, which Pearce knew opened into the dinette.

Pearce stepped inside and waited for his eyes to adjust to the dim light. "There," Arne said, pointing to what looked like a mound of blankets in the living room. "There she is."

Pearce moved closer until he could make out tufts of blond hair protruding above the blankets. He shoved away an overturned coffee table and snatched the covers back.

Twenty-two-year-old Jody Kaarsten lay absolutely still beneath them. She was face down and wore only a pair of bikini panties and a short quilted robe that was bunched up around her shoulders. Her panties had been pulled down just below her buttocks.

Numbly, Pearce touched her wrist. It was still warm, but he couldn't feel any reassuring pulse to show that her heart was still beating. He knew that she needed a doctor, but he could not imagine what might have happened to her. He wondered if she had somehow injured herself falling off the couch. While Arne stood there silently, Pearce ran to the phone and picked up the receiver.

There was no dial tone.

"Stay here, Arne," he said. "I'll run next door and call an ambulance."

Pearce was back within minutes. Arne hadn't moved. He seemed to be in shock.

"Ted, I think there's something around her neck," Kaarsten said quietly.

Pearce looked, but he couldn't see anything. He had to pull the blankets down and lift Jody's long blond hair away from her neck before he saw the man's necktie that cut deep into the tender flesh there. He tried to loosen it, but the garrote had been twisted around her throat so tightly that he could not even get his fingers beneath it.

Suddenly Arne cried out, "I forgot about the baby!" Pearce knew he was speaking of seven-month-old Peri Lynn, whose room was just down a narrow hallway leading from the living area. Arne ran now toward his younger daughter.

"Oh, my god!" Kaarsten's voice chilled Pearce. "The baby, too!"

Hoping against hope, Pearce ran to the nursery. He found Arne staring down at the motionless baby. "No, no," Pearce began, "she's just sleeping." But then he saw the pink satin ribbon—the kind used to decorate stuffed toys. It was embedded in Peri Lynn's neck just as the necktie encircled her mother's throat. Instinctively he reached out to get it off the baby's neck. But like the necktie, the ribbon was cinched too tightly for him to remove it by hand.

"Quick, get me a knife," he said to Arne Kaarsten. Understandably, Kaarsten seemed to be too stunned to help much. Instead, he led Pearce into the kitchen and pointed at the cabinets. Pearce rummaged through unfamiliar drawers until he came up with a paring knife. He ran back to the baby and cut the ribbon. Still, Peri Lynn did not move.

Now Pearce returned to Jody Kaarsten. He sliced once, twice, and once again at the tie that was wound three times around her neck. Finally it fell free.

But Jody Kaarsten did not move either.

Pearce knew that they needed all the help they could get. Again he ran home and called the Kent Police. However, the dispatcher determined that the Kaarsten home lay outside the boundaries of the small Seattle suburb and transferred the call to King County Police. He learned that the county police had been dispatched at the same time the ambulance call was logged and were already on their way.

It seemed as though hours had passed, but it had only been five or ten minutes. Ted Pearce returned to his stricken neighbor. He noted idly that Arne Kaarsten wore trousers, a T-shirt, and a bulky plaid robe. Arne kept repeating a litany: "Why did it have to happen to *her?* Why did it have to happen to *her?*"

Pearce didn't know if Arne was talking about his wife or his baby. Despite his neighbor's pleas that he go next door, Arne was adamant about remaining in his own home. He stared at his dead wife fixedly, as if he could will her back to life.

Two ambulance attendants came hurrying up the front walk, carrying a resuscitator. Skillfully the EMT turned Jody Kaarsten over and fitted an airway into her throat so that they could force air into her lungs. The machine made her breasts rise and fall artificially as air filled her lungs. Arne stood nearby and watched, transfixed, as his wife seemed to have miraculously come back to life.

"Is she breathing? *Is she breathing?*" he asked sharply.

The EMT shook his head, explaining that the breathing was really just an illusion, dependent on the machine. There were no signs of life at all. Arne sighed deeply.

Neither Jody nor Peri Lynn responded to the desperate efforts of the rescue team to save them. They had been dead too long before their bodies were discovered.

No one yet had asked why or how. It was hard enough just to accept that it had happened at all.

King County Patrol Officer Bill Gorsline arrived at the neat ranch home a moment later, followed shortly by fellow Patrolman Ken Trainor. Both urged Arne Kaarsten to leave his home. Finally he agreed to go next door with Pearce.

Gorsline glanced around the living room and saw that it was basically clean—the carpet vacuumed, the furniture dusted—but now it was in disarray. A woman's purse, its contents spilled out, lay on the floor beside the overturned coffee table; the change purse appeared to have been opened and pawed through. A diaper bag rested untouched on one chair, but a can of baby powder lay on the floor next to Jody Kaarsten's head. A copy of a book, *The Hospital War,* was on the floor nearby.

As Gorsline and Trainor waited for detectives from the Major Crimes Unit in downtown Seattle to respond, they moved carefully around the house. They saw that the bathroom floor was littered with curlers, bobby pins, and a diaper pin; the bathroom rug was twisted and had been pushed or pulled partway into the hallway.

Ken Trainor posted himself at the front door of the Kaarsten home to keep anyone from contaminating the crime scene. He heard a loud rapping sound and turned around. He was startled to see that Arne Kaarsten had returned to the house and was knocking on the living room window to attract his attention. Fighting exasperation because he knew the distraught widower was probably not responsible, Trainor beckoned to Kaarsten to come outside.

But Kaarsten shook his head and signaled for Trainor to
follow him.

"I've got something important to show you in the backyard," Kaarsten insisted.

"Look here," Kaarsten said, as they walked over the
damp grass. "I was walking toward the house and I dropped
my cigarette lighter. Then I kicked it accidentally, and it
slid up against the house."

Trainor nodded, perplexed, wondering what Kaarsten
was trying to say.

"So I bent over," Kaarsten said excitedly, "and when I
looked up I could see the reflection of broken wires in the
telephone connection into the house. See?" He pointed
toward the lower part of the home's siding.

Trainor didn't see. The wires were protected by a cover,
and he couldn't see any break at all. Only when he placed
his fingers beneath the plastic box and pulled it clear of the
house a bit was he able to discern a break.

"I'll point that out to the detectives," Trainor promised,
leading Kaarsten away from the home once more. "Now, I
think you'll be more comfortable next door."

Kaarsten left, but he came back several times, anxious to
assist the investigators in their assessment of what had
happened. Every time they turned around, he seemed to be
in their way. It was a hell of a thing, they realized, for a man
to lose his wife *and* one of his children like this, and he had
to be in shock, but neither of them had ever seen a family
member so determined to be part of the investigation.

Detective Sergeant George Helland and Detective Robert
Andrews reached the Kaarsten home shortly before 9:00
A.M. They saw that the 1,000-square-foot house was built on
an open plan: the kitchen, dining area, and living room were
actually one large room partially divided by counters. A
door to the garage from the dining area stood half open. So
did an outside door leading from the garage to the backyard.

A short central hallway led from the living-dining room to
the nursery and then to Anna's room on the right. The
bathroom and master bedroom were on the left. Someone,

probably Jody Kaarsten, had apparently been sleeping on the convertible sofa in the living room, because it was folded down to the bed position.

The bed in the master bedroom was unmade, and a man's plaid bathrobe had been tossed across the end. A clock showing the correct time hummed away beside the bed.

Dirty glasses and ashtrays covered the tabletop in the dinette area. A single bowl half full of cereal stood amid the clutter.

Andrews photographed the interior while Helland made triangulation measurements. By measuring from Jody Kaarsten's body to fixed points in the house, he could establish exactly where the body and pertinent evidence had been found—if he ever needed to do so—even after her body was moved to the medical examiner's office. The two investigators dusted the exposed surfaces for prints.

They knew already that they were dealing with a case that defied any predictable pattern. A woman and a baby had been strangled in their own home—while an adult male and a small girl slept only a few feet away. While it was certainly possible for an intruder to enter a home and commit such brutal killings, the immediate question dealt with motive. The Kaarsten home was like any subdivision home a young couple just starting out might buy. The furniture was neat but inexpensive. There were no objets d'art, no jewels, furs, stereos, cameras—nothing to lure a burglar. Yes, Jody Kaarsten's purse had been rifled, but they wondered how much money the young wife could have had?

If the motive had been a sexual attack, surely Jody Kaarsten would have cried out to her husband for help. But Arne Kaarsten hadn't mentioned hearing screams. At this point, it didn't look like a rape that had progressed to murder. Jody's clothing was in disarray, but it had not been removed.

The clutter in the bathroom was odd. The rug rested halfway into the hall, and the curlers had been knocked to the floor, making it look rather as if she had been attacked while she was putting up her hair and then dragged to where she lay.

Even if rape *had* been the original motive, why would the

killer have strangled little Peri Lynn? A seven-month-old baby could hardly have been a threat; she wasn't even old enough to stand up in her crib, much less crawl out of it. She couldn't talk. How could she have identified a killer?

Two-and-a-half-year-old Anna would have been more dangerous as a witness, but not much more. Two baby girls. Why would the murderer have killed the baby and left the toddler sleeping? Why hadn't Arne Kaarsten heard anything during the night?

Helland and Andrews went over the exterior of the home meticulously to see if any doors or windows had been jimmied or forced. None of them bore any marks. Sergeant Helland knelt to examine the cut telephone line. Like Trainor, Helland was unable to see the severed wires until he lifted the plastic cap that covered the terminal ends. As the single lead from the outside wall entered the plastic cap, it split into two segments, each leading to a terminal. One of these leads had been cut a few inches from the terminal. This would have caused the phone inside to go dead instantly.

Helland carefully cut this segment at the terminal end so that the severed end could be examined by the FBI laboratories. Then he made a temporary connection so that detectives could use the phone during their preliminary investigation. It had already been dusted for fingerprints.

The bodies of Jody and Peri Lynn Kaarsten were removed to the King County Medical Examiner's Office to await autopsy. The detectives stayed behind to bag and label everything in the house that might bear some trace evidence left by their killer.

As the morning progressed, more and more King County detectives spread out over the area, questioning neighbors in an ever widening circle around the Kaarsten home. The Pearces, living right next door, were the first people interviewed. They were almost as shocked as Kaarsten himself; they said they had seen Jody Kaarsten at midnight the night before. They could scarcely believe that she was dead.

"Jody was over last night," Patti Pearce said. "They'd all gone down to Oregon for the Fourth of July. While she was down there, she had her hair bleached really blond, and she wanted to show us. Besides that, their phone was out of order, and she wanted to report it and call for the exact time because Arne said that all the clocks in the house had stopped."

It seemed that the Kaarstens' first day back from the long weekend had been marked by several unusual circumstances. The Pearces recalled Jody saying that Arne had told her he'd seen a man peering through their glass patio door earlier in the day. Arne Kaarsten evidently had not seen the man's face—only his legs. Then the peeper had run to the fence around their backyard and disappeared.

Patti Pearce said that Jody had arrived at their home about 10:00 P.M. Tuesday night and stayed until midnight.

Detective Ted Forrester was assigned the task of getting a statement from the widower. He offered to drive Kaarsten downtown to King County Police headquarters in the courthouse where he could give a formal statement about the events of the night and early morning. The Pearces volunteered to care for Anna, and Kaarsten rode into Seattle with Forrester.

Forrester is a kind, low-key man, and he was sympathetic to the young husband who had awakened to inexplicable horror. During the forty-five-minute drive to Seattle, Kaarsten spoke over and over about his loss. He explained that he and Jody had had a wonderful marriage. "We were the perfect family," he said. "I can't understand why she's been taken from me—in such a terrible way."

At headquarters, Chief of Detectives T. T. Nault talked with the grief-stricken young husband. Handsome, almost boyish-looking Arne Kaarsten had thick brown hair combed in a smooth pompadour. He told Chief Nault that he and Jody had been high school sweethearts. He had been nineteen and she a year younger when they married in November 1962. The teenage couple became parents the next year, when Anna was born.

"When was Peri Lynn born?" Nault asked.

Kaarsten looked down and bit his lip. "She was born on December 16, 1965. Last year."

Kaarsten said he was employed as a draftsman for a concrete conduit company. His avocation and his main interest, however, was race-car driving. Although he could not afford to own one of the expensive cars he raced, he said he drove for the president of a manufacturing firm who owned several cars.

Nault asked Kaarsten to recall the events leading up to the murder of half his family. Kaarsten sighed and began.

He recalled that the weekend just past had been particularly pleasant for his family. They had rented a car so they could drive to southern Oregon to spend the Fourth of July with Jody's relatives. The trip had been relaxing and fun, and he said he had been pleased when one of Jody's relatives bleached her hair for her. He said he loved the way she looked as a strawberry blonde.

They had driven home on Monday because Kaarsten had to work Tuesday. That afternoon—July 5—Jody had phoned her husband at work and asked him to pick up some supplies at the drugstore and bring them home on his lunch hour. He had gone to pick up Anna first, made the pharmacy trip in fifteen minutes, and come home to find that the door was locked.

"Locked?" Nault said.

Kaarsten nodded. "This was strange. Jody never locks the door in the daytime." He went on to say that she was very frightened. While he was gone, she had seen a man "in his twenties" and wearing work clothes prowling around outside their home.

Kaarsten said he went at once to the sliding patio doors to the backyard. He caught just a glimpse of a man's legs outside the patio doors, but the man disappeared before Arne could get outside and give chase. Pressed for more details, he shook his head. The glare of the sun on the glass doors had kept him from seeing more than the prowler's legs.

"Did you go back to work yesterday afternoon?"

"No, Jody was frightened, and both she and the babies were sick," Arne Kaarsten said. "I decided to take a half sick day from work so I could stay home and take care of them."

Later in the afternoon his wife and daughters apparently felt better. Kaarsten said they visited relatives, ate supper at a restaurant, and did some shopping at a discount store before returning home around 10:00 P.M.

It was only then, he said, that Jody had picked up the phone to call her family in Oregon and discovered the line was dead. She decided to run next door to the Pearces' and report it.

Kaarsten was struggling to recall the evening before in sequence. "I began to feel sick myself at that point," he said. He and Jody had agreed they would get a better night's sleep if he slept alone in the bedroom and she slept on the fold-down couch in the living room. They thought they had probably picked up some kind of twenty-four-hour flu while they were in Oregon.

He said one of his relatives was a nurse and had given him some sleeping pills. They had worked so well that he fell asleep almost immediately. He didn't know what time Jody had come back from the Pearces', and since she planned to sleep in the living room, she didn't disturb him when she got home.

"You hear anything last night?"

Kaarsten shook his head. "Nothing. I even slept past my usual wake-up time of six forty-five. I didn't wake up until a quarter to eight. Usually Peri Lynn wakes us at six forty-five."

But of course Peri Lynn did not wake up. Kaarsten said he had been half asleep when he wandered down the hall toward the living room. He had seen the pile of blankets on the floor, but he didn't immediately register what he was seeing. Only when he saw the blond hair poking out of the bedclothes did he realize that Jody was underneath.

He said he pulled the blankets back, then panicked at what he saw. "I grabbed Anna and ran next door to get help."

Nault wondered why Kaarsten had not grabbed Peri Lynn, too. Maybe he'd been afraid that Anna would wander out of her bedroom and find her mother dead. Maybe he just hadn't been thinking straight.

Arne Kaarsten told Nault that he was quite sure burglary had been the motive; Jody had had $100 in cash in her purse, and it was missing.

Nault wondered aloud why burglars had neglected to take Jody's diamond ring and her expensive watch. She was still wearing both when detectives arrived.

Kaarsten said he had no idea. None of this made much sense. But he was sure it had to do with the prowler who had been watching Jody though the patio doors. "I saw him," he said again. "I saw his legs. If only I'd managed to catch him . . ."

Arne Kaarsten thought the voyeur must have been the one who cut the phone line—so no one could call the police if he was caught inside the house. But the grieving widower was at a loss to understand why a burglar had picked his modest home.

Nault was puzzled, too—more than puzzled. There were elements here that made the skin prickle at the back of his neck. Burglars didn't break into little ranch houses when people were sleeping inside. It wasn't worth the risk. Also, burglars rarely killed when they were discovered; they ran. And burglars would have had no reason to kill a little baby. Furthermore, why would Kaarsten have bothered to check his wife's purse to see if the cash was missing? Wouldn't the motive for her murder have been the last thing on his mind when he was so filled with shock and grief?

Tactfully Nault questioned Kaarsten further about his marriage. He wondered if it was really the perfect union that Kaarsten had described. And slowly the picture of unblemished wedded bliss began to crumble. Kaarsten admitted that it had not been as idyllic as he had first described it.

Perhaps they had married too young; perhaps Jody had needed to know she was still attractive to other men. He said she had been unfaithful to him—something that he was embarrassed to admit but felt he had to explain, since her adultery might have had something to do with her murder.

Kaarsten said that Jody took a vacation—alone—to Oregon in April of 1965. While she was there she met another man. She spent a weekend with him. Her physical attraction to him was so consuming that she changed from the faithful wife she had always been. It was not like Jody to be unfaithful, but it happened. A week later, Kaarsten said, she flew back to Oregon to meet the man again. Her lover, Jack Kane,* seemed to have an almost hypnotic hold over his wife. In July, Jody actually left Arne and moved in with Kane in Oregon.

But Jody didn't stay long with Kane. She discovered she was pregnant. The baby would have been conceived in March—before she met Jack Kane; it was clearly Arne's baby. When Jody told her husband she wanted to come home and try again, he said he welcomed her with open arms. They reconciled, and according to the distraught man in front of Nault, their renewed marriage had been perfect ever since. Peri Lynn had been born six months later.

Nault had to ask an obvious question: "Did you ever think that Peri Lynn might not be your child?"

Kaarsten said the thought had crossed his mind several times. But he had decided it was destructive to worry, so he'd put it out of his mind. Born in mid-December, Peri Lynn was a full-term baby; that meant she had been conceived in March. As far as Kaarsten was concerned, Peri Lynn was his, and he accepted her just as he'd accepted Anna. Once he did so, the marriage had seemed to get better and better.

When he was asked to take a lie-detector test, Arne Kaarsten agreed readily. However, when the polygrapher, Norm Matzke, started to attach the leads of the machine that would register blood pressure, respiration, galvanic skin response, and heart rate, he could see that Arne Kaarsten was much too nervous and emotionally upset for his responses to be registered and evaluated accurately. It was just too soon. They would have to try again at a later date.

Kaarsten told the detectives that the necktie used to strangle Jody had been one of his own. It had to have been a weapon of opportunity. He remembered that he had taken it off, along with his sweater and jacket, when they came home the night before. He had draped the tie and his other clothing on the railing of Peri Lynn's playpen, which sat next to the couch.

Nault noted that Kaarsten had a Band-Aid on the back of his right hand. "You hurt your hand?" he asked casually.

"Yeah, I was roughhousing with Anna last night, and she scratched me accidentally."

"Can I take a look at it?"

When Kaarsten took the bandage off, Tom Nault could see that Kaarsten had two deep fresh scratches along the tendons between his middle and ring fingers. He jotted the information down but said nothing more.

It was noon—four hours after the bodies were found— when King County Medical Examiner Dr. Gale Wilson began the autopsies on Jody and Peri Lynn Kaarsten.

Jody was very slender at five feet six inches and 100 pounds. As Wilson had suspected, she had died of asphyxia by ligature. There were cruel bruises and indentations on the flesh of her neck where the necktie had cut in, and she had the characteristic pinpoints of petechial hemorrhages on her face and in her eyes, which were common to strangulation victims. The only other marks on her body were a bruise on the lower left side of her chin and vertical splits in the two middle fingernails of her left hand. It looked as if she had tried to fight off a hand that held the garrote that squeezed out her life. By measuring the degree of rigor mortis, lividity, and loss of body heat, Dr. Wilson determined that Jody Kaarsten had died between midnight and 2:00 A.M. the previous night.

Peri Lynn had died of the same cause, but she had no broken fingernails. She had probably been sound asleep when the ribbon from her teddy bear was placed around her neck and tightened.

The Kaarsten investigation was to become one of the strangest marathons King County Police detectives had ever participated in. They never fell victim to the tunnel vision that affects some departments. They eliminated all possible suspects, winnowing their theories down until there was only one possibility left.

They compiled a thick case file on every aspect in the double murder. They located Jack Kane, Jody's ex-lover, and Detectives George Helland and Len Randall brought him to Seattle for a secret preliminary hearing. The results of that hearing were announced through local news media, leaving the public even more bewildered than before.

It was a perfectly legal finding, though it was rarely used: "The deceased were killed by person or persons *known.*" People were accustomed to hearing that victims of unsolved murder cases were "killed by person or persons *unknown.*" That phrase was often used on television mysteries. If the police and the prosecuting attorney *knew* who the killer was, why hadn't they arrested someone?

Not surprisingly, murder cases are the most difficult to try; the defendant's life—either literally or figuratively—is in the hands of twelve jurors. If he or she is convicted, he will either be sentenced to death or be sent to prison for life. Ideally, the prosecution team wants to have a plethora of physical evidence to show the jury—something they can see, feel, hear, touch, or have explained to them by an expert witness.

Circumstantial evidence is helpful, but it is most effective as an adjunct to physical evidence. With only circumstantial evidence, the most confident prosecutor may have a few pangs of anxiety. If a defendant is acquitted of a crime, he cannot be tried again—other than civilly, as in the O. J. Simpson case—because double jeopardy will attach. Otherwise, defendants could be tried over and over for the same crime, and that would not be fair.

Most prosecutors prefer to play a waiting game, gathering as much evidence—both physical and circumstantial—as possible before they bring charges. Prosecutors often become the target of brickbats from reporters, who respond to a public demanding action.

An agonizing decision had been made in the case of Jody and Peri Lynn Kaarsten. Initially, there was not enough evidence to win a murder case. That did not mean the case was over, however, or that the victims had been forgotten by the detectives who had worked many overtime hours. They knew the name of the "person known," and they were biding their time until everything came together.

Three-year-old Anna Kaarsten went to live with relatives

in another state. Arne Kaarsten picked up the threads of his life. He lost himself in his obsession with racing cars. He soon became better known as a racing celebrity than as the tragic widower who had lost his wife and infant daughter in a double homicide. Driving an English-built Chevrolet-powered Lola Formula A racer that cost $30,000, Arne Kaarsten became well known in racing circles in the Northwest. For true racing buffs, his fame extended to the rest of America. Arne wasn't the best, but he was good. He was described as a "fierce competitor" but a "temperamental loser."

The memory of the Kaarsten murders faded from the minds of the public, but not from the minds of King County detectives and prosecutors. George Helland, who had been promoted to lieutenant, often dropped into the Pacific Raceways track, where Kaarsten raced. There seemed to be no overt enmity between the two men. Kaarsten always greeted Helland with a grin and a handshake. If there was something beneath the surface of the greetings exchanged, it would have taken more than a casual observer to detect it.

Four years passed, and county elections brought a new King County prosecuting attorney and a new regime. A grand jury probe took the wraps off a number of cases that had lain dormant and almost forgotten in dusty King County files. The Kaarsten murders were among the cases that were reviewed.

Grand jury testimony is secret. Even the suspects' attorneys are not allowed into the inner sanctum where witnesses give testimony that may or may not lead to indictment. Among the witnesses called when the Kaarsten case was reopened was a married couple who had been extremely close to Arne Kaarsten. Knute Martin* owned Martin Marine Supplies and a stable of expensive racing cars; his much younger wife, Lily,* was an enthusiastic racing buff too. They had employed Arne to drive their Formula A, and he also worked in their marine products firm. Although they would continue to stand behind him both financially and emotionally, the testimony they gave behind the doors of the grand jury chambers was electrifying.

Twenty-nine-year-old Special Prosecutor Richard McBroom and his associates, Gary Wagner and Jack Merrit, now urged that Arne Kaarsten be indicted for the murder of Jody and Peri Lynn Kaarsten. (Tragically, McBroom, a brilliant young special prosecutor, would not live to see the denouement of the indictment he had spearheaded; he died of a rare blood disease a year after the grand jury hearings of 1971.)

Deputy Prosecuting Attorney Jim Warme conferred with Lieutenant George Helland, and the two men agreed that they were morally bound to go into trial, even if the King County Prosecutor's Office had to do so armed only with the circumstantial evidence available.

Physical evidence that would have been invaluable if they were prosecuting a stranger for the murder of Jody and Peri Lynn was useless when the suspect was their own husband and father. Hairs, fibers, body fluids, and fingerprints found at the crime scene and traced to Arne Kaarsten meant nothing. He had lived in the same house with the victims. It was to be expected that he had left traces of himself there. Unless Kaarsten had left his fingerprint in his victims' blood, it would be of no evidentiary value. And his alleged victims had not bled. They had been strangled.

With his necktie. With the ribbon from Peri Lynn's own teddy bear.

On August 30, 1971—more than five years after the crimes of which he was accused—King County Detectives George Helland and Ted Forrester arrested Arne Kaarsten. He was charged with two counts of first-degree murder. He quickly posted $10,000 bail (10 percent of the $100,000 bail ordered) and walked away free. Although he was facing the most serious charge possible, Kaarsten would spend most of his time outside jail in the years to come. If he began to feel invincible, it was not surprising.

Arne Oscar Kaarsten's trial date was set for December 13, 1971.

A huge Christmas tree glittered in the lobby of the King

County Courthouse as participants and spectators flocked to Kaarsten's trial. It was a bizarre trial. The defendant was not led into the courtroom in leg irons and handcuffed. He was not in jail during his trial. Instead, he was free to go to lunch at a local restaurant with his relatives and friends, and free to sleep in his own bed each night. Detectives, reporters, and the defendant often nodded across their lunch plates before returning to the courtroom.

Arne Kaarsten appeared to view his trial on two murder charges as only a slight interruption in his usual pursuits. He was confident and expansive—the very picture of a man who had been placed in a ridiculous position by some accident of fate. His attitude suggested that he would surely triumph. He smiled often and took voluminous notes during testimony. He betrayed neither dread nor sorrow.

The testimony elicited, however, was reminiscent of the classic film noir starring Barbara Stanwyck and Fred MacMurray, *Double Indemnity*. There was a story here—a story far more convoluted than the arguments between a young husband and wife living in a little ranch house in Kent, Washington.

Warme and his fellow prosecutor, Lee Yates, presented Arne Kaarsten in a new light. He was not, they suggested, the poised defendant the jury saw before them, not a man who allowed nothing to ruffle him or anger him. Instead, they described him as a man who was so enraged by his wife's infidelity that he had vowed to kill her for it. Moreover, they maintained that he had accomplished his revenge with a careful plan to gain financially from Jody's and little Peri Lynn's murder.

According to the prosecution, Jody Kaarsten's affair with Jack Kane was not as brief as Kaarsten had said it was. It was far from over when she returned to Kaarsten in June of 1965. Arne Kaarsten had been consumed with rage toward the couple who had cuckolded him. During a period when the Kaarstens had separated again, Jack Kane had the effrontery to come to Washington and actually spend several days with Jody in the home Kaarsten had provided for her. When Arne Kaarsten found them together, he was enraged, and he shouted, "One day I'll get you both!"

Even after Jody had returned to Kaarsten, ostensibly for good, she met with Jack Kane one last time, and they made love. By carefully backtracking her movements in 1965, the King County detectives had uncovered this information. Whether Kaarsten had found out about this final tryst before he learned of it in his murder trial was a moot question.

Had he ever forgiven Jody for betraying him? Warme and Yates suggested that he had not. He was, they said, a man who could put on a mask—a mask that hid his real feelings so flawlessly that Jody believed they had begun their married life again with a clean slate.

But Arne Kaarsten had wanted something far more than he wanted Jody. And the prosecutors said he had left a paper trail that detailed a meticulous plot to achieve two goals.

On March 27, 1966—little more than three months before Jody and Peri Lynn Kaarsten were murdered—Arne had answered an ad in a Portland, Oregon, paper. The ad offered a 1957 300SL Mercedes-Benz for $3,500. On March 29, Knute Martin, Kaarsten's racing sponsor, took out a note to buy that car. The car was for Arne, who would somehow have to come up with the money to pay off the note.

Ten days later, on April 6, Arne Kaarsten bought insurance policies on the lives of his wife and two daughters. Jody was insured for $7,500 and the youngsters for $15,000 each. The insurance was double indemnity. In case of accidental or other violent death, the policies would pay off twice as much.

During that period in 1966, Arne Kaarsten made slightly over $700 a month as a draftsman, adequate in that era to support a small family. But a salary of $9,000 a year could not satisfy a taste for expensive cars. And Arne Kaarsten had come to care for flashy cars far more than he cared for Jody.

On June 24 he attempted to borrow $3,800 from a bank. He explained to the loan officer that he wanted the money to exercise an option on a piece of property. As collateral, he listed a 1957 Mercedes-Benz, the car that he did not yet own. His listing of his assets continued as a work of fiction. He confided that he was being groomed for the presidency of his company, a blatant lie, and that he was a partner in another business, which had netted him $9,400 in 1965—another lie. To cinch the loan, he explained that he would receive a large bonus from his company within a month and could pay off the loan then—yet another lie.

The loan was denied when the bank found that the Mercedes did not belong to Kaarsten. Indeed, he wanted the loan to *buy* the car.

Twelve days after Kaarsten attempted to borrow $3,800 and three months to the day from the time he bought the insurance policies on their lives, Jody and Peri Lynn Kaarsten were dead.

An old friend of the Kaarstens testified for the prosecution. She had known Arne and Jody Kaarsten since they were newlyweds. They had been very happy then. Arne had been in her home, the woman said, on the day he found his murdered wife. He'd had a handkerchief folded over two deep scratches on his hand, which were still bleeding. When she asked what had happened, he told her that little Anna had accidentally scratched him. The next day Kaarsten had asked this female witness not to talk about the case to anyone but his attorney. She had found this request oddly troubling.

Even more troubling, however, was a conversation she had with Arne Kaarsten on the evening after they had attended the double funeral for Jody and Peri Lynn. Arne had suddenly pulled his insurance policies out of his coat pocket and said, "Hey, I didn't know it was double indemnity."

The witness had been shocked that he would actually be carrying the policies in his suit jacket when half of his family was being buried. She was even more shocked when he seemed so elated to find that they had double indemnity clauses.

Arne Kaarsten had filed his claims quickly and had collected an initial payment of $16,722.26 in insurance money.

* * *

Deputy Prosecuting Attorney Warme spoke to the jury and reconstructed the murders as he had deduced the sequence of events from the investigation.

"Jody Kaarsten returned from her neighbors' at midnight and went to the bedroom where Kaarsten slept," Warme explained. "She took off her dress, put on a robe, and then went to the bathroom to fix her hair. In the small bathroom a man came up behind her. She didn't scream. That man put Arne Kaarsten's necktie around her neck. She reached up with her hands to save her life—she split two fingernails fighting to breathe. She fell then . . . striking her chin, probably on the vanity. . . .

"Then she was possibly dragged or carried to the living room and covered with blankets. Maybe she was already dead; maybe she was still unconscious and dying. Seven-month-old Peri Lynn Kaarsten slept in her nursery. Someone's hand took a pink ribbon from a stuffed toy and put it around that baby girl's neck and strangled the life from her body."

The young deputy prosecutor didn't name names; he didn't have to—every eye in the courtroom was on Arne Kaarsten. But Kaarsten remained serene. When he looked up, he could see the photographs of Jody's and Peri Lynn's bodies; prosecutors had pinned the pictures to a corkboard at the front of the courtroom. Still, he continued to smile and chat with his coterie of supporters during breaks.

Other witnesses from the Kaarstens' neighborhood testified. It soon became clear that the "prowler" had been spotted by Arne and Arne alone. The jury had only his statement that Jody had seen the window-peeper too; Jody was dead and could not testify about what she had and had not seen.

The detectives who had been at the crime scene on that long-ago July morning testified that Arne Kaarsten had been "overly" helpful in providing them with information about peculiar events around his home prior to his wife's murder. It was Arne Kaarsten who saw the prowler's legs outside the patio doors. It was Arne who had led Ken Trainor to the severed phone wires. Although two detectives had to get down to ground level and lift the opaque cover

over the wires, Arne had somehow been able to tell they were cut without raising the lid. Arne Kaarsten was the only one who knew how much money Jody had had in her purse. He was the one who said $100 was missing.

There were other bits of circumstantial evidence that marked Arne Kaarsten as a liar. Jody Kaarsten had told her neighbors that Arne said all the clocks in the house had stopped. Arne said that he had overslept because his alarm didn't go off. Why, then, had detectives found the clock in the master bedroom working perfectly the next morning? Jody had allegedly come home and gone to sleep in the living room without even going into the master bedroom. Had Kaarsten himself stopped to reset the bedroom clock in the morning before running to the Pearces for help?

A neighbor living directly across the street testified that he had been up preparing for work at 6:45 A.M. on that Wednesday in July. When he glanced through the front window of the Kaarsten house he saw a man wearing a bulky coat or robe in the Kaarsten living room. That was more than an hour before Arne Kaarsten, wearing his bulky bathrobe, ran for help to the Pearses' home shortly before 8:00 A.M. And even though detectives found that robe on the end of the bed in the master bedroom, Kaarsten insisted he had not worn it in months. Was it within the realm of credulity that an intruder—a man who had killed a woman and a baby—would still be lingering in the house long after daylight?

And who had prepared a bowl of cereal that morning and eaten half of it—only feet away from the body of Jody Kaarsten? Would a burglar-killer have been so brazen?

One of Arne Kaarsten's acquaintances testified about a strange conversation. When Arne learned that scrapings had been taken from Jody's nails, he had explained to his friend, "They'll probably find some of my skin. Anna scratched me, roughhousing, and then Jody cleaned Anna's nails with her own when she put her to bed."

This statement was inconsistent with his earlier statements. He had told police that *he* had put Anna to bed.

There were other discrepancies. Taken singly, they didn't
mean that much. Considered all together, they suggested
that Arne Kaarsten had concocted a plan that didn't fit, and
so he had made it fit by continually changing his explanations.

If Arne Kaarsten's family had been sick enough for him
to take a half-day off from work, why did he take them out
to dinner, shopping, and visiting on that same day?

Even more difficult to understand was Jody's change in
attitude. According to Arne, Jody had been so terrified of
the prowler that she had locked her doors in the middle of
the day. Wasn't it peculiar, then, that she had gone outdoors
and through the dark yard to visit the Pearces? She had
come home alone at midnight, too; she didn't ask Ted
Pearce to see her safely home. She hadn't been at all afraid.
And if Kaarsten had seen a prowler's legs and attempted to
chase him earlier that day, why had he gone peacefully to
sleep while Jody was out there in the dark?

When the defense began its case, Kaarsten's attorneys,
Carl Richey and Larry Barokas, presented a number of
character witnesses who attested to the harmony in the
Kaarsten marriage at the time of the double murder. They
also presented witnesses who said that Kaarsten was known
to be a very sound sleeper. Again and again the defense
attorneys stressed the fact that there was no physical
evidence linking the twenty-three-year-old widower to the
crime. Under the laws of the United States, Richey and
Barokas were not saddled with the burden of proof. They
did not have to prove that Arne Kaarsten was innocent; it
was up to the prosecutors to prove beyond a reasonable
doubt and moral certainty that he was guilty.

Richey and Barokas threw down their ace card when they
called Jody's alleged lover, Jack Kane, to the stand. He was
an attractive man in a carny-cowboy kind of way whose
testimony often made jurors and the gallery smile.

Kane was only too happy to go into detail about his affair
with Jody Kaarsten. He was obviously a ladies' man, and he
admitted that he had been married several times. He also

acknowledged that he had once been a patient in a mental facility. But he certainly did not appear at all deranged on the witness stand, and he told his story in a straight-forward—albeit colorful—way.

Kane said he had first met Jody in April of 1965. "I fell somewhat in love with her that weekend," he testified. "The next Friday she called and said she was flying to Eugene [Oregon]. I met her, and we spent the weekend in a motel room. I saw her again at the Kaarsten home in May of 1965. I was shaving in the bathroom when Kaarsten came in. We shook hands and started making small talk. Anna came in and ran to me and said, 'Hi, Daddy!'"

"And what happened then?"

Jack Kane testified that Arne Kaarsten had stopped being civil at that point. "Kaarsten said, 'What the hell's going on?' Then he left and said, 'Okay. You guys go back to your funny little games. Someday, I'll fix both of you.'"

Larry Barokas focused on Kane's history of mental illness: "Didn't you tell your psychiatrist that you planned to blow up your in-laws with a detonator?"

"I may have," the witness admitted casually, explaining that he was angry with them at the time, but he insisted that he wouldn't really have harmed them.

"What was the reason you went to the hospital in the first place?" Barokas pressed. "Wasn't it for rape?"

Kane wriggled uncomfortably in his chair. "Well . . . I was only sixteen, and this older woman invited me over. When I walked in . . . well, she came out in hardly any clothes and I was scared . . . so I . . . Well, I just hit her."

It was clear that Barokas was attempting to set Jack Kane up as a viable suspect in the murders. But Kane insisted that he was not angry when Jody left him to go back to Kaarsten. He testified that she was pregnant and needed a husband to take care of her and that he was in no position to marry her. They had parted reluctantly but by mutual agreement.

"Where were *you* on July 6?" Barokas asked suddenly.

"I was working in the woods in Casper, Wyoming," Kane answered. He admitted that he had been on a drinking binge during that whole week. Jack Kane, as charming a rogue as he appeared to be, was clearly not blessed with good judgment. He confided to an utterly fascinated jury that his memory had failed him during that time. One of the main reasons he had been unable to marry Jody Kaarsten was that—in the summer of 1966—he was already married to one of his many wives. But on July 16 he had completely forgotten he was currently married, and he had wed a beautiful teenage girl.

He continued his testimony, which sounded like nothing so much as a cross-country movie comedy script. He and his new, if bigamous, bride were headed for their honeymoon in South Dakota's Badlands National Park when they had a mishap.

"A buffalo attacked my sports car," Kane testified.

"I beg your pardon," Barokas said.

"He came at us and crushed both doors, and we couldn't drive it, and we couldn't get out of it, either. We had to wait until the state police found us."

After a long uneasy time trapped in the battered little car, Kane said he and his teenage bride were rescued by a highway patrolman. The incident got much tongue-in-cheek coverage in local papers and hit the AP wires. It was a natural for human interest: "Buffalo Attacks Sports Car of Honeymooning Couple."

Unfortunately for Jack Kane, the parents of his latest *legal* wife read the news stories with interest. They learned that their son-in-law had remarried without benefit of divorce and then had been roughed up by a buffalo. They didn't find it as funny as the reading public. When they told their daughter, she brought charges against Jack Kane and had him arrested for bigamy.

The double murder trial, which was now edging dangerously close to Christmas, continued through Saturday, December 18. On the advice of counsel, defendants in murder cases rarely take the witness stand. But Arne Kaarsten insisted on testifying. His demeanor continued to be that of a supremely confident man. He might well have been the toastmaster at a banquet for close friends. He smiled and spoke easily to the jury, turning often to include them in his answers to questions. After the lunch break, however, Kaarsten seemed a changed man. Either he'd had time to think about the enormity of the charges against him or his legal counsel had suggested that he should act a little more somber, considering the occasion. Now his face sagged, and he spoke in a low, almost humble tone.

"What happened to that smile?" Deputy Prosecutor Lee Yates asked with a bite in his voice.

"I guess I'm just surprised at being called to the witness stand today," Kaarsten responded weakly.

When he was shown a picture of his wife, Kaarsten broke into sobs. That seemed peculiar, since it certainly wasn't the first time he had seen the photograph. Kaarsten had gazed at pictures of the bodies of Jody and Peri Lynn on the corkboard in front of the courtroom through most of the trial and had never shown a trace of emotion. Now it was as if he were seeing for the very first time this picture of his wife lying dead in a tangle of blankets.

It was late afternoon on December 21, 1971, when the jurors retired to begin deliberation. It would not be a quick verdict. The rule of thumb that attorneys and court watchers live by is that a quick verdict is a guilty verdict; the longer a jury stays out, the more likely it is that there will be an acquittal. When the jurors were still weighing the testimony and evidence more than forty hours later, the defense camp felt optimistic. In the end, it took Arne Kaarsten's jury almost forty-eight hours to reach a verdict. It was two days before Christmas when Kaarsten walked into the courtroom to hear the jury's decision. He walked arm in arm with one of Jody Kaarsten's closest relatives; her family was supporting his innocence. If Jody's own family believed in him, how could a jury find otherwise?

Arne Kaarsten was shocked and turned stark white when the jury foreman read the verdicts. In the death of Jody Kaarsten: "Guilty of murder in the first degree."

In the death of Peri Lynn Kaarsten: "Guilty of murder in the first degree."

The jury did, however, recommend against the death

penalty. Arne Kaarsten was sentenced instead to two concurrent life sentences; with good behavior, he could be out of jail in thirteen years and four months.

The Kaarsten saga was far from over. Arne Kaarsten's legal team appealed the guilty verdicts on the basis of prejudicial testimony by a witness. The witness in question was the owner of a Kent ambulance service, also an EMT, who was the man who had tried in vain to bring Jody Kaarsten back to life. He had testified that, in his opinion, Kaarsten had not seemed as concerned or as grief-stricken as other husbands he had observed when he worked over their stricken mates. He said that Kaarsten grew concerned only when it looked as if Jody was breathing—when her chest began to rise and fall as a result of air being forced into her lungs by the resuscitator. At that point—and that point only—did the ambulance owner detect panic in Kaarsten.

The prosecution had inferred that Arne Kaarsten was afraid his wife was still alive and might tell who had choked her.

The defense attorneys claimed that the ambulance driver was not an expert in human behavior and that his testimony should have been deemed prejudicial and should have been stopped, or else the jury should have been advised to disregard it. Although the EMT had seen scores of worried relatives in accident and sudden death situations and had become a kind of intuitive judge of human nature in such cases, he was not—in the accepted legal sense—an expert witness.

On March 5, 1973, the Washington State Court of Appeals reversed Arne Kaarsten's convictions and ordered a new trial. Kaarsten had been released from the Monroe, Washington, Reformatory on a $35,000 appeal bond on July 31, 1972, pending a State Supreme Court hearing on the issue of whether or not he should be allowed bond. The state subsequently ruled that Kaarsten could not be freed because of the capital nature of the crime, but, ironically, that decision did not take effect until his convictions had been reversed.

Arne Kaarsten remained free for sixteen months.

The Killer Who Never Forgot . . . or Forgave

In December 1973, almost exactly two years after his first trial, Arne Kaarsten once again went on trial for the murder of his wife and baby. Once more, a Christmas tree dominated the lobby of the courthouse. The courtroom was different, and the judge and jury were different, but one got the feeling of déjà vu. It seemed that all of this had happened before. As indeed it had.

Kaarsten himself, still a popular race-car driver, appeared scarcely changed. His hair was a bit grayer, but his full face was unlined. Interestingly, the strain of the marathon legal ordeal showed strongly on relatives and friends of Jody and Peri Lynn, both now dead for seven years. Little Peri Lynn would have been in the fourth grade by now. Anna was in the sixth.

Some of the witnesses had died, although the ones whose testimony was vital to a conviction had been located and brought to the trial.

Carl Richey once again represented Kaarsten, and Lee Yates would again prosecute for the state. The mere passage of time had made the Kaarsten case less newsworthy. This time there were no headlines on the front page—only short articles in the back sections of local papers. Kaarsten spoke expansively to an attractive television newswoman and was filmed smiling broadly as he strode into the courtroom. One reporter studied the jury and remarked, "It's possible that Kaarsten may seem innocent now just because so much time has gone by since they died. That alone might be enough to sway a jury."

Lieutenant George Helland once again sat behind the prosecutors to aid in the case as a "friend of the court." Those of us who had been there for the first trial felt that we were seeing a movie for the second time.

The testimony was repeated. Everything was the same—except for one thing. Lee Yates had felt there was one loose end dangling in the first trial. That raveling concerned Jody Kaarsten's lover, Jack Kane. The defense had done its best to plant a veiled implication that Kane might have been the killer—that Jack Kane, consumed by jealousy, might have come skulking around the Kaarsten home and then attacked Jody and the baby after Kaarsten was asleep. Had it not been for Jody's discovery that she carried Arne's baby, Peri Lynn, she might have continued her affair with Jack Kane. That was something the defense had run with as a motive to suggest Kane was the killer.

Yates was sure that the defense would employ the same tactics this time. Kane had testified he was "working in the woods in Casper, Wyoming," but the prosecution had been unable to locate a witness who could substantiate this in the first trial.

Now Yates undertook an all-out campaign to find someone who could place Kane several states away from Washington on the day of the murders. Kane had mentioned that he'd gotten paid on July 6 and that his boss would remember he was there. But efforts to find the boss, Arnold Schillings, had always resulted in blind alleys.

Yates figured that a contractor with a business as large as the one Kane had described was probably a fairly solid citizen. It was likely that Schillings still maintained a business somewhere in the western states. "Arnold Schilling" wasn't the most common name in the world, but it wasn't that unusual, either. The young prosecuting attorney decided to forgo a night's sleep and search for Schilling.

Lee Yates began calling information operators in Wyoming, Montana, and Idaho. He called every town in each of the three states and inquired about a listing for "Arnold Schilling," "A. Schilling," "Schilling Construction," or anything similar. With the cooperation of patient information operators, Yates found that Schilling did not live in Wyoming or in Montana.

Then Yates hit it lucky. An operator checking in a statewide directory for Idaho found a listing for an Arnold Schilling in Twin Falls. He was the only Arnold Schilling in the state. Holding his breath, Yates asked to be put through to the number.

Lee Yates was elated when he realized he had found the right Arnold Schilling. Surprisingly, Schilling said he had heard about the Kaarsten murders. He happened to have been traveling through Washington State on vacation a few weeks after the homicides, and he remembered hearing about it on a radio news broadcast. But of course, he'd had no reason to connect the killings to Jack Kane, the man who worked for him.

"Could you tell me if Kane was working for you in Wyoming on July 6, 1966?" Yates asked. It was such a long shot. The IRS wouldn't require Schilling to keep employment records for seven years and a half years.

"Sure . . . sure," Schilling said. "You know, I think he was. I could check some pay records."

In the end, Schilling's records verified that he had handed Jack Kane a check on July 6, 1966. The check itself, returned after cancellation, had been lost in a flood. But Schilling was prepared to swear on the witness stand that he had seen Kane on that day, paid him, and that Kane could not have been in Kent, Washington, at the time of the murders.

This may have been the turning point in Arne Kaarsten's second trial.

Once again, as Christmas lights twinkled outside, a jury found Arne Kaarsten guilty on two counts of first-degree murder. Judge Janice Niemi allowed Arne Kaarsten to remain free on his $35,000 appeal bond when his lawyers said he would appeal yet again.

Lee Yates moved that the bail be revoked, however, and six days later Judge Niemi ruled that criminal procedure guidelines prohibited bail for a person convicted of capital offenses.

Kaarsten was ordered back to jail.

On January 21, 1974, Arne Kaarsten was once again sentenced to two concurrent life terms. On February 5, he was again denied bail pending appeal—with the court citing, ironically, the case of *The State vs. Kaarsten* as a precedent.

The State Supreme Court released Kaarsten from the Washington State Reformatory on March 14, pending the appeal of his conviction, with the posting of $10,000 in cash and a $100,000 appearance bond. The court action followed a recent statute issued by the U.S. Supreme Court, which gave trial judges discretion in granting bail in capital crimes such as murder. Immediately he was rearrested and was back in the King County Jail on March 15.

On December 23, 1975, Arne Kaarsten was sent to the

Washington State Reformatory in Monroe to begin serving his life sentence. He was later transferred to a federal prison on McNeil Island, Washington. He was paroled to a halfway house on April 11, 1989, and discharged from parole permanently on July 26, 1993—twenty-seven years after his wife and baby were murdered. His conviction for the double murder had kept him in prison for only the standard "life sentence" of that era: thirteen and a half years.

More than two decades after Arne Kaarsten's conviction, Senior Deputy Prosecuting Attorney Lee Yates—who is now assigned to the Appeals Division of the King County Prosecuting Attorney's Office—remembers Kaarsten's two trials as if they had happened only last week. He was not surprised to learn that Kaarsten was out of prison. "He was lucky in his timing," Yates said with acceptance tinged with a trace of bitterness. "If he committed the murders of his wife and baby today, he would be charged with aggravated murder and he would have received a mandatory sentence of life without parole."

Yates was, however, a bit startled to hear that Arne Kaarsten was living a highly successful post-prison life. He served three years as president of a local Sons of Norway Lodge. In that position, Arne Kaarsten was the chosen escort for the king and queen of Norway when they visited Seattle a few years ago. Kaarsten remains as charming, personable, and confident as he appeared in his two trials. Although his hair has turned white in the years since 1966, Kaarsten is still handsome and wears the same perfect pompadour that he did then. He has a successful career and, presumably, a good life with a woman he knew before he went to prison.

Ironically, although Arne Kaarsten was the race-car driver in the 1970s, it is Prosecutor Lee Yates who races today—in his classic Porsche.

Had she lived, Jody Kaarsten would be fifty-three today. Peri Lynn would be thirty-one in December. A necktie and a pink ribbon ended their future three decades ago.

Other bestselling Warner titles available by mail: